ACT

ACT 答案词

盛会杰 | 王鑫◎编著

中国人民大学出版社
·北京·

前　言

ACT（American College Test）即"美国大学入学考试"，是对学生综合能力的测试，ACT 考试成绩既是美国大学的入学条件之一，又是大学发放奖学金的主要依据之一。ACT 由五部分组成：文章改错（English）、数学（Math）、阅读（Reading）、科学推理（Science）和写作（Writing），其中写作为选考部分。

结合 ACT 的组成部分来看，对于广大备战 ACT 的考生来说，攻克 ACT 词汇难关有一定的难度。而且，很多考生在背单词这个环节存在误区，认为一本词汇书走天下，没有意识到不同部分的单词应该分开记忆。为了帮助广大考生备考 ACT，攻克 ACT 词汇难关，我们出版了《ACT 答案词》一书。

首先，本书的词汇全部来自 ACT 历年考试题目。经过对 ACT 历年考试题目的精析，我们汇总了历年考试题目中出现的单词，对其进行科学甄选以及按难度精选，最终形成了本书的单词。

其次，本书按英语阅读、数学、科学三个科目对词汇进行科学分类。结合 ACT 的组成部分，我们将本书的词汇科学且精准地分为英语阅读词汇（24 个 List）、数学词汇（11 个 List）以及科学词汇（11 个 List）。

再次，本书从 ACT 历年考试题目中为每个单词匹配了原汁原味的真题例句，以便于考生在理解与记忆单词的同时，掌握单词用法并熟悉考试难度。

最后，本书为每个单词的例句配备了地道贴切的中文翻译。例句中难免会有比较专业的词汇，尤其是数学和科学部分，中文翻译可以协助考生快速理解单词例句。

衷心希望《ACT 答案词》一书能成为广大考生备战 ACT 的得力助手，助力考生全面、科学、高效地掌握 ACT 词汇。

目　录

第一部分　英语阅读词汇 ·· 1

    List 1 ··· 2

    List 2 ··· 13

    List 3 ··· 25

    List 4 ··· 37

    List 5 ··· 49

    List 6 ··· 61

    List 7 ··· 73

    List 8 ··· 85

    List 9 ··· 97

    List 10 ·· 109

    List 11 ·· 121

    List 12 ·· 133

    List 13 ·· 144

    List 14 ·· 155

    List 15 ·· 167

    List 16 ·· 179

    List 17 ·· 190

    List 18 ·· 202

    List 19 ·· 214

    List 20 ·· 226

    List 21 ·· 238

    List 22 ·· 250

    List 23 ·· 261

    List 24 ·· 273

第二部分　数学词汇 ·· 279

    List 1 ··· 280

    List 2 ··· 283

List 3 ·· 289

List 4 ·· 291

List 5 ·· 305

List 6 ·· 308

List 7 ·· 318

List 8 ·· 320

List 9 ·· 321

List 10 ·· 323

List 11 ·· 325

第三部分　科学词汇 ·· 327

List 1 ·· 328

List 2 ·· 338

List 3 ·· 349

List 4 ·· 357

List 5 ·· 370

List 6 ·· 381

List 7 ·· 391

List 8 ·· 400

List 9 ·· 404

List 10 ·· 409

List 11 ·· 413

第一部分
英语阅读词汇

List 1

1 **aback**

[ə'bæk]

义 *adv.* 吃惊地；向后地

例 She was completely taken aback by his anger.

译 她完全被他的愤怒吓了一跳。

2 **abandonment**

[ə'bændənmənt]

义 *n.* 放弃；放纵

例 Constant rain forced the abandonment of the next day's competitions.

译 持续降雨迫使第二天的各项比赛中途停止。

3 **abbey**

['æbɪ]

义 *n.* 修道院，修道院教堂

例 Next to the abbey, there is a big new church.

译 在修道院的旁边，有一座新的大教堂。

4 **abbreviate**

[ə'bri:vɪeɪt]

义 *v.* 缩写；使简略

例 We shall abbreviate the "directed graph" to digraph.

译 我们将把"有方向的图"简称为方向图。

5 **abdomen**

['æbdəmən]

义 *n.* 腹部

例 He went into the hospital to undergo tests for a pain in his abdomen.

译 他因腹部疼痛而进了医院接受检查。

6 **abide**

[ə'baɪd]

义 *v.* 遵守；坚持

例 They have got to abide by the rules.

译 他们必须遵守规则。

7 **ably**

['eɪblɪ]

义 *adv.* 能干地；巧妙地

例 We were ably assisted by a team of volunteers.

译 我们得到一组志愿者的有力帮助。

8 **abnormally**

[æb'nɔ:rməlɪ]

义 *adv.* 异常地，例外地

例 Abnormally low or high body temperature effect a variety of physiologic responses including lowered metabolic rate.

译 不正常的低或高体温会影响动物体各种不同的生理反应，包括低代谢率。

9 **abort**

[ə'bɔ:rt]

义 *v.* 流产；中止

例 When the decision was made to abort the mission, there was great confusion.

译 当决定中止这次任务时，引起了很大的混乱。

---

10 abortion
[ə'bɔ:rʃn]

义 *n.* 流产，堕胎；（计划等）失败

例 I've always been anti-abortion.

译 我一直反对堕胎。

---

11 abruptly
[ə'brʌptlɪ]

义 *adv.* 突然地；莽撞地

例 The sky darkened abruptly.

译 天空突然暗了下来。

---

12 absentminded
['æbsənt'maɪndɪd]

义 *adj.* 心不在焉的；恍惚的

例 Tell him never be absentminded.

译 告诉他不要心不在焉。

---

13 absorption
[əb'sɔ:rpʃn]

义 *n.* 吸收；合并

例 This controls the absorption of liquids.

译 这控制了液体的吸收。

---

14 absurd
[əb's3:rd]

义 *adj.* 荒唐的，不合理的　*n.* 荒诞，荒诞的事物

例 He has a good sense of the absurd.

译 他对荒诞事物有较强的识别能力。

---

15 abut
[ə'bʌt]

义 *v.* 邻接；毗连；紧靠

例 His land abuts on to a road.

译 他的土地紧靠公路。

---

16 accede
[ək'si:d]

义 *v.* 同意；继承

例 I think we could accede to that.

译 我想我们可以同意这一点。

---

17 acceleration
[ək͵selə'reɪʃn]

义 *n.* 加速；加速度

例 Acceleration and velocity are both vectors.

译 加速度和速度都是矢量。

---

18 accost
[ə'kɔ:st]

义 *v.* 搭话；搭讪

例 The child was told how to accost the servants and the governess.

译 那孩子被告知如何与仆人和家庭教师搭话。

---

19 accumulative

[əˈkjuːmjələtɪv]

义 *adj.* 积聚的，累积的

例 The consensus is that risk factors have an accumulative effect.

译 一致意见认为多种危险因素有累积的效果。

20 accusatory

[əˈkjuːzətɔːrɪ]

义 *adj.* 指责的；控告的

例 Don't be angry or accusatory with Laura.

译 不要对劳拉生气或指责她。

21 acetic

[əˈsiːtɪk]

义 *adj.* 醋的，乙酸的

例 Vinegar contains acetic acid.

译 醋中含有醋酸。

22 aciding

[ˈæsɪdɪŋ]

义 *n.* 酸蚀法

例 Through effect analyzing and evaluating, the acid and sand fracturings are considered to be better than bed rock aciding.

译 通过效果分析和评价，认为酸携砂压裂优于基岩酸化。

23 acknowledgement

[əkˈnɑːlɪdʒmənt]

义 *n.* 确认；感谢

例 The flowers were a small acknowledgement of your kindness.

译 这些花聊表谢意，感谢你的好心帮助。

24 acoustical

[əˈkuːstɪkl]

义 *adj.* 听觉的；声学的

例 This fat tissue has some rather fascinating acoustical properties.

译 这个脂肪组织具有相当独特的声学特征。

25 acquiesce

[ˌækwɪˈes]

义 *v.* 默许；勉强同意

例 Steve seemed to acquiesce in the decision.

译 史蒂夫似乎默许了这个决定。

26 acrid

[ˈækrɪd]

义 *adj.* 苦味的；刺鼻的

例 He hauled himself up onto the tracks and caught the acrid scent of creosote.

译 他爬上铁轨，闻到了木馏油的刺鼻气味。

27 acrobatic

[ˌækrəˈbætɪk]

义 *adj.* 杂技的

例 We got a lot of acrobatic types of people.

译 我们有很多杂技演员。

28 acronym
['ækrənɪm]

义　*n.* 首字母缩略词

例　The name is not an acronym.

译　此称呼不是只取首字母的缩略词。

---

29 acrylic
[ə'krɪlɪk]

义　*adj.* 丙烯酸的

例　Acrylic paints can be used to create large, flat blocks of color.

译　丙烯酸涂料可以用来绘制大而平的色块。

---

30 actuality
[ˌæktʃʊ'æləti]

义　*n.* 现实；事实

例　In actuality, Ted did not have a disorder but merely a difficult temperament.

译　事实上，泰德并没有什么疾病，只是脾气不好。

---

31 adaptable
[ə'dæptəbl]

义　*adj.* 能适应的；可改编的

例　Human beings are infinitely adaptable.

译　人类的适应能力是无限的。

---

32 adapter
[ə'dæptər]

义　*n.* 适配器

例　About 60,000 subscribers have special adapters to receive and decode the signals.

译　大约有 6 万用户使用特殊的适配器接收并解码信号。

---

33 adhesive
[əd'hi:sɪv]

义　*n.* 黏合剂

例　She gingerly secured the loose paint flakes around the rip with a liquid adhesive.

译　她小心翼翼地用一种液体黏合剂把裂缝周围松散的油漆片固定住。

---

34 adjoin
[ə'dʒɔɪn]

义　*v.* 邻接，毗连

例　Our two houses adjoin.

译　我们的两所房子邻接着。

---

35 adjustable
[ə'dʒʌstəbl]

义　*adj.* 可调整的

例　The bags have adjustable shoulder straps.

译　这些包有可调整的肩带。

---

36 adorn
[ə'dɔ:rn]

义　*v.* 装饰；佩戴

例　Gold was considered divine in ancient Greece and was used to adorn temples and as an offering to the gods.

译　在古希腊，黄金被认为是神圣的，它被用于装饰庙宇和用作给神的祭品。

37 adulteration

[ə,dʌltə'reɪʃn]

义 *n.* 掺假；次品

例 The Congress should not encourage, let alone facilitate, such efforts by holding open the Patriot Act for further revision and adulteration.

译 国会不应该鼓励让《爱国者法案》公开以供进一步修订和掺假，更不用说促进这样的努力了。

---

38 advancement

[əd'vænsmənt]

义 *n.* 进步；升任

例 Today, the pace of life is increasing with technological advancements.

译 今天，随着科技的进步，生活的节奏越来越快。

---

39 adventurer

[əd'ventʃərər]

义 *n.* 冒险家

例 Cendrars is an adventurer.

译 桑德拉尔是一位冒险家。

---

40 advisor

[əd'vaɪzər]

义 *n.* 顾问

例 The sons and grandsons of Theodosius were too young when they came to power to rule without the assistance of older advisors.

译 狄奥多西的子孙辈在掌权时还太小，没有年长顾问的帮助就无法统治。

---

41 aeronautical

[,eərə'nɔːtɪkl]

义 *adj.* 航空的，航空学的

例 Many of the pilots were to achieve eminence in the aeronautical world.

译 许多飞行员都在航空界取得了卓越的成就。

---

42 aerospace

['erəʊspeɪs]

义 *n.* 宇宙空间，航空航天工业

例 One could also mention the aerospace industry, which uses cork for its qualities of lightness coupled with good thermal insulation.

译 人们还提到航空航天工业，它使用软木是因为它具有轻盈的品质和良好的隔热性。

---

43 affable

['æfəbl]

义 *adj.* 和蔼可亲的

例 He was affable at one moment, choleric the next.

译 他一会儿和蔼可亲，一会儿暴躁易怒。

---

44 affectation

[,æfek'teɪʃn]

义 *n.* 假装；做作

例 Kay has no affectation at all.

译 凯一点也不做作。

---

45 affirm

[ə'fɜːrm]

义 *v.* 证实，肯定

例 I can affirm that no one will lose their job.

译 我可以肯定，没有人会失业。

46 affordance

[ə'fɔːrdəns]

义 *n.* 功能可见性

例 There are only a few manual affordances.

译 那里只有一些手动提示。

---

47 afoot

[ə'fʊt]

义 *adj.* 徒步的；在进行中

例 Changes were afoot.

译 变化在进行之中。

---

48 aft

[æft]

义 *adv.* 向船尾，在船尾

例 I went aft to take my turn at the helm.

译 我走到船尾去掌舵。

---

49 agate

['æɡət]

义 *n.* 玛瑙；玛瑙制工具

例 It is round, like the size of a small yellow agate.

译 它是圆的，大小很像一个小的黄色的玛瑙。

---

50 agglomeration

[ə,ɡlɑːmə'reɪʃn]

义 *n.* 结块，凝聚

例 Addition of coagulants promotes agglomeration of particles.

译 混凝剂的加入促进了颗粒的凝聚。

---

51 agile

['ædʒl]

义 *adj.* 灵活的，机灵的

例 At 20 years old he was not as strong, as fast, as agile as he is now.

译 20 岁时，他不像现在这样强壮、快速、灵活。

---

52 agitator

['ædʒɪteɪtər]

义 *n.* 煽动者，鼓动者；搅拌器

例 The agitator is inclined to exaggerate trivial matters.

译 那个煽动者有夸大琐碎事物的倾向。

---

53 aglow

[ə'ɡləʊ]

义 *adj.* 发光的；兴奋的

例 The night skies will be aglow with fireworks.

译 夜晚的天空将被烟花照亮。

---

54 ahold

[ə'həʊld]

义 *adv.* 迎风行驶　*n.* 抓，握

例 I'm going to have to get ahold of myself.

译 我得控制一下自己。

---

55 aide

[eɪd]

义 *n.* 助手，副官

例 An aide avowed that the President had known nothing of the deals.

译 总统的一位助手承认，总统对这些交易一无所知。

---

56 airfield

['erfɪeld]

义 *n.* 飞机场

例 He attempted to return downwind to the airfield.

译 他试图顺风返回机场。

---

57 airlift

['erlɪft]

义 *n.* 空运；空中补给线

例 The airlift was conducted in force ten winds.

译 空运是在十级大风中进行的。

---

58 alchemist

['ælkəmɪst]

义 *n.* 炼金术士

例 He and his alchemist precursors discovered that the weight of the products in a chemical reaction equal the weight of the reactants.

译 他和他的炼金术士先驱们发现，化学反应中产物的重量等于反应物的重量。

---

59 alertness

[ə'lɜ:rtnəs]

义 *n.* 警觉；机敏

例 Alcohol causes a loss of judgment and alertness.

译 酒精会使人丧失判断力和警觉性。

---

60 alight

[ə'laɪt]

义 *adj.* 燃烧着的

例 Several buildings were set alight.

译 几座建筑被点燃。

---

61 alignment

[ə'laɪnmənt]

义 *n.* 结盟；准线

例 The church should have no political alignment.

译 教会不应该有政治结盟。

---

62 allegory

['æləgɔ:rɪ]

义 *n.* 寓言

例 The book is a kind of allegory of Latin American history.

译 这本书有点像是对拉丁美洲历史的一种寓言。

---

63 alley

['ælɪ]

义 *n.* 胡同，小巷

例 She parked her bike in the alley.

译 她把自行车停在小巷里。

---

64 allusion

[ə'lu:ʒn]

义 *n.* 暗指，暗示，典故

例 Her poetry is full of obscure literary allusion.

译 她的诗充满了晦涩的文学典故。

---

65 aloft

[ə'lɔ:ft]

义 *adv.* 在高处，在空中

例 He held the trophy proudly aloft.

译 他骄傲地把奖杯举向空中。

---

66 amassment

[ə'mæsmənt]

义 *n.* 积聚

例 The accumulation of capital refers simply to the gathering or amassment of objects of value, the increase in wealth, or the creation of wealth.

译 资本积累仅仅是指价值对象的聚集或积累、财富的增加或者财富的创造。

---

67 amphibious

[æm'fɪbɪəs]

义 *adj.* 具有双重性的，【生】两栖的

例 A third brigade is at sea, ready for an amphibious assault.

译 第三旅已在海上，准备进行海陆双重攻击。

---

68 amplifier

['æmplɪfaɪər]

义 *n.* 放大器；扩音机

例 The amplifier exploded in a fountain of sparks.

译 放大器爆炸，喷射出火星。

---

69 amplitude

['æmplɪtu:d]

义 *n.* 广阔；振幅

例 This is the amplitude.

译 这是振幅。

---

70 analyst

['ænəlɪst]

义 *n.* 分析家

例 Analysts forecast huge profits this year.

译 分析家预测今年的利润会非常丰厚。

---

71 anatomical

[ˌænə'tɑ:mɪkl]

义 *adj.* 结构上的；解剖的

例 The superior nuchal line is not always a reliable external anatomical mark.

译 上项线并不总是一个可靠的外部解剖标记。

---

72 anew

[ə'nu:]

义 *adv.* 重新，再

例 And now, as you graduate to begin anew, I wish that for you.

译 现在，在你们即将毕业、开始新的旅程的时候，我希望你们也能这样。

---

73 anguished

['æŋgwɪʃd]

义 *adj.* 很痛苦的

例 She let out an anguished cry.

| 译 | 她发出了一声极为痛苦的叫喊。 |

74 animation
[ˌænɪˈmeɪʃn]

义 *n.* 动画片，动漫

例 The films are a mix of animation and full-length features.

译 这些电影是动画和情节长片的混合体。

75 annotate
[ˈænəteɪt]

义 *v.* 注解

例 Historians annotate, check and interpret the diary selections.

译 历史学家对日记选篇进行注解、核查以及阐释。

76 annoyance
[əˈnɔɪəns]

义 *n.* 烦恼；生气

例 His annoyance won't last.

译 他不会烦恼很久的。

77 antagonist
[ænˈtæɡənɪst]

义 *n.* 敌手，对手

例 He had never previously lost to his antagonist.

译 他之前从未输给过他的对手。

78 ante
[ˈæntɪ]

义 *n.* 赌注；款项

例 In February, Reagan upped the ante.

译 2 月，里根加大了赌注。

79 anthem
[ˈænθəm]

义 *n.* 国歌；圣歌；赞美诗

例 The band played the Czech anthem.

译 乐队演奏了捷克国歌。

80 anthology
[ænˈθɑːlədʒɪ]

义 *n.* 选集，文选

例 The anthology has a surprising sense of coherence.

译 整本选集有着惊人的连贯性。

81 anthropic
[ænˈθrɑːpɪk]

义 *adj.* 人类的

例 The form of subject is divided into individual subject, aggregative subject, anthropic subject and so on.

译 主体形式分为个体主体、集团主体和人类主体等。

82 anthropomorphic
[ˌænθrəpəˈmɔːrfɪk]

义 *adj.* 被赋予人形的；拟人化的

例 Instead of attributing its creation to anthropomorphic gods, they sought rational explanations.

译 他们不是把世界看作拟人化的神的创造，而是要寻求一个合理的解释。

83 antiquated
['æntəˌkweɪtɪd]

义 *adj.* 旧式的；过时的

例 Many factories are so antiquated they are not worth saving.

译 许多工厂太旧了，不值得挽救。

---

84 apathy
['æpəθɪ]

义 *n.* 冷漠

例 They told me about isolation and public apathy.

译 他们向我讲述了孤立感与公众的冷漠。

---

85 aperture
['æpərtʃʊr]

义 *n.* 光圈；缝隙

例 Through the aperture he could see daylight.

译 透过缝隙，他能看到日光。

---

86 aplenty
[ə'plentɪ]

义 *adj.* 丰富的

例 There were problems aplenty at work.

译 工作中有很多问题。

---

87 apologetic
[əˌpɑːlə'dʒetɪk]

义 *adj.* 道歉的，愧疚的

例 They were very apologetic about the trouble they'd caused.

译 他们对所惹的麻烦深感愧疚。

---

88 apparel
[ə'pærəl]

义 *n.* 衣服，服装

例 The store sells women's and children's apparel.

译 这家商店出售女装和童装。

---

89 append
[ə'pend]

义 *v.* 附加，添加

例 Footnotes have been appended to the document.

译 该文件附加了脚注。

---

90 appetizer
['æpɪtaɪzər]

义 *n.* 开胃食品；开胃菜

例 Would you like any appetizer?

译 您要开胃菜吗？

---

91 apprehension
[ˌæprɪ'henʃn]

义 *n.* 理解；忧虑

例 It reflects real anger and apprehension about the future.

译 它反映了对未来的真正愤怒和忧虑。

---

92 apprenticeship
[ə'prentɪʃɪp]

义 *n.* 学徒期；学徒身份

例 He served a one-year apprenticeship.

译 他曾经当过一年的学徒。

---

93 approbation

[ˌæprəˈbeɪʃn]

义 *n.* 认可；赞许

例 The proposal met his approbation.

译 这项建议得到了他的赞许。

---

94 apron

[ˈeɪprən]

义 *n.* 围裙；停机坪

例 She wiped her floury hands on her apron.

译 她在围裙上擦了擦沾满面粉的手。

---

95 aquaculturist

[ˌɑːkwəˈkʌltʃərɪst]

义 *n.* 水产养殖者

例 Aquaculturists work to bring a variety of healthy fish, lobsters, crabs and more from aquatic environments to our dinner table.

译 水产养殖工作者致力于将各种健康的鱼类、龙虾、螃蟹等从水生环境带到我们的餐桌上。

---

96 aquamarine

[ˌɑːkwəməˈriːn]

义 *n.* 碧绿色；海蓝宝石

例 The stunning gemstones include aquamarine, amethyst, sugilite and etc.

译 令人惊叹的宝石有海蓝宝石、紫水晶、紫杉石等。

---

97 arcade

[ɑːrˈkeɪd]

义 *n.* 拱廊；游乐中心；室内购物中心

例 We know this new shopping arcade is ready for lease.

译 我们知道这栋新的购物商场已准备好出租。

---

98 archetype

[ˈɑːrkɪtaɪp]

义 *n.* 原型，典型

例 She is the archetype of an American movie star.

译 她是典型的美国影星。

---

99 argumentative

[ˌɑːrgjuˈmentətɪv]

义 *adj.* 爱争论的，好辩论的

例 It was because he was of an argumentative mind that in their cabin at night he permitted himself to carp.

译 正是因为他爱争论，所以晚上在他们的舱房里，他才允许自己吹毛求疵。

---

100 aria

[ˈɑːrɪə]

义 *n.* 咏叹调，唱腔；唱段

例 Listen to this aria from the opera.

译 听下面这首歌剧中的咏叹调。

List 2

1 **aristocratic**

[əˌrɪstə'krætɪk]

义 *adj.* 贵族的

例 Nabokov was the scion of an aristocratic family.

译 纳博科夫是一个贵族家庭的后代。

2 **arrogant**

['ærəgənt]

义 *adj.* 傲慢的，自大的

例 He's an arrogant little boy.

译 他是个傲慢的小男孩。

3 **arrowhead**

['ærəʊhed]

义 *n.* 箭头

例 The Indians chipped flint arrowhead.

译 印第安人凿制燧石箭头。

4 **artificiality**

[ˌɑːrtɪˌfɪʃɪ'æləti]

义 *n.* 人工制造；人为状态

例 It will seem rather a monument of artificiality.

译 这似乎是一座人造的纪念碑。

5 **ascent**

[ə'sent]

义 *n.* 上升；上坡路

例 Burke pushed the button and the lift began its slow ascent.

译 伯克按下按钮，电梯开始缓慢上升。

6 **assorted**

[ə'sɔːrtɪd]

义 *adj.* 组合的；各种各样的

例 The meat is served with salad or assorted vegetables.

译 端上的肉配有色拉或什锦蔬菜。

7 **astound**

[ə'staʊnd]

义 *v.* 使惊骇，使大吃一惊

例 He used to astound his friends with feats of physical endurance.

译 他过去常以惊人的体力耐力使他的朋友们感到吃惊。

8 **attired**

[ə'taɪərd]

义 *adj.* 穿着……衣服的

例 He was attired in a plain, mud-flecked uniform.

译 他身穿一件朴素而沾有泥点的制服。

9 **audible**

['ɔːdəbl]

义 *adj.* 听得见的

例 His words were barely audible.

译 他的话勉强听得见。

10 aurora

[ɔːˈrɔːə]

义 *n.* 曙光，极光

例 She stood on the balcony and shone as the aurora borealis shines.

译 她站在阳台上，像北极光一样闪闪发光。

---

11 authenticate

[ɔːˈθentɪkeɪt]

义 *v.* 证明……为真，验证

例 The system might use a smart identity card, or a digital credential linked to a specific computer and would authenticate users at a range of online services.

译 该系统可能使用智能身份证或与特定电脑相连的数字证书，并在一系列在线服务中认证用户。

---

12 automaker

[ˈɔːtəʊmeɪkər]

义 *n.* 汽车制造者

例 A certain automaker aims to increase its market share by deeply discounting its vehicles' prices for the next several months.

译 某汽车制造商计划在未来几个月大幅降价，以增加其市场份额。

---

13 avant

[æˈvɑːt]

义 *adj.* 先锋的，前卫的；激进的

例 They wanted to create something at once avant-garde and classical.

译 他们想立刻制造前卫经典的产品。

---

14 avert

[əˈvɜːrt]

义 *v.* 转开；避免

例 He did his best to avert suspicion.

译 他尽量避免嫌疑。

---

15 awaken

[əˈweɪkən]

义 *v.* 醒；意识到

例 As soon as you awaken, identify what is upsetting about the dream.

译 一旦你醒来，找出梦中令人不安的地方。

---

16 awash

[əˈwɒʃ]

义 *adj.* 被淹没的，泛滥的

例 The city is awash with drugs.

译 这个城市毒品泛滥。

---

17 awhile

[əˈwaɪl]

义 *adv.* 片刻，一会儿

例 The trend has been around for a while but has recently really started to take off on social media.

译 这股潮流其实出现了有一阵子了，但直到最近才突然在社交媒体上火起来。

---

18 babysit

[ˈbeɪbɪsɪt]

义 *v.* 临时代为照看婴孩

例 He's babysitting the neighbor's children.

译 他在临时照看邻居的孩子。

---

19 backfire

[ˌbæk'faɪər]

义 *v.* 产生事与愿违的结果

例 The president's tactics could backfire.

译 总统的策略可能会事与愿违。

---

20 backlist

['bæklɪst]

义 *n.* 库存书籍目录

例 It can consult its own backlist.

译 它可以查阅自己的库存目录。

---

21 backup

['bækʌp]

义 *n.* 后备；备份

例 You should make a copy of the disk as a backup.

译 你应该复制磁盘作为备份。

---

22 bade

[beɪd]

义 *v.* 命令（bid 的过去式）

例 He summoned all the huntsmen together, and bade them go out into the forest with him.

译 他把所有的猎人召集在一起，命令他们和他一起到森林里去。

---

23 baffle

['bæfl]

义 *v.* 使困惑，难倒

例 You can't baffle me with that.

译 你不能用那件事来难倒我。

---

24 balding

['bɔːldɪŋ]

义 *adj.* 变秃的

例 He wore a straw hat to keep his balding head from getting sunburned.

译 他戴了一顶草帽，以免他的秃头被太阳晒伤。

---

25 ballot

['bælət]

义 *n.* 投票；选票；投票用纸

例 She won 58.8% of the ballot.

译 她赢得了 58.8% 的选票。

---

26 balmy

['bɑːmɪ]

义 *adj.* 芳香的；温和的

例 It was April, balmy and warm.

译 那是四月，天气温暖和煦。

---

27 bandstand

['bændstænd]

义 *n.* 露天音乐台，舞台

例 The crowd cheered as she went up the steps to the bandstand.

译 当她走上舞台的台阶时，人群欢呼起来。

---

28 barbed

['bɑ:rbd]

义 *adj.* 有刺的；讽刺的

例 Plots of land have been demarcated by barbed wire.

译 一块块土地都用带刺的铁丝网圈了起来。

---

29 barbershop

['bɑ:rbərʃɑ:p]

义 *n.* 理发店

例 Gabriel's family soon helped him open his first barbershop in San Isidro, Peru, which he worked at for one and a half years.

译 加布里尔的家人很快就帮他在秘鲁的圣伊西德罗开了第一家理发店，他在那里工作了一年半。

---

30 barter

['bɑ:rtər]

义 *v.* 物物交换，以货易货　*n.* 物物交易制度；用于易物的物品

例 Overall, barter is a very inefficient means of organizing transactions.

译 总的来说，物物交易制度是一种非常低效的组织交易的方式。

---

31 bashful

['bæʃfl]

义 *adj.* 害羞的，羞怯的

例 She is bashful in doing anything.

译 她干什么事都害羞。

---

32 batter

['bætər]

义 *v.* 猛击

例 The passengers were battered by flying luggage and cargo as the cabin lost pressure.

译 当机舱失压时，乘客们受到飞落的行李和货物的猛击。

---

33 battlefield

['bætlfi:ld]

义 *n.* 战场

例 The castle stands on the site of an ancient battlefield.

译 这座城堡坐落在一个古代战场的遗址上。

---

34 bawl

[bɔ:l]

义 *v.* 大哭；大声训斥

例 She puts her head in her hands and starts to bawl.

译 她双手抱头大哭起来。

---

35 bayside

['beɪsaɪd]

义 *n.* 海边

例 Listen to the ad for the Bayside Hotel.

译 听一听海湾酒店的广告。

---

36 beckon

['bekən]

义 *v.* 吸引

例 Seen from afar, its towering buildings beckon the visitor in.

译 从远处望去，其高耸的建筑吸引着来访者。

37　bedsheet

[bedʃiːt]

义 *n.* 床单

例 Born in New York City in 1923, this now-retired art professor began his career drawing on the walls, floors, and even the bedsheets in his parents' house.

译 这位现已退休的艺术教授于 1923 年出生于纽约市，他的职业生涯始于在父母家的墙壁、地板甚至床单上作画。

38　beep

[biːp]

义 *n.* 哔哔声

例 There is also a short door closing beep.

译 还有一声短促的关门哔哔声。

39　befall

[bɪˈfɔːl]

义 *v.* 发生；降临

例 The things that befall us are often due to a lack of social support.

译 发生在我们身上的事情往往是由于缺乏社会支持。

40　befit

[bɪˈfɪt]

义 *v.* 适宜；对……适当

例 He shall restore the dwellings of the saints throughout the lands and settle the pastors in places which befit them.

译 他将在全国恢复圣徒的住所，并将牧师安置在适合他们的地方。

41　behalf

[bɪˈhæf]

义 *n.* 利益；代表

例 The guardian signed the contract on behalf of the minor child.

译 监护人代表未成年的孩子在合同上签了字。

42　behavior

[bɪˈheɪvjər]

义 *n.* 行为，举止

例 His behaviors are very French.

译 他的行为很像法国人。

43　beige

[beɪʒ]

义 *adj.* 米黄色的　*n.* 米黄色

例 The beige of his jacket toned in with the cream shirt.

译 他的米黄色夹克与乳白色衬衫很相配。

44　belated

[bɪˈleɪtɪd]

义 *adj.* 迟来的

例 Soon after their belated dinner, the grandfather was seen climbing up the Alp.

译 在他们迟来的晚餐后不久，有人看见祖父爬上高山。

---

45 beloved

[bɪˈlʌvd]

义 *adj.* 心爱的　*n.* 心爱的人

例 It was a gift from her beloved.

译 这是她心爱的人送给她的礼物。

46 benign

[bɪˈnaɪn]

义 *adj.* 仁慈的；温和的

例 It wasn't cancer, only a benign tumor.

译 那不是癌症，只是良性肿瘤。

47 bequeath

[bɪˈkwiːð]

义 *v.* 遗赠，遗留

例 She said if the world did not act conclusively now, it would only bequeath the problem to future generations.

译 她说，如果现在不采取果断行动，就只会把这个问题遗留给后代。

48 bestow

[bɪˈstəʊ]

义 *v.* 授予，给予

例 It was a title bestowed upon him by the king.

译 那是国王授予他的头衔。

49 betrayal

[bɪˈtreɪəl]

义 *n.* 背叛；暴露

例 Others saw it as a betrayal.

译 其他人则认为这是一种背叛。

50 bewilder

[bɪˈwɪldər]

义 *v.* 使迷惑，使……不知所措

例 So many questions bewilder me.

译 如此多的问题使我迷惑不解。

51 bid

[bɪd]

义 *v./n.*（买方）出价，投标

例 After more than 11 hours of bids and counter bids, ABC (American Broadcasting Company) won in the sixth round.

译 经过 11 个多小时的竞价和还价之后，ABC（美国广播公司）在第六轮中取得了胜利。

52 bidding

[ˈbɪdɪŋ]

义 *n.* 出价，投标

例 Several companies remained in the bidding.

译 几家公司仍在投标中。

53 binary

[ˈbaɪnərɪ]

义 *adj.* 二进位的；二元的

例 The computer performs calculations in binary and converts the results to decimal.

译 计算机以二进位进行计算，而后把计算结果转换为十进制数。

---

54 binding

['baɪndɪŋ]

义 *adj.* 有约束力的；捆绑的

例 It is set out in a legally binding protocol which forms part of the treaty.

译 这在有法律约束力的且构成条约一部分的附件中有说明。

---

55 binocular

[bɪ'nɑːkjələr]

义 *adj.* 双眼的，两眼用的

例 This is a 20 power binocular microscope.

译 这是一架 20 倍的双目显微镜。

---

56 biofuel

['baɪəʊfjuːəl]

义 *n.* 生物燃料

例 Biofuels can be mixed with conventional fuels.

译 生物燃料可以与传统燃料混合使用。

---

57 biograph

['baɪəʊɡræf]

义 *n.* 传记

例 In his 1985 album *Biograph*, Dylan wrote about the appeal of folk music to him.

译 在他 1985 年的专辑《传记》中，迪伦写到了民谣音乐对他的吸引力。

---

58 biomimicry

[ˌbaɪəʊ'mɪmɪkrɪ]

义 *n.* 仿生，仿生学

例 Janine Benyus of the Biomimicry Institute describes how seashells form layers of mineral and polymer from seawater.

译 生物仿生研究所的珍妮·班亚斯描述了贝壳是如何从海水中吸收形成矿物和聚合物层的。

---

59 biosphere

['baɪəʊsfɪr]

义 *n.* 生物圈

例 Biocycle is the cycling of chemicals through the biosphere.

译 生物循环是化学物质在生物圈内的循环。

---

60 biplane

['baɪpleɪn]

义 *n.* 双翼飞机

例 He arrives in his biplane and crash-lands in a tree.

译 他驾驶双翼飞机到达，在一棵树上紧急降落。

---

61 bisect

[baɪ'sekt]

义 *v.* 平分，切分为二

例 The new road will bisect the town.

译 新马路将把城市分成两部分。

---

62 bitterness

义 *n.* 苦味；苦难；悲痛

['bɪtənəs]　　例 But underneath the humor is an edge of bitterness.

译 但在幽默的背后却是苦难。

---

63 biz

[bɪz]

义 *n.* 商业，生意

例 The environment biz is fickle.

译 商业环境变幻无常。

---

64 blackish

['blækɪʃ]

义 *adj.* 带黑色的

例 Katy has long blackish hair.

译 凯蒂有一头黑色的长发。

---

65 blare

[bler]

义 *n.* 巨响；吼叫声

例 The source of this paradox is electronic anti-noise which creates sound waves to cancel out unwanted noise, such as rattles, blare, etc.

译 这个矛盾的来源是电子抗噪，它产生声波来抵消不需要的噪声，如响尾声、刺耳的鸣响声等。

---

66 blindly

['blaɪndlɪ]

义 *adv.* 盲目地；蛮干地

例 Don't just blindly follow what the banker says.

译 不要盲目地听从这位银行家的话。

---

67 blocky

['blɑːkɪ]

义 *adj.* 短而结实的；块状结构的

例 The blocky box body is thin fan shaped.

译 块状箱体为薄扇形。

---

68 blog

['blɑːg]

义 *v.* 写博客

例 He spends his time traveling through the countryside in search of old recipes, trying them himself, and blogging about his experiences.

译 他花时间在乡村旅行，寻找旧的食谱并亲自尝试，并将自己的经历写在博客上。

---

69 blooded

['blʌdɪd]

义 *adj.* 纯种的；有血的

例 The cat and dog belong to the warm-blooded animals.

译 猫和狗属于温血动物。

---

70 blueberry

['bluːberɪ]

义 *n.* 蓝莓

例 While I've piled on the praise for his creation, please be aware of the following: firstly, *Blueberry Garden* will not be for everyone.

译 虽然我对他的创作赞不绝口，但请注意以下几点：首先，《蓝莓花园》并不适合所有人。

---

71 blurt

[blɜ:rt]

义 *v.* 脱口说出，突然说出

例 I managed to blurt out.

译 我设法脱口而出。

---

72 blush

[blʌʃ]

义 *n.* 脸红；羞愧

例 "The most important thing is to be honest," she says, without the trace of a blush.

译 "最重要的是要诚实，"她一点也不脸红地说。

---

73 boisterous

['bɔɪstərəs]

义 *adj.* 喧闹的；狂暴的

例 With boisterous mirth they dropped upon their knees in a body and did mock homage to their prey.

译 他们欢天喜地，跪倒在地，假装对他们的猎物表示敬意。

---

74 bole

[bəʊl]

义 *n.* 树干

例 The most unusual thing about the Eastern Redwood is that the flowers grow directly on the bole.

译 东部红杉最特别的地方是它的花直接长在树干上。

---

75 bony

['bəʊnɪ]

义 *adj.* 多骨的；瘦骨嶙峋的

例 She suddenly held up a small, bony finger and pointed across the room.

译 她突然举起一根瘦小的手指，指着房间的另一头。

---

76 bookkeeping

['bʊkki:pɪŋ]

义 *n.* 簿记，记账

例 The new mandates also present auditing and bookkeeping challenges.

译 新的规定同样提出审计和记账的问题。

---

77 bottleneck

['bɑ:tlnek]

义 *n.* 瓶颈

例 He pushed everyone full speed ahead until production hit a bottleneck.

译 他催促每个人全速前进，直到生产遇到瓶颈。

---

78 bouquet

[bʊ'keɪ]

义 *n.* 花束；称赞

例 The woman carried a bouquet of dried violets.

译 那女人拿着一束干紫罗兰。

---

79 boyhood

义 *n.* 少年时代

[ˈbɔɪhʊd]   例 They are rivals who have known each other since boyhood.

译 他们是少年时代就相识的对手。

---

80 brag

[bræg]

义 *v.* 吹嘘，自夸

例 One secret I learned very early on was not to brag about success.

译 我很早就学会了一个秘诀，那就是不要吹嘘自己的成功。

---

81 brainpower

[ˈbreɪnpaʊər]

义 *n.* 脑力，聪明才智

例 She admired Robert's brainpower.

译 她钦佩罗伯特的才智。

---

82 brainstorm

[ˈbreɪnstɔːm]

义 *n.* 好主意；脑猝病   *v.* 集体讨论，头脑风暴

例 The women meet twice a month to brainstorm and set business goals for each other.

译 她们每个月见两次以进行头脑风暴，并为彼此设商业目标。

---

83 brandish

[ˈbrændɪʃ]

义 *v.* 挥，挥舞

例 To fight darkness you don't brandish a sword but you light a candle.

译 要想击败黑暗，你需要的不是挥剑，而是一支点亮的蜡烛。

---

84 brash

[bræʃ]

义 *adj.* 傲慢的，无礼的，自以为是的

例 On stage she seems hard, brash and uncompromising.

译 在舞台上，她显得冷酷、傲慢、毫不妥协。

---

85 brawl

[brɔːl]

义 *n.* 喧闹，斗殴

例 He had been in a drunken street brawl.

译 他曾在街上醉酒斗殴。

---

86 brazier

[ˈbreɪzɪər]

义 *n.* 火盆

例 You will find a brazier within a shallow cave there.

译 你会在那里的一个小山洞里能找到一个火盆。

---

87 breadth

[bredθ]

义 *n.* 宽度

例 The breadth of the whole camp was 400 paces.

译 整个营地的宽度是 400 步。

---

88 breakage

[ˈbreɪkɪdʒ]

义 *n.* 破损，打破，破坏；破碎物品

例 Brushing wet hair can cause stretching and breakage.

译 梳湿头发会导致头发拉伸和破损。

---

89 breakup

['breɪkʌp]

义 *n.* 崩溃；解体；分手

例 If you cannot imagine your ex with someone else and are not over the breakup, it might be better not to go.

译 如果你无法想象你的前任和别人在一起，而且还没有从分手中恢复过来，那么最好还是不要去。

---

90 breast

[brest]

义 *n.* 乳房，胸脯

例 Her mother died of breast cancer.

译 她的母亲死于乳腺癌。

---

91 breathtaking

['breθteɪkɪŋ]

义 *adj.* 令人赞叹的，吃惊的

例 He spoke with breathtaking arrogance.

译 他说话傲慢得令人吃惊。

---

92 brilliance

['brɪlɪəns]

义 *n.* 才华；光辉

例 She loved his brilliance and his generous heart.

译 她爱他的才华和慷慨的心。

---

93 brim

[brɪm]

义 *n.* 边；边缘

例 Her glass was filled right up to the brim.

译 她的杯子装得满满的。

---

94 brisk

[brɪsk]

义 *adj.* 活泼的，轻快的

例 A brisk walk should blow the cobwebs away.

译 轻快的散步可以使人头脑清醒。

---

95 broad

[brɔːd]

义 *adj.* 宽广的，宽阔的

例 The hills rise green and sheer above the broad river.

译 这些小山碧绿陡峭，矗立在这条宽阔的河流之上。

---

96 bruise

[bruːz]

义 *n.* 瘀青，挫伤 *v.* 打击，挫伤；碰伤

例 Strawberries bruise easily.

译 草莓容易碰伤。

---

97 brushstroke

['brʌʃstrəʊk]

义 *n.* 一笔；笔法

例 He paints with harsh, slashing brushstrokes.

| 译 | 他画画笔锋粗犷凌厉。 |

---

98 brutally

['bru:təlɪ]

义	*adv.* 残忍地，冷酷无情地
例	A stormy night at sea, even in the tropics, can be brutally chilling.
译	即使是在热带地区，海上的暴风雨之夜也冷得令人难以忍受。

---

99 buildup

['bɪld‚ʌp]

义	*n.* 集结；增长
例	Amyloid buildup often affects the kidneys, damaging their filtering system.
译	淀粉样蛋白的积聚通常会影响肾脏，损害肾脏的过滤系统。

---

100 bulky

['bʌlkɪ]

义	*adj.* 庞大的；笨重的
例	These sorts of products are heavy and bulky and the cost of transporting them relatively high.
译	这类产品笨重、庞大，运输成本也比较高。

List 3

1 bulldozer

['bʊldəʊzər]

义 *n.* 推土机；欺凌者

例 There would be one machine, one bulldozer for the entire area.

译 整个地区会有一台机器——一台推土机。

2 bumpy

['bʌmpɪ]

义 *adj.* 颠簸的，崎岖不平的

例 In addition, the rough, bumpy roads of the time made maneuvering the carts difficult.

译 此外，当时的道路崎岖不平，使车辆很难操纵。

3 bunny

['bʌnɪ]

义 *n.* 小兔子

例 The Happy Bunny club was heaving.

译 快乐兔俱乐部正在解散。

4 buoyancy

['bɔɪənsɪ]

义 *n.* 浮力

例 Air can be pumped into the diving suit to increase buoyancy.

译 可以把空气泵入潜水衣以增加浮力。

5 burner

['bɜːrnər]

义 *n.* 燃烧器；火炉

例 It's like an old charcoal burner.

译 它就像一个旧的炭炉。

6 buttress

['bʌtrəs]

义 *v.* 支持

例 We firmly buttress up our football team.

译 我们坚决支持我们的足球队。

7 buzzy

['bʌzɪ]

义 *adj.* 时尚的，生动的

例 The café has an intimate but buzzy atmosphere.

译 这个咖啡馆很温馨，但又有一种时尚的氛围。

8 calibration

[ˌkælɪ'breɪʃn]

义 *n.* 标定，校准；刻度

例 The instrument is very delicate for general calibration purposes.

译 这种仪器作为一般的标定是很精确的。

9 callous

['kæləslɪ]

义 *adj.* 无情的；硬结的

例 She was selfish, arrogant and often callous.

译 她自私傲慢，而且常常冷酷无情。

10 calmly
[ˈkɑːmlɪ]

义 *adv.* 平静地，安静地
例 The wise man replied calmly.
译 智者平静地回答。

11 campfire
[ˈkæmpfaɪər]

义 *n.* 营火，篝火
例 My mother cooks over a campfire.
译 我妈妈用营火做饭。

12 capitalist
[ˈkæpɪtəlɪst]

义 *n.* 资本家，资本主义者
例 Individual capitalists are typically wealthy people who have a large amount of capital (money or other financial assets) invested in business.
译 个人资本家通常是指那些拥有大量可投资于商业的资金（金钱或其他金融资产）的富人。

13 captivate
[ˈkæptɪveɪt]

义 *v.* 迷住，迷惑
例 Though the 1920s was the time and age when crosswords were at the peak of the public's obsession with crosswords, the puzzles and their cryptic clues continue to captivate audiences.
译 尽管 20 世纪 20 年代是公众对填字游戏痴迷的巅峰时期，但现在谜题及其神秘的线索仍然吸引着观众。

14 carefree
[ˈkerfriː]

义 *adj.* 无忧无虑的，轻松愉快的
例 Chantal remembered carefree summers at the beach.
译 尚塔尔回忆起在海滩上无忧无虑的夏天。

15 caregiver
[ˈkergɪvər]

义 *n.* 看护者
例 If it has to hire a caregiver for every two children, it can't really achieve any economies of scale on labor to save money when other expenses go up.
译 如果不得不为每两个孩子雇佣一名看护者，那么当其他费用上升时，就无法在劳动力成本上面真正实现任何经济上的节约。

16 cartoonist
[kɑːrˈtuːnɪst]

义 *n.* 漫画家
例 He was a cartoonist.
译 他是一位漫画家。

17 carve
[kɑːrv]

义 *v.* 雕刻
例 They used thousand-year-old methods and replicas of Viking tools, which meant carving each of the ship's oak planks with axes, wedges, and hammers.

> **译** 他们使用了有上千年历史的方法和维京人工具的复制品，这意味着用斧子、楔子和锤子雕刻每一块船上的橡木板。

18 cast

[kæst]

义 *v.* 掷；选定演员

例 The play is being cast in both the US and Britain.

译 目前正在英美两国挑选这部戏的演员。

19 casualty

['kæʒʊəltɪ]

义 *n.* 事故；伤亡人员

例 There are fears that the casualty toll may be higher.

译 人们担心伤亡人数可能会更高。

20 cataclysmic

[ˌkætə'klɪzmɪk]

义 *adj.* 灾难性的

例 Few had expected that change to be as cataclysmic as it turned out to be.

译 很少有人预料到这种变化会像结果那样具有灾难性。

21 catalyze

['kætəˌlaɪz]

义 *v.* 催化

例 It is proved that ACF is a type of catalyzing electrode material.

译 研究表明，ACF 是一种催化电极材料。

22 cauliflower

['kɔːlɪflaʊər]

义 *n.* 花椰菜

例 I'll give you a nice dish of cauliflower with white sauce on it.

译 我给您上一盘白汁花椰菜。

23 cautionary

['kɔːʃənerɪ]

义 *adj.* 警戒的，警告的

例 In her conclusion, the author sounds a cautionary note.

译 在作者的结论中，她敲响了警钟。

24 ceaseless

['siːsləs]

义 *adj.* 不绝的，不停的

例 There is a ceaseless struggle from noon to night.

译 斗争从中午一直持续到晚上。

25 cede

[siːd]

义 *v.* 放弃，割让（领土，权利）

例 They feel invisible, so they cede responsibility.

译 他们觉得自己被忽视了，所以他们放弃了责任。

26 celebratory

['seləbrətɔːrɪ]

义 *adj.* 庆祝的

例 That night she, Nicholson, and the crew had a celebratory dinner.

译 那天晚上，她、尼科尔森和工作人员吃了一顿庆功宴。

---

27 cemetery

['semətərɪ]

义 *n.* 墓地

例 He was buried in Highgate Cemetery.

译 他被葬在海格特公墓。

---

28 centerpiece

['sentə,piːs]

义 *n.* 中心装饰品；核心

例 The reconstructed boat, as a symbol of the maritime connections that bound together the communities either side of the channel, was the centerpiece.

译 重造的船是航海联络的象征，把海峡两岸的群体联结到一起，这便是它的核心意义所在。

---

29 chandelier

[,ʃændə'lɪr]

义 *n.* 枝形吊灯（烛台）

例 A crystal chandelier lit the room.

译 一盏水晶枝形吊灯照亮了房间。

---

30 changeover

['tʃeɪndʒəʊvər]

义 *n.* 转换，逆转；大变更

例 He again called for a faster changeover to a market economy.

译 他再次呼吁加快向市场经济的转换。

---

31 chapped

[tʃæpt]

义 *adj.* 裂开的，有裂痕的

例 Apparently from constant rubbing of her nose and mouth with the back of her hand, her cheeks were chapped and red.

译 显然是由于她不停地用手背摩擦鼻子和嘴巴，她的脸颊皲裂发红。

---

32 charcoal

['tʃɑːrkəʊl]

义 *n.* 木炭；炭笔

例 We recommend using alternative sources of fuel such as charcoals.

译 我们建议使用替代燃料资源，如木炭。

---

33 charisma

[kə'rɪzmə]

义 *n.* 非凡的领导力；魅力

例 The president has great personal charisma.

译 总统有很强的个人魅力。

---

34 chatty

['tʃætɪ]

义 *adj.* 爱闲聊的；非正式的

例 She's quite a chatty person.

译 她是个爱闲聊的人。

35　cheekbone

['tʃiːkbəʊn]

义　*n.* 颊骨，颧骨

例　She was very beautiful, with high cheekbones.

译　她颧骨高高的，非常漂亮。

36　cheerfulness

['tʃɪəfəlnəs]

义　*n.* 高兴，快活

例　Cheerfulness is health.

译　高兴就是健康的体现。

37　cheerleader

['tʃɪrliːdər]

义　*n.* 拉拉队长；支持者

例　I'm talking about next head cheerleader.

译　我说的是下一届拉拉队队长的人选。

38　chilly

['tʃɪlɪ]

义　*adj.* 寒冷的；冷淡的

例　It was a chilly afternoon.

译　那是一个寒冷的下午。

39　chimp

[tʃɪmp]

义　*n.* 黑猩猩

例　The chimp pulls off the leaves and chews the stick.

译　黑猩猩扯下树叶，咀嚼树枝。

40　chin

[tʃɪn]

义　*n.* 颏，下巴

例　He rested his chin in his hands.

译　他双手托着下巴。

41　chitchat

['tʃɪtˌtʃæt]

义　*n.* 闲谈，聊天

例　Not being a mother, I found the chitchat exceedingly dull.

译　由于我不是一个母亲，我觉得这种闲聊非常无聊。

42　choke

[tʃəʊk]

义　*v.* 窒息；说不出话

例　Very small toys can choke a baby.

译　很小的玩具会使婴儿窒息。

43　chore

[tʃɔːr]

义　*n.* 讨厌的工作，琐事

例　Shopping's a real chore for me.

译　购物对我来说真是件讨厌的事。

44　choreograph

义　*v.* 设计舞蹈动作；设计，筹划

['kɔ:rɪəgræf] 　例 What I would really like to do is to choreograph other people. It would be an exciting career.

译 我真正想做的是为别人设计舞蹈动作，这将是个令人兴奋的工作。

45　chronicler

['krɑ:nɪklər]

义 *n.* 年代史编者，记录者

例 The chronicler sets down every detail, believing all to be of ultimate significance.

译 记录者把每一个细节都记录了下来，相信它们最终都会是珍贵史料。

46　chuckle

['tʃʌkl]

义 *v.* 轻声笑，暗自笑

例 Oracle must chuckle every time an open-source operating system company reports its paltry profits or losses.

译 每当一家开源操作系统公司报告其微薄的利润或亏损时，甲骨文公司肯定会窃笑。

47　churn

[tʃɜ:rn]

义 *v.* 剧烈，搅动，（使）猛烈翻滚

例 The water churned beneath the huge ship.

译 水在巨轮下面剧烈翻滚。

48　cipher

['saɪfər]

义 *n.* 密码；零

例 All important plans were sent to the police in cipher.

译 所有重要计划都以加密形式送交警方。

49　civilian

[sə'vɪljən]

义 *adj.* 平民的　*n.* 平民，百姓

例 A civilian was killed by a stray bullet.

译 一名平民被流弹打死。

50　clamor

['klæmə]

义 *n.* 喧闹

例 The clamor of traffic gave me a headache.

译 交通的喧闹声使我头痛。

51　clarification

[ˌklærəfɪ'keɪʃn]

义 *n.* 澄清，阐明

例 I made some clarifications to my initial post.

译 我对最初的帖子做了一些澄清。

52　clarity

['klærətɪ]

义 *n.* 清楚，透明

例 It was a model of clarity.

译 这是清楚的典范。

---

53 cleanup

['kliːnˌʌp]

义 *n.* 清除，大扫除

例 We need to do a full household cleanup.

译 我们得好好做做全家大扫除了。

---

54 clink

[klɪŋk]

义 *v.* 使发出叮当声；碰杯

例 They clink glasses and drink.

译 他们碰杯喝酒。

---

55 clipping

['klɪpɪŋ]

义 *n.* 剪报；剪取物

例 So, that was called coupon clipping.

译 这被称为优惠券剪报。

---

56 clog

[klɑːg]

义 *v.* 阻塞，堵塞

例 Within a few years the pipes began to clog up.

译 几年之内，管道开始堵塞。

---

57 closeness

['kləʊsnəs]

义 *n.* 亲密；密闭；接近

例 Intimacy is the feeling of closeness, of connectedness with someone, of bonding.

译 亲密感是一种亲密的感觉，是与某人的连接，是黏合的感觉。

---

58 clunky

['klʌŋkɪ]

义 *adj.* 笨重的，笨拙的

例 The movie is ruined by wooden acting and clunky dialogue.

译 这部电影被木讷的表演和笨拙的对白给毁了。

---

59 clutter

['klʌtər]

义 *v.* 弄乱，混乱 *n.* 杂乱，混乱

例 There was a clutter of bottles and tubes on the shelf.

译 架子上乱七八糟地堆放着瓶子和管子。

---

60 coauthor

[kəʊˈɔːθə]

义 *n.* 合著者，共同执笔者 *v.* 合著

例 For example, you can write a query that retrieves the coauthored psychology books.

译 例如，你可以编写一个检索合著的心理学书籍的查询系统。

---

61 coax

[kəʊks]

义 *v.* 哄；诱骗

例 The officer spoke yesterday of her role in trying to coax vital information from the young victim.

译 该官员昨天谈起她的职责：设法诱骗那个年轻受害人提供重要信息。

62 cogitation

[ˌkɒdʒɪ'teɪʃn]

义 *n.* 慎重考虑；苦思

例 After much cogitation, we decided to move to the Bahamas.

译 经过再三考虑，我们决定搬到巴哈马群岛去。

63 coherence

[kəʊ'hɪrəns]

义 *n.* 一致；连贯

例 The anthology has a surprising sense of coherence.

译 这部选集有着惊人的连贯性。

64 cohesive

[kəʊ'hiːsɪv]

义 *adj.* 团结的，有凝聚力的；黏性的

例 An island country, a whole continent, Australia has remarkably cohesive personality.

译 作为一个岛国、一个大洲，澳大利亚具有显著的凝聚力。

65 coincident

[kəʊ'ɪnsɪdənt]

义 *adj.* 同时发生的；一致的

例 Their aims are coincident with ours.

译 他们的目标与我们的一致。

66 collaboration

[kəˌlæbə'reɪʃn]

义 *n.* 合作；通敌

例 The government worked in close collaboration with teachers on the new curriculum.

译 政府和教师就新的课程进行了紧密合作。

67 collection

[kə'lekʃn]

义 *n.* 收集，收取

例 I need one more stamp before my collection is completed.

译 我还需要一张邮票我的集邮就完成了。

68 collegial

[kə'liːdʒɪəl]

义 *adj.* 学院的；共同掌权的

例 Therefore, the research on the collegial P. E. culture in campus has important meaning.

译 因此，对校园体育文化的研究有着重大的意义。

69 colorfully

['kʌləfəllɪ]

义 *adv.* 多彩地；绚烂地

例 A clean cyberspace will paint our lives more colorfully.

译 一个干净的网络空间将使我们的生活更加丰富多彩。

70 coloring

['kʌlərɪŋ]

义 *n.* 着色，染色

例 Not only the coloring genes, but lots of other genes are getting mixed up, too.

译 不仅是染色基因，很多其他基因也在混合。

71 colorless

['kʌlələs]

义 *adj.* 无色的

例 The colorless liquid seeped into the ground and continues even now to foul the local water supply.

译 无色的液体渗入地下，甚至现在还在污染当地的供水系统。

---

72 color

['kʌlər]

义 *v.* 给……着色；脸红

例 Andrew couldn't help noticing that she colored slightly.

译 安德鲁不禁注意到她微微有些脸红。

---

73 combative

[kəm'bætɪv]

义 *adj.* 好斗的

例 He conducted the meeting yesterday in his usual combative style, refusing to admit any mistakes.

译 他昨天以他一贯的好斗风格主持了会议，拒绝承认任何错误。

---

74 commonsense

[ˌkɑ:mən'sens]

义 *adj.* 有常识的；明白事理的

例 These are commonsense reforms that respond to the obvious problems exposed by the financial crisis.

译 这些都是应对金融危机暴露的明显问题的常识性改革。

---

75 commotion

[kə'məʊʃn]

义 *n.* 骚动，喧闹

例 Tolstoy was hardly aware of all the commotion.

译 托尔斯泰几乎没有意识到这一切骚动。

---

76 communicative

[kə'mju:nɪkeɪtɪv]

义 *adj.* 健谈的；交流的

例 I don't find him very communicative.

译 我不觉得他很健谈。

---

77 communion

[kə'mju:nɪən]

义 *n.* 交流；共享

例 Prayer is regarded as a form of communion with God.

译 祈祷被视为是与上帝进行交流的一种方式。

---

78 commuter

[kə'mju:tər]

义 *n.* 每日往返上班者

例 She accidentally stepped on his foot on a crowded commuter train.

译 在拥挤的通勤火车上，她不小心踩了他的脚。

---

79 companionship

[kəm'pænɪənʃɪp]

义 *n.* 友谊；陪伴

例 I depended on his companionship and on his judgment.

译 我依赖他的陪伴和他的判断。

80 compassionate

[kəm'pæʃənət]

义 *adj.* 有同情心的

例 She has a wise, compassionate face.

译 她有一张睿智、富有同情心的脸。

---

81 compatibility

[kəm,pætə'bɪlətɪ]

义 *n.* 协调；兼容

例 This is for compatibility with current browsers.

译 这是为了与当前浏览器兼容。

---

82 completeness

[kəm'pli:tnəs]

义 *n.* 完成；完整

例 For the sake of completeness, all names are given in full.

译 为完整起见，所有名称均用全名。

---

83 compression

[kəm'preʃn]

义 *n.* 压缩，浓缩

例 The compression of the wood is easily achieved.

译 木材的压缩很容易实现。

---

84 computerize

[kəm'pju:təraɪz]

义 *v.* 用电脑处理；使电脑化

例 Let's totally computerize the operation.

译 让我们把操作完全电脑化。

---

85 conceit

[kən'si:t]

义 *n.* 自负；个人观点

例 Reyes emits confidence without conceit.

译 罗伊斯散发着自信但不自负。

---

86 conceptualize

[kən'septʃʊəlaɪz]

义 *v.* 概念化

例 How we conceptualize things has a lot to do with what we feel.

译 我们如何概念化事物与我们的感觉有很大关系。

---

87 concerted

[kən's3:rtɪd]

义 *adj.* 协定的；一致的

例 We need to make a concerted effort to finish on time.

译 我们需要齐心协力按时完成。

---

88 concise

[kən'saɪs]

义 *adj.* 简明的，简要的

例 Burton's text is concise and informative.

译 伯顿的文章文字简要，内容丰富。

---

89 concoction

[kən'kɑ:kʃən]

义 *n.* 混合；调和物

例 This new drink, a concoction of the sorghum beer, was popular with chiefs and commoners alike.

译 这种新饮料，一种高粱啤酒的调和物，广受首领和平民欢迎。

---

90 condemnation

[ˌkɑ:ndem'neɪʃn]

义 *n.* 谴责；定罪

例 There was widespread condemnation of the invasion.

译 那次侵略遭到了普遍的谴责。

---

91 condensation

[ˌkɑ:nden'seɪʃn]

义 *n.* 浓缩，凝结

例 It's constantly being recycled through evaporation and condensation.

译 它通过蒸发和凝结不断循环利用。

---

92 conductor

[kən'dʌktər]

义 *n.* (乐队等的)指挥；导体

例 The conductor beat time with a baton.

译 指挥用指挥棒打拍子。

---

93 confederate

[kən'fedərət]

义 *n.* 同盟者；同伙　*adj.* 联邦的；联合的

例 Finally the Confederate army had to surrender, ending the war in May, 1865.

译 最后，南部联邦军队不得不投降，战争在 1865 年 5 月结束。

---

94 confession

[kən'feʃən]

义 *n.* 供认，供状；承认，坦白；表白；忏悔

例 I have a confession to make.

译 我要坦白一件事。

---

95 confidential

[ˌkɑ:nfɪ'denʃl]

义 *adj.* 秘密的，机密的

例 My letter is, of course, strictly private and confidential.

译 当然，我的信属于私人信件，是严格保密的。

---

96 confinement

[kən'faɪnmənt]

义 *n.* 拘禁；分娩；关押

例 Last night he was being held in solitary confinement in Douglas jail.

译 昨晚他被单独关押在道格拉斯监狱。

---

97 conflagration

[ˌkɑ:nflə'greɪʃən]

义 *n.* 大火；爆发

例 Now that a great financial blaze has taken hold, the eurozone is facing its 1666 moment. Unless tamed, the conflagration might not spare anybody.

译 如今一场金融大火席卷而来，欧元区面临着如同 1666 年那样的时刻。除非将其扑灭，否则大火之下，无人能够幸免。

98 confluence

['kɑːnfluəns]

义 *n.* 合流，汇合

例 The peak stands at the confluence of three major storm tracks, and its steep slopes force rising winds to accelerate.

译 这座山峰位于三大风暴路径的汇合处，陡峭的山坡迫使上升的风加速。

---

99 congeal

[kən'dʒiːl]

义 *v.* (使)凝结，凝固

例 The blood had started to congeal.

译 血开始凝固了。

---

100 conical

['kɑːnɪkl]

义 *adj.* 圆锥形的

例 Belugas have 40 small conical teeth which they use to grasp fish.

译 白鲸有 40 个用来捕食鱼的圆锥形小牙齿。

List 4

1 conjecture

[kən'dʒektʃər]

义 *n.* 推测，臆测；猜测

例 That was a conjecture, not a fact.

译 那只是猜测，不是事实。

---

2 connotation

['kɑːnə'teɪʃən]

义 *n.* 含义；内涵

例 The meaning of children's books lies in conveying the profound connotation behind the story.

译 儿童读物的意义在于传达故事背后的深刻内涵。

---

3 consciously

['kɑːnʃəslɪ]

义 *adv.* 有意识地；自觉地

例 I found a seat in the corner, sat down, and leaned my head back against the window frame, half-consciously watching for the station to recede slowly into the distance.

译 我在角落里找了个座位坐了下来，将头靠在窗框上，不太有意识地望着车站慢慢远去。

---

4 conservator

[kən'sɜːrvətər]

义 *n.* 保护者，管理员

例 The stabilization of "bronze disease" remains a major challenge for the archaeological conservator.

译 "青铜病"的稳定问题对文物保护者来说仍是一个挑战。

---

5 conserve

[kən'sɜːrv]

义 *v.* 节省；保护

例 If no one owns the resource concerned, no one has an interest in conserving it or fostering it: fish is the best example of this.

译 如果没有人拥有相关的资源，就没有人有兴趣保护或培育它：鱼类就是最好的例子。

---

6 consign

[kən'saɪn]

义 *v.* 把……委托给，交付，托管；托售，寄售

例 I think you can consign it here.

译 您可以把它寄存在这儿。

---

7 console

[kən'səʊl]

义 *v.* 安慰，慰藉

例 I can console myself with the fact that I'm not alone.

译 我可以安慰自己，我并不孤单。

---

8 conspire

[kən'spaɪər]

义 *v.* 协力；共谋，合谋

例 People always conspire to keep the truth from me.

译 人们总是合谋不把真相告诉我。

9 constrained

[kən'streɪnd]

义 *adj.* 不自然的；强迫的；过于受拘束的，拘泥的

例 The boy felt constrained in her presence.

译 那男孩在她面前感到不自然。

---

10 constrict

[kən'strɪkt]

义 *v.* 束紧，使收缩

例 A major change is that my eyes constrict normally now.

译 一个主要的变化是我的眼睛现在正常收缩了。

---

11 consultant

[kən'sʌltənt]

义 *n.* 顾问，咨询者

例 She is a consultant to the government.

译 她是政府顾问。

---

12 contaminant

[kən'tæmɪnənt]

义 *n.* 污染物质，沾染物

例 The passage most strongly suggests that nitrate can act as both a contaminant and a nutrient.

译 这篇文章强烈地表明硝酸盐既是污染物又是营养物质。

---

13 contention

[kən'tenʃn]

义 *n.* 争论；争夺

例 Exactly where the apple came from had long been a matter of contention and discussion among people who study plant origins.

译 苹果的确切产地一直是研究植物起源的人们争论和探讨的问题。

---

14 controllable

[kən'trəʊləbl]

义 *adj.* 可管理的；可控制的

例 This makes the surfboards more controllable.

译 这使冲浪板更加可控。

---

15 convene

[kən'viːn]

义 *v.* 召集，集合，开会；传唤

例 We'd convene probably at least every week.

译 我们可能至少每周都要开会。

---

16 convention

[kən'venʃn]

义 *n.* 协定；惯例

例 It is remarkable how effective these conventions are in creating the impression of a loud and noisy medium.

译 值得注意的是，这些惯例在制造一种喧闹的媒体印象方面是多么有效。

---

17 convergence

[kən'vɜːrdʒəns]

义 *n.* 收敛，汇聚；趋同

例 A survey conducted earlier this year shows how this convergence on similar types of work has blurred class boundaries.

译 今年早些时候进行的一项调查显示，相似工作类型上的趋同是如何模糊阶级界限的。

---

18 convergent

[kən'vɜːrdʒənt]

义 *adj.* 会聚性的，聚合性的；收敛的

例 Convergent questions have one correct answer.

译 聚合性问题只有一个正确答案。

---

19 convertible

[kən'vɜːrtəbəl]

义 *adj.* 可改变的，可转换的，可兑换的

例 The bonds are convertible into ordinary shares.

译 债券可兑换为普通股。

---

20 conveyance

[kən'veɪəns]

义 *n.* 运输；运输工具，交通工具

例 Mahoney had never seen such a conveyance before.

译 马奥尼以前从未见过这样的交通工具。

---

21 corny

['kɔːrnɪ]

义 *adj.* 陈词滥调的，老生常谈的

例 I know it sounds corny, but I'm really not motivated by money.

译 我知道这听起来有点老生常谈，但我真的不是为了钱。

---

22 corrective

[kə'rektɪv]

义 *adj.* 纠正的，矫正的

例 Scientific institutions have been reluctant to take corrective action.

译 科学机构一直都不愿采取纠正的行动。

---

23 corrosive

[kə'rəʊsɪv]

义 *adj.* 腐蚀的，蚀坏的

例 Sodium and sulphur are highly corrosive.

译 钠和硫具有很强的腐蚀性。

---

24 councilor

['kaʊnsələ]

义 *n.* 议员，顾问

例 Amanda's mother employs a personal trainer, a bodyguard, a singing coach and a councilor to look after all her fifteen-year-old daughter's needs.

译 阿曼达的母亲雇用了一名私人教练、一名保镖、一名歌唱教练和一名顾问来满足她 15 岁女儿的所有需要。

---

25 courageous

[kə'reɪdʒəs]

义 *adj.* 勇敢的，有勇气的

例 The children were very courageous.

译 孩子们非常勇敢。

---

26 covet

['kʌvət]

义 *v.* 觊觎，垂涎

例 You covet this throne too much.

| | | 译 | 你太觊觎这个宝座了。 |

---

27 cozy

['kəʊzɪ]

义 *adj.* 舒适的，惬意的

例 This cozy workplace no longer exists here.

译 这个舒适的工作场所在这里已经不复存在了。

---

28 cram

[kræm]

义 *n.* （应考）突击准备；填鸭式学习

例 Zealous parents send their kids to the expensive cram schools.

译 热心的父母把他们的孩子送到昂贵的补习班。

---

29 cramp

[kræmp]

义 *n.* 抽筋，痉挛

例 Hillsden was complaining of a cramp in his calf muscles.

译 希尔斯登说他的小腿肌肉抽筋。

---

30 craving

['kreɪvɪŋ]

义 *n.* 渴望，热望

例 This craving is, of course, the bane of many ex-alcoholics' existence.

译 这种渴望当然是许多前酒徒生活的烦恼之源。

---

31 creamer

['kri:mər]

义 *n.* 植脂末，奶精

例 I don't like creamer, I prefer natural milk instead.

译 我不喜欢奶精，我更喜欢自然的牛奶。

---

32 creamy

['kri:mɪ]

义 *adj.* 含乳脂的，乳脂状的

例 Its limestone face was a creamy gold against the lowering sun, and he felt the bite of nostalgia.

译 在落日的映衬下，它那石灰石般的面孔呈现出乳脂般的金黄色，他感到了一种怀旧的感觉。

---

33 crease

[kri:s]

义 *n.* 折痕，皱痕　*v.* 起皱

例 Most outfits crease a bit when you are traveling.

译 大多数的外套在旅行中都会有些起皱。

---

34 creek

[kri:k]

义 *n.* 小湾，小溪

例 On summer afternoons, my sister and I used to go on creek walks.

译 夏天的下午，我和姐姐常去小溪边散步。

---

35 crescent

['kresnt]

义 *n.* 新月；新月形之物

例 The moon was a brightly shining crescent.

译 当时月亮是一弯明亮的新月。

---

36 cripple

['krɪpl]

义 *v.* 使残废；严重损坏，严重削弱

例 A total cutoff of supplies would cripple the country's economy.

译 全面终止供给将严重削弱该国经济。

---

37 crisp

[krɪsp]

义 *adj.* 脆的

例 The celery is fresh and crisp.

译 这芹菜新鲜脆嫩。

---

38 crook

[krʊk]

义 *n.* 骗子

例 That salesman is a real crook.

译 那个推销员是个十足的骗子。

---

39 crossbeam

['krɔːsˌbiːm]

义 *n.* 大梁，横梁

例 The long corridor has over 14,000 traditional Chinese paintings on the beams and crossbeams.

译 长廊的梁柱和横梁上有 1 万 4 千多幅中国画。

---

40 crudeness

[kruːdnəs]

义 *n.* 未成熟；生硬；粗野

例 Without art the crudeness of reality would make the world unbearable.

译 如果没有艺术，现实的粗野将使世界变得无法忍受。

---

41 cryptic

['krɪptɪk]

义 *adj.* 秘密的，隐晦的

例 He has issued a short, cryptic statement denying the spying charges.

译 他发表了一份简短而隐晦的声明，否认间谍指控。

---

42 cubism

['kjuːbɪzəm]

义 *n.* 立体派，立体主义

例 Cubism was equally the creation of Picasso and Braque.

译 立体主义是由毕加索和布拉克共同创造的。

---

43 cubist

['kjuːbɪst]

义 *n.* 立体派艺术家　*adj.* 立体派的

例 She can understand cubist pictures.

译 她能理解立体派的画作。

---

44 cumbersome

['kʌmbərsəm]

义 *adj.* 笨重的；不方便的

例 Although the machine looks cumbersome, it is actually easy to use.

译 虽然这台机器看起来很笨重，但实际上很容易使用。

---

45 curb

[kɜ:rb]

义 *v.* 控制，抑制

例 He needs to learn to curb his temper.

译 他需要学会控制自己的脾气。

---

46 curd

[kɜ:rd]

义 *n.* 凝乳

例 We had all kinds of peddlers who went from house to house, selling fresh bean curd and steamed buns, twisted dough and colorful candies.

译 我们有各种各样的小贩，挨家挨户地叫卖新鲜的豆腐、馒头、面团和彩糖。

---

47 cutter

['kʌtər]

义 *n.* 裁剪者，切割机

例 The cutters are opened by turning the knob anticlockwise.

译 逆时针转动旋钮可以开启切割机。

---

48 cyclically

['saɪklɪklɪ]

义 *adv.* 循环地，环形地

例 Kuike calls mercury "huandan, a cyclically transformed regenerative elixir" associated with longevity.

译 奎可称水银为"环丹，一种循环转化的再生灵丹"，与长寿有关。

---

49 cynicism

['sɪnɪsɪzəm]

义 *n.* 愤世嫉俗，玩世不恭

例 He was dismayed at the cynicism of the youngsters.

译 他为年轻人的玩世不恭感到沮丧。

---

50 cypher

['saɪfər]

义 *n.* 解码；无足轻重的人

例 Do you think he is a cypher, Curly?

译 你认为他是个无足轻重的人吗，科利？

---

51 dancehall

['dɑ:nsˌhɔ:l]

义 *n.* 舞厅

例 Bob Marley's musical legacy may be waning 30 years after his death as Jamaica's youth prefers dancehall to reggae, but the singer remains a cult, if highly commercialized, figure.

译 鲍勃·马利逝世30周年后，他的音乐遗产正在消亡，因为比起雷鬼乐，牙买加的年轻人更加青睐舞厅音乐，然而，如果对马利的形象进行高度的商业化运作，身为歌手的马利将继续成为人们崇拜的偶像。

---

52 dank

[dæŋk]

义 *adj.* 阴湿的

例 After this day we would spend the rest of the season in a dank and moldy indoor pool.

译 过了这一天，剩下的季节我们就要在潮湿发霉的室内游泳池里度过了。

---

53 dazzle
['dæzl]

义 *n.* 耀眼；令人赞叹的特质

例 Of course she had her good bones and bright looks, all that fair dazzle of skin and hair.

译 当然，她的骨骼很好，容貌亮丽，皮肤和头发光彩夺目。

---

54 dealer
['di:lər]

义 *n.* 商人，经销商

例 You are well advised to buy your car through a reputable dealer.

译 建议你通过信誉好的经销商购买汽车。

---

55 debut
[deɪ'bju:]

义 *n.* 首次露面，初次登场

例 His debut album was hugely successful stateside.

译 他的首张专辑在美国大获成功。

---

56 deceptive
[dɪ'septɪv]

义 *adj.* 欺骗性的，骗人的

例 Looks can be deceptive.

译 外表可能是有欺骗性的。

---

57 decisiveness
[dɪ'saɪsɪvnəs]

义 *n.* 坚决，果断

例 Now here's real decisiveness.

译 这才是真正的果断。

---

58 decompress
[ˌdi:kəm'pres]

义 *v.* 减压

例 I went to Hawaii for a week to decompress.

译 为了减压，我去夏威夷玩了一星期。

---

59 dedication
[ˌdedɪ'keɪʃn]

义 *n.* 奉献

例 Her colleagues could not fault her dedication to the job.

译 她的同事认为她的敬业精神是无可挑剔的。

---

60 defective
[dɪ'fektɪv]

义 *adj.* 有问题的，有缺陷的

例 Retailers can return defective merchandise.

译 零售商可以退回有问题的商品。

---

61 defence
[dɪ'fens]

义 *n.* 防御；辩护

例 Nobody spoke out in his defence.

译 没有人站出来替他辩护。

---

62 defender

[dɪ'fendər]

义 *n.* 防卫者；辩护者

例 Lewis was the NFL's top defender in the 2000 season.

译 刘易斯是 2000 年赛季美国国家足球联盟的最佳防守球员。

---

63 deficient

[dɪ'fɪʃnt]

义 *adj.* 不足的，不充分的；有缺陷的

例 Deaf people are sometimes treated as being mentally deficient.

译 失聪的人有时被认为有智力缺陷。

---

64 delectable

[dɪ'lektəbl]

义 *adj.* 快乐的；美味的

例 These apples look delectable.

译 这些苹果看起来很美味。

---

65 deletion

[dɪ'liːʃn]

义 *n.* 删除

例 Information must be stored so that it is secure from accidental deletion.

译 必须保存信息以防止意外删除。

---

66 delirious

[dɪ'lɪrɪəs]

义 *adj.* 神志昏迷的；发狂的

例 The crowds were delirious with joy.

译 人群欣喜若狂。

---

67 deluxe

[dɪ'lʌks]

义 *adj.* 豪华的；高级的

例 Deluxe editions of this biography are available now.

译 这本传记的精装本现在有售。

---

68 demo

['deməʊ]

义 *n.* 样本唱片；演示

例 They all went on the demo.

译 他们都参加了演示。

---

69 demystify

[ˌdiː'mɪstɪfaɪ]

义 *v.* 使简单化，使非神秘化

例 This book aims to demystify medical treatments.

译 这本书旨在使医学治疗简单化。

---

70 denial

[dɪ'naɪəl]

义 *n.* 否认，拒绝

例 Joanna's denial rang true.

译 乔安娜的否认听起来是真的。

---

71 dentistry

['dentɪstrɪ]

义 *n.* 牙科学；牙科

例 In those days, dentistry was basic. Extractions were carried out without anaesthetic.

译 那时牙科刚起步，拔牙是在没有麻药的情况下进行的。

---

72 dependency

[dɪ'pendənsɪ]

义 *n.* 依赖；属国

例 Their aim is to reduce people's dependency on the welfare state.

译 他们的目标是减少人们对福利国家的依赖。

---

73 deputy

['depjʊtɪ]

义 *n.* 代表；副手；代理人

例 His brother was acting as his deputy in America.

译 他的兄弟充当他在美国的代理人。

---

74 descendent

[dɪ'sendənt]

义 *n.* 后裔，后代，子孙

例 She has at least 111 descendents, including Shelagh Rogers.

译 她至少有 111 个后代，包括谢拉赫·罗杰斯。

---

75 descent

[dɪ'sent]

义 *n.* 下降，衰落；斜坡

例 There is a gradual descent to the sea.

译 有一个逐渐下降到海边的斜坡。

---

76 destructive

[dɪ'strʌktɪv]

义 *adj.* 破坏性的；有害的；否定的，消极的

例 He was unable to contain his own destructive feelings.

译 他无法克制自己的消极情绪。

---

77 detachment

[dɪ'tætʃmənt]

义 *n.* 冷漠，超然

例 She felt a sense of detachment from what was going on.

译 她对所发生的一切有一种超然的感觉。

---

78 detain

[dɪ'teɪn]

义 *v.* 扣留；拘押；留住

例 He caught her arm in a subconscious attempt to detain her.

译 他下意识地抓住她的胳膊，想留住她。

---

79 devastation

[ˌdevə'steɪʃn]

义 *n.* 毁坏，破坏；荒废

例 It's a scene of complete devastation.

| 译 | 那是一幅满目疮痍的景象。 |

80 devour

[dɪˈvaʊər]

义 *v.* 吞食；吞噬，毁灭

例 Rats devour most seeds before they can germinate.

译 老鼠在种子发芽前吃掉了大部分种子。

81 diction

[ˈdɪkʃn]

义 *n.* 措辞；用语，用词

例 Its fossilization can be found in phonetics, dictions, and grammar.

译 它的僵化现象可以在语音、用语和语法中找到。

82 diffident

[ˈdɪfɪdənt]

义 *adj.* 缺少的；羞怯的

例 John was as bouncy and ebullient as Helen was diffident and reserved.

译 约翰活泼、热情，而海伦却羞怯、矜持。

83 digress

[daɪˈgres]

义 *v.* 走向岔道；离开本题

例 My thoughts were beginning to digress.

译 我的思想开始开小差了。

84 dike

[daɪk]

义 *n.* 堤坝，排水沟

例 The authorities have mobilized vast numbers of people to drain flooded land and build or repair dikes.

译 政府动员了大批民众为遭受洪灾的地区排涝并修建或修复堤坝。

85 diminutive

[dɪˈmɪnjətɪv]

义 *adj.* 小的，小型的

例 He's a diminutive figure, less than five feet tall.

译 他身材矮小，不足 5 英尺高。

86 dimness

[dɪmnəs]

义 *n.* 微暗，昏暗

例 It took a while for his eyes to adjust to the dimness.

译 过了一段时间他的眼睛才适应了昏暗。

87 disability

[ˌdɪsəˈbɪlətɪ]

义 *n.* 残疾

例 We all fear disability or infirmity.

译 我们都害怕残疾或虚弱。

88 disband

[dɪsˈbænd]

义 *v.* 解散，遣散

例 The council voted to disband and reform as a confederation.

译 委员会投票解散并改革为一个联盟。

89 disclosure

[dɪs'kləʊʒər]

义 *n.* 揭发，公开，透露；披露

例 The new's disclosure shocked the public.

译 新消息的披露震惊了公众。

90 discomfort

[dɪs'kʌmfərt]

义 *n.* 不适，不安

例 She hears the discomfort in his voice.

译 她听出他声音里的不安。

91 discord

['dɪskɔ:rd]

义 *n.* 不和；不和谐音

例 A note of discord has crept into relations between the two countries.

译 两国关系中悄然出现了不和谐的音符。

92 discourse

['dɪskɔ:rs]

义 *n.* 谈话，讨论；演讲

例 He was hoping for some lively political discourse at the meeting.

译 他希望在会上听到些生动的政治演讲。

93 disdainful

[dɪs'deɪnfl]

义 *adj.* 不屑一顾的，轻蔑的

例 She had an affected air and a disdainful look.

译 她的神态矫揉造作，神情不屑一顾。

94 disembark

[ˌdɪsɪm'bɑ:rk]

义 *v.* (使)上岸，(使)登陆

例 Seven second-class passengers prepared to disembark.

译 7 名二等舱乘客准备上岸。

95 dishearten

[dɪs'hɑ:rtn]

义 *v.* (使)使去信心，使沮丧

例 He was disheartened by their hostile reaction.

译 他被他们有敌意的反应弄得沮丧了。

96 disinclined

[ˌdɪsɪn'klaɪnd]

义 *adj.* 不愿的，不想的

例 He was disinclined to talk about himself, especially to his students.

译 他不愿意谈论自己，尤其是在学生面前。

97 disorderly

[dɪs'ɔ:rdərlɪ]

义 *adj.* 无秩序的，乱的

例 The marchers were charged with disorderly conduct and later released.

译 游行者们被控扰乱社会治安罪，后被释放。

98　dispatch

[dɪ'spætʃ]

义　*v.* 派遣；发送；迅速完成　*n.* 派遣；急件

例　The dispatch of the task force is purely a contingency measure.

译　派遣特遣队纯粹是应急措施。

99　disposition

[ˌdɪspə'zɪʃn]

义　*n.* 性情；倾向

例　She is mild in disposition.

译　她性情温和。

100　disrepair

[ˌdɪsrɪ'per]

义　*n.* 破损；失修

例　The building was in a general state of disrepair.

译　整座建筑处于失修状态。

List 5

1　disrespect
[ˌdɪsrɪ'spekt]

义 *n.* 不敬，无礼

例 Folded arms signal pride in Finland, but disrespect in Fiji.

译 抱臂在芬兰表示骄傲，但在斐济则表示不尊重。

2　dissimilarity
[ˌdɪsɪmɪ'lærətɪ]

义 *n.* 不同，相异

例 The person who comes from the dissimilarity nation usually becomes the friend after a game.

译 来自不同国家的人在一场比赛后常常成为朋友。

3　dissolution
[ˌdɪsə'luːʃn]

义 *n.* 瓦解，解散

例 He stayed on until the dissolution of the firm in 1948.

译 他一直待到 1948 年公司解散。

4　dissonance
['dɪsənəns]

义 *n.* 不一致；不和谐

例 There may be evolutionary forces behind cognitive dissonance reduction.

译 减少认知失调的背后可能有进化的力量。

5　dissonant
['dɪsənənt]

义 *adj.* 不一致的；刺耳的

例 They chose to include all of these dissonant voices together.

译 他们选择把所有这些不和谐的声音包罗在一起。

6　distributive
[dɪ'strɪbjətɪv]

义 *adj.* 分布的；分配的

例 Distributive justice is not about moral desert.

译 公平分配不是道义缺失。

7　distributor
[dɪ'strɪbjətər]

义 *n.* 经销商；配电器

例 Denmark has few natural resources, limited manufacturing capability; its future in Europe will be as a broker, banker, and distributor of goods.

译 丹麦自然资源少，制造能力有限；未来，它在欧洲的角色将是经纪人、银行家和货物分销商。

8　divine
[dɪ'vaɪn]

义 *adj.* 神圣的，神的　*n.* 天意；上帝

例 In ancient mythology there was no impassable gulf separating the divine from the human beings.

译 在上古神话中，神与人之间没有不可逾越的鸿沟。

9 divinity

[dɪ'vɪnətɪ]

义 *n.* 神性；神学

例 This is stupidity, not divinity.

译 这是愚昧，不是神圣。

10 dizziness

['dɪzɪnəs]

义 *n.* 头昏眼花，眩晕

例 A sudden dizziness overpowered him.

译 一阵突然的眩晕令他难以忍受。

11 domicile

['dɑ:mɪsaɪl]

义 *n.* 住所，住宅

例 My domicile place is Nanjing.

译 我的户籍地是南京。

12 donor

['dəʊnər]

义 *n.* 捐献者，捐赠者

例 The donor prefers to remain anonymous.

译 捐赠者不愿透露姓名。

13 doubly

['dʌblɪ]

义 *adv.* 加倍地，二倍地

例 In pregnancy a high fiber diet is doubly important.

译 怀孕期间高纤维饮食倍加重要。

14 downplay

[ˌdaʊn'pleɪ]

义 *v.* 对……轻描淡写；不予重视

例 Aboard his plane, the secretary tries to downplay the importance of the budget votes.

译 在飞机上，国防部长试图淡化预算投票的重要性。

15 downriver

[ˌdaʊn'rɪvər]

义 *adj.* 下游的

例 Restarting the engine, we motored downriver.

译 我们重新启动马达，沿河而下。

16 doze

[dəʊz]

义 *v.* 打瞌睡

例 He was dozing in front of the TV.

译 他在电视机前打瞌睡。

17 dragonfly

['dræɡənflaɪ]

义 *n.* 蜻蜓

例 The dragonfly feeds on mosquitoes and flies.

译 蜻蜓捕食蚊蝇。

18 dreamlike

['dri:mlaɪk]

义 *adj.* 梦一般的，梦幻的

例 Her paintings have a naive, dreamlike quality.

译 她的画有种天真、梦幻的感觉。

---

19 dreamy

['dri:mɪ]

义 *adj.* 梦幻般的；心不在焉的

例 The music has a dreamy, elegiac quality.

译 那音乐听上去有一种梦幻般的哀伤感。

---

20 dresser

['dresər]

义 *n.* 化妆台，梳妆台

例 Ivy leaves embellish the front of the dresser.

译 常春藤叶子装饰着梳妆台的正面。

---

21 dropping

['drɑ:pɪŋ]

义 *n.* 滴下物；动物粪便

例 Large amounts of the virus are known to be excreted in the droppings from infected birds.

译 已知大量病毒会从受感染鸟类的粪便中排出。

---

22 drumbeat

['drʌmbi:t]

义 *n.* 鼓声，鼓点

例 By understanding these constraints, we begin to understand why some people march to a different drumbeat.

译 通过了解这些限制，我们开始理解为什么有些人踩着不同的鼓点行走。

---

23 dryer

['draɪər]

义 *n.* 烘干机；干燥剂

例 What a sweet day it will be when I move into an apartment with a washer and dryer connected.

译 当我搬进一座有相连着的洗衣机和烘干机的公寓时，那将是多么甜蜜的一天。

---

24 duct

[dʌkt]

义 *n.* 管道，导管

例 Air ducts and electrical cables were threaded through the complex structure.

译 通风管和电缆从这幢结构复杂的建筑物中穿过。

---

25 ducted

[dʌktɪd]

义 *adj.* 管道中的；输送的

例 In the propulsion performance of the icebreaker, we mainly use the ducted propeller as the main propulsion.

译 在破冰船的推进性能方面，我们主要采用导管螺旋桨作为主推进器。

---

26 duplication

[ˌdju:plɪ'keɪʃn]

义 *n.* 复制；副本

例 There could be a serious loss of efficiency through unnecessary duplication of resources.

译 不必要的资源重复可能会导致严重的效率损耗。

---

27 dutiful

['duːtɪfl]

义 *adj.* 顺从的；尽职的

例 A teacher should be patient and dutiful.

译 老师应该有耐心和责任心。

---

28 dynastic

[dɪ'næstɪk]

义 *adj.* 王朝的

例 If descriptions of the first dynastic festival of the Ptolemies around 280 B.C. are accurate, the party would cost millions of dollars today.

译 如果关于公元前 280 年左右托勒密王朝的第一个节日的描述是准确的，那么那个宴会的花费相当于现在的数百万美元。

---

29 eagerness

['iːgərnɪs]

义 *n.* 渴望；热心

例 I couldn't hide my eagerness to get back home.

译 我掩饰不住想回家的渴望。

---

30 earthy

['ɜːrθɪ]

义 *adj.* 朴实的；世俗的

例 I'm attracted to warm, earthy colors.

译 我喜欢温暖、朴实的颜色。

---

31 eatable

['iːtəbl]

义 *adj.* 可以吃的

例 Though there are more eatable plants, there may also be wild animals, poisonous snakes, and other hazards.

译 虽然这有更多的可食用植物，但也可能存在野生动物、毒蛇和其他危险。

---

32 eccentricity

[ˌeksen'trɪsətɪ]

义 *n.* 古怪，怪癖

例 She is unusual to the point of eccentricity.

译 她不同寻常到古怪的地步。

---

33 ecotourist

['iːkəʊtʊːrɪst]

义 *n.* 生态旅游者

例 Ideally, ecotourists learn about the habitats that they visit, provide donations to conserve them, and generate income for host communities.

译 理想情况下，生态旅游者了解他们所访问的栖息地，提供捐款来保护它们，并为当地社区创造收入。

---

34 ecstasy

['ekstəsɪ]

义 *n.* 狂喜；入迷

例 You should see the bright ecstasy in the eyes of a nesting thrush.

译 你应该能从一只正在筑巢的画眉的眼睛里看到喜悦。

---

35 ecstatic

[ɪk'stætɪk]

义 *adj.* 狂喜的

例 Sally was ecstatic about her new job.

译 萨莉对她的新工作欣喜若狂。

---

36 edibility

[edɪ'bɪlɪtɪ]

义 *n.* 适食性，可食性

例 Besides their edibility, mushrooms have long been considered to have medicinal properties.

译 除了食用性，蘑菇长期以来被认为具有药用价值。

---

37 educational

[ˌedʒʊ'keɪʃənl]

义 *adj.* 教育的，有教育意义的

例 We carry a range of educational software.

译 我们有一系列的教育软件。

---

38 educator

['edʒʊkeɪtər]

义 *n.* 教育工作者

例 The television producer today has to be part news person, part educator.

译 今天的电视制作人必须一半是新闻人，一半是教育者。

---

39 efficiency

[ɪ'fɪʃnsɪ]

义 *n.* 效率；功率

例 There was much debate on the relative efficiencies of different types of waterwheels.

译 关于不同类型水车的相对效率有很多争论。

---

40 effortlessly

['efətləslɪ]

义 *adv.* 毫不费力地，轻易地

例 Schumacher adapted effortlessly to his new surroundings.

译 舒马赫毫不费力地适应了新环境。

---

41 ego

['iːgəʊ]

义 *n.* 自我，自负

例 I thought I could control myself, but my ego came into play.

译 我以为我能控制自己，但我的自负起了作用。

---

42 elaboration

[ɪˌlæbə'reɪʃn]

义 *n.* 详细阐述；精心完成的东西

例 The importance of the plan needs no further elaboration.

译 这个计划的重要性无须进一步阐述。

---

43 elated

[ɪ'leɪtɪd]

义 *adj.* 兴高采烈的

例 For my part, I feel elated and close to tears.

译 就我而言，我感到很高兴，几乎要哭了。

44　elective

[ɪ'lektɪv]

义 *adj.* 选举的；随意选择的；选修的

例 Most of the students of our class take Japanese as an elective course.

译 我们班大多数学生选修日语。

45　electoral

[ɪ'lektərəl]

义 *adj.* 选修的；选举的，选举人的

例 Franklin had won with a plurality in electoral votes of 449.

译 富兰克林在选举团投票中以 449 票的优势获胜。

46　elegance

['elɪgəns]

义 *n.* 高雅，典雅

例 She dresses with casual elegance.

译 她穿着休闲优雅。

47　elemental

[ˌelɪ'mentl]

义 *adj.* 元素的；基本的

例 Each elemental unit has a simple layout consisting of a rectangular box and a triangular roof.

译 每个基本单元都有一个简单的布局，由一个矩形的盒子和一个三角形的屋顶组成。

48　elimination

[ɪˌlɪmɪ'neɪʃn]

义 *n.* 消除；淘汰

例 Though it may give some benefit to the poor, its key component is the elimination of tax on dividends.

译 尽管它可能会给穷人带来一些好处，但它的关键部分是取消股利税。

49　elude

[ɪ'luːd]

义 *v.* 逃避，躲避

例 The two men managed to elude the police for six weeks.

译 这两个人设法躲避了警察六个星期。

50　emanate

['eməneɪt]

义 *v.* 散发，发出

例 Marital problems emanate from selfishness and pride.

译 婚姻的问题，来自我们的自私和骄傲。

51　emancipate

[ɪ'mænsɪpeɪt]

义 *v.* 释放，解放

例 To emancipate all mankind, we will balk at no sacrifice.

译 为了全人类的解放，我们不惜一切代价。

52　embarrassment

[ɪm'bærəsmənt]

义 *n.* 尴尬，难堪

例 I think I would have died of embarrassment.

译 我想我会尴尬 "死" 的。

53 embodiment
[ɪmˈbɑ:dɪmənt]

义 *n.* 化身，体现
例 Since his "action" is in the past, the photograph is its sole embodiment.
译 因为他的 "行为" 是在过去的，所以照片是它唯一的体现。

54 emphatically
[ɪmˈfætɪklɪ]

义 *adv.* 断然地；强调地
例 The proposal was emphatically defeated.
译 这项建议遭到断然否决。

55 empirically
[ɪmˈpɪrɪklɪ]

义 *adv.* 经验主义地
例 They approached this part of their task empirically.
译 他们以经验为依据处理这部分任务。

56 empowerment
[ɪmˈpaʊəmənt]

义 *n.* 授权，权利赋予
例 More female-empowerment projects are needed.
译 人们需要更多的女性赋权项目。

57 empress
[ˈemprəs]

义 *n.* 女皇，皇后
例 He'll also meet the emperor and the empress at a lunch on Tuesday.
译 他还将在周二的午餐会上见到皇帝和皇后。

58 enclosure
[ɪnˈkləʊʒər]

义 *n.* 附件；围栏
例 They decided not to let their new dog run loose, confining it to a fenced enclosure during the day.
译 他们决定不让他们的新狗乱跑，白天把它关在围栏里。

59 encore
[ˈɑ:ŋkɔ:r]

义 *n.* 加演
例 She played a Chopin waltz as an encore.
译 她应听众的要求又加奏了一首肖邦的圆舞曲。

60 encroachment
[ɪnˈkrəʊtʃmənt]

义 *n.* 侵蚀，侵犯
例 The problem was to safeguard sites from encroachment by property development.
译 问题是要保护遗址免受房地产开发商的侵占。

61 endeavor
[ɪnˈdevər]

义 *v.* 尽力，努力
例 The girl feverishly endeavored to open the window, the glass apparently proving to be too heavy for her.

译 女孩拼命地试图打开窗户，显然玻璃对她来说太重了。

---

62 endowment

[ɪnˈdaʊmənt]

义 *n.* 天赋，才能

例 It's called the endowment effect.

译 这被称为禀赋效应。

---

63 enfold

[ɪnˈfəʊld]

义 *v.* 包裹；拥抱

例 I enjoy with something of sadness, remembering that this melodious silence is but the prelude of that deeper stillness that waits to enfold us all.

译 想起这悠扬的寂静不过只是那更深沉的静寂的前奏，那静寂等待着拥抱我们所有人，我就有些伤感地享受着。

---

64 enhancer

[ɪnˈhænsər]

义 *n.* 增强器，增强剂

例 Cinnamon is an excellent flavor enhancer.

译 肉桂是一种绝佳的提味料。

---

65 enlightenment

[ɪnˈlaɪtnmənt]

义 *n.* 启示，启蒙

例 His speech gave us some enlightenment.

译 他的演讲给了我们一些启示。

---

66 enrichment

[ɪnˈrɪtʃmənt]

义 *n.* 丰富

例 I think it promises enrichment for any reader from those who know little about science to the career physicists.

译 我认为它为任何读者都提供了丰富的知识，不论是对科学知之甚少的人，还是职业物理学家。

---

67 enterprising

[ˈentərpraɪzɪŋ]

义 *adj.* 有事业心的，有进取心的

例 To realize this vision, Ricci is mounting one of the most lavish, enterprising, and expensive promotional campaigns in magazine-publishing history.

译 为了实现这一愿景，里奇正在发起杂志出版史上最奢侈、最富有进取精神、最昂贵的促销活动之一。

---

68 entice

[ɪnˈtaɪs]

义 *v.* 诱使，引诱

例 They'll entice thousands of doctors to move from the cities to the rural areas by paying them better salaries.

译 他们将以更高的工资吸引成千上万的医生从城市搬到农村。

---

69 entrust

[ɪnˈtrʌst]

义 *v.* 信赖，交托

例 Either you come in person, or you entrust someone with the matter.

译 你要么自己来，要么就托人办理这件事。

---

70 entryway

['entrɪweɪ]

义 *n.* 入口

例 I stood just beyond the entryway hoping he would notice me.

译 我站在入口通道外，希望他会注意到我。

---

71 enviable

['envɪəbl]

义 *adj.* 令人羡慕的

例 He is in the enviable position of having two job offers to choose from.

译 他有两个工作机会可供选择，真令人羡慕。

---

72 envious

['envɪəs]

义 *adj.* 羡慕的

例 Everyone is so envious of her.

译 每个人都很羡慕她。

---

73 epitomize

[ɪ'pɪtəmaɪz]

义 *v.* 概括；成为……的缩影

例 These movies seem to epitomize the 1950s.

译 这些电影似乎是 20 世纪 50 年代的缩影。

---

74 erasure

[ɪ'reɪʒər]

义 *n.* 擦除，抹掉，消除

例 Globalization is the erasure of national borders for economic purposes.

译 全球化是为了经济目的而消除国界。

---

75 erosive

[ɪ'rəʊsɪv]

义 *adj.* 腐蚀的，冲蚀的

例 Erosive wear is one of main reasons of barrel life.

译 烧蚀磨损是影响枪管寿命的主要原因之一。

---

76 errand

['erənd]

义 *n.* 任务，差事

例 He ran off to the village on his errand of mercy.

译 他跑到村里去行善。

---

77 escalate

['eskəleɪt]

义 *v.* 升级

例 We do not want to escalate the war.

译 我们不想让战争升级。

---

78 estimation

[ˌestɪ'meɪʃn]

义 *n.* 判断，评价；估计

例 Lyell's strategy for estimation of geologic dates was not very accurate.

译 莱尔估测地质年代的方法不是很准确。

79 eternity
[ɪ'tɜ:rnətɪ]

义 *n.* 极长的时间；永恒，不朽

例 It keeps things alive from itself, so the problem with art is its eternity.

译 它让事物能脱离自身而永存，所以艺术的问题在于它的永恒。

80 ethnicity
[eθ'nɪsətɪ]

义 *n.* 种族特点；种族渊源

例 Keyssar also scrutinizes unemployment patterns according to skill level, ethnicity, race, age, class, and gender.

译 凯萨还根据技能水平、族群、人种、年龄、阶级和性别仔细研究了失业模式。

81 ethos
['i:θɑ:s]

义 *n.* 理念

例 The whole ethos of the hotel is effortless service.

译 该宾馆的整体理念是轻松服务。

82 evaporation
[ɪ,væpə'reɪʃn]

义 *n.* 蒸发

例 Our bodies can sweat, thereby losing heat by evaporation.

译 我们的身体会出汗，从而通过蒸发失去热量。

83 evasive
[ɪ'veɪsɪv]

义 *adj.* 逃避的；含糊其词的

例 Tessa was evasive about why she had not been at home that night.

译 泰莎对她那天晚上不在家的原因含糊其词。

84 everlasting
[,evər'læstɪŋ]

义 *adj.* 永恒的；持久的

例 To his everlasting credit, he never told anyone what I'd done.

译 值得永远赞扬的是，他从来没有告诉任何人我做了什么。

85 excerpt
['eksɜ:rpt]

义 *n./v.* 摘录，引用

例 This is excerpts from a novel.

译 这是一部小说的摘录。

86 exhaustion
[ɪg'zɔ:stʃən]

义 *n.* 疲惫，筋疲力尽

例 She was in a state of nervous exhaustion.

译 她处于神经极度疲劳的状态。

87 exhaustive
[ɪg'zɔ:stɪv]

义 *adj.* 彻底的；消耗的

例 We've performed an exhaustive scan on your computer, but we couldn't find any malicious software.

译 我们对你的电脑进行了彻底扫描，但没有发现任何恶意软件。

---

88 exhibitor

[ɪɡ'zɪbɪtər]

义 *n.* 参展者；提出人

例 Many exhibitors have even printed out pamphlets written in Chinese.

译 许多参展商甚至打印出用中文写的宣传册子。

---

89 exhilaration

[ɪɡˌzɪlə'reɪʃn]

义 *n.* 高兴，兴奋

例 We experience relief, exhilaration and freedom.

译 我们体验到放松、兴奋和自由。

---

90 exile

['ekzaɪl]

义 *n.* 放逐，流放

例 During his exile, he also began writing books.

译 在流放期间，他也开始了写书。

---

91 explanatory

[ɪk'splænətɔːrɪ]

义 *adj.* 说明的，解释的

例 These statements are accompanied by a series of explanatory notes.

译 这些说明附有一系列解释性说明。

---

92 explicitly

[ɪk'splɪsɪtlɪ]

义 *adv.* 明白地，明确地

例 The report states explicitly that the system was to blame.

译 报告明确指出应该归咎于体制。

---

93 extant

[ek'stænt]

义 *adj.* 现存的

例 The oldest extant document is dated 1492.

译 现存最古老的文献是 1492 年的。

---

94 extravagant

[ɪk'strævəgənt]

义 *adj.* 奢侈的；不切实际的，放肆的

例 She's got very extravagant tastes.

译 她的品位很奢侈。

---

95 extroverted

['ekstrəvɜːrtɪd]

义 *adj.* 性格外向的

例 Some young people who were easygoing and extroverted as children become self-conscious in early adolescence.

译 一些童年时期随和外向的年轻人在青春期早期变得有自我意识。

---

96 extrusion

[ɪk'struːʒn]

义 *n.* 挤出；推出；逐出

例 Extrusion punches must be coated to prevent galling.

译 挤压冲头必须涂上涂层以防止磨损。

---

97 exuberant

[ɪɡ'zuːbərənt]

义 *adj.* 兴高采烈的，充满活力的；丰富的

例 She gave an exuberant performance.

译 她的表演充满活力。

---

98 exude

[ɪɡ'zuːd]

义 *v.* 流露，显露；流出，渗出

例 The guerrillas exude confidence.

译 游击队员们展现出信心。

---

99 fabrication

[ˌfæbrɪ'keɪʃn]

义 *n.* 制造；虚构的谎言

例 She described the interview as a "complete fabrication".

译 她把这次采访描述为"纯属虚构"。

---

100 facade

[fə'sɑːd]

义 *n.* 建筑物的正面

例 The elaborate facade contrasts strongly with the severity of the interior.

译 精致的门面同室内的简朴形成强烈的反差。

List 6

1 factuality
[fæktjʊˈælɪtɪ]

义 *n.* 实在性，事实性

例 And this factuality is only effective to this consciousness.

译 而这个实在性只对这种意识有效。

---

2 faithful
[ˈfeɪθfl]

义 *adj.* 忠诚的，忠实的

例 Throughout his career, he remained faithful to the principles of classical art.

译 在他的整个职业生涯中，他始终忠实于古典艺术的原则。

---

3 fallout
[ˈfɔ:laʊt]

义 *n.* 辐射尘；后果，余波

例 The financial fallout has begun, and the political fallout may not be far behind.

译 金融方面的后果已经开始，政治方面的后果可能也不远了。

---

4 famed
[feɪmd]

义 *adj.* 著名的

例 She is famed for playing dizzy blondes.

译 她以扮演令人眩晕的金发美女而闻名。

---

5 fantasia
[fænˈteɪzɪə]

义 *n.* 幻想曲

例 Way back in 1939, an HP product was used to help construct the amazing audio in *Fantasia*.

译 早在 1939 年，一款惠普产品就被用来在《幻想曲》中营造惊人的音效。

---

6 fantastical
[fænˈtæstɪkəl]

义 *adj.* 奇异的，虚构的

例 The book has many fantastical aspects.

译 这本书有很多虚构的内容。

---

7 farewell
[ˌferˈwel]

义 *n./adj./v./int.* 再会，告别(的)

例 I bade all my friends farewell.

译 我告别了所有的朋友。

---

8 fated
[ˈfeɪtɪd]

义 *adj.* 命中注定的

例 We were fated never to meet again.

译 我们命中注定永远不能再见面。

---

9 fatherland
[ˈfɑ:ðərlænd]

义 *n.* 祖国，故土

例 They were willing to serve the fatherland in its hour of need.

译 他们愿意在祖国需要的时候为祖国服务。

---

10 fating

['feɪtɪŋ]

义 *n.* 命运，归宿

例 This study provided a theory basis for the researching of forming, transportation, transformation and fating of organic pollution in soil.

译 本研究为研究土壤中有机污染物的形成、运输、转化和归宿提供了理论依据。

---

11 fatten

['fætn]

义 *v.* 养肥，使肥胖

例 She's very thin after her illness—but we'll soon fatten her up.

译 她生病后很瘦，但我们很快就会把她养胖。

---

12 favor

['feɪvə]

义 *n.* 帮助；赞同

例 The margin in favor was 280 to 153.

译 赞成票以 280 票比 153 票的优势领先。

---

13 fearless

['fɪrləs]

义 *adj.* 无畏的，勇敢的

例 Only the selfless can be fearless.

译 只有无私的人才能无畏。

---

14 feisty

['faɪstɪ]

义 *adj.* 易怒的；活跃的

例 At 66, she was as feisty as ever.

译 66 岁时，她依然精力充沛。

---

15 feminism

['femənɪzəm]

义 *n.* 女权主义

例 Feminism is currently the fashionable topic among the chattering classes.

译 女权主义是时下好议时政的闲聊阶层热议的话题。

---

16 ferment

[fər'ment]

义 *v.* 发酵

例 Fruit juices ferment if they are kept for too long.

译 果汁如果存放时间过长就会发酵。

---

17 ferocity

[fə'rɑ:sətɪ]

义 *n.* 凶猛性；狂暴的行为

例 The winds howled too fiercely, the storms blew up without warning, the waves were of a scale and ferocity never seen in the Mediterranean.

译 狂风呼啸，风暴毫无预兆地爆发了，海浪的规模和凶猛程度在地中海是前所未见的。

18 festive

['festɪv]

义 *adj.* 欢乐的，喜庆的

例 The town has a festive holiday atmosphere.

译 这个城镇充满了欢乐的节日气氛。

---

19 fetal

['fiːtl]

义 *adj.* 胎儿的

例 There are three types of continuous fetal monitoring.

译 有三种类型的持续胎儿监护。

---

20 fiber

['faɪbər]

义 *n.* 纤维

例 In the last class, we started talking about useful plant fibers.

译 上节课，我们开始讨论有用的植物纤维。

---

21 fiberglass

['faɪbəˌglɑːs]

义 *n.* 玻璃纤维

例 The pool's fiberglass sides had cracked and the water had leaked out.

译 泳池四周的玻璃钢面开裂，水渗了出来。

---

22 figuratively

['fɪgjərətɪvlɪ]

义 *adv.* 比喻地，借喻地

例 She is, figuratively speaking, holding a gun to his head.

译 打个比方说，她正拿枪对着他的脑袋。

---

23 figurehead

['fɪgjərhed]

义 *n.* 装饰船头的人像；傀儡领袖

例 Otherwise Miller would become a dispensable figurehead.

译 否则米勒就会变成可有可无的傀儡。

---

24 finalize

['faɪnəlaɪz]

义 *v.* 完成，确定

例 The prime minister is holding consultations with his colleagues to finalize the deal.

译 总理正在和他的同事们进行磋商，以最终敲定这笔交易。

---

25 firmness

[fɜːmnəs]

义 *n.* 坚固；坚定

例 He was a man of intelligence and of firmness of will.

译 他是一个聪明而意志坚定的人。

---

26 fistful

['fɪstfʊl]

义 *n.* 一把

例 Mandy handed him a fistful of coins.

译 曼迪递给他一把硬币。

27 flamboyant

[flæm'bɔɪənt]

义 *adj.* 艳丽的；炫耀的

例 Critics attack his lavish spending and flamboyant style.

译 批评者抨击他的挥霍无度和浮华风格。

---

28 flatness

[flætnəs]

义 *n.* 平坦；平淡

例 The main design is used for the flatness measurement.

译 设计主要用于水平度测量。

---

29 flaunt

[flɔ:nt]

义 *v.* 飘扬；炫耀

例 It's not an externally observable characteristic unless you want to flaunt it.

译 除非你想炫耀它，否则它不是一个外在可见的特征。

---

30 flavored

['fleɪvəd]

义 *adj.* 风味的；经过调味的

例 Flavored coffee is sold at gourmet food stores and coffee shops.

译 调味咖啡可在美食店和咖啡店买到。

---

31 fleet

[fli:t]

义 *v.* 疾驰，飞逝，掠过

例 The pain eventually fleeted off over time.

译 随着时间的推移，疼痛最终消失了。

---

32 fleeting

['fli:tɪŋ]

义 *adj.* 短暂的；疾驰的

例 We paid a fleeting visit to Paris.

译 我们短暂地游览了巴黎。

---

33 flier

['flaɪər]

义 *n.* 传单

例 These days, we are bombarded with endless junk mail, fliers, and general bumf.

译 如今我们被铺天盖地的垃圾邮件、广告传单和无用的公文轰炸。

---

34 flimsy

['flɪmzɪ]

义 *adj.* 脆弱的，已损坏的；不足信的

例 The evidence against him is pretty flimsy.

译 对他不利的证据很站不住脚。

---

35 flippant

['flɪpənt]

义 *adj.* 轻率的；没礼貌的

例 He now dismisses that as a flippant comment.

译 他现在把那当作一个轻率的评论。

36 flirtation
['flɜːr'teɪʃn]

义 *n.* 调情；一时兴起，逢场作戏；短暂的风流韵事

例 After a brief flirtation with politics, he went into business.

译 对政治有过一阵兴趣后，他转向了商业。

---

37 floppy
['flɑːpɪ]

义 *adj.* 松软的；懒散的　*n.* 软磁盘，软盘

例 Today's floppy disc drives are tolerant of poor quality disc.

译 现在的软驱也能读取质量低劣的软盘。

---

38 flounder
['flaʊndər]

义 *v.* 不知所措；挣扎

例 What a pity that his career was left to flounder.

译 真遗憾，他的事业陷入了困境。

---

39 flowering
['flaʊərɪŋ]

义 *adj.* 开花的　*n.* 开花

例 Sadly, bamboo plants die after flowering.

译 令人遗憾的是，竹子开花后会死亡。

---

40 fluted
['fluːtɪd]

义 *adj.* 有凹槽的

例 The teak table has fluted legs.

译 这张柚木桌子的桌腿有凹槽纹饰。

---

41 foam
[fəʊm]

义 *n.* 泡沫，气泡

例 He used a foam template to assemble a group of corks into a pretty interesting shape.

译 他用泡沫板将一组软木塞组装成一个非常有趣的形状。

---

42 folklore
['fəʊklɔːr]

义 *n.* 民间传说；民俗学

例 The story rapidly became part of family folklore.

译 这个故事很快成为家庭民间传说的一部分。

---

43 folktale
['fəʊkˌteɪl]

义 *n.* 民间故事

例 I thought that a fairy tale was just a written version of an oral folktale.

译 我以为童话只是那些民间故事的书面版本。

---

44 fondness
['fɑːndnəs]

义 *n.* 爱好，喜爱

例 I've always had a fondness for chocolate cake.

译 我一直喜欢吃巧克力蛋糕。

45 foolishness

['fuːlɪʃnəs]

义 *n.* 可笑；愚蠢

例 Jenny had to laugh at her own foolishness.

译 珍妮不得不为自己的愚蠢而自嘲。

46 footnote

['fʊtnəʊt]

义 *n.* 脚注；补充说明

例 As a footnote, I should add that there was one point on which his bravado was more than justified.

译 作为补充说明，我应该再加一点，他表现得过于逞强。

47 forceful

['fɔːrsfl]

义 *adj.* 有力的；强烈的

例 He was forceful, but by no means a zealot.

译 他很有说服力，但绝不是狂热分子。

48 forecaster

['fɔːrkæstər]

义 *n.* (天气) 预报员，预测者

例 Forecasters say the storms may not be as bad as they initially predicted.

译 天气预报员说风暴可能没有他们最初预测得那么严重。

49 foreclose

[fɔːrˈkləʊz]

义 *v.* 取消抵押品的赎回权

例 The bank foreclosed on the mortgage for his previous home.

译 银行取消了他先前住所的抵押赎回权。

50 forego

[fɔːrˈgəʊ]

义 *v.* 放弃，在……之前

例 Many skiers are happy to forego a summer holiday to go skiing.

译 许多滑雪者愿意放弃暑假去滑雪。

51 forerunner

['fɔːrʌnər]

义 *n.* 先驱；先驱者

例 Developments in the late Tang served as a forerunner for future events that profoundly influenced China.

译 唐朝后期的发展为中国古代社会的巨大变革开了先河。

52 foretell

[fɔːrˈtel]

义 *v.* 预言，预测

例 That data will help us do remarkable things like foretell the future.

译 这些数据将帮助我们做一些非凡的事情，比如预测未来。

53 forewarn

[fɔːrˈwɔːrn]

义 *v.* 预先警告；事先告知

例 Perhaps he should forewarn customers with a little sign.

译 也许他应该用一个小提示来预先告知顾客。

54 format

['fɔ:rmæt]

义 *n.* 总体安排，计划；设计；开本，版式

例 They've brought out the magazine in a new format.

译 他们以新的版式出版这杂志。

---

55 formative

['fɔ:rmətɪv]

义 *adj.* 形成的；造型的；影响发展的

例 My father was a sunday painter, and his art books played a formative role in my childhood.

译 我的父亲是一个业余画家，他的艺术图书对我的童年产生了很深的影响。

---

56 formless

['fɔ:rmləs]

义 *adj.* 无定形的；没有形状的

例 He was a worshipper of the formless God.

译 他是无形之神的崇拜者。

---

57 forum

['fɔ:rəm]

义 *n.* 讨论会；论坛

例 His goal was to provide a forum for writers to express their political views and to promote increased social awareness.

译 他的目标是为作家提供一个论坛来表达他们的政治观点，并提高社会意识。

---

58 foundry

['faʊndrɪ]

义 *n.* 铸造；铸造厂

例 The moulds for the foundry are made in the tool-room area.

译 铸造车间的模具是在工具间生产的。

---

59 foyer

['fɔɪər]

义 *n.* 门厅，休息室

例 I went and waited in the foyer.

译 我走到门厅里等着。

---

60 fray

[freɪ]

义 *v.* 磨损

例 The stitching had begun to fray at the edges.

译 边上的针脚已经开始磨损了。

---

61 freelancer

['fri:lænsər]

义 *n.* 自由职业者

例 I'm working as a freelancer now.

译 我现在是个自由职业者。

---

62 freeze

[fri:z]

义 *v.* 冷冻；冻结；凝固

例 Strawberry cannot be freezed.

译 草莓不能冷冻。

63 frenetic

[frə'netɪk]

义 *adj.* 发狂的，狂热的

例 In 2011, many shoppers opted to avoid the frenetic crowds and do their holiday shopping from the comfort of their computer.

译 2011 年，许多购物者选择避开狂热的人群，用电脑舒适地进行假日购物。

64 freshen

['freʃn]

义 *v.* 变新鲜；（天气）变凉爽；增强变冷

例 The wind will freshen tonight.

译 今晚风力将会增强。

65 freshness

[freʃnəs]

义 *n.* 新鲜

例 We guarantee the freshness of all our produce.

译 我们保证所有农产品的新鲜。

66 frightful

['fraɪtfl]

义 *adj.* 可怕的，吓人的

例 A frightful traffic disaster was avoided.

译 避免了一场可怕的交通事故。

67 frivolous

['frɪvələs]

义 *adj.* 轻佻的；无聊的；轻率的

例 I just decided I was a bit too frivolous to be a doctor.

译 我只是觉得自己有点过于轻率，不适合做医生。

68 frugal

['fruːgl]

义 *adj.* 节俭的，省钱的

例 Everyone says this, but it really is a top tip for frugal eaters.

译 每个人都这么说，但对于节俭的食客来说，这确实是一个最好的建议。

69 fruitful

['fruːtfl]

义 *adj.* 多产的；富有成效的

例 Our farm boasts hundreds of fruitful peach trees.

译 我们农场有数百棵硕果累累的桃树。

70 fuel

['fjuːəl]

义 *n.* 燃料　*v.* 给……提供燃料；增强，加强

例 Hopefulness fueled America's baby boom.

译 希望推动了美国的婴儿潮。

71 futile

['fjuːtl]

义 *adj.* 无效的，无用的

例 It would be futile to protest.

译 抗议是无效的。

72 fuzz

[fʌz]

义 *n.* 细毛，绒毛

例 I saw it as a dim fuzz through the binoculars.

译 我通过双筒望远镜看到它是一团模糊的绒毛。

---

73 fuzzy

['fʌzɪ]

义 *adj.* 毛茸茸的；模糊的

例 The lettering is fuzzy and indistinct.

译 字迹模糊不清。

---

74 gangster

['gæŋstər]

义 *n.* 匪徒，歹徒

例 He was obsessed with gangster movies.

译 他那时迷上了警匪片。

---

75 gape

[geɪp]

义 *v.* 目瞪口呆地凝视；张口结舌地看

例 His secretary stopped taking notes to gape at me.

译 他的秘书停止记笔记，目瞪口呆地看着我。

---

76 gash

[gæʃ]

义 *n.* 深的伤口

例 He was bleeding from a gash on his head.

译 他头上的伤口在流血。

---

77 gasp

[gæsp]

义 *n.* 喘气，喘息；渴望

例 At last, I hear a soft thud, a gasp, and silence.

译 最后，我听到一声轻轻的撞击声，一声喘息，然后是一片寂静。

---

78 gatehouse

['geɪthaʊs]

义 *n.* 警卫室；门楼

例 John was on the uppermost floor of the three-storey gatehouse.

译 约翰在三层门房的最高层。

---

79 gatekeeper

['geɪtki:pər]

义 *n.* 看门人，门卫

例 His secretary acts as a gatekeeper, reading all mail before it reaches her boss.

译 老板的秘书就像一个看门人一样把关，看过所有邮件后再呈送给他。

---

80 gatherer

['gæðərər]

义 *n.* 收集者，收集器

例 There were a few disadvantages to the hunter-gatherer lifestyle.

译 狩猎采集生活也有一些不利之处。

81 generalization

[ˌdʒenrələˈzeɪʃn]

义 *n.* 一般化；概括

例 Yet it is doubtful whether the proposition is strong enough to bear the vast weight of generalization that has been placed on it.

译 然而，这一概括是否足以承受其被赋予的广泛概括的重量，这是值得怀疑的。

82 genial

[ˈdʒiːnɪəl]

义 *adj.* 友好的

例 His genial personality endeared him to other musicians, but his career suffered when he spent more time socializing than practicing.

译 他和蔼可亲的性格使他深受其他音乐家的喜爱，但当他把更多的时间花在社交而不是练习上时，他的事业受到了影响。

83 geniality

[ˌdʒiːnɪˈælətɪ]

义 *n.* 和蔼，亲切

例 Even to himself the geniality rang false and he came to a stop.

译 这种亲切的语气他自己听来都觉得虚伪，于是他停了下来。

84 genteel

[dʒenˈtiːl]

义 *adj.* 文雅的，有教养的；上流社会的

例 It was a place to which genteel families came in search of health and quiet.

译 这是上流社会家庭寻求健康和宁静的地方。

85 geophysical

[ˌdʒiːəʊˈfɪzɪkl]

义 *adj.* 地球物理学的

例 It now appears that they also have an important influence on the geophysical processes that propel the plates across the globe.

译 现在看来，它们对推动板块在地球上移动的地球物理过程也有重要影响。

86 giddy

[ˈgɪdɪ]

义 *adj.* 眼花的；头晕的

例 When I looked down from the top floor, I felt giddy.

译 当我从顶楼往下看时，我感到头晕目眩。

87 giveaway

[ˈgɪvəweɪ]

义 *n.* 泄露；免费样品

例 The only giveaway was the look of amusement in her eyes.

译 唯独她俏皮的眼神暴露了她。

88 glamorous

[ˈglæmərəs]

义 *adj.* 富有魅力的，迷人的

例 The show demonstrates how glamorous ballroom dancing is.

译 这个节目展示了交际舞的魅力。

89　gleam

[gli:m]

义　*v.* 闪烁；隐约地闪现　*n.* 反光，闪光；微光

例　I saw the gleam of the knife as it flashed through the air.

译　我看到了刀子在空中划过时发出的闪光。

90　glean

[gli:n]

义　*v.* 收集

例　To glean the safety of the income offered by a stock, investors look at dividend cover.

译　为了确保股票收益的安全性，投资者会关注股息保障倍数。

91　glibly

[glɪblɪ]

义　*adj.* 能说善道的，圆滑的　*adv.* 流畅地；流利地；油嘴滑舌地

例　He speaks glibly.

译　他说话油腔滑调。

92　glint

[glɪnt]

义　*n.* 闪烁，闪光

例　He had a wicked glint in his eye.

译　他的眼睛里闪烁着邪恶的光芒。

93　glisten

['glɪsn]

义　*v.* 闪光，闪耀

例　The leaves glisten with dew.

译　叶子上的露水闪闪发光。

94　glitch

[glɪtʃ]

义　*n.* 小故障；小失误

例　A computer software glitch fouled up their presentation.

译　一个小小的电脑软件故障毁掉了他们的展示会。

95　glob

[glɑ:b]

义　*n.* 一滴；小滴水珠

例　It probably feels like a little glob of water drop under your skin.

译　它可能感觉像你皮肤下的一滴小水滴。

96　globule

['glɑ:bju:l]

义　*n.*（液体的）小球体

例　Our bone marrow contains fat in the form of small globules.

译　我们骨髓里有小球状的脂肪。

97　gloomy

['glu:mɪ]

义　*adj.* 阴暗的，幽暗的；沮丧的，忧伤的

例　They found him in a gloomy, downbeat mood.

译　他们发现他情绪低落、闷闷不乐。

98 glorify

['glɔːrɪfaɪ]

义 *v.* 美化；赞美

例 In their works these authors tended to glorify women's contributions to frontier life.

译 在他们的作品中，这些作者倾向于赞美女性对边疆生活的贡献。

99 glossy

['glɑːsɪ]

义 *adj.* 光滑的；有光泽的

例 Her hair was thick, glossy and in tiptop condition.

译 她的头发浓密而有光泽，状态极佳。

100 goggle

['gɑːgl]

义 *n.* 护目镜

例 The company will design and develop a digitally enhanced night vision goggle.

译 该公司将设计并研发一款数字化增强夜视护目镜。

List 7

1 gory
['gɔ:rɪ]

义 *adj.* 血淋淋的，血腥的
例 I can't bear gory films.
译 我受不了血腥电影。

2 gossip
['gɑ:sɪp]

义 *n.* 流言蜚语，闲话
例 He spent the first hour talking gossip.
译 他头一个小时尽在说人闲话。

3 governmental
[ˌgʌvərn'mentl]

义 *adj.* 政府的；政治的
例 These refugees are taken care of by the combined efforts of the host countries and non-governmental organizations.
译 这些难民在东道国和非政府组织的共同努力下得到照顾。

4 gracious
['greɪʃəs]

义 *adj.* 亲切的，和蔼的
例 She is a lovely and gracious woman.
译 她是一个可爱而亲切的女人。

5 gradation
[grə'deɪʃn]

义 *n.* 渐变；阶段
例 But TV images require subtle gradations of light and shade.
译 但是，电视影像要求有十分细微的光影变化。

6 graphical
['græfɪkl]

义 *adj.* 图形的；生动的
例 The system uses an impressive graphical interface.
译 该系统使用了一个令人印象深刻的图形界面。

7 grassy
['græsɪ]

义 *adj.* 长满草的，像草的
例 The buildings are hidden behind grassy banks.
译 建筑物隐藏在长满青草的堤岸后面。

8 grate
[greɪt]

义 *n.* 栅；壁炉
例 A wood fire burned in the grate.
译 柴火在炉栅里燃烧。

9 gravitate
['grævɪteɪt]

义 *v.* 受吸引；重力吸引
例 Many young people gravitate to the cities in search of work.
译 许多年轻人被吸引到城市寻找工作。

10 Greece

[gri:s]

义 *n.* 希腊

例 They met while on holiday in Greece.

译 他们是在希腊度假时相遇的。

11 grid

[grɪd]

义 *n.* 栅栏；网格

例 The grid gives it organization and structure.

译 网格赋予它组织和结构。

12 grief

[gri:f]

义 *n.* 悲痛，忧伤

例 She was out of her mind with grief.

译 她悲痛得精神失常了。

13 grieve

[gri:v]

义 *v.* 使伤心，使悲伤

例 I didn't have any time to grieve.

译 我没有任何时间去悲伤。

14 grim

[grɪm]

义 *adj.* 严峻的；冷酷的

例 They painted a grim picture of growing crime.

译 他们描绘了犯罪率不断上升的严峻景象。

15 groove

[gru:v]

义 *n.* 槽，纹

例 The cupboard door slides open along the groove.

译 柜门沿槽滑开。

16 gust

[gʌst]

义 *n.* 一阵强风

例 A gust of wind blew my hat off.

译 一阵强风把我的帽子吹掉了。

17 gymnastic

[dʒɪm'næstɪk]

义 *adj.* 体操的，体育的

例 Trent Dimas won gold in the final men's gymnastic event.

译 特伦特·迪马斯在男子体操决赛中获得金牌。

18 handlebar

['hændlbɑ:r]

义 *n.* 车把

例 Motorcycle-style handlebar gives you tight control of rudders, which steer using airflow.

译 摩托车式的车把使你能严格控制方向盘，它是利用气流转向的。

19 handwritten

['hænd'rɪtn]

义 *adj.* 手写的

例 A brief, handwritten postscript lay beneath his signature.

译 他的签名下面有一段简短的手写附言。

---

20 harshness

['hɑ:rʃnəs]

义 *n.* 粗糙的事物；严肃

例 As the wine ages, it loses its bitter harshness.

译 随着酒的陈酿，它失去了苦涩的涩味。

---

21 haze

[heɪz]

义 *n.* 薄雾；迷糊

例 They vanished into the haze near the horizon.

译 他们消失在地平线附近的薄雾中。

---

22 headlamp

['hedlæmp]

义 *n.* 头灯，（车）前照灯

例 Electrics are upgraded from 6 volt to 12 volt allowing separate side-lights within the headlamp units.

译 电气系统从 6 伏升级到 12 伏，允许前照灯位置有单独的侧灯。

---

23 headwind

['hedwɪnd]

义 *n.* 逆风，顶风

例 One potential headwind is jobs.

译 一个潜在的不利问题是失业。

---

24 hearsay

['hɪrseɪ]

义 *n.* 传闻

例 We can't make a decision based on hearsay and guesswork.

译 我们不能根据传言和猜测做决定。

---

25 heartbroken

['hɑ:rtbrəʊkən]

义 *adj.* 悲伤的

例 Was your daddy heartbroken when they got a divorce?

译 你父母离婚的时候你爸爸伤心吗？

---

26 hearten

['hɑ:rtn]

义 *v.* 激励；振作

例 This reminder did not hearten the servants much; they still held back.

译 这个提醒并没有使仆人们感到多大的振奋，他们仍然犹豫不决。

---

27 heartwarming

['hɑ:rt,wɔ:mɪŋ]

义 *adj.* 暖人心房的，感人的

例 The walls there were adorned in which there were heartwarming messages in frames.

译 墙上装饰着镶在相框里的暖心留言。

28 heavyweight

['hevɪweɪt]

义 *n.* 超过平均重量的人或物；重量级选手

例 The heavyweight champion will be given a shot at Holyfield's world title.

译 这位重量级冠军将有机会挑战霍利菲尔德的世界冠军头衔。

---

29 hefty

['heftɪ]

义 *adj.* 重的；异常大的

例 This is one of the reasons why some males birds have exotic plumes, why elk carry hefty antlers, and why male fiddler crabs have such large claws.

译 这就是为什么一些雄性鸟类有奇异的羽毛，为什么雄麋鹿有巨大的鹿角，为什么雄性招潮蟹有如此大的爪子的原因之一。

---

30 hexagonal

[heks'ægənl]

义 *adj.* 六角形的，六边的

例 As I exited the final display, I entered a hexagonal room.

译 当我离开最后的展览时，我进入了一个六角形的房间。

---

31 hierarchical

[ˌhaɪə'rɑːrkɪkl]

义 *adj.* 按等级划分的

例 This is certainly a little difficult for people who are more used to a hierarchical system.

译 对于那些更习惯于等级制度的人来说，这当然有点困难。

---

32 highland

['haɪlənd]

义 *n.* 高地

例 They're found in sweltering mangrove swamps in Southeast Asia and in blizzard-lashed highlands in the Himalayas.

译 在东南亚闷热的红树林沼泽以及喜马拉雅山脉暴风雪肆虐的高地上都能找到它们。

---

33 hilltop

['hɪltɑːp]

义 *n.* 山顶

例 Over centuries, these layers created the hilltop.

译 几个世纪以来，这些岩层形成了山顶。

---

34 hither

['hɪðər]

义 *adv.* 到此处

例 Refugees run hither and thither in search of safety.

译 难民为了寻求安全四处奔逃。

---

35 homegrown

['həʊm'grəʊn]

义 *adj.* 自家种植的，土生的

例 Martinelli reminds visitors often that he uses 100 percent homegrown fruit from California's Bajaro Valley.

译 马蒂内利经常提醒游客，他百分之百使用来自加州巴加罗山谷产的本土水果。

36 homemade

['həʊm'meɪd]

义 *adj.* 自制的；国产的

例 Then we finished the last of the homemade muffins from Pam.

译 然后我们吃完了帕姆自制的最后一块松饼。

---

37 hone

[həʊn]

义 *v.* 训练（尤指技艺）；磨（刀）

例 Leading companies spend time and money on honing the skills of senior managers.

译 龙头公司会花费时间和金钱提高高层管理人员的技能。

---

38 honk

[hɑːŋk]

义 *n.* 汽车喇叭声

例 She pulled to the right with a honk.

译 她按了一声喇叭，把车往右开了。

---

39 honored

['ɑːnərd]

义 *adj.* 深感荣幸的；受尊敬的

例 I feel honored to be your guest.

译 能成为你的客人我很荣幸。

---

40 horrify

['hɔːrɪfaɪ]

义 *v.* 使恐惧，使惊骇

例 The whole country was horrified by the killings.

译 全国都对这些凶杀案感到大为震惊。

---

41 horsehair

['hɔːrsher]

义 *n.* 马毛，马鬃

例 The handles were carved out of cattle bones and the bristles were made from wild boar or horsehair.

译 手柄由牛骨雕刻而成，鬃毛则由野猪或马毛制成。

---

42 houseboat

['haʊsbəʊt]

义 *n.* 游艇；船屋

例 The plane was catapulted from a houseboat in the Potomac but instead of rising into the air, it plunged into the frigid waters.

译 这架飞机从波托马克河的一艘游艇上弹射而出，但它没有升到空中，而是坠入了冰冷的水中。

---

43 hover

['hʌvər]

义 *v.* 盘旋；徘徊

例 Seagulls hover over the surging waves.

译 海鸥在汹涌的波涛上方翱翔。

---

44 howl

[haʊl]

义 *n.* 长嚎；高声叫喊；呼啸

例 They listened to the howl of the wind through the trees.

译 他们听着风吹过树林的呼啸声。

45 humane

[hjuːˈmeɪn]

义 *adj.* 仁慈的，人道的

例 We shall urge humane principles and use our influence to promote justice.

译 我们将推行人权原则并运用我们的影响力去促进正义。

46 humerus

[ˈhjuːmərəs]

义 *n.* 肱骨，肱部

例 The objective was to provide the exact dimensions of the intertubercular sulcus of the humerus.

译 目的是提供肱骨结节间沟的确切尺寸。

47 humiliation

[hjuːˌmɪlɪˈeɪʃn]

义 *n.* 耻辱，丢脸

例 They frequently plumb the depths of loneliness, humiliation, and despair.

译 他们常常陷入孤独、屈辱和绝望的深渊。

48 humpback

[ˈhʌmpbæk]

义 *n.* 座头鲸

例 Human beings borrow ideas in music from humpback whales.

译 人类从座头鲸身上得到了音乐灵感。

49 hurtle

[ˈhɜːrtl]

义 *v.* 飞驰，猛冲；猛烈碰撞

例 Motorbikes and trucks hurtle along the roads.

译 摩托车和卡车沿路飞驰。

50 hutch

[hʌtʃ]

义 *n.* 笼；小屋

例 Their pet rabbit had gone to the great rabbit hutch in the sky.

译 他们的宠物兔已去世（回到西天的兔宫）了。

51 hydrophone

[ˈhaɪdrəˌfəʊn]

义 *n.* 水听器，水诊器

例 A Marine detector is a hydrophone.

译 海洋探测器是一种水听器。

52 hysteria

[hɪˈstɪrɪə]

义 *n.* 歇斯底里，不正常的兴奋

例 She felt an anxiety bordering on hysteria.

译 她感到近乎歇斯底里的焦虑。

53 identifier

[aɪˈdentɪfaɪər]

义 *n.* 标识符；鉴定人

例 We introduce fragment identifiers for the speakers.

译 我们为演讲者引入片段标识符。

54　idolization

[ˌaɪdəlaɪˈzeɪʃn]

义　*n.* 偶像化；盲目的崇拜

例　The idolization of celebrity also became a part of mainstream culture in cities.

译　对名人的崇拜也成为城市主流文化的一部分。

55　ignition

[ɪgˈnɪʃn]

义　*n.* 点火；点火器

例　Abruptly he turned the ignition key and started the engine.

译　他突然转动点火钥匙，启动了发动机。

56　illegible

[ɪˈledʒəbl]

义　*adj.* 难辨认的；（字迹）模糊的

例　Entries which are illegible or otherwise not in accordance with the rules will be disqualified.

译　难以辨认或不符合规则的条目将被取消资格。

57　illusionary

[ɪˈluːʒənərɪ]

义　*adj.* 幻觉的，错觉的

例　In summary, space and time are varying and illusionary phenomena.

译　总之，时空是变化的、虚幻的现象。

58　illustrative

[ɪˈlʌstrətɪv]

义　*adj.* 说明的

例　The charts in this article are for illustrative purposes only.

译　本文中的图表仅供说明之用。

59　illustrator

[ˈɪləstreɪtər]

义　*n.* 插图画家

例　She models for an illustrator.

译　她为一位插图画家当模特。

60　imitator

[ˈɪmɪteɪtər]

义　*n.* 模仿者

例　For many, Rome is at best the imitator and the continuator of Greece on a larger scale.

译　对许多人来说，罗马充其量是希腊的模仿者和延续者，只是规模更大。

61　immaterial

[ˌɪməˈtɪrɪəl]

义　*adj.* 无形的；不重要的

例　Whether we like him or not is immaterial.

译　我们喜不喜欢他无关紧要。

62　immemorial

[ˌɪməˈmɔːrɪəl]

义　*adj.* 远古的，久远的

例　It has remained virtually unchanged since time immemorial.

译　自远古以来，它几乎没有改变过。

63 **immensity**

[ɪ'mensətɪ]

义 *n.* 无限，巨大

例 We were overwhelmed by the sheer immensity of the task.

译 任务太重，把我们都吓倒了。

---

64 **immerse**

[ɪ'mɜːrs]

义 *v.* 浸；沉浸，陷入

例 Their commitments do not permit them to immerse themselves in current affairs as fully as they might wish.

译 他们的承诺不允许他们像自己希望的那样完全沉浸在时事中。

---

65 **immersion**

[ɪ'mɜːrʃn]

义 *n.* 专心，投入；沉浸，浸入

例 The wood had become swollen from prolonged immersion.

译 木头因长期浸泡而膨胀。

---

66 **immigrate**

['ɪmɪɡreɪt]

义 *v.* 移居入境

例 He immigrated from India at age 18.

译 他 18 岁时从印度移民过来。

---

67 **immortalize**

[ɪ'mɔːrtəlaɪz]

义 *v.* 使不朽，使名垂千古

例 He would immortalize her in a poem.

译 他会在诗歌里让她不朽。

---

68 **imperil**

[ɪm'perəl]

义 *v.* 使陷于危险中；危及

例 Pesticides, pollution, parasites, and disease imperil the insects, which rank among the top pollinators on Earth.

译 杀虫剂、污染、寄生虫和疾病都威胁着昆虫，而昆虫是地球上最重要的授粉者之一。

---

69 **imperiled**

[ɪm'perəld]

义 *adj.* 处于危险中的

例 The biggest was the Endangered Species Act of 1973, which protects imperiled animal species from extinction.

译 其中最著名的是 1973 年的《濒危物种保护法》，该法案旨在保护濒临灭绝的动物物种。

---

70 **impersonate**

[ɪm'pɜːrsəneɪt]

义 *v.* 扮演，假冒

例 He was caught trying to impersonate a security guard.

译 他假扮警卫被抓获。

---

71 **impetuous**

[ɪm'petʃuəs]

义 *adj.* 冲动的；鲁莽的；猛烈的

例 He tended to react in a heated and impetuous way.

| 译 | 他往往反应激烈，急躁冲动。 |

72 importune

[ˌɪmpɔːrˈtuːn]

义 *v.* 强求，硬要

例 I importune you to help them.

译 我求你帮帮他们。

73 imprecision

[ˌɪmprɪˈsɪʒn]

义 *n.* 不精确，不正确

例 There is considerable imprecision in the terminology used.

译 所用的术语相当不准确。

74 impressionism

[ɪmˈpreʃənɪzəm]

义 *n.* 印象派，印象主义

例 Manet is a painter of impressionism.

译 莫奈是印象派画家。

75 impressionist

[ɪmˈpreʃənɪst]

义 *n.* 印象主义者，印象派作家

例 The blurred imagery of impressionist paintings seems to stimulate the brain's amygdala.

译 印象派绘画中模糊的意象似乎刺激了大脑中的杏仁核。

76 impromptu

[ɪmˈprɑːmptuː]

义 *adj.* 即席的，临时的

例 This afternoon the Palestinians held an impromptu press conference.

译 今天下午巴勒斯坦国人召开了一场临时记者招待会。

77 inanimate

[ɪnˈænɪmət]

义 *adj.* 无生命的

例 A rock is an inanimate object.

译 岩石是无生命的物体。

78 incandescence

[ˌɪnkænˈdesns]

义 *n.* 炽热

例 She burned with an incandescence that had nothing to do with her looks.

译 她光彩照人，但这与其容貌无关。

79 incandescent

[ˌɪnkænˈdesnt]

义 *adj.* 辉耀的，炽热的；发白热光的

例 It cost far more than a regular incandescent bulb.

译 它比普通的白炽灯泡贵得多。

80 incessant

[ɪnˈsesnt]

义 *adj.* 不断的，无尽的

例 Incessant rain made conditions almost intolerable.

译 阴雨绵绵使得情况几乎无法忍受。

---

81 incidental

[ˌɪnsɪ'dentl]

义 *adj.* 附带的

例 The discovery was incidental to their main research.

译 这一发现是他们主要研究中的附带收获。

---

82 incompetence

[ɪn'kɑːmpɪtəns]

义 *n.* 不合格；不能胜任

例 The government was accused of incompetence.

译 政府被指控不称职。

---

83 incorporation

[ɪnˌkɔːrpə'reɪʃn]

义 *n.* 合并；公司

例 Signing a pre-incorporation contract is a universal phenomenon before the establishment of a corporation.

译 在公司成立之前，签订公司成立前合同是一种普遍现象。

---

84 indecipherable

[ˌɪndɪ'saɪfrəbl]

义 *adj.* 辨读不出的，无法破译的

例 Majid's writing was virtually indecipherable.

译 马吉德的字迹几乎无法辨认。

---

85 indecisive

[ˌɪndɪ'saɪsɪv]

义 *adj.* 犹豫不决的，非决定性的

例 The president's flip-flops on taxes made him appear indecisive.

译 总统在税收问题上改变立场使他看起来有些优柔寡断。

---

86 indiscriminate

[ˌɪndɪ'skrɪmɪnət]

义 *adj.* 任意的；不加选择的

例 Doctors have been criticized for their indiscriminate use of antibiotics.

译 医生们因滥用抗生素而受到批评。

---

87 indissoluble

[ˌɪndɪ'sɑːljəbl]

义 *adj.* 不能溶解的；不能毁损的；牢不可破的

例 For the waste material, we bury those dissoluble ones and burn those indissoluble ones.

译 对于废弃物，我们掩埋那些可溶性的，焚烧那些不溶性的。

---

88 induct

[ɪn'dʌkt]

义 *v.* 使就职；引导；带领

例 In new Cambridge economic growth model, we induct a new variable, technology labor.

译 在新剑桥经济增长模型中，我们引入了技术劳动者这一新的变量。

---

89 inductee

[ˌɪndʌk'tiː]

义 *n.* 就任者；应召入伍的士兵

例 In 2002, he became the first inductee into *Guitar World* magazine's Hall of Fame.

译 2002 年，他成为《吉他世界》杂志名人堂的第一位入选者。

---

90 indulgence

[ɪn'dʌldʒəns]

义 *n.* 沉溺；放纵

例 He leads a life of indulgence.

译 他过着放纵的生活。

---

91 inevitability

[ɪnˌevɪtə'bɪlətɪ]

义 *n.* 必然性，不可避免性

例 There is a certain inevitability that ebook sales have now overtaken paperback sales on Amazon's US site.

译 在美国亚马逊网站上，电子书的销量必然会超过平装书。

---

92 inextinguishable

[ˌɪnɪk'stɪŋgwɪʃəbəl]

义 *adj.* 不能消灭的；压不住的

例 Human beings have an inextinguishable capacity to be cruel to one another, particularly in groups.

译 人类有一种无法消灭的能力，那就是对彼此残忍，尤其是在群体中。

---

93 infamous

['ɪnfəməs]

义 *adj.* 无耻的；臭名昭著的

例 He was infamous for his anti-feminist attitudes.

译 他因反女权主义而臭名昭著。

---

94 infinitely

['ɪnfɪnətlɪ]

义 *adv.* 无限地，无穷地

例 Human beings are infinitely adaptable.

译 人类的适应能力是无限的。

---

95 inflame

[ɪn'fleɪm]

义 *v.* 激怒；加剧

例 His comments have inflamed teachers all over the country.

译 他的评论激怒了全国教师。

---

96 inflammability

[ɪnˌflæmə'bɪlɪtɪ]

义 *n.* 可燃性；易兴奋性

例 Its inflammability is accord with requirement, and has high precision.

译 其燃烧性能符合要求，且精度高。

---

97 inflect

[ɪn'flekt]

义 *v.* 弯曲；改变

例 The results inflect the precise of the whole bridge state analysis.

译 这些结果改变了整个桥梁状态分析的精度。

---

98 informality

[ˌɪnfɔː'mælətɪ]

义 *n.* 非正式；不拘礼节

例 She enjoyed the relative informality of island life.

译 她喜欢岛上相对随意的生活。

99 infra
['ɪnfrə]

义 *adv.*（书等的）下文；在下面

例 A partnership agreement must accompany account application, and a partnership addendum enclosed infra must be completed and signed.

译 申请账户必须附有合伙协议，且必须填写并签署下文所附的合伙附录。

100 inheritance
[ɪn'herɪtəns]

义 *n.* 遗传；遗产

例 She spent all her inheritance in a year.

译 她在一年之内就花光了所有的遗产。

List 8

1 inlet
['ɪnlet]

义 *n.* 水湾；入口
例 Water will be observed draining from the inlet connection of the device.
译 从装置的进口连接处应该可以观察到水的排放。

2 inn
[ɪn]

义 *n.* 客栈，小旅店
例 I always feel at home at Ye Olde Starre Inn.
译 在老斯塔尔酒店，我总有一种家的感觉。

3 innkeeper
['ɪnkiːpər]

义 *n.* 旅馆老板，客栈老板
例 It was the innkeeper who had come to tell him that midnight had struck.
译 原来是旅馆老板来告诉他已经午夜了。

4 insane
[ɪn'seɪn]

义 *adj.* 疯狂的，精神错乱的
例 This job is driving me insane.
译 这份工作快要把我逼疯了。

5 inseparable
[ɪn'seprəbl]

义 *adj.* 不能分的
例 He firmly believes liberty is inseparable from social justice.
译 他坚信自由与社会正义是分不开的。

6 inshore
['ɪnʃɔːr]

义 *adj.* 近海岸的；向陆的
例 A barge was close inshore about a hundred yards away.
译 一艘驳船离岸边大约一百码远。

7 insinuate
[ɪn'sɪnjueɪt]

义 *v.* 暗示；含沙射影地说
例 What are you trying to insinuate?
译 你想暗示什么？

8 insistent
[ɪn'sɪstənt]

义 *adj.* 坚持的；迫切的
例 The doctor demurred, but Piercey was insistent.
译 医生不同意，但是皮尔西坚持不懈。

9 inspirational
[ˌɪnspə'reɪʃnəl]

义 *adj.* 带有灵感的，鼓舞人心的
例 Our new brochure is crammed full of inspirational ideas.
译 我们新的小册子中振奋人心的妙计比比皆是。

10 instill

[ɪnˈstɪl]

义 *v.* 逐渐灌输；滴注

例 She instilled in the children the virtues of good hard work, and making the best of what you have.

译 她慢慢给孩子们灌输勤奋工作的品德，教导他们充分利用现有的条件。

11 instructional

[ɪnˈstrʌkʃənl]

义 *adj.* 教育的；教学的

例 You may wish to take advantage of our instructional session.

译 你应该充分利用我们的教学课程。

12 insure

[ɪnˈʃʊr]

义 *v.* 保险；确保

例 We strongly recommend insuring against sickness or injury.

译 我们强烈建议投伤病保险。

13 insurmountable

[ˌɪnsərˈmaʊntəbl]

义 *adj.* 不能克服的；难以对付的

例 The crisis doesn't seem like an insurmountable problem.

译 这场危机似乎不是一个无法克服的问题。

14 intensity

[ɪnˈtensətɪ]

义 *n.* 强度；强烈

例 Finally, the Raman scattering intensities are discussed.

译 最后讨论了拉曼效应强度。

15 intentness

[ɪnˈtentnɪs]

义 *n.* 专心

例 He sat up suddenly and listened with a passionate intentness.

译 他忽然坐直了身子，神情激动，聚精会神地侧耳倾听。

16 interactive

[ˌɪntərˈæktɪv]

义 *adj.* 相互作用的；交互的

例 The school believes in interactive teaching methods.

译 这所学校信奉互动式教学方法。

17 intercept

[ˌɪntərˈsept]

义 *v.* 拦截，截取

例 It is illegal to intercept radio messages.

译 拦截无线电信息是违法的。

18 interdependent

[ˌɪntərdɪˈpendənt]

义 *adj.* 相互依赖的　*v.* 互助的

例 We live in an increasingly interdependent world.

译 我们生活在一个日益相互依赖的世界。

19 interglacial

[ˌɪntə'gleɪʃəl]

义 *adj.* 间冰期的

例 Earth was already in one of its warm interglacial periods when we started burning fossil fuels.

译 当我们开始燃烧化石燃料时，地球已经处于温暖的间冰期。

---

20 internment

[ɪn'tɜːrnmənt]

义 *n.* 拘禁

例 He was confined in an internment camp in Utah.

译 他被关押在犹他州的一个拘留营。

---

21 interpretive

[ɪn'tɜːprɪtɪv]

义 *adj.* 说明的；解释的

例 History is an interpretive process.

译 历史是一个解释的过程。

---

22 intimacy

['ɪntɪməsɪ]

义 *n.* 亲密；亲昵的言语（或行为）

例 The opening of the scene depicts Akhnaten and his family in a moment of intimacy.

译 开头场景描绘了阿克那吞和他的家人的亲密时刻。

---

23 intrepid

[ɪn'trepɪd]

义 *adj.* 无畏的，刚毅的

例 The intrepid are richly rewarded with new discoveries.

译 无畏的人收获了大量的新发现。

---

24 intricately

['ɪntrɪkətlɪ]

义 *adv.* 杂乱地；复杂地，精细地

例 Franklin made his mother an intricately detailed scale model of the house.

译 富兰克林给他母亲做了一个按这座房子比例缩小的精巧逼真的模型。

---

25 introspective

[ˌɪntrə'spektɪv]

义 *adj.* 反省的，内省的

例 We humans are introspective.

译 我们人类会反观自省。

---

26 intuit

[ɪn'tuːɪt]

义 *v.* 由直觉知道

例 They would confidently intuit your very thoughts.

译 他们会自信地凭直觉感知你的想法。

---

27 inundate

['ɪnʌndeɪt]

义 *v.* 淹没

例 The flood inundated the whole district.

译 洪水淹没了整个地区。

---

28 inventory

['ɪnvəntɔːrɪ]

义 *n.* 详细目录；存货（清单）

例 They're likely to hold big fire sales to liquidate their inventory.

译 他们可能会进行大减价以清理库存。

---

29 investigation

[ɪnˌvestɪ'geɪʃn]

义 *n.* 调查，审查

例 Investigations have never turned up any evidence.

译 调查没能发现任何证据。

---

30 invigorate

[ɪn'vɪgəreɪt]

义 *v.* 鼓舞，激励

例 Take a deep breath in to invigorate you.

译 深吸一口气，让自己振作起来。

---

31 invoice

['ɪnvɔɪs]

义 *n.* 发货单；发票

例 We will be pleased to delete the charge from the original invoice.

译 我们将愿意将这笔费用从原来的发票中删去。

---

32 involuntary

[ɪn'vɑːləntərɪ]

义 *adj.* 无意的；不由自主的

例 The drug's side effects can include involuntary defecation.

译 这种药物的副作用包括无意识排便。

---

33 involution

[ˌɪnvə'luːʃən]

义 *n.* 退化

例 Involution is the descent of spirit into matter.

译 退化是精神向物质的下降。

---

34 irrefutable

[ˌɪrɪ'fjuːtəbl]

义 *adj.* 不能反驳的，不可否认的

例 The pictures provide irrefutable evidence of the incident.

译 这些照片为这一事件提供了无可辩驳的证据。

---

35 irreplaceable

[ˌɪrɪ'pleɪsəbl]

义 *adj.* 不可替代的

例 Although cork is a dead bark, it should be considered a noble plant material since its intrinsic properties are numerous and irreplaceable by any single synthetic material of the same cost.

译 尽管软木是一种枯死的树皮，但它应该被视为一种高贵的植物材料，因为它有大量内在价值，并且任何一种同等成本的合成材料都无法替代它。

---

36 irresistibly

[ˌɪrɪ'zɪstəblɪ]

义 *adv.* 不可抵抗地；压制不住地

例 They were irresistibly drawn to each other.

译 他们不可抵挡地相互倾心。

37　irreverent

['ɪ'revərənt]

义 *adj.* 不敬的，无礼的

例 Taylor combined great knowledge with an irreverent attitude to history.

译 泰勒知识渊博，但对历史却持不尊重态度。

38　irreversibly

[,ɪrɪ'vɜ:rsəblɪ]

义 *adv.* 不可逆转地

例 It is this irreversibly modified world, from the polar caps to the equatorial forests, that is all the nature we have.

译 从极地冰盖到赤道森林，我们所拥有的就是这个变化不可逆转的世界。

39　jagged

['dʒægɪd]

义 *adj.* 参差不齐的

例 They clambered back under the falls to detach the raft from a jagged rock.

译 他们爬回瀑布下面，把木筏从一块参差不齐的岩石上分离出来。

40　janitor

['dʒænɪtər]

义 *n.* 门卫，门警

例 Ed Roberts had been a school janitor for a long time.

译 埃德·罗伯茨在学校当了很长时间的门卫。

41　jeer

[dʒɪr]

义 *v.* 嘲弄，奚落

例 They began to jeer and insult him more than the other boys.

译 他们开始嘲笑和侮辱他，比其他男孩更甚。

42　jot

[dʒɑ:t]

义 *n.* 少量

例 There's not a jot of truth in what he says.

译 他没有一句实话。

43　joyfulness

['dʒɔɪflnəs]

义 *n.* 欢喜，快乐

例 Color glowed in his face and his strange eyes widened with joyfulness.

译 他的脸涨得通红，那双奇怪的眼睛睁得大大的，眼里充满了快乐。

44　jurisdiction

[,dʒʊrɪs'dɪkʃn]

义 *n.* 司法权，审判权；管辖权；管辖区域，管辖范围

例 This case falls outside my jurisdiction.

译 这个案子不在我的管辖范围之内。

45　jury

['dʒʊrɪ]

义 *n.* 陪审团，评委会

例 Has the jury reached a verdict?

译 陪审团做出裁决了吗？

---

46 kickball

['kɪkbɔ:l]

义 *n.* 踢球（儿童足球）

例 I was never really into playing kickball.

译 我从来没有真正喜欢过踢球。

---

47 kidnap

['kɪdnæp]

义 *v./n.* 绑架

例 He admitted the charge of kidnap.

译 他对绑架的指控供认不讳。

---

48 kiwifruit

['kɪwɪˌfru:t]

义 *n.* 猕猴桃，奇异果

例 Cangxi Red kiwifruit industry has a bright prospect.

译 苍溪红猕猴桃产业前景广阔。

---

49 kneel

[ni:l]

义 *v.* 跪

例 We knelt down on the ground to examine the tracks.

译 我们跪在地上察看足迹。

---

50 label

['leɪbl]

义 *v.* 贴标签

例 She even labeled everything.

译 她甚至给所有东西都贴上了标签。

---

51 labor

['leɪbər]

义 *n.* 工人，劳工

例 I think Milton is encouraging us to question, to wrestle with the theological certainties that the rest of the poem labors to establish.

译 我认为米尔顿是在鼓励我们去质疑，去与劳工们努力在这首诗其余部分中建立的神学确定性搏斗。

---

52 laborer

['leɪbərər]

义 *n.* 劳动者，劳工

例 The Japanese provided the labor and the crop was divided between laborers and landowners.

译 日本人提供劳力，作物由劳工和地主分配。

---

53 lament

[lə'ment]

义 *v.* 对……感到悲痛　*n.* 悲叹，悼词

例 Ken began to lament the death of his only son.

译 肯为他独生子的去世开始感到悲痛。

---

54 landfill

['lændfɪl]

义 *n.* 垃圾填埋地

例 The rubbish in modern landfills does not rot.

译 现代垃圾埋填场里的垃圾不会腐烂。

55　landscape
['lændskeɪp]

义 *n.* 风景；风景画

例 He enjoyed the fair landscape of his hometown.

译 他喜欢家乡美丽的风景。

56　lash
[læʃ]

义 *v.* 怒斥；鞭打

例 She went quiet for a moment while she summoned up the words to lash him.

译 她沉默了一会儿，想了些话来怒斥他。

57　lassitude
['læsɪtuːd]

义 *n.* 无力，疲倦

例 Symptoms of anaemia include general fatigue and lassitude.

译 贫血的症状包括全身疲劳和无力。

58　launchpad
['lɔːntʃpæd]

义 *n.* (火箭等的) 发射台

例 Here, the shuttle is mounted on a mobile launchpad weeks before its liftoff.

译 在这里，发射前几周航天飞机是安装在移动发射台上的。

59　laundress
['lɔːndrɪs]

义 *n.* 洗衣女

例 She affirmed that the British laundress was not a mistress of her art.

译 她还断言，英国的洗衣妇没有掌握这一行的本领。

60　lave
[leɪv]

义 *v.* 洗涤，洗掉

例 She ran cold water in the basin, laving her face and hands.

译 她在脸盆里放了凉水，洗了洗脸和手。

61　layover
['leɪəʊvər]

义 *n.* 短暂停留，逗留

例 She booked a plane for Denver with a layover in Dallas.

译 她订了去丹佛的飞机，中途在达拉斯转机。

62　laziness
['leɪzɪnəs]

义 *n.* 懒惰

例 It's laziness, pure and simple.

译 这纯粹是懒惰。

63　leach
[liːtʃ]

义 *v.* 过滤

例 The nutrient is quickly leached away.

译 营养物质很快就被过滤掉了。

---

64 lean

['liːn]

义 *v.* 倾斜

例 She walked slowly, leaning on her son's arm.

译 她倚着儿子的胳膊慢慢地走着。

---

65 leash

[liːʃ]

义 *n.* (系狗的)皮带；控制，约束

例 One Sunday he began trying to teach the two puppies to walk on a leash.

译 一个星期天，他开始试着教两只幼犬拴着狗绳走路。

---

66 legally

['liːgəlɪ]

义 *adv.* 合法地，法律上地

例 It could be a bit problematic, legally speaking.

译 从法律上讲，这可能有点问题。

---

67 legendary

['ledʒəndərɪ]

义 *adj.* 传说的；著名的

例 The hill is supposed to be the resting place of the legendary King Lud.

译 这座山被认为是传说中的路德国王的安息之地。

---

68 legislate

['ledʒɪsleɪt]

义 *v.* 制定法律，用立法规定

例 They promised to legislate to protect people's right to privacy.

译 他们承诺立法保护人们的隐私权。

---

69 legislature

['ledʒɪsleɪtʃər]

义 *n.* 立法机关

例 It was originally planned as a reference library for the federal legislature.

译 最初，它被计划用来作为联邦立法机构的参考图书馆。

---

70 lengthy

['leŋθɪ]

义 *adj.* 冗长的，漫长的

例 A deal was struck after lengthy negotiations.

译 长时间谈判后，协议达成了。

---

71 lick

[lɪk]

义 *v.* 击败

例 Tom said, "I can lick you!"

译 汤姆说："我能打败你！"

---

72 lieutenant

[luːˈtenənt]

义 *n.* 中尉，副官

例 The lieutenant stopped and stood stock-still.

译 中尉停了下来，一动不动地站着。

---

73 lifelike

['laɪflaɪk]

义 *adj.* 逼真的；栩栩如生的

例 The horse he painted is very lifelike.

译 他画的马非常逼真。

---

74 lifestyle

['laɪfstaɪl]

义 *n.* 生活方式

例 People's lifestyles are usually fixed by generational habits and fashions.

译 人们的生活方式通常是由一代人的习惯和时尚所决定的。

---

75 lighthouse

['laɪthaʊs]

义 *n.* 灯塔

例 A lighthouse marks the entrance to the harbor.

译 灯塔标志着港口的入口。

---

76 lightness

['laɪtnəs]

义 *n.* 亮度；（颜色）浅淡

例 The dark green spare bedroom is in total contrast to the lightness of the large main bedroom.

译 深绿色的备用卧室与明亮的主卧室形成了鲜明的对比。

---

77 likeness

['laɪknəs]

义 *n.* 相像；相似物

例 These myths have a startling likeness to one another.

译 这些神话有着惊人的相似之处。

---

78 limelight

['laɪmlaɪt]

义 *n.* 众人注目的中心；聚光灯

例 Tony has now been thrust into the limelight, with a high-profile job.

译 托尼有一份令人注目的工作，现在已成为人们关注的焦点。

---

79 linkage

['lɪŋkɪdʒ]

义 *n.* 联系，连合

例 There is no formal linkage between the two agreements.

译 这两份协约间无正式关联。

---

80 listless

['lɪstləs]

义 *adj.* 无精打采的

例 She looked washed out and listless.

译 她看上去疲惫不堪，无精打采。

---

81 locale

[ləʊ'kæl]

义 *n.* 现场，场所

例 An amusement park is the perfect locale for youngsters to have all sorts of adventures.

译 游乐园是年轻人进行各种冒险活动的最佳场所。

---

82 localize

['ləʊkəlaɪz]

义 *v.* 集中；局部化

例 Few officers thought that the war could be localized.

译 没几个军官认为这场战争会是局部战争。

---

83 locust

['ləʊkəst]

义 *n.* 蝗虫

例 There were millions of locusts around us—a locust sandstorm.

译 我们周围有数百万只蝗虫——这是一场蝗虫沙尘暴。

---

84 lodestar

['ləʊdstɑːr]

义 *n.* 指示方向之星，北极星

例 At the same time, it's our lodestar.

译 同时，这也是我们的指导方针。

---

85 lodger

['lɑːdʒər]

义 *n.* 房客

例 Jennie took in a lodger to help with the mortgage.

译 詹妮收留了一名房客来帮她分担房屋贷款。

---

86 lodging

['lɑːdʒɪŋ]

义 *n.* 寄宿处，借宿

例 He was given free lodging.

译 他得到了免费住宿。

---

87 loftily

['lɔːftɪlɪ]

义 *adv.* 高尚地；傲慢地

例 Love in tragedies was for the most part loftily, romantic.

译 悲剧中的爱情大多是高尚而浪漫的。

---

88 loneliness

['ləʊnlɪnəs]

义 *n.* 孤独，寂寞

例 He felt a sudden inexpressible loneliness.

译 他突然感到一种说不出的孤独。

---

89 lonesome

['ləʊnsəm]

义 *adj.* 寂寞的，孤单的

例 I felt lonesome in the strange land.

译 在这个陌生的地方我感到很孤独。

---

90 longstanding

['lɔːŋ'stændɪŋ]

义 *adj.* (已持续)长时间的，为时甚久的

例 Whether you can successfully change your personality as an adult is the subject of a longstanding psychological debate.

译 作为一个成年人，你能否成功地改变自己的个性是一个长期存在的心理学争论的话题。

---

91 lookout

['lʊkaʊt]

义 *n.* 瞭望台；瞭望员；注意

例 He denied that he'd failed to keep a proper lookout that night.

译 他否认那天晚上他未能小心警戒的事实。

---

92 loosen

['luːsn]

义 *v.* 松开；放松；放宽

例 He reached up to loosen the scarf around his neck.

译 他伸出手松开围在脖子上的围巾。

---

93 lopsidedness

['lɑpˌsaɪdədnəs]

义 *n.* 倾斜边；不匀称；不平衡

例 Part of that lopsidedness was the huge pile of international reserves emerging countries built up during the boom on the back of strong exports.

译 全球金融的失衡部分是由于新兴国家在繁荣时期依靠发达的出口而累积了大量外汇储备。

---

94 lore

[lɔːr]

义 *n.* 学问，知识；传说

例 He has wedded to lore and logic long ago.

译 他早已跟学问与逻辑私订终身。

---

95 lotion

['ləʊʃn]

义 *n.* 乳液，护肤液

例 The lotion cools and refreshes the skin.

译 这种乳液能使皮肤凉爽、清爽。

---

96 loudness

[laʊdnəs]

义 *n.* 响亮；音量

例 The first point I'd like to address is loudness.

译 我想说的第一点是响度。

---

97 loudspeaker

[ˌlaʊd'spiːkər]

义 *n.* 扬声器，喇叭

例 One boy did an imitation of a soldier with a loudspeaker.

译 一个男孩拿着扬声器学着士兵的样子。

---

98 lovelorn

['lʌvlɔːrn]

义 *adj.* 失恋的；害相思病的

例 He was acting like a lovelorn teenager.

译 他表现得像一个患有相思病的少年。

99　lubrication

[ˌluːbrɪˈkeɪʃn]

义 *n.* 润滑

例 We shall require more lubrication oil this month to move the massive stones quickly and safely.

译 这个月我们需要更多的润滑油，以便快速安全地搬运这些巨石。

100　lug

[lʌg]

义 *v.* 用力拉或拖；拖累

例 I managed to lug the wet clothes to the laundromat.

译 我设法把湿衣服拖到自助洗衣店。

List 9

1 luminescent
[ˌluːmɪˈnesnt]

义 *adj.* 发冷光的

例 The discharge vessel is provided with a luminescent layer comprising a mixture of at least a red and a green luminescent material.

译 放电容器配备有发光层，该发光层包含至少一种红色和绿色发光材料的混合物。

---

2 luminous
[ˈluːmɪnəs]

义 *adj.* 发光的；清楚的

例 They painted the door a luminous green.

译 他们把门漆成了亮绿色。

---

3 lumpy
[ˈlʌmpɪ]

义 *adj.* 粗笨的；多块状物的

例 When the rice isn't cooked properly it goes lumpy and gooey.

译 如果米饭没有煮熟，就会结块、黏稠。

---

4 lunatic
[ˈluːnətɪk]

义 *n.* 疯子

例 The man's a raving lunatic.

译 那人是个胡言乱语的疯子。

---

5 lusterless
[ˈlʌstəlɪs]

义 *adj.* 无光泽的

例 She wore her lusterless hair drawn up into a bun, in the traditional shape of a ginkgo leaf.

译 她把毫无光泽的头发挽成传统的银杏叶形状的发髻。

---

6 lyrical
[ˈlɪrɪkl]

义 *adj.* 抒情的；抒情诗的

例 This juxtaposition of brutal reality and lyrical beauty runs through Park's stories.

译 残酷的现实和抒情的美并存贯穿于帕克的故事中。

---

7 lyricism
[ˈlɪrɪsɪzəm]

义 *n.* 抒情诗体；抒情性

例 We English do not run to lyricism.

译 我们英国人不喜欢用抒情体。

---

8 lyricist
[ˈlɪrɪsɪst]

义 *n.*（流行歌曲的）歌词作者；抒情诗人

例 I think you may be a born lyricist.

译 我认为你天生就是个作曲家。

---

9 madman
[ˈmædmən]

义 *n.* 疯子；精神病患者

例 He wanted to jump up and run outside, screaming like a madman.

译 他想在外面跑跳，像疯子似的尖叫。

10　magnification

[ˌmægnɪfɪˈkeɪʃn]

义 *n.* 放大；夸张

例 The telescope has a magnification of 50.

译 这架望远镜可以放大 50 倍。

11　magnificence

[mægˈnɪfɪsns]

义 *n.* 豪华，宏伟

例 The greatest splendor and the greatest magnificence one can imagine await them.

译 人们所能想象到的最伟大的辉煌在等着他们。

12　maiden

[ˈmeɪdn]

义 *adj.* 首次的

例 The Titanic sank on its maiden voyage.

译 泰坦尼克号首航便沉没了。

13　mainline

[ˈmeɪnlaɪn]

义 *adj.* 主流的；传统的

例 We observe a striking shift away from a labor theory among all mainline economists.

译 我们发现在所有主流经济学家中出现了一种背离劳动理论的惊人变化。

14　majestic

[məˈdʒestɪk]

义 *adj.* 宏伟的，壮丽的

例 The setting, at the foot of the Alps, is majestic.

译 阿尔卑斯山脚的环境雄伟壮丽。

15　makeshift

[ˈmeɪkʃɪft]

义 *adj.* 临时的

例 A few cushions formed a makeshift bed.

译 几个靠垫临时搭成一张床。

16　malevolence

[məˈlevələns]

义 *n.* 恶意；狠毒

例 But he did not know what malevolence was.

译 但他不知道什么是恶意。

17　malignant

[məˈlɪgnənt]

义 *adj.* 有恶意的；恶性的

例 She developed a malignant breast tumor.

译 她患了恶性乳腺肿瘤。

18　malleable

[ˈmælɪəbl]

义 *adj.* 可塑的；易改变的

例 She was young enough to be malleable.

译 她还年轻，有一定的可塑性。

19　malnourishment

[mæl'nʌrɪʃm(ə)nt]

义 *n.* 营养不良

例 There is famine in many countries, and people are dying of malnourishment, of starvation, and of related diseases.

译 许多国家都在闹饥荒，那里的人民因为营养不良、饥饿以及由此引发的疾病而纷纷死去。

20　mandate

['mændeɪt]

义 *v.* 强制执行，颁布

例 Not everyone will agree with the authors' policy ideas, which range from mandating more holiday time to reducing tax incentives for American homebuyers.

译 并不是每个人都同意作者的政策观点，其中包括强制增加休假时间，以及减少对美国购房者的税收优惠等。

21　maneuver

[mə'nu:vər]

义 *v.* 机动；演习　*n.* 细致巧妙的移动；机动动作

例 He was kept pausing in order to look at the sceneshifters' maneuvers.

译 他一直停下来观察换布景者的动作。

22　manicure

['mænɪkjʊr]

义 *n.* 修指甲；修指甲的人

例 I have a manicure occasionally.

译 我偶尔会修指甲。

23　mantled

['mæntld]

义 *adj.* 披着斗篷的；罩上的　*v.* 覆盖；（脸）发红，涨红

例 Her face mantled with shame.

译 她羞愧得满脸通红。

24　manufacturer

[,mænjʊ'fæktʃərər]

义 *n.* 制造商

例 There were several possibilities open to each manufacturer.

译 每个制造商都面临几种可能。

25　marshmallow

['mɑ:rʃmeləʊ]

义 *n.* 棉花糖

例 This family set up fire and grill marshmallow for kids.

译 这个家庭点起了火，给孩子们烤棉花糖吃。

26　masculine

['mæskjələn]

义 *adj.* 男性的

例 "He" and "him" are masculine pronouns.

译 "he" 和 "him" 是男性代词。

27 masque

[mæsk]

义 *n.* 化装舞会；面膜

例 You should use this facial masque often.

译 你应该经常使用这种面膜。

28 masterful

['mæstərfl]

义 *adj.* 傲慢的；熟练的

例 Big successful moves need bold, masterful managers.

译 重大而成功的举措需要大胆而熟练的管理者。

29 materialize

[mə'tɪrɪəlaɪz]

义 *v.* 成为现实，实现

例 A rebellion by radicals failed to materialize.

译 激进分子的一次叛乱未能实现。

30 mathematician

[ˌmæθəmə'tɪʃn]

义 *n.* 数学家

例 I'm not a very good mathematician.

译 我不是一个很好的数学家。

31 matriarch

['meɪtrɑːrk]

义 *n.* 女家长，女族长

例 And, her mother is definitely the matriarch of the bigger family.

译 而且，她的母亲绝对是这个大家庭的女家长。

32 matrilineal

[ˌmætrɪ'lɪnɪəl]

义 *adj.* 母系的

例 They are the world's largest matrilineal society.

译 她们是世界上最大的母系社会。

33 maturation

[ˌmætʃʊ'reɪʃn]

义 *n.* 成熟

例 The brain's level of physiological maturation may support these types of memories, but not ones requiring explicit verbal descriptions.

译 大脑的生理成熟水平可能支持这些类型的记忆，而不是需要明确语言描述的。

34 mealtime

['miːltaɪm]

义 *n.* 进餐时间，开饭时间

例 To reduce inflammation, take an aspirin or ibuprofen at mealtime.

译 为了减轻发炎，吃饭时候服用阿司匹林或布洛芬。

35 measurably

['meʒərəblɪ]

义 *adv.* 可以测定的程度；适度地

例 Employees who participate in corporate fitness programs are not measurably less healthy than people who exercise on their own.

译 参加企业健身计划的员工的健康状况一定程度上并不比独自锻炼的员工差。

---

36 meatless

['miːtləs]

义 *adj.* 素食的；无肉的

例 There are Meatless Mondays, Beefless Thursdays and Farm Fridays in the dining halls.

译 餐厅里有"无肉星期一""无牛肉星期四"和"农场星期五"。

---

37 mechanically

[mə'kænɪklɪ]

义 *adv.* 机械地

例 I'm not mechanically minded.

译 我没有机械方面的头脑。

---

38 melodrama

['melədrɑːmə]

义 *n.* 情节剧，音乐剧；传奇剧式的事件

例 Instead of tragedy, we got melodrama.

译 我们看的是情节剧，而不是悲剧。

---

39 memoir

['memwɑːr]

义 *n.* 传记；实录

例 His 1998 memoir is a delightful trip down memory lane.

译 他 1998 年的回忆录是一次愉快的怀旧之旅。

---

40 memorial

[mə'mɔːrɪəl]

义 *n.* 纪念碑；纪念仪式

例 The memorial featured nineteen statues of soldiers arranged in a triangular formation.

译 纪念碑以三角形排列的十九尊士兵雕像为特色。

---

41 mentoring

['mentɔːrɪŋ]

义 *n.* 指导

例 Men score higher starting salaries, have more mentoring, and have better odds of being hired.

译 男性的起薪更高，得到的指导更多，被聘用的概率也更高。

---

42 methodically

[mə'θɑːdɪklɪ]

义 *adv.* 有条不紊地；有条理地

例 Cussane worked quickly and methodically.

译 库珊工作迅速，有条不紊。

---

43 meticulous

[mə'tɪkjələs]

义 *adj.* 一丝不苟的，缜密的

例 Their room had been prepared with meticulous care.

译 他们的房间是经过细心布置的。

---

44 metropolitan

义 *adj.* 大都市的

[ˌmetrəˈpɑːlɪtən] 例 Two years ago, he signed over his art collection to the New York Metropolitan Museum of Art.

译 两年前，他与纽约大都会艺术博物馆签署了他的艺术收藏协议。

---

45 microgram

[ˈmaɪkrəʊɡræm]

义 *n.* 微克

例 This paper describes a rapid method for the separation and determination of microgram amounts of scandium and thorium.

译 本文介绍了一种快速分离测定微量钪、钍的方法。

---

46 midplane

[ˈmɪdpleɪn]

义 *n.* 中平面

例 The exact formula set for the midplane of the uniform-field wedge magnet is derived.

译 本文推导了匀强电场楔形磁铁在中心平面的精确公式。

---

47 midship

[ˈmɪdʃɪp]

义 *n.* 船体中央部

例 A design of midship section is one of the most important part of ship structure design.

译 船中剖面设计是船舶结构设计的重要组成部分。

---

48 midsummer

[ˌmɪdˈsʌmər]

义 *n.* 仲夏；夏至

例 It was a lovely midsummer morning.

译 这是一个美好的仲夏清晨。

---

49 migrant

[ˈmaɪɡrənt]

义 *n.* 移居者；候鸟

例 Migrant workers move from city to city in search of work.

译 农民工从一个城市迁移到另一个城市以寻找工作。

---

50 migratory

[ˈmaɪɡrətɔːrɪ]

义 *adj.* 迁移的

例 The differences in feeding preferences lead, in turn, to differences in migratory habits.

译 食物偏好的差异又反过来导致了迁徙习性的差异。

---

51 mildly

[ˈmaɪldlɪ]

义 *adv.* 柔和地，和善地；适度地

例 The result was unfortunate, to put it mildly.

译 说得好听一点，结果是不幸的。

---

52 milligram

[ˈmɪlɪɡræm]

义 *n.* 毫克

例 A new hair-growing drug is being sold for three times the price, per milligram, as the drug's maker charges for another product with the same active ingredient.

译 一种新的生发药每毫克的售价是该药物制造商另一种含有相同活性成分的产品的售价的三倍。

---

53 millimeter

['mɪləˌmi:tər]

义 *n.* 毫米

例 Each tentacle is about two millimeters long.

译 每条触须大约两毫米长。

---

54 mimicry

['mɪmɪkrɪ]

义 *n.* 模仿；（动物等）拟态伪装

例 One of his few strengths was his skill at mimicry.

译 他为数不多的长处之一就是善于模仿。

---

55 mindful

['maɪndfl]

义 *adj.* 深切注意的；记住的

例 We must be mindful of the consequences of selfishness.

译 我们必须注意自私的后果。

---

56 mint

[mɪnt]

义 *n.* 薄荷

例 She popped a mint into her mouth.

译 她迅速地把一片薄荷糖塞进嘴里。

---

57 misbehave

[ˌmɪsbɪ'heɪv]

义 *v.* 行为无礼貌；行为不端

例 I struggle to keep my temper with the kids when they misbehave.

译 孩子们不听话时，我会努力控制住自己的脾气。

---

58 miscalculation

[ˌmɪskælkjʊ'leɪʃn]

义 *n.* 算错，误算；判断错误

例 That is a grave miscalculation.

译 这是一个严重的误判。

---

59 mischievous

['mɪstʃɪvəs]

义 *adj.* 调皮的，恶作剧的

例 Berg tilts his head and a mischievous look crosses his face.

译 贝格歪着头，脸上闪过一丝调皮的神色。

---

60 miscommunication

[ˌmɪskəˌmju:nɪ'keɪʃən]

义 *n.* 错误传达

例 If we are not aware of and sensitive to cultural differences, the possibilities for miscommunication and conflict are enormous.

译 如果我们没有意识并对文化差异不敏感，那么造成沟通误解和冲突的可能性是特别大的。

---

61 misfit

['mɪsfɪt]

义 *n.* 不适合

例 She always felt a bit of a misfit in the business world.

译 她总觉得自己在商界有些不适应。

---

62 misfortune

[ˌmɪsˈfɔːrtʃuːn]

义 *n.* 不幸，灾祸

例 His story is a catalogue of misfortune.

译 他的经历中充满了接二连三的厄运。

---

63 misgiving

[ˌmɪsˈɡɪvɪŋ]

义 *n.* 疑虑，怀疑

例 It's a freedom that, of course, parliament had pushed for, but now what they've got there is some misgiving.

译 当然，这是一种议会一直在推动的自由，但现在他们收获的是一些疑虑。

---

64 mismanagement

[ˌmɪsˈmænɪdʒmənt]

义 *n.* 管理不善；处理不当

例 His gross mismanagement left the company desperately in need of restructuring.

译 他处理事务的严重不当使得公司急需重组。

---

65 misquote

[ˌmɪsˈkwəʊt]

义 *v.* 误引，错误地引用

例 Did the *Wall Street Journal* misquote him?

译 《华尔街日报》是不是引用错了他的话？

---

66 misshapen

[ˌmɪsˈʃeɪpən]

义 *adj.* 畸形的

例 Her hands were misshapen by arthritis.

译 她的手因关节炎而变形。

---

67 mistrust

[ˌmɪsˈtrʌst]

义 *n.* 不信任，疑惑

例 Mistrust was written large on her face.

译 她脸上流露出明显的不信任。

---

68 misty

['mɪstɪ]

义 *adj.* 有雾的；模糊的，不清晰的

例 They got misty-eyed listening to records of Ruby Murray singing *Danny Boy*.

译 听着鲁比·默里演唱《丹尼男孩》的唱片，他们泪眼蒙眬。

---

69 mitten

['mɪtn]

义 *n.* 连指手套

例 There is a hole in the thumb of his mitten.

译 他手套的拇指位置有个洞。

---

70 moderateness

['mɑːdərətnəs]

义 *n.* 温和；适度性

例 It is believed to have verve of optimism, moderateness, or pessimism.

译 它被认为具有乐观、温和或悲观的神韵。

---

71 moderator

['mɑːdəreɪtər]

义 *n.* 调解人，仲裁人；主持人

例 She also acted as a moderator at a UNICEF event last December.

译 她还在去年 12 月的一次联合国儿童基金会活动中担任过主持人。

---

72 modernity

[məˈdɜːrnətɪ]

义 *n.* 现代性；现代性的东西

例 He accepts the western cultural current open-mindedly and walks at the edge between tradition and modernity.

译 他以开放的心态接受西方文化潮流，游走在传统与现代的边缘。

---

73 modernize

['mɑːdərnaɪz]

义 *v.* (使) 现代化

例 The country badly needs aid to modernize its outmoded industries.

译 这个国家迫切需要援助以对其过时的产业进行现代化。

---

74 modulate

['mɑːdʒəleɪt]

义 *v.* 调整；调节

例 These chemicals modulate the effect of potassium.

译 这些化合物可以调节钾的功效。

---

75 modulation

[ˌmɑːdʒəˈleɪʃn]

义 *n.* 调节，转调

例 The famine turned the normal modulation of climate into disaster.

译 饥荒使得正常的气候变化变成了灾难。

---

76 mold

[məʊld]

义 *n.* 模子，模型

例 What they did was they made plaster casts from molds of the sculptures.

译 他们所做的就是用雕塑的模子制作石膏模型。

---

77 momenta

[məʊˈmentə]

义 *n.* 动量

例 A falling object gains momentum as it falls.

译 物体下落增加动量。

---

78 momentary

['məʊmənterɪ]

义 *adj.* 短暂的，瞬间的

例 The lights go off, and the din of the tourists turns from a momentary grumble of protest to a greedy growl and finally to whispered disappointment.

译 灯光熄灭了，一时间游客的噪声从短暂的抗议的抱怨声变成了贪婪的咆哮声，最后变成了失望的低语声。

---

79 momentum

[məʊˈmentəm]

义 *n.* 【物】动量

例 A falling object gains momentum as it falls.

译 物体下落增加动量。

---

80 moniker

['mɑːnɪkər]

义 *n.* 名字，绰号

例 The moniker "Mother Jones" was conferred on Jones by members of the American Railway Union.

译 "琼斯母亲"的称号是由美国铁路联盟的成员授予琼斯的。

---

81 monologue

['mɑːnəlɔːg]

义 *n.* 独白；独角戏

例 This is a monologue by a mower.

译 这是一个割草者的独白。

---

82 monopolize

[mə'nɑːpəlaɪz]

义 *v.* 独占；垄断

例 Wheat had come to nearly monopolize the region, but it was particularly vulnerable to the locusts.

译 小麦几乎垄断了这一地区，但它特别容易受到蝗虫的袭击。

---

83 monotone

['mɑːnətəʊn]

义 *n.* (说话或唱歌)单调　*adj.* 单调的

例 He spoke in a monotone drawl.

译 他用慢吞吞又单调的语气说话。

---

84 monstrous

['mɑːnstrəs]

义 *adj.* 骇人听闻的；远大的；荒谬的

例 She endured the monstrous behavior for years.

译 她忍受这种骇人听闻的行为多年。

---

85 montage

[ˌmɑːn'tɑːʒ]

义 *n.* 蒙太奇

例 Montage directed more and more of the popular science and education programs.

译 蒙太奇手法被越来越多地应用于科教节目。

---

86 montane

['mɑːnteɪn]

义 *adj.* 山区的

例 Montane rain forest is a zonal forest type in the northern tropical monsoon climate.

译 山地雨林是热带北缘季风气候中的地带性森林类型。

---

87 moonlit

['muːnlɪt]

义 *adj.* 月光照耀的

例 As she speaks, her emotional gaze shifts from the ground, to my eyes, to the moonlit sky, to the ground, and back to my eyes again.

译 她说话时，充满感情的目光从地面转向我的眼睛，转向月光照耀着的天空，转向地面，然后又回到我的眼睛。

88 motherhood

['mʌðərhʊd]

义 *n.* 母亲身份，母性

例 Motherhood suits her.

译 她很适合做母亲。

---

89 motivation

[ˌməʊtɪ'veɪʃn]

义 *n.* 动机

例 He hailed this week's arms agreement but in the same breath expressed suspicion about the motivations of the United States.

译 他对本周达成的武器协议表示开心，但同时也对美国的动机表示怀疑。

---

90 motorist

['məʊtərɪst]

义 *n.* 驾车的人；乘车旅行的人

例 While road testing the car, a mechanic injures another motorist and is sued for $50,000.

译 在道路测试时，一名机械师伤到了另一名司机，并被起诉要求赔偿 5 万美元。

---

91 motorized

['məʊtəraɪzd]

义 *adj.* 装上发动机的

例 Around 1910 motorized carriages were beginning to replace horse-drawn cabs.

译 大约在 1910 年，装有发动机的四轮车开始取代马车。

---

92 mound

[maʊnd]

义 *n.* 小丘；一堆

例 I've got a mound of paperwork to do.

译 我有一大堆文件要做。

---

93 mournful

['mɔːrnfl]

义 *adj.* 悲恸的，悲哀的

例 He looked mournful, even near to tears.

译 他看上去很悲伤，几乎要哭了。

---

94 mouthy

['maʊθɪ]

义 *adj.* 说大话的，大声叫嚣的

例 I can't stand those mouthy brats.

译 我无法忍受那些吵吵闹闹的小孩。

---

95 mower

['məʊər]

义 *n.* 割草机；除草人

例 This lawn mower is driven by a small electric motor.

译 这割草机是由一台小型电动机驱动的。

---

96 multiplication

[ˌmʌltɪplɪ'keɪʃn]

义 *n.* 增加；加法

例 There will be simple tests in addition, subtraction, multiplication, and division.

译 将会有简单的加减乘除测试。

---

97 muscularity

[ˌmʌskjəˈlærətɪ]

义 *n.* 肌肉发达，强壮

例 This may explain why men have such a range of muscularity.

译 这或许可以解释为何男性拥有大量发达的肌肉组织。

---

98 musculature

[ˈmʌskjələtʃər]

义 *n.* 肌肉系统，肌肉组织

例 The shoulders are strong and well laid back with smooth musculature.

译 肩膀结实而向后倾斜，肌肉平滑。

---

99 muse

[mju:z]

义 *n.* 沉思；灵感；缪斯

例 I want to be a better writer and maybe my muse will provide the motivation.

译 我想成为一个更好的作家，也许我的灵感会提供动力。

---

100 muster

[ˈmʌstər]

义 *v.* 集合；鼓起

例 The men mustered before their clan chiefs.

译 男人们聚集在族长们面前。

List 10

1 mutuality

['mjuːtʃʊ'ælətɪ]

义 *n.* 相互关系，相互依存；亲密

例 But strong bonds of mutuality are not built in this way.

译 但是牢固的相互关系不是以这种方式建立的。

2 mystical

['mɪstɪkl]

义 *adj.* 神秘的；神秘主义的

例 That was clearly a deep mystical experience.

译 这显然是一次深刻而神秘的经历。

3 narration

[nə'reɪʃn]

义 *n.* 叙述；旁白，解说

例 He has recorded the narration for the production.

译 他录制了这部作品的解说词。

4 nationalistic

[ˌnæʃnə'lɪstɪk]

义 *adj.* 民族主义的；国家的；民族的

例 Nationalistic fervor is running high.

译 民族主义热情高涨。

5 nautical

['nɔːtɪkl]

义 *adj.* 海上的，航海的

例 The museum houses a fascinating miscellany of nautical treasures.

译 该博物馆收藏了各种吸引人的航海珍品。

6 naval

['neɪvl]

义 *adj.* 海军的；军舰的

例 He was the senior serving naval officer.

译 他是现役海军高级军官。

7 navigational

[ˌnævɪ'geɪʃənl]

义 *adj.* 导航的，航行的

例 I entered the command into my navigational computer.

译 我在导航计算机里输入指令。

8 needlework

['niːdlwɜːrk]

义 *n.* 针线活，缝纫手艺

例 She did beautiful needlework and she embroidered table napkins.

译 她会做漂亮的针线活，还会绣餐巾。

9 nefarious

[nɪ'feriəs]

义 *adj.* 违法的；邪恶的

例 Why make a whole village prisoner if it was not to some nefarious purpose?

译 如果不是为了什么邪恶的目的，为什么要把整个村子的人都关起来呢？

10 negligible
['neglɪdʒəbl]

义 *adj.* 可以忽略的

例 The company says the cost of relocation will be negligible.

译 该公司表示，搬迁的成本可以忽略不计。

---

11 neighboring
['neɪbərɪŋ]

义 *adj.* 附近的；邻接的

例 Progress has been made towards a political compromise between the two neighboring countries.

译 这两个邻国之间的政治和解已经取得进展。

---

12 neurologist
[nʊ'rɑːlədʒɪst]

义 *n.* 神经病学家

例 Doctor Freud was trained as a neurologist.

译 弗洛伊德医生被培养成一名神经学家。

---

13 neutrality
[nuː'trælətɪ]

义 *n.* 中立

例 We have tried to pursue a policy of neutrality.

译 我们试图奉行中立的政策。

---

14 newbie
['nuːbɪ]

义 *n.* 新手，菜鸟

例 You will be a newbie forever.

译 你永远都是新手。

---

15 newfound
['njuːˌfaʊnd]

义 *adj.* 新发现的

例 She savored her newfound freedom.

译 她尽情享受她新获得的自由。

---

16 newness
[njuːnəs]

义 *n.* 崭新；新奇；不熟悉

例 This newness just left me wanting more.

译 这种新鲜感让我想要更多。

---

17 newsletter
['nuːzletər]

义 *n.* 时事通讯，业务通讯，内部通讯，新闻信札

例 We issue a monthly newsletter.

译 我们每月发行一份时事通讯。

---

18 newsprint
['nuːzprɪnt]

义 *n.* 新闻用纸；油墨；报纸上的文字

例 They get their hands covered in newsprint.

译 他们的手上沾满了油墨。

---

19 newsroom

义 *n.* 编辑部；报章杂志阅览室；报纸贩卖部

['nu:zru:m]

例 The American Society of News Editors reckons that 13,500 newsroom jobs have gone since 2007.

译 美国新闻编辑协会估测，自 2007 年以来，已有 13 500 位编辑人员失业。

---

20 newsstand

['nju:zˌstænd]

义 *n.* 报摊，杂志摊

例 You can buy it at newsstand.

译 你可以在书报摊买到它。

---

21 newsworthy

['nu:zwɜːrðɪ]

义 *adj.* 有新闻价值的

例 This situation might develop into an even more newsworthy item if the police were involved.

译 如果警方介入的话，这个局面就会变得更有新闻价值了。

---

22 nightly

['naɪtlɪ]

义 *adj.* 每晚的，夜间的

例 She appears nightly on the television news.

译 她每晚都在电视新闻上出现。

---

23 nightmarish

['naɪtˌmerɪʃ]

义 *adj.* 噩梦似的，可怕的

例 The party began to take on an unreal, almost nightmarish quality.

译 聚会开始呈现出一种不真实的、几乎是噩梦般的气氛。

---

24 nighttime

['naɪtˌtaɪm]

义 *n.* 夜间

例 Antidiuretic prescriptions can reduce nighttime urination.

译 抗利尿处方药可减少夜间排尿。

---

25 nit

[nɪt]

义 *n.* 虱子；没用的人，笨蛋

例 I'd rather leave the business than work with such a nit.

译 我宁愿离开公司，也不愿和这样的笨蛋一起工作。

---

26 noiseless

['nɔɪzləs]

义 *adj.* 无声的，寂静的

例 In 1839, in the first scientific treatise on the sperm whale, Thomas Beale, a surgeon aboard a whaler, wrote that it was "one of the most noiseless of marine animals".

译 1839 年，在第一篇关于抹香鲸的科研论文中，捕鲸船上的外科医生托马斯·比尔写道，抹香鲸是"海洋中最无声的动物之一"。

---

27 noncommercial

[ˌnɑnkə'mɜːrʃəl]

义 *adj.* 非营利的

例 It is free for noncommercial use.

译 它可免费用于非商业用途。

28　nonexistent

[ˌnɑːnɪɡ'zɪstənt]

义　*adj.* 不存在的

例　Pollution control measures are either not strict or nonexistent, leading to choking clouds of smog.

译　污染控制措施不严格或有空白，导致烟雾弥漫。

29　nonfiction

[ˌnɑːn'fɪkʃən]

义　*n.* （非小说的）写实文学

例　The series will include both fiction and nonfiction.

译　这个系列将包括小说和纪实作品。

30　noninvasive

[ˌnɑːnɪn'veɪsɪv]

义　*adj.* 非侵害的；非侵袭的；无创

例　Today, we can map the brain with noninvasive scanners.

译　今天，我们可以用无创扫描仪来探测大脑。

31　nonlinear

[nɑːn'lɪniːə]

义　*adj.* 非线性的

例　Environmental systems tend to be nonlinear, and therefore not easy to predict.

译　环境系统往往是非线性的，因此不容易预测。

32　nonperishable

[nɑːn'perɪʃəbəl]

义　*adj.* 不易损坏的　*n.* 不易损坏之物

例　Today, the theater acknowledges its bartering tradition by collecting nonperishable food items in exchange for tickets for at least one performance per year.

译　如今，这家剧院认可了其以物易物的传统，每年收集不易腐烂的食物以换取至少一场演出的门票。

33　nonprofit

[ˌnɑːn'prɑːfɪt]

义　*adj.* 非营利的

例　The consortium is a nonprofit group affiliated with the University of Chicago.

译　该联盟是一个隶属于芝加哥大学的非营利组织。

34　nonrepresentational

[ˌnɑːnreprɪzen'teɪʃənəl]

义　*adj.* 非写实的；抽象的

例　The modern culture is not nonrepresentational culture but idiographic culture linked close with some substantial form.

译　现代文化不是抽象文化，而是与某种物质形态紧密相连的具象文化。

35　nonstop

[nɑːn'stɑːp]

义　*adj.* 直达的；不间断的

例　This is a nonstop bus.

译　这是一趟能直达的公共汽车。

36　nostalgic

义　*adj.* 怀旧的；乡愁的

[nɑ:'stældʒɪk] 　例 He made a nostalgic return visit to Hawaii.

译 他对夏威夷进行了一次怀旧的回访。

37　nosy

['nəʊzɪ]

义 *adj.* 好管闲事的；爱追问的

例 He was having to whisper in order to avoid being overheard by their nosy neighbors.

译 他不得不低声说话，以免被他们爱管闲事的邻居听到。

38　notate

['nəʊteɪt]

义 *v.* 把……写成标志

例 Even a work that had already been notated was subject in the heat of the moment to total transformation motivated solely by the whim of the composer.

译 即使一个已经被记录下来的作品，也会因为作曲家一时的心血来潮而得到彻底改变。

39　notepad

['nəʊtpæd]

义 *n.* 记事本，笔记本

例 A notepad is the only equipment you need.

译 而你唯一需要的设备是一本笔记本。

40　nourishment

['nɜ:rɪʃmənt]

义 *n.* 营养；滋养品

例 The mother provides the embryo with nourishment and a place to grow.

译 母亲为胚胎提供营养和发育的场所。

41　novella

[nə'velə]

义 *n.* 短篇故事，中篇小说

例 The novella is marked with distinct theme, far reaching meaning, and narrative techniques in particular.

译 这部中篇小说主题鲜明，意义深远，叙事技巧特别突出。

42　novice

['nɑ:vɪs]

义 *n.* 新手，新信徒

例 I'm a complete novice at skiing.

译 滑雪方面，我完全是个新手。

43　nutritionist

[njʊ'trɪʃənɪst]

义 *n.* 营养学家

例 However, some nutritionists advise against switching to a totally strict vegetarian diet.

译 然而，一些营养学家建议不要转向完全严格的素食。

44　nylon

['naɪlɑ:n]

义 *n.* 尼龙

例 The strap's black nylon label boasts a "W", which might stand for "Wilson", except it doesn't.

译 带子上的黑色尼龙标签上写着 "W"，这也许代表 "威尔逊"，但事实并非如此。

---

45 oasis

[əʊˈeɪsɪs]

义 *n.* 绿洲；宜人之地

例 It hovered before his eyes like the mirage of an oasis.

译 它在他眼前晃动，好像海市蜃楼里的绿洲。

---

46 obedience

[əˈbiːdɪəns]

义 *n.* 服从，顺从

例 Isabella had been taught unquestioning obedience.

译 伊莎贝拉被教导要绝对服从。

---

47 obligated

[ˈɑːblɪɡeɪtɪd]

义 *adj.* 有义务的；有责任的

例 He felt obligated to help.

译 他觉得有义务帮忙。

---

48 oblivion

[əˈblɪvɪən]

义 *n.* 遗忘，忘却

例 Most of his inventions have been consigned to oblivion.

译 他的大部分发明都已被遗忘。

---

49 oblong

[ˈɑːblɔːŋ]

义 *adj.* 椭圆形的；长方形的　*n.* 椭圆形；长方形

例 The plum is the slightly oblong central bulge, protruding about 3,000 light-years above and below the galactic plane, comprised mostly of older stars.

译 "梅子"是银河系平面上方和下方约 3 000 光年处略微呈椭圆形的中央凸起部分，主要由较老的恒星组成。

---

50 obscurity

[əbˈskjʊrətɪ]

义 *n.* 晦涩；不出名

例 He spent most of his life working in obscurity.

译 他大半生都在默默无闻地工作。

---

51 observant

[əbˈzɜːrvənt]

义 *adj.* 观察力敏锐的

例 The husband is not usually so observant.

译 丈夫通常不那么善于观察。

---

52 obsessive

[əbˈsesɪv]

义 *adj.* 渴望的；强迫性的

例 His son had an obsessive drive to gain his father's approval.

译 他儿子渴望得到他的赞赏。

---

53 obstruction

[əbˈstrʌkʃn]

义 *n.* 障碍，妨碍；闭塞

例 The boy was suffering from a bowel obstruction.

译 这个男孩患有肠梗阻。

---

54 oceanographer

[ˌəʊʃə'nɑːɡrəfər]

义 *n.* 海洋学家

例 How she was this great oceanographer!

译 她是多么伟大的海洋学家！

---

55 odious

['əʊdɪəs]

义 *adj.* 可憎的；讨厌的

例 Odious debt is not repayable.

译 恶债不予偿还。

---

56 odorless

['əʊdərləs]

义 *adj.* 无臭的；没有气味的

例 Install a CO detector to alert you of the presence of the deadly, odorless, colorless gas.

译 安装一氧化碳检测器来提示你是否存在这种致命的、无色无味的气体。

---

57 odorous

['əʊdərəs]

义 *adj.* 有气味的；芳香的；难闻的

例 The microbiological deodorization efficiency for odorous sulfur compounds, especially for dimethyl sulfide, is relatively low.

译 用生物脱臭的方法处理致臭的含硫化合物，尤其是二甲基硫化物的效率较低。

---

58 offshoot

['ɔːfʃuːt]

义 *n.* 分枝，支派；衍生物

例 Psychology began as a purely academic offshoot of natural philosophy.

译 心理学形成之初是作为自然哲学的一个纯学术分支。

---

59 offstage

[ˌɔːf'steɪdʒ]

义 *adj./adv.* 不在舞台上的(地)，戏外的(地)

例 There was a lot of noise offstage.

译 舞台下有很多噪声。

---

60 oily

['ɔɪlɪ]

义 *adj.* 含油的，像油的；油腔滑调的

例 He was wiping his hands on an oily rag.

译 他用一块油乎乎的破布擦手。

---

61 onboard

['ɑːn'bɔːd]

义 *adj.* 机上的，装载的

例 The vehicle is covered by onboard Wi-Fi and 5G network for faster data transmission.

译 车内覆盖有车载 WiFi，可接入 5G 网络，以实现更快的数据传输。

---

62 oncoming

['ɑːnkʌmɪŋ]

义 *adj.* 接近的；即将到来的

例 He strayed into the path of an oncoming car.

译 他误入了有一辆迎面而来的汽车的车道。

---

63 onlooker

['ɑ:nlʊkər]

义 *n.* 旁观者

例 His manner is that of an onlooker.

译 他的态度像个旁观者。

---

64 onslaught

['ɑ:nslɔ:t]

义 *n.* 猛攻，攻击；抨击

例 Sometimes I think Jack's is a tough slot, given the never-ending onslaught of instant information and the general wisdom these days that if you don't "grow" your business at a certain heady rate it will wither and die.

译 鉴于即时信息源源不断的冲击，以及如今普遍的观点，即如果你不以一定的速度"发展"你的业务，它将会枯萎和死亡，有时我会认为杰克的职位很艰难。

---

65 openness

['əʊpənnəs]

义 *n.* 公开，开放

例 It says the information should be released with openness and transparency.

译 应公开透明地发布信息。

---

66 opportunistic

[,ɑ:pərtu:'nɪstɪk]

义 *adj.* 机会主义的；投机取巧的

例 Many of the strongly opportunistic plants are the common weeds of fields and gardens.

译 许多坚定的机会主义植物是田野和花园中常见的杂草。

---

67 orchestrate

['ɔ:rkɪstreɪt]

义 *v.* 精心安排，密谋

例 The colonel was able to orchestrate a rebellion from inside an army jail.

译 上校得以在陆军监狱里精心策划了一场叛乱。

---

68 orderly

['ɔ:rdərlɪ]

义 *adj.* 有秩序的；整齐的

例 It's a beautiful, clean and orderly city.

译 这是一座干净美丽、秩序井然的城市。

---

69 ordinance

['ɔ:rdɪnəns]

义 *n.* 法令，条例

例 The present Road Traffic Ordinance states clearly that the limit of alcohol concentration.

译 现行的《道路交通条例》明确规定了酒精含量的限制标准。

---

70 organizer

['ɔ:gənaɪzər]

义 *n.* 组织者

例 We need fewer organizers and more doers.

译 我们需要少一些组织者，多一些实干者。

---

71 originality

[ə,rɪdʒə'næləti]

义 *n.* 独创性；创造力

例 I give it ten out of ten for originality.

译 我给它的创意打满分。

72 outbuilding

['aʊtbɪldɪŋ]

义 *n.* 附属建筑物；外屋

例 An outbuilding at the Palace of Versailles was converted into a 23-key luxury hotel, set to open in 2011.

译 凡尔赛宫的一间外屋被改成拥有 23 间客房的豪华旅馆，并在 2011 年开业。

73 outburst

['aʊtbɜːrst]

义 *n.* 爆发，突发；（感情）迸发

例 There was an extraordinary outburst of applause from every corner of the auditorium.

译 观众席的每个角落都爆发出热烈的掌声。

74 outcrop

['aʊtkrɑːp]

义 *n.*（岩石）露头；露出

例 The outcrop that we found proved to be very rich in gold.

译 我们发现的露头岩石被证明富含金矿。

75 outfit

['aʊtfɪt]

义 *n.* 设备；服装

例 She was wearing an outfit she'd bought the previous day.

译 她穿着前一天买的一套衣服。

76 outlive

[,aʊt'lɪv]

义 *v.* 比……活得长；比……经久

例 I'm sure Rose will outlive many of us.

译 我相信罗斯会比我们中的很多人活得更久。

77 outmoded

[,aʊt'məʊdɪd]

义 *adj.* 过时的

例 The political system has become thoroughly outmoded.

译 这种政治制度已经完全过时了。

78 outpost

['aʊtpəʊst]

义 *n.* 前哨；警戒部队

例 The soldiers trenched an outpost.

译 士兵们用战壕防御前哨。

79 outpouring

['aʊtpɔːrɪŋ]

义 *n.* 流露；涌现

例 The news of his death produced an instant outpouring of grief.

译 他去世的消息立即引起了一阵悲痛。

80 outreach

[ˈaʊtriːtʃ]

义 *v.* 比……到达更远；超过

例 The singer's talent outreaches that of others.

译 这位歌手的才华超过了其他人。

---

81 outrigger

[ˈaʊtrɪgər]

义 *n.*（承力外伸）支架，伸臂梁

例 During the work they use an outrigger or a front blade to ensure machine stability.

译 作业时他们通过使用悬臂架或前叶以保证机械稳定性。

---

82 outspoken

[aʊtˈspəʊkən]

义 *adj.* 直言不讳的，坦率的

例 She was outspoken in her criticism of the plan.

译 她直言不讳地批评那项计划。

---

83 outstretched

[ˌaʊtˈstretʃt]

义 *adj.* 扩张的；伸长的

例 She was staring into the fire muttering, and holding her arms outstretched to warm her hands.

译 她凝视着炉火，嘴里喃喃自语，接着伸出双臂来取暖。

---

84 overact

[ˌəʊvərˈækt]

义 *v.* 做得过火，演得过火

例 A good actor or actress does not overact on stage.

译 一个好的演员不会在舞台上过度表演。

---

85 overbear

[ˈəʊvəˌbeə]

义 *v.* 威压，压服

例 With his huge body, he overbore his opponent under him.

译 他用他那庞大的身躯将对手压在身下。

---

86 overconfident

[ˌəʊvərˈkɑːnfɪdənt]

义 *adj.* 自负的；过于自信的

例 He proved overconfident on the witness stand, misremembering a key piece of evidence.

译 他在证人席上过于自信，记错了一项关键证据。

---

87 overemotional

[əʊvərɪˈməʊʃənl]

义 *adj.* 多愁善感的

例 At the graduation party, everyone got a bit overemotional.

译 毕业晚会上，每个人都有点情绪激动。

---

88 overflow

[ˌəʊvərˈfləʊ]

义 *v.* 泛滥，溢出

例 The bath is overflowing.

译 浴盆溢水了。

89 overgrown

[ˌəʊvər'grəʊn]

义 *adj.* (草等) 丛生的；成长过快的

例 The yard was overgrown with weeds.

译 院子里杂草丛生。

---

90 overhear

[ˌəʊvər'hɪr]

义 *v.* 无意中听到；偷听

例 They were shut away in a little room where nobody could overhear.

译 他们被关在一个小房间里，谁也无法偷听。

---

91 overheat

[ˌəʊvər'hiːt]

义 *v.* 使过热，过热

例 For early August in Iowa the weather is cool and won't overheat the crew.

译 八月初的艾奥瓦州天气凉爽，不会使船员感觉太热。

---

92 overpay

[ˌəʊvər'peɪ]

义 *v.* 多付，多给报酬

例 Management has to make sure it does not overpay its staff.

译 管理层必须确保不会给员工多支付工资。

---

93 overpopulation

[ˌəʊvəˌpɑːpjʊ'leɪʃn]

义 *n.* 人口过剩

例 I strongly agree that overpopulation has placed an enormous burden on each citizen and the environment.

译 我强烈认同人口过剩给每个公民和环境带来了巨大的负担。

---

94 overrate

[ˌəʊvər'reɪt]

义 *v.* 评价过高，高估

例 I believe you overrate his abilities.

译 我认为你高估了他的能力。

---

95 overshadow

[ˌəʊvər'ʃædəʊ]

义 *v.* 遮阴；使黯然失色

例 Hester is overshadowed by her younger and more attractive sister.

译 赫斯特那更年轻而且更有魅力的妹妹使得她黯然失色。

---

96 overspend

[ˌəʊvər'spend]

义 *v.* 过度使用；花费过多

例 The company has overspent on marketing.

译 这个公司在市场推广方面开支过多。

---

97 overtly

[əʊ'vɜːtlɪ]

义 *adv.* 明显地；公开地

例 He never overtly expressed his feelings about the issue.

译 他从未公开表达过自己对这个问题的看法。

98　overtone

['əʊvərtəʊn]

义　*n.* 弦外音；寓意

例　The word has a pejorative overtone.

译　这个单词有点贬义。

99　owlishly

['aʊlɪʃlɪ]

义　*adv.* 猫头鹰般地；警觉地

例　She blinked at them owlishly.

译　她警觉地向他们眨了眨眼。

100　pact

[pækt]

义　*n.* 契约，协定，条约

例　They have made a pact with each other not to speak about their differences in public.

译　他们彼此达成协议，不公开谈论他们的分歧。

List 11

1 paintbrush
['peɪntbrʌʃ]

义 *n.* 画笔
例 I use a paintbrush to paint.
译 我用画笔画画。

2 paleontologist
[,peɪlɪn'tɑ:lədʒɪst]

义 *n.* 古生物学者
例 Among the thousands of fossils that paleontologists have recovered at Messel Pit are specimens representing nearly 45 different mammal species.
译 在古生物学家在麦塞尔化石坑发现的数千块化石中，有代表近 45 种不同哺乳动物的样本。

3 palisade
[,pælɪ'seɪd]

义 *n.* 篱笆，栅栏
例 The plants' interlocking roots stop riverborne sediments from coursing out to sea, and their trunks and branches serve as a palisade that diminishes the erosive power of waves.
译 这种植物的根系相互缠绕，阻止了河流带来的沉积物流入大海，它们的树干和树枝就像一道屏障，减弱了海浪的侵蚀力。

4 pamper
['pæmpər]

义 *v.* 纵容，溺爱
例 "Mother, don't pamper him," he called after her.
译 "妈妈，不要纵容他。" 他在她身后喊道。

5 panelled
['pænld]

义 *adj.* 镶框式的，有饰板的
例 The panelled walls were covered with portraits.
译 镶有嵌板的墙上挂满了肖像画。

6 panoramic
[,pænə'ræmɪk]

义 *adj.* 全景的
例 The terrain's high points provide a panoramic view of Los Angeles.
译 从这一地带的制高点可以看见洛杉矶的全景。

7 pantry
['pæntrɪ]

义 *n.* 食品储藏室；餐具室
例 His mother used cardboard to section off a small pantry.
译 他母亲用硬纸板隔出了一个小食品储藏室。

8 paperback
['peɪpərbæk]

义 *n.* 纸封面本，平装书；普及本
例 The novel was reissued in paperback.
译 这本小说重新发行了平装本。

9 paperless
['peɪpərləs]

义 *adj.* 无纸传输信息（或数据）的
例 Paperless trading can save time and money.

译 无纸交易能够省时省钱。

---

10 parachute

['pærəʃuːt]

义 *n.* 降落伞

例 Garnerin safe journey was regarded as the first trial parachute jump.

译 加纳林的安全之旅被视为首次试航跳伞。

---

11 paradoxically

[ˌpærə'dɑːksɪklɪ]

义 *adv.* 自相矛盾地；反常地

例 Paradoxically, the less you have to do the more you may resent the work that does come your way.

译 矛盾的是，你需要做的事情越少，你可能就越讨厌自己的工作。

---

12 paralysis

[pə'ræləsɪs]

义 *n.* 瘫痪

例 The strike caused total paralysis in the city.

译 罢工使这个城市完全陷入瘫痪。

---

13 parch

[pɑːrtʃ]

义 *v.* 烘，烤干，炙烤

例 These grains may parch, but they will not pop.

译 这些谷物可能会烤焦，但不会爆裂。

---

14 pare

[per]

义 *v.* 削减；剥或削（某物）的皮

例 The luxury tax won't really do much to pare down the budget deficit.

译 奢侈税对削减预算赤字并没有太大作用。

---

15 parish

['pærɪʃ]

义 *n.* 教区；地方行政区

例 He is vicar of a large rural parish.

译 他是乡下一个大教区的牧师。

---

16 passerby

['pæsər'baɪ]

义 *n.* 过路人，行人

例 A passerby described what he saw moments after the car bomb had exploded.

译 一名行人描述了汽车炸弹爆炸后他看到的情景。

---

17 pastry

['peɪstrɪ]

义 *n.* 面粉糕饼

例 The bread, pastry and mayonnaise are homemade.

译 面包、糕点和蛋黄酱都是自制的。

---

18 patchwork

['pætʃwɜːrk]

义 *n.* 修补工作；拼凑的东西

例 For centuries, quilting and patchwork have been popular needlecrafts.

译 几个世纪以来，绗缝和拼布一直是流行的针线工艺。

19 pathologist
[pə'θɑːlədʒɪst]

义 *n.* 病理学家
例 The pathologist found that the cause of death was status asthmaticus.
译 病理学家发现死因是哮喘。

20 patsy
['pætsɪ]

义 *n.* 容易受骗的人
例 Davis was nobody's patsy.
译 戴维斯不会上任何人的当。

21 paw
[pɔː]

义 *n.* 脚爪，爪子
例 The dog had hurt its paw.
译 狗弄伤了自己的爪子。

22 payday
['peɪdeɪ]

义 *n.* 发薪日；支付日；交割日
例 Friday is payday.
译 周五是发薪日。

23 peaceable
['piːsəbl]

义 *adj.* 不争吵的，和平的，温顺的
例 A peaceable settlement has been reached.
译 已经达成和解。

24 peacefulness
['piːsflnəs]

义 *n.* 温和，平静
例 Peacefulness is one of the delights of country life.
译 宁静是乡村生活的乐趣之一。

25 peal
[piːl]

义 *n.* 响亮的声音；钟声
例 I heard a peal of laughter.
译 我听到一阵响亮的笑声。

26 pearly
['pɜːrlɪ]

义 *adj.* 珍珠似的；珍贵的
例 Her skin was pearly white.
译 她的皮肤如珍珠般白皙。

27 peek
[piːk]

义 *v.* 偷看，窥视　*n.* 一瞥，偷偷地一看
例 I took a quick peek inside.
译 我快速地瞥了一眼里面。

28 peeper

['pi:pə]

义 *n.* 窥视者；嘀咕的人

例 What began in the early 1990s as a place with a few hundred curious visitors has now become a tourism destination that attracts 10,000 penguin peepers a year.

译 20 世纪 90 年代初，这个地方只有几百名好奇的游客，现在这个地方已经成为一个每年吸引一万名游客来观看企鹅的旅游目的地。

---

29 peephole

['pi:phəʊl]

义 *n.* 窥孔，门镜

例 He squinted through the peephole.

译 他眯起眼睛靠近窥视孔看了看。

---

30 peg

[peg]

义 *n.* 钉；支柱；借口

例 His work jacket hung on the peg in the kitchen.

译 他的工作服挂在厨房里的挂钩上。

---

31 pendant

['pendənt]

义 *n.* 垂饰，悬挂物

例 We envision the camera becoming so small that it integrates into clothing, such as the button of a shirt, a brooch, or a pendant.

译 我们想象一下，如果这个摄影机非常小巧，我们就可以把它放进衣服里，像衬衫扣子、胸针或是项链的坠子一样。

---

32 penniless

['penɪləs]

义 *adj.* 身无分文的

例 They'd soon be penniless and homeless if she couldn't find suitable work.

译 如果她找不到合适的工作，他们很快就会身无分文、无家可归。

---

33 pentathlon

[pen'tæθlən]

义 *n.* 五项全能运动

例 Modern pentathlon became an Olympic event in 1912.

译 现代五项全能运动在 1912 年被列为奥运会比赛项目。

---

34 penultimate

[pen'ʌltɪmət]

义 *adj.* 倒数第二的

例 The methane concentration nearly doubled, for example, between the peak of the penultimate glacial period and the following interglacial period.

译 例如，在倒数第二个冰期的高峰和接下来的间冰期之间，甲烷浓度几乎翻了一番。

---

35 percolate

['pɜːrkəleɪt]

义 *v.* 过滤；渗透；浸透

例 Water had percolated down through the rocks.

译 水从岩缝间渗漏了下去。

---

36 perfectionist

义 *n.* 十全十美主义者；至善论者

[pər'fekʃənɪst]

例 Like Vermeer, Saenredam was a perfectionist and his output was fairly small.

译 和维米尔一样，萨恩雷丹也是一个完美主义者，他的作品很少。

---

37 perfumed

['pərfju:md]

义 *adj.* 香味的

例 She lay in the deep bath for a long time, enjoying its sensuously perfumed water.

译 她在浴缸里躺了很长时间，享受着香喷喷的水。

---

38 perplexity

[pər'pleksəti]

义 *n.* 困惑；使人困惑的事物

例 The school stared in perplexity at this incredible folly.

译 全校师生困惑地盯着这不可思议的愚蠢行为。

---

39 persecution

[ˌpɜ:rsɪ'kju:ʃn]

义 *n.* 迫害

例 It is the memory and threat of persecution that binds them together.

译 遭受迫害的记忆和威胁把他们紧紧联系在一起。

---

40 perseverance

[ˌpɜ:rsə'vɪrəns]

义 *n.* 毅力，坚韧不拔

例 He has never stopped trying and showed great perseverance.

译 他从未停止尝试，并表现出极大的毅力。

---

41 persistence

[pər'sɪstəns]

义 *n.* 坚持，毅力

例 Skill comes only with practice, patience, and persistence.

译 只有通过练习、耐心和坚持不懈才能掌握技能。

---

42 personage

['pɜ:rsənɪdʒ]

义 *n.* 名流；人物；角色

例 There is no evidence for such a historical personage.

译 没有证据表明有这样一位历史人物。

---

43 personal

['pɜ:rsənl]

义 *adj.* 私人的，个人的

例 That's my personal opinion.

译 这是我的个人意见。

---

44 personalize

['pɜ:rsənəlaɪz]

义 *v.* 个人化，私人化

例 The mass media tends to personalize politics.

译 大众媒体倾向于把政治个人化。

---

45 personify

[pər'sɑ:nɪfaɪ]

义 *v.* 是……的典型，体现；拟人化

例 These children personify all that is wrong with the education system.

译 这些儿童充分体现了教育制度的缺陷。

---

46 persuasion

[pər'sweɪʒn]

义 *n.* 说服，劝说；信念

例 She has great powers of persuasion.

译 她的游说能力极强。

---

47 pertain

[pər'teɪn]

义 *v.* 适合

例 Those laws no longer pertain.

译 那些法律已不再适用。

---

48 perturb

[pər'tɜ:rb]

义 *v.* 使烦恼，使不安

例 Her sudden appearance did not seem to perturb him in the least.

译 她的突然出现似乎一点也没有令他不安。

---

49 perverse

[pər'vɜ:rs]

义 *adj.* 任性的；有悖常理的

例 It would be perverse to stop this healthy trend.

译 阻止这一健康的趋势是有悖常理的。

---

50 petition

[pə'tɪʃn]

义 *n.* 请愿书；祈求

例 Jill volunteered to organize a petition.

译 吉尔自愿组织请愿。

---

51 petrify

['petrɪfaɪ]

义 *v.* 使石化；使发呆

例 The literal meaning of "petrify" is "turn to stone".

译 "石化" 的字面意思是 "变成石头"。

---

52 phenom

[fə'nɑ:m]

义 *n.* 杰出人才

例 But the 12-year-old phenom turned out to be two years older, making him ineligible for Little League play.

译 但后来证实，这位 12 岁的杰出选手实际上 14 岁了，没有参加少年联赛的资格。

---

53 phenomenal

[fə'nɑ:mɪnl]

义 *adj.* 显著的，杰出的，不寻常的，惊人的；感觉得到的，可感知的

例 It is predicted that this phenomenal growth will have a great impact on our society and economy.

译 据预测，这种惊人的增长将对我们的社会和经济产生巨大的影响。

---

54 phony

['fəʊni:]

义 *adj.* 假的，欺骗的；伪造的

例 He'd telephoned with some phony excuse she didn't believe for a minute.

> **译** 他用一些她根本就不信的假借口打电话。

55　photojournalist

[ˌfəʊˌtəʊ'dʒenəlɪst]

义 *n.* 摄影记者

例 To be a photojournalist, you should be informed.

译 作为一名摄影记者，你应该了解情况。

56　photometer

[fəʊ'tɑ:mətər]

义 *n.* 光度计，光度测定器

例 Photometers are specifically designed to measure emitted, reflected or transmitted light in photometric terms of luminous flux, luminance, illuminance or luminous intensity.

译 光度计是专门设计以光通量、亮度、照度或发光强度的光度来测量发射、反射或透射光的。

57　pictorial

[pɪk'tɔ:rɪəl]

义 *adj.* 绘画的；用图片的

例 The layout of the pictorial is fresh and lively.

译 画报的版面清新活泼。

58　pictorially

[pɪk'tɔ:rɪəlɪ]

义 *adv.* 绘画般地

例 Each section is explained pictorially.

译 每一部分都做了图示说明。

59　picturesque

[ˌpɪktʃə'resk]

义 *adj.* 如画的；生动的；奇特的

例 Anthony Ward's picturesque set immediately submerges us in a gorgeous world of folk innocence.

译 安东尼·沃德的风景如画的布景立即将我们淹没在民俗纯真的美丽世界中。

60　pier

[pɪr]

义 *n.* 码头；桥墩

例 The pier is a wooden structure.

译 这个码头是一个木结构建筑。

61　pilfer

['pɪlfər]

义 *v.* 盗，偷，窃

例 He pilfer from a cash register.

译 他偷收银机里的钱。

62　pinon

['pɪnjən]

义 *n.* 矮松；矮松果

例 The high, flat mountaintop is covered with many green juniper and pinon pine trees.

译 这座高而平的山顶覆盖着许多绿色的杜松和矮松。

---

63 pinprick

['pɪnprɪk]

义 *n.* 针刺；针孔；小烦恼

例 "The drill hole is just a pinprick on an elephant's back," he said.

译 他说："钻孔不过是大象背上的一个针孔。"

---

64 plaintive

['pleɪntɪv]

义 *adj.* 哀伤的，可怜的

例 They lay on the firm sands, listening to the plaintive cry of the seagulls.

译 他们躺在坚实的沙子上，听着海鸥的哀鸣。

---

65 plait

[plæt]

义 *n.* 辫子；皱褶

例 Her plait has been clipped last week.

译 她的辫子在上周被剪掉了。

---

66 plank

[plæŋk]

义 *n.* 木板；平板支撑

例 She sawed the plank in half.

译 她把木板锯成两半。

---

67 plat

[plæt]

义 *n.* 一小块地；地区图

例 Could you tell me where the plat books for the northwest valley are?

译 请问西北峪的地图册放在什么地方？

---

68 playoff

['pleɪɔːf]

义 *n.* 延长赛；季后赛

例 Playoff bonus system improved the quality of the game objective.

译 季后赛奖金制度客观上提高了比赛的质量。

---

69 pleading

['pliːdɪŋ]

义 *n.* 恳求，呼吁

例 Despite our pleadings to be allowed to leave, they kept us there for several more hours.

译 尽管我们恳求允许我们离开，他们还是让我们在那里多待了几个小时。

---

70 pleasantry

['plezntrɪ]

义 *n.* 幽默；开玩笑；客气话

例 I seem to be in evil case, and all for an innocent and thoughtless pleasantry.

译 我似乎陷入了不幸的境地，而这一切都是因为一句天真而轻率的玩笑。

---

71 pleat

[pliːt]

义 *n.* 褶；褶状物

例 Each pleat was stitched in place by hand.

译 每条褶裥都是手工缝制出来的。

72 plop

[plɑ:p]

义 *n.* 扑通声

例 Another drop of water fell with a soft plop.

译 又一滴水轻轻滴答一声落下。

---

73 plow

[plaʊ]

义 *n.* 犁；耕地

例 Low till farming limits the use of plows.

译 低耕农业限制了犁的使用。

---

74 plowing

[plaʊɪŋ]

义 *n.* 耕作

例 The season for spring plowing has come.

译 春耕时节来到了。

---

75 plumber

['plʌmər]

义 *n.* 管道工

例 We had to call in a plumber to unblock the drain.

译 我们只得叫个水管工来疏通下水道。

---

76 plunder

['plʌndər]

义 *v.* 掠夺，抢劫

例 She faces charges of helping to plunder her country's treasury of billions of dollars.

译 她面临协助窃取国库中数十亿美元的指控。

---

77 plywood

['plaɪwʊd]

义 *n.* 夹板，胶合板

例 This plywood addition helps to strengthen the structure.

译 添加的胶合板有助于加固结构。

---

78 pocked

[pɑ:kt]

义 *adj.* (表面)布满小洞的

例 The surface of the moon is pocked with craters.

译 月亮的表面布满陨石坑。

---

79 pointer

['pɔɪntər]

义 *n.* 指针；教鞭

例 She tapped on the world map with her pointer.

译 她用教鞭轻敲着世界地图。

---

80 poised

[pɔɪzd]

义 *adj.* 泰然自若的；保持平衡的

例 Clearly, the situation remains delicately poised.

| 译 | 显然，局势仍保持微妙的平衡。 |

---

81 poisonous

['pɔɪzənəs]

义 *adj.* 有毒的；恶意的

例 This gas is highly poisonous.

译 这种气体毒性很大。

---

82 polestar

['pəʊlstɑ:r]

义 *n.* 北极星；指导原则

例 We styled that as "Polestar".

译 我们将其命名为"北极星"。

---

83 politeness

[pə'laɪtnəs]

义 *n.* 礼貌

例 Respect and politeness are things they should learn at home.

译 尊重和礼貌是他们应该在家里学习的东西。

---

84 pomegranate

['pɑ:mɪɡrænɪt]

义 *n.* 石榴；石榴树

例 Red pomegranates like red lantern.

译 红红的石榴像红灯笼。

---

85 ponderous

['pɑ:ndərəs]

义 *adj.* 笨拙的；乏味的

例 Having said that, there's really nothing so dead as *The Norton Anthology of English Literature*, or ponderous.

译 话虽如此，没有什么比《诺顿英国文学选集》更死板，或者更沉闷的了。

---

86 pooh-pooh

[ˌpu:'pu:]

义 *v.* 蔑视，对……不屑一顾（或嗤之以鼻）

例 In the past he has pooh-poohed suggestions that he might succeed Isaacs.

译 过去，他对自己或许接替艾萨克斯的说法嗤之以鼻。

---

87 popcorn

['pɑ:pkɔ:rn]

义 *n.* 爆米花

例 Linda lay face down on a living room couch, nibbling popcorn.

译 琳达脸朝下躺在客厅的沙发上，啃着爆米花。

---

88 poplar

['pɑ:plər]

义 *n.* 白杨；白杨木

例 Strange fruits hang from the poplar trees.

译 杨树上挂着奇异的果实。

---

89 populist

['pɑ:pjəlɪst]

义 *adj.* 平民主义的，平民化的　*n.* 平民主义者，平民论者

例 He is a self-declared populist.

译 他自称是平民主义者。

90　populous

[ˈpɑːpjələs]

义 *adj.* 人口多的，人口稠密的

例 Indonesia, with 262 million people, is the fourth most populous country in the world.

译 印度尼西亚有 2.62 亿人口，是世界第四人口大国。

91　porch

[pɔːrtʃ]

义 *n.* 门廊，走廊

例 A small boy tumbled off the porch.

译 一个小男孩从门廊上摔了下来。

92　port

[pɔːrt]

义 *n.* 港口　　*v.* 转移；（计算机）移植（软件）

例 No one has ported that application yet.

译 还没有人移植过那个应用程序。

93　porter

[ˈpɔːrtər]

义 *n.* 搬运工，杂务工

例 A porter relieved her of the three large cases.

译 一个行李搬运工替她扛了 3 个大包。

94　portfolio

[pɔːrtˈfəʊlɪəʊ]

义 *n.* 文件夹；投资组合

例 Each client's portfolio is tailor-made.

译 每个客户的投资组合都是量身定制的。

95　porthole

[ˈpɔːrthəʊl]

义 *n.* 舷窗，舱口

例 The tiny voltmeters at each porthole all register the voltage as "normal" for their porthole.

译 每个舷窗上的微小电压表都将其舷窗上的电压记录为"正常"。

96　portico

[ˈpɔːrtɪkəʊ]

义 *n.* 柱廊；门廊

例 It's a palace with a huge marble portico.

译 那是一座有巨大大理石门廊的宫殿。

97　portraitist

[ˈpɔːrtrətɪst]

义 *n.* 肖像画家；人像摄影家

例 Rembrandt began to work as a professional portraitist about 1631.

译 伦勃朗大约在 1631 年开始从事职业肖像画家的工作。

98　posthumously

[ˈpɑːstʃəməslɪ]

义 *adv.* 在死后

例 He was buried with full military honors and posthumously awarded a Purple Heart.

译 他以最高军事荣誉下葬，并在死后被授予紫心勋章。

---

99 postmaster

['pəʊstmæstər]

义 *n.* 邮政局局长

例 She was appointed postmaster of the city of York.

译 她被任命为约克市邮政局局长。

---

100 potency

['pəʊtnsɪ]

义 *n.* 效力，潜能；权力

例 If you keep a medicine too long, it may lose its potency.

译 一种药如果放得太久，就会失去药效。

List 12

1 potter
['pɑ:tər]

义 *n.* 陶工，陶艺家

例 The potter shaped and squeezed the lump of clay into a graceful shape.

译 陶工把泥块捏成优美的形状。

---

2 practically
['præktɪklɪ]

义 *adv.* 实际上；几乎

例 It sounds like a good idea, but I don't think it will work practically.

译 这个主意听起来不错，但我认为它实际上行不通。

---

3 prank
[præŋk]

义 *n.* 开玩笑，恶作剧；戏谑

例 The prank crammed his mailbox with computer-delivered electronic junk mail.

译 该恶作剧使他的邮箱里塞满了计算机发送的电子垃圾邮件。

---

4 prearrange
[ˌpri:ə'reɪndʒ]

义 *v.* 预先安排

例 When you prearrange your funeral, you can pick your own flowers and music.

译 当你预先准备自己的葬礼时，你可以挑选自己喜欢的鲜花和音乐。

---

5 precession
[prɪ'seʃən]

义 *n.* 先行；岁差

例 There is a third movement the hypothesis covers called precession.

译 该假说还涵盖了第三种运动，称为岁差。

---

6 preconception
[ˌpri:kən'sepʃn]

义 *n.* 预想；先入之见；偏见

例 He did not allow his preconceptions to compromise his scientific work.

译 他不允许自己的偏见破坏自己的科学工作。

---

7 predetermined
[ˌpri:dɪ'tɜ:rmɪnd]

义 *adj.* 预先确定的

例 The capsules can be made to release the pesticides at a predetermined time.

译 这种胶囊可以在预定的时间释放农药。

---

8 predicament
[prɪ'dɪkəmənt]

义 *n.* 困境

例 Hank explained our predicament.

译 汉克解释了我们的困境。

---

9 predilection
[ˌpredl'ekʃn]

义 *n.* 偏好，袒护

例 They later showed the same unusual predilection for drawing on paper imported from the Far East.

译 他们后来表现出同样不寻常的偏好，即喜欢在从远东进口的纸上作画。

---

10 preeminent

[pri'emɪnənt]

义 *adj.* 卓越的；超群的

例 He is preeminent in the field of surgery.

译 他在外科领域出类拔萃。

---

11 prepackaged

[pri'pækɪdʒd]

义 *adj.* 预先包装好的

例 Prepackaged deli meats have a long shelf life if they remain unopened.

译 预先包装的熟食肉如果不开封，保质期会很长。

---

12 presage

['presɪdʒ]

义 *v.* 预示，预兆；预言，预感　*n.* 预感，预兆；预知

例 The lowering clouds presage a storm.

译 乌云低垂预示着暴风雨即将来临。

---

13 preservationist

[ˌprezər'veɪʃənɪst]

义 *n.* 保护主义者

例 Preservationists in Iowa reckon they are losing 1,000 barns each year.

译 艾奥瓦州的保护主义者估计他们每年损失 1 000 个谷仓。

---

14 preserver

[prɪ'zɜːrvər]

义 *n.* 保存人，保护者；救生用具

例 Are you a food preserver?

译 你喜欢储存食物吗？

---

15 presidential

[ˌprezɪ'denʃl]

义 *adj.* 总统的；总统制的

例 A presidential election was scheduled for last December.

译 总统选举原定于去年 12 月举行。

---

16 pressurize

['preʃəraɪz]

义 *v.* 对……施加压力，逼迫……

例 She was pressurized into accepting the job.

译 她被迫接受了这份工作。

---

17 presumption

[prɪ'zʌmpʃn]

义 *n.* 推测；可能性

例 There is a general presumption that the doctor knows best.

译 一般人都以为医生最了解情况。

---

18 presuppose

[ˌpriːsə'pəʊz]

义 *v.* 预先假定；预料

例 Teachers sometimes presuppose a fairly high level of knowledge by the students.

译 教师有时假定学生有相当高的知识水平。

---

19 pretentious
[prɪ'tenʃəs]

义 *adj.* 自负的；矫饰的
例 His response was full of pretentious nonsense.
译 他的回答满是矫揉造作的废话。

---

20 preview
['pri:vju:]

义 *n.* 预习，预告
例 He had gone to see the preview of a play.
译 他去看了一出戏的预演。

---

21 prickle
['prɪkl]

义 *n.* (动物或植物上的)刺，棘；刺痛
例 A porcupine is covered with prickles.
译 豪猪身上长满了刺。

---

22 prideful
['praɪdfəl]

义 *adj.* 自傲的，高傲的
例 As much as we try to deny it, we are prideful people.
译 无论我们多么努力要否认，我们都是骄傲的人。

---

23 prim
[prɪm]

义 *adj.* 规规矩矩的；古板的
例 You can't tell her that joke—she's much too prim and proper.
译 你不能跟她讲那个笑话——她太故作正经了。

---

24 primal
['praɪml]

义 *adj.* 最初的，原始的；主要的
例 Jealousy is a primal emotion.
译 嫉妒是一种原始的情感。

---

25 prise
[praɪz]

义 *v.* 强行使分开；强迫某人披露某事
例 She used a knife to prise open the lid.
译 她用刀把盖子撬开了。

---

26 privately
['praɪvətlɪ]

义 *adv.* 私下地；秘密地
例 Most of the apartments are privately owned.
译 大部分公寓都是私人所有的。

---

27 privy
['prɪvɪ]

义 *adj.* 私下知情的；私人的；秘密的
例 She was not privy to any information contained in the letters.
译 她未获准知晓那些信的内容。

28 procedural

[prə'si:dʒərəl]

义 *adj.* 程序的

例 A Spanish judge rejected the suit on procedural grounds.

译 一名西班牙法官以程序为由驳回了该诉讼。

---

29 prod

[prɑ:d]

义 *n.* 戳，捅；刺激

例 She gave him a sharp prod with her umbrella.

译 她用伞猛地捅了他一下。

---

30 prodigious

[prə'dɪdʒəs]

义 *adj.* 巨大的；惊人的，奇异的

例 This business generates cash in prodigious amounts.

译 这项业务产生了巨额现金。

---

31 profane

[prə'feɪn]

义 *adj.* 亵渎的；不敬神的；世俗的

例 Cardinal Daly has said that churches should not be used for profane or secular purposes.

译 戴利主教说过，教堂不应该用于非宗教或世俗目的。

---

32 professionalism

[prə'feʃənəlɪzəm]

义 *n.* 职业水准或特性；职业化

例 We were impressed by the professionalism of the staff.

译 工作人员的专业精神给我们留下了深刻的印象。

---

33 professionally

[prə'feʃənəlɪ]

义 *adv.* 职业上；专业地

例 Having curtains made professionally can be costly.

译 专业制作窗帘可能会很昂贵。

---

34 profitability

[ˌprɑ:fɪtə'bɪlətɪ]

义 *n.* 收益性；盈利能力

例 An income statement can indicate the profitability of the business.

译 收益表能反映企业的获利能力。

---

35 profusion

[prə'fju:ʒn]

义 *n.* 丰多，大量；浪费

例 Roses grew in profusion against the old wall.

译 老墙边遍生玫瑰。

---

36 programmatic

[ˌprəʊɡrə'mætɪk]

义 *adj.* 标题音乐的；节目的；计划性的

例 Agencies, the ad holding companies in particular, have driven a lot of the programmatic revolution.

译 机构，尤其是广告控股公司，已经推动了许多纲领性变革。

37 programmer

['prəʊɡræmər]

义 *n.* 程序员；程序器

例 To make the computer work at full capacity, the programmer has to think like the machine.

译 为了使计算机满负荷工作，程序员必须像机器一样思考。

---

38 progressively

[prə'ɡresɪvlɪ]

义 *adv.* 前进地；渐进地，逐渐地

例 Her symptoms became progressively worse.

译 她的症状逐渐恶化。

---

39 prolifically

[prə'lɪfɪklɪ]

义 *adv.* 多产地；丰富地

例 Eurasian watermilfoil, a weed not native to Frida Lake, has reproduced prolifically since being accidentally introduced there.

译 欧亚水叶草，一种并非弗里达湖原生植物的杂草，自从被意外引进后，就大量繁殖。

---

40 prominently

['prɑ:mɪnəntlɪ]

义 *adv.* 显著地

例 The photographs were prominently displayed on her desk.

译 照片显著地陈列在她的书桌上。

---

41 promoter

[prə'məʊtər]

义 *n.* 促进者；启动子

例 She became a leading promoter of European integration.

译 她成为欧洲一体化的主要促进者。

---

42 promptly

['prɑ:mptlɪ]

义 *adv.* 迅速地；立即地；敏捷地

例 He deals with emergencies promptly.

译 他迅速处理紧急情况。

---

43 promptness

[prɑ:mptnəs]

义 *n.* 敏捷；迅速

例 This method has the advantages of accuracy, promptness and convenience.

译 这种分析方法具有准确、快速、方便的优点。

---

44 pronged

[prɔ:ŋd]

义 *adj.* 尖端分叉的

例 She picked up a pronged branch.

译 她拾起一根尖端分叉的树枝。

---

45 propaganda

[ˌprɑ:pə'ɡændə]

义 *n.* 宣传；宣传的内容

例 Art may be used as a vehicle for propaganda.

译 艺术可以用作宣传的工具。

46	prophecy	义	*n.* 预言
	['prɑ:fəsɪ]	例	Will the teacher's prophecy be fulfilled?
		译	老师的预言会应验吗？

47	prophetically	义	*adv.* 预言性地
	[prə'fetɪklɪ]	例	He prophetically warned of the dangers of progress.
		译	他有先见之明地告诫人们要注意进程的危险性。

48	proportional	义	*adj.* 成比例的；相称的
	[prə'pɔ:rʃənl]	例	Their system seems to combine the two ideals of strong government and proportional representation.
		译	他们的制度似乎结合了强大的政府和比例代表制这两种理想状况。

49	propriety	义	*n.* 正当；得体
	[prə'praɪətɪ]	例	Nobody questioned the propriety of her being there alone.
		译	没有人怀疑她一个人在那里是否妥当。

50	prosaic	义	*adj.* 单调乏味的；无想象力的
	[prə'zeɪɪk]	例	His instructor offered a more prosaic explanation for the surge in interest.
		译	他的老师对利率的急剧上升给出了一个更枯燥乏味的解释。

51	prostrate	义	*adj.* 卧倒的；拜倒的
	['prɑ:streɪt]	例	They fell prostrate in worship.
		译	他们拜倒在地。

52	protagonist	义	*n.* 主角；支持者
	[prə'tægənɪst]	例	The chief protagonists in the row are Visa and Mastercard, the world's leading credit card brands.
		译	这场纠纷的主角是世界两大信用卡品牌——维萨和万事达。

53	protectorate	义	*n.* 摄政；受保护国；护民官之职
	[prə'tektərət]	例	In 1914 the country became a British protectorate.
		译	1914年该国成为英国的保护国。

54	protester	义	*n.* 抗议者；提出异议者
	[prə'testər]	例	A woman protester was killed by a ricochet (bullet).
		译	一名女抗议者被跳弹（子弹）打死。

55　protrude

[prəʊ'truːd]

义 *v.* 突出，伸出

例 He hung his coat on a nail protruding from the wall.

译 他把上衣挂在钉在墙面的一根钉子上了。

56　prow

[praʊ]

义 *n.* (飞机)机头；船头

例 He stands on the prow, looking at the sea.

译 他站在船头望着大海。

57　prudently

['pruːdntlɪ]

义 *adv.* 谨慎地，慎重地

例 I believe it is essential that we act prudently.

译 我认为我们必须谨慎行事。

58　psychoanalysis

[ˌsaɪkəʊə'næləsɪs]

义 *n.* 精神分析，心理分析

例 Psychoanalysis is a pseudoscience.

译 精神分析是一门伪科学。

59　publicist

['pʌblɪsɪst]

义 *n.* 国际法学家；政治评论家；宣传人员

例 Pitt's personal publicist, Cindy Guagenti, confirmed the donation.

译 皮特的私人公关辛迪·瓜根蒂证实了这一捐赠。

60　publicize

['pʌblɪsaɪz]

义 *v.* 宣传；公布；广告

例 The author appeared on television to publicize her latest book.

译 那位作家上电视宣传她的新书。

61　pucker

['pʌkər]

义 *v.* 使折叠；起皱　*n.* 皱纹；皱褶

例 His morning-coat fits him without a pucker.

译 他的晨礼服非常合身，穿起来连一条皱褶也没有。

62　puddle

['pʌdl]

义 *n.* 水坑，地上积水

例 Careful you don't tread in that puddle.

译 小心，别踩着那水坑。

63　pudgy

['pʌdʒɪ]

义 *adj.* 矮胖的

例 This was a pudgy man with thinning hair.

译 这是一个矮胖的男人，头发稀疏。

64　puff

[pʌf]

义 *v.* 喷出；吹捧　*n.* 吸，抽；(烟、气等的)一缕，少量

例 The magician vanished in a puff of smoke.

译 魔术师在一股烟雾中消失了。

65 pulsate

['pʌlseɪt]

义 *v.* 搏动；悸动；有规律地跳动

例 The Pole Star appears to be changing from a star that pulsates.

译 北极星似乎由一颗脉动的恒星衍变而来。

66 pun

[pʌn]

义 *n.* 双关语；俏皮话

例 He is a master of the pun and the double entendre.

译 他精通俏皮话和双关语。

67 punctuality

[ˌpʌŋktʃʊ'æləti]

义 *n.* 准时

例 He's becoming more and more obsessive about punctuality.

译 他对守时越来越执着。

68 punctuation

[ˌpʌŋktʃʊ'eɪʃn]

义 *n.* 标点

例 Our teacher is very fussy about punctuation.

译 我们老师对标点符号十分挑剔。

69 pungent

['pʌndʒənt]

义 *adj.* 刺鼻的；辛辣的

例 It is a pungent reminder of the fish market that operated here on Fulton Street for nearly two centuries.

译 这刺鼻的气味让人想起富尔顿街上经营了近两个世纪的鱼市。

70 punk

[pʌŋk]

义 *n.* 朋克

例 I was never really into punk.

译 我从未真正喜欢过朋克摇滚乐。

71 punster

['pʌnstər]

义 *n.* 喜欢说双关语的人，爱说俏皮话的人

例 Language meant a lot to him, and though I never shared his fondness for punsters or a certain kind of briskly witty columnist, I could see that he liked words to crackle on the page.

译 语言对他来说很重要，虽然我从来没有像他那样喜欢爱开玩笑或诙谐的专栏作家，但我看得出他喜欢文字在纸上噼啪作响。

72 punt

[pʌnt]

义 *n.* 方头或平底船；踢悬空球　*v.* 踢悬空球

例 The referee told him to punt or kick the ball off the ground.

译 裁判让他开悬空球，或将球踢出场地。

73 puppet

['pʌpɪt]

义 *n.* 木偶；傀儡

例 The occupying forces set up a puppet government.

| 译 | 占领军建立了一个傀儡政府。 |

74 puppeteer
[ˌpʌpɪˈtɪr]

义 *n.* 拉线木偶表演者
例 A wandering puppeteer goes to a town.
译 一个流浪的木偶表演者去了一个小镇。

75 puppetry
[ˈpʌpɪtrɪ]

义 *n.* 木偶；木偶戏
例 But learning puppetry is very hard.
译 但是学习木偶戏是非常困难的。

76 purist
[ˈpjʊrɪst]

义 *n.* 纯粹主义者
例 To some extent, he is a purist.
译 在某种程度上，他是一个纯粹主义者。

77 purl
[pɜːrl]

义 *n.* 用反针编织
例 The basic stitches are knit and purl.
译 基本的针法是平织和反织。

78 purposeful
[ˈpɜːrpəsfl]

义 *adj.* 有决心的；果断的；有意义的
例 She looked purposeful and determined.
译 她看上去胸有成竹、意志坚定。

79 purr
[pɜːr]

义 *v.* （猫等满足地）呜呜叫；（机器等）发出低沉震颤声
例 Carmela heard the purr of a motorcycle coming up the drive.
译 卡梅拉听到摩托车开上快车道的嗡嗡声。

80 pus
[pʌs]

义 *n.* 脓；脓汁
例 The wound is still discharging pus.
译 伤口仍在流脓。

81 pushy
[ˈpʊʃɪ]

义 *adj.* 固执己见的，强求的；野心勃勃的，有进取心的
例 She was a confident and pushy young woman.
译 她是个自信、有进取心的年轻女性。

82 pyramidal
[ˈpɪrəmɪdl]

义 *adj.* 金字塔形的；角锥状的
例 The shape is actually trigonal pyramidal.
译 它的形状实际上是三角金字塔形。

83 pyrotechnic

[ˌpaɪrəˈteknɪk]

义 *adj.* 烟火制造术的；辉煌灿烂的

例 Prior to this, rockets were used only in pyrotechnic displays.

译 在此之前，火箭仅仅用于展示烟火。

---

84 quadrillion

[kwɑːˈdrɪljən]

义 *n.* 千的五次方

例 The magic number is 6.3 quadrillion electron-volts.

译 这个神奇的数字是 6.3 万亿电子伏。

---

85 quail

[kweɪl]

义 *v.* 畏缩，胆怯；感到恐惧

例 The very words make many of us quail.

译 这些话让我们中的许多人畏缩不前。

---

86 quake

[kweɪk]

义 *v.* 震动；颤抖　*n.* 地震；颤抖

例 The quake destroyed mud buildings in many remote villages.

译 地震摧毁了许多偏远村庄的泥土房屋。

---

87 Quaker

[ˈkweɪkər]

义 *n.* 教友派信徒

例 I went to this Quaker wedding once and it was fantastic.

译 我参加过一次教友派信徒的婚礼，感觉特别棒。

---

88 qualm

[kwɑːm]

义 *n.* 疑虑；晕眩；紧张不安

例 He had been working very hard so he had no qualms about taking a few days off.

译 他一直辛勤工作，所以休息几天他觉得心安理得。

---

89 quarry

[ˈkwɔːrɪ]

义 *n.* 猎物，被追逐的目标

例 The hunters lost sight of their quarry in the forest.

译 猎人在森林里跟丢了猎物。

---

90 quart

[kwɔːrt]

义 *n.* 夸脱（容量单位）

例 He stepped out to buy a quart of milk.

译 他出去买了一夸脱奶。

---

91 quarterback

[ˈkwɔːrtərbæk]

义 *n.*（橄榄球赛中指挥反攻的）四分卫

例 Foley tackled the quarterback.

译 弗利擒住了四分卫。

---

92 quarterly

[ˈkwɔːrtərlɪ]

义 *adj.* 季度的

例 Their quarterly meetings were anodyne affairs.

译 他们的季度会议都是些平淡的事情。

93 quench
[kwentʃ]

义 *v.* 解渴

例 He stopped to quench his thirst at a stream.

译 他停在一条小溪边喝水解渴。

94 queuing
[kjʊɪŋ]

义 *n.* 排队

例 Queuing means you are putting the needs of others before your own.

译 排队意味着你把他人的需求放在自己的前面。

95 quietness
['kwaɪətnəs]

义 *n.* 平静，安定，安静

例 To free ourselves from physical and mental tensions, we all need deep thought and inner quietness.

译 为了把自己从身体和精神的紧张中解放出来，我们每个人都需要进行深刻思考，并保持内心平静。

96 quill
[kwɪl]

义 *n.* 羽毛笔；纬管

例 She dipped a quill in ink, then began to write.

译 她把羽毛笔蘸进墨水中，然后开始写字。

97 quilted
['kwɪltɪd]

义 *adj.* 絮有棉花的

例 She stood hugging her quilted jacket round her.

译 她紧裹棉衣站在那里。

98 quilting
['kwɪltɪŋ]

义 *n.* 缝纫；缝被子

例 She does a lot of quilting.

译 她缝了很多被子。

99 quip
[kwɪp]

义 *v.* 说俏皮话；嘲讽

例 The chairman quipped that he would rather sell his airline than his computer systems.

译 主席风趣地说，他宁可卖掉他的航空公司，也不愿出售他的计算机系统。

100 quirk
[kwɜːrk]

义 *n.* 怪癖；急转；奇事

例 By a tantalizing quirk of fate, the pair have been drawn to meet in the first round of the championship.

译 由于命运的捉弄，这对选手被抽中在锦标赛的第一轮相遇。

List 13

1 quitter
['kwɪtər]

义 *n.* 半途而废的人
例 I am a fighter, not a quitter.
译 我是一个斗士，不是一个半途而废的人。

2 quiver
['kwɪvər]

义 *v.* 颤抖；振动　*n.* 颤抖，颤音
例 Jane couldn't help the quiver in her voice.
译 简不禁声音颤抖。

3 racehorse
['reɪshɔːrs]

义 *n.* 赛马用的马
例 His latest acquisition is a racehorse.
译 他最近购得一匹赛马。

4 racetrack
['reɪstræk]

义 *n.* 赛车道，赛车场；赛马场
例 You can't cross the road—it's like a racetrack.
译 你不要横过这条马路——它像赛车道。

5 racial
['reɪʃl]

义 *adj.* 种族的，人种的
例 He was chased here a decade ago, by racial prejudice, by the lack of work, by television and rock and roll, by free jazz.
译 十年前，他因种族偏见、缺少工作、电视和摇滚乐、自由爵士乐等因素被赶到这里。

6 racism
['reɪsɪzəm]

义 *n.* 种族主义
例 Racism has been a scar on the game.
译 种族主义行为给这项运动抹了黑。

7 racquet
['rækɪt]

义 *n.* 球拍
例 I hope you enjoy the racquet.
译 希望你喜欢这张球拍。

8 radiant
['reɪdɪənt]

义 *adj.* 发光的；明亮的
例 She was radiant with health.
译 她身体健康，容光焕发。

9 radically
['rædɪklɪ]

义 *adv.* 根本地；完全地；过激地
例 Increased professionalism has changed the game radically.
译 职业化程度的提高从根本上改变了比赛。

10 radish

['rædɪʃ]

义 *n.* (小)萝卜

例 This radish has gone spongy.

译 这萝卜变软了。

---

11 rafter

['ræftər]

义 *n.* 椽，屋梁

例 The big rafter is visible in this room.

译 这间屋子粗大的屋梁可以看得见。

---

12 rafting

['ræftɪŋ]

义 *n.* 漂流运动

例 We went white-water rafting on the Colorado River.

译 我们在科罗拉多河上漂流。

---

13 raider

['reɪdər]

义 *n.* 袭击者，侵入者

例 With a deft flick of his foot, Mr. Worth tripped one of the raiders up.

译 沃思先生机敏地把脚一伸，将其中一个袭击者给绊倒了。

---

14 railing

['reɪlɪŋ]

义 *n.* 栏杆

例 She gripped on to the railing with both hands.

译 她双手紧紧抓住栏杆。

---

15 railroad

['reɪlrəʊd]

义 *n.* 铁路

例 The railroad finally reached Santa Barbara in 1877.

译 铁路终于在 1877 年修到了圣塔芭芭拉。

---

16 rainstorm

['reɪnstɔːrm]

义 *n.* 暴雨，暴风雨

例 The cars collided during a heavy rainstorm.

译 汽车在暴雨中相撞。

---

17 RAM

[ræm]

义 *abbr.* 内存，随机存取存储器

例 The system has 256MB RAM, expandable to 2GB.

译 该系统有 256MB 内存，可扩展到 2GB。

---

18 ramble

['ræmbl]

义 *v.* 漫步；漫谈　*n.* 漫游；闲逛

例 She went into a long ramble about the evils of television.

译 她开始长篇大论地谈论电视的害处。

19　ramification

[ˌræmɪfɪ'keɪʃn]

义　*n.* 衍生物；分支机构

例　The bank has ramification throughout the world.

译　这家银行在世界各地都有分行。

20　ramshackle

['ræmʃækl]

义　*adj.* 要倒塌似的，摇摇欲坠的

例　These eateries were often a little more than ramshackle sheds or hastily erected tents.

译　这些餐馆往往比摇摇欲坠的棚子或仓促搭起的帐篷稍好些。

21　ranching

[ræntʃɪŋ]

义　*n.* 经营牧场

例　Ranching is serious business in Australia.

译　牧场在澳大利亚是一项很重要的产业。

22　rancor

['ræŋkə]

义　*n.* 敌意，恨意

例　I have no rancor against them.

译　我对他们没有怨恨。

23　ranger

['reɪndʒər]

义　*n.* 看守人；护林员

例　Bill Justice is a park ranger at the Carlsbad Caverns National Park.

译　比尔·贾斯蒂斯是卡尔斯巴德洞窟国家公园的管理员。

24　ransack

['rænsæk]

义　*v.* 彻底搜索，洗劫

例　The house had been ransacked by burglars.

译　这房子遭到了盗贼的洗劫。

25　rant

[rænt]

义　*v.* 咆哮，大声地说

例　As the boss began to rant, I stood up and went out.

译　当老板开始咆哮时，我站起来走了出去。

26　rappel

[ræ'pel]

义　*v.* 绕绳下降

例　They learned to rappel down a cliff.

译　他们学会了沿绳索从悬崖上滑下。

27　rapt

[ræpt]

义　*adj.* 全神贯注的；入迷的；出神的

例　All over the country, people listened in rapt attention.

译　全国各地的人都聚精会神地听着。

28　rarity

['rerətɪ]

义　*n.* 稀有；罕见的人或物，珍品

例　Women are still something of a rarity in senior positions in business.

译 在商界担任高级职位的女性仍属罕见。

---

29 raspberry

['ræzberɪ]

义 *n.* 覆盆子

例 Eugene was concocting Rossini Cocktails from champagne and pureed raspberries.

译 尤金当时正在用香槟和覆盆子泥调配罗西尼鸡尾酒。

---

30 rattan

[ræ'tæn]

义 *n.* 藤

例 The ball is made of rattan—a natural fiber.

译 这个球是用藤做的，藤是一种天然纤维。

---

31 rattle

['rætl]

义 *v.* 嘎嘎作响；喋喋不休

例 Every time a bus went past, the windows rattled.

译 每逢公共汽车经过这里，窗户都格格作响。

---

32 rattlesnake

['rætlsneɪk]

义 *n.* 响尾蛇

例 I see a rattlesnake sliding by me.

译 我看见一条响尾蛇从我身边滑过。

---

33 raucous

['rɔːkəs]

义 *adj.* 沙哑的，粗声的；刺耳的

例 The raucous voices of the other men died away.

译 其他人刺耳的声音渐渐消失了。

---

34 ravage

['rævɪdʒ]

义 *v./n.* 毁坏，破坏

例 Her looks had not survived the ravages of time.

译 她的容颜未能幸免于时间的摧残。

---

35 rave

[reɪv]

义 *v.* 极力赞扬；说胡话；咆哮

例 The critics raved about his performance.

译 评论家们热情赞扬了他的表演。

---

36 rawhide

['rɔːhaɪd]

义 *n.* (牛的)生皮；生牛皮鞭

例 At his belt he carried a rawhide whip.

译 他腰间挎着一根生牛皮鞭子。

---

37 reacquaint

[ˌriːə'kweɪnt]

义 *v.* 重新认识，重新熟悉

例 Syrnikov hopes to help Russians reacquaint themselves with the country's agrarian roots.

译 西尔尼科夫希望帮助俄罗斯人重新认识这个国家的农业根源。

---

38 reactive

[rɪ'æktɪv]

义 *adj.* 反应的；反作用的；活性的

例 I want our organization to be less reactive and more proactive.

译 我希望我们组织少些被动，多些主动。

---

39 realist

['riːəlɪst]

义 *n.* 现实主义者；唯实论者

例 I see myself not as a cynic but as a realist.

译 我认为自己不是一个愤世嫉俗的人，而是一个现实主义者。

---

40 reanimation

['riːˌænɪ'meɪʃən]

义 *n.* 复活；鼓舞，鼓励

例 Stem cell and nanotechnology research offer real possibilities for the reanimation of tissue.

译 干细胞和纳米技术研究为组织再生提供了真正的可能性。

---

41 rearward

['rɪrwərd]

义 *adv.* 在背后；向后方

例 The center of pressure moves rearward and the plane becomes unbalanced.

译 气压中心后移，飞机失去平衡。

---

42 reassemble

[ˌriːə'sembl]

义 *v.* 重装；再聚集

例 We will now try to reassemble pieces of the wreckage.

译 我们现在要把残骸碎片重新组装起来。

---

43 reawaken

[ˌriːə'weɪkən]

义 *v.* 使回忆；再次唤醒

例 The place reawakened childhood memories.

译 这个地方唤起了童年的回忆。

---

44 rebellious

[rɪ'beljəs]

义 *adj.* 叛逆的；难以控制的

例 Ginny was irrepressibly rebellious.

译 金妮无法抑制地叛逆。

---

45 reborn

[ˌriː'bɔːrn]

义 *adj.* 再生的，新生的

例 This country was being reborn as a great power.

译 这个国家经过复兴成了一个强国。

---

46 rebut

[rɪ'bʌt]

义 *v.* 反驳，辩驳，举反证

例 He spent most of his speech rebutting criticisms of his foreign policy.

译 他大部分的演讲都用来反驳他在外交政策上受到的各种批评。

47 recapitulate

[ˌriːkəˈpɪtʃʊleɪt]

义 *v.* 概括；重述要点

例 Let's just recapitulate the essential points.

译 让我们重述一下要点吧。

---

48 recast

[ˌriːˈkæst]

义 *v.* 改动

例 She recast her lecture as a radio talk.

译 她把她的演讲改成了广播讲话。

---

49 receptacle

[rɪˈseptəkl]

义 *n.* 容器

例 The seas have been used as a receptacle for a range of industrial toxins.

译 海洋被用作一系列工业毒素的容器。

---

50 receptor

[rɪˈseptər]

义 *n.* 感受器；受体

例 There are at least two classes of these receptors, which have been designated A1 and A2.

译 这些受体至少有两类，分别称为 A1 和 A2。

---

51 recess

[rɪˈses]

义 *n.* 休息

例 She decides to visit the school library during recess.

译 她决定在课间休息时参观学校图书馆。

---

52 reciprocate

[rɪˈsɪprəkeɪt]

义 *v.* 互换，交换；报答

例 Some day I will reciprocate your kindness to me.

译 总有一天我会报答你对我的恩情。

---

53 recitation

[ˌresɪˈteɪʃn]

义 *n.* 背诵；详述；吟诵

例 The boy stumbled through his recitation.

译 这男孩结结巴巴地背诵。

---

54 reckoning

[ˈrekənɪŋ]

义 *n.* 计算；算账

例 By my reckoning we were seven or eight miles from the campground.

译 据我估算我们离露营地大约七八英里远。

---

55 recliner

[rɪˈklaɪnər]

义 *n.* 斜倚物；斜靠着的人；装有软垫的躺椅

例 I sat in my father's chair, a mustard-colored recliner.

译 我坐在父亲的褐黄色的躺椅上。

---

56 recluse

[ˈrekluːs]

义 *n.* 隐士

例 His widow became a virtual recluse for the remainder of her life.

译 实际上他的遗孀余生都过着隐居生活。

---

57 recognizable

['rekəgnaɪzəbl]

义 *adj.* 可认识的；可辨别的

例 The building was easily recognizable as a prison.

译 很容易看出这座建筑是所监狱。

---

58 recommit

[,ri:kə'mɪt]

义 *v.* 重犯；重新提出

例 So let us recommit ourselves to this cause.

译 因此，让我们再次致力于这一事业。

---

59 recreational

[,rekrɪ'eɪʃənl]

义 *adj.* 娱乐的，消遣的

例 These areas are set aside for public recreational use.

译 这些地方已经划出来用于公共娱乐。

---

60 recruiter

[rɪ'kru:tər]

义 *n.* 招募者，招聘人员

例 A real estate recruiter we worked with illustrates the positive difference such training can make.

译 一位与我们合作过的房地产招聘人员向我们展示了这种培训所能带来的积极影响。

---

61 recruitment

[rɪ'kru:tmənt]

义 *n.* 征募新兵；补充；招聘

例 In future, staff recruitment will fall within the remit of the division manager.

译 今后，人员招聘将由部门经理负责。

---

62 rectangle

['rektæŋgl]

义 *n.* 长方形，矩形

例 Pencil-box is a rectangle.

译 铅笔盒是长方形的。

---

63 recurrent

[rɪ'kɜ:rənt]

义 *adj.* 再发生的；周期性的；循环的

例 Race is a recurrent theme in the work.

译 种族是这部作品中反复出现的主题。

---

64 redefine

[,ri:dɪ'faɪn]

义 *v.* 重新定义

例 We need to redefine what we mean by democracy.

译 我们需要重新定义民主的含义。

---

65 redemption

[rɪ'dempʃn]

义 *n.* 赎回；救赎

例 He craves redemption for his sins.

译 他渴望能够赎罪。

---

66 redirect

[ˌriːdəˈrekt]

义 **v. 使改方向；重定向**

例 Controls were used to redistribute or redirect resources.

译 采取了管制措施来重新分配资源或转变资源投放方向。

---

67 redistribution

[ˌriːdɪstrɪˈbjuːʃn]

义 **n. 重新分配；再区分**

例 In the process of this wealth redistribution, risk is also building up.

译 在财富重新分配的过程中，风险也在增加。

---

68 redouble

[ˌriːˈdʌbl]

义 **v. 加倍；再折叠；重复**

例 The campaign has redoubled its efforts to win the backing of women.

译 该竞选活动已经加大努力，以赢取女性选民支持。

---

69 reducer

[rɪˈdjuːsə]

义 **n. 减径管；缩减者；减速器**

例 It is prohibited to lift the gear reducer with bolt holes on output drive flange.

译 严禁用减速机输出传动法兰上的螺栓孔起吊齿轮减速器。

---

70 redwood

[ˈredwʊd]

义 **n. 红杉，红木树**

例 Members of the research group stand atop the stump of a giant redwood tree.

译 研究小组的成员站在一棵巨大的红杉树桩上。

---

71 reeducate

[riːˈedʒəˌkeɪt]

义 **v. 再教育**

例 We are having to reeducate the public very quickly about something they have always taken for granted.

译 我们必须尽快地对公众进行再教育，让他们了解一些他们一直认为理所当然的事情。

---

72 reedy

[ˈriːdɪ]

义 **adj. 芦苇丛生的；芦苇做的；细长的**

例 To my right was the small loch, edged with reedy banks.

译 在我的右边是一个小湖，湖边芦苇丛生。

---

73 reflexivity

[rɪflekˈsɪvɪtɪ]

义 **n. 自反性；反身性**

例 Sarraute's work combines representation with reflexivity.

译 萨洛特的作品结合了再现性和自反性。

74　refolding

[reˈfəʊldɪŋ]

义 *v.* 重折叠

例 The recent research progress of recombinant protein refolding was reviewed.

译 本文对近年来重组蛋白复性技术的研究进行进行了评述。

75　reformer

[rɪˈfɔːrmər]

义 *n.* 改革家，改革运动者

例 True adaptation to society comes automatically when the adolescent reformer attempts to put his ideas to work.

译 当青少年改革家试图将自己的想法付诸实践时，真正的社会适应就会自动到来。

76　reformulate

[ˌriːˈfɔːrmjuleɪt]

义 *v.* (想法、计划等)重新规划

例 It is never too late to reformulate your goals.

译 重定目标决不会为时过晚。

77　refract

[rɪˈfrækt]

义 *v.* (使)折射

例 As we age, the lenses of the eyes thicken, and thus refract light differently.

译 随着我们年龄的增长，眼睛的晶状体变厚，因此对光线的折射也会发生变化。

78　refrain

[rɪˈfreɪn]

义 *n.* (诗歌的)叠句，(歌曲的)副歌；经常重复的评价(或抱怨)

例 Rosa's constant refrain is that she doesn't have a life.

译 罗莎老是重复说她没有自己的生活。

79　refreshment

[rɪˈfreʃmənt]

义 *n.* 茶点，点心；恢复活力

例 Light refreshments will be served during the break.

译 休息期间将有点心供应。

80　refueling

[riːˈfjuːəlɪŋ]

义 *n.* 加燃料，加油

例 Refueling is done right in the air.

译 加油是在空中完成的。

81　refurbish

[ˌriːˈfɜːrbɪʃ]

义 *v.* 整修，翻新；修改，完善

例 We also need to refurbish our old buildings.

译 我们还需要翻新旧的教学楼。

82　refusal

[rɪˈfjuːzl]

义 *n.* 拒绝，回绝

例 Her answer amounted to a complete refusal.

译 她的回答等于完全拒绝。

83 regale

['rɪ'geɪl]

义 *n.* 宴请，款待

例 This is the regale of the thought.

译 这是思想的盛宴。

---

84 regally

['riːgəlɪ]

义 *adv.* 为王；像帝王地

例 In these days, of course, we live regally, practically doing nothing.

译 在这些日子里，我们过着帝王般的生活，几乎什么都不用做。

---

85 reggae

['regeɪ]

义 *n.* 雷鬼，雷盖（西印度群岛一种节奏强烈的流行音乐）

例 I like all kinds of music from opera to reggae.

译 我喜欢各种音乐，从歌剧到雷盖都喜欢。

---

86 regimen

['redʒɪmən]

义 *n.* 养生法；生活规则；训练课程

例 Gradually, he deviated from his training regimen.

译 渐渐地，他不再坚持自己的训练计划。

---

87 reincarnation

[,riːɪnkɑːr'neɪʃn]

义 *n.* 转世，再生

例 He believed in reincarnation.

译 他相信转世再生。

---

88 rejoice

[rɪ'dʒɔɪs]

义 *v.* （使）高兴，（使）欢喜

例 The motor industry is rejoicing at the cut in car tax.

译 汽车工业对汽车减税感到非常高兴。

---

89 rejuvenate

[rɪ'dʒuːvəneɪt]

义 *v.* 使……年轻；使……恢复精神

例 Shelley was advised that the Italian climate would rejuvenate him.

译 雪莱被告知意大利的气候能使他恢复活力。

---

90 rekindle

[,riː'kɪndl]

义 *v.* 重新点燃

例 There are fears that the series could rekindle animosity between the two countries.

译 有人担心，这部电视剧可能会重新点燃两国之间的仇恨。

---

91 relaunch

[,riː'lɔːntʃ]

义 *v.* 重新开张；重新发动

例 Analysts said that it's very likely the game will be relaunched in late August or early September.

译 分析人士表示，这款游戏很可能会在 8 月底或 9 月初重新发布。

92 relent

['rɪ'lent]

义 *v.* 变宽容，变温和；（坏天气）变好

例 The police will not relent in their fight against crime.

译 警方在同犯罪分子的斗争中决不手软。

---

93 relish

['relɪʃ]

义 *n.* 享受，乐趣

例 She savored the moment with obvious relish.

译 她显然很享受这一时刻。

---

94 relocation

[ˌriːləʊˈkeɪʃn]

义 *n.* 再定位，搬迁；重新配置

例 The company says the cost of relocation will be negligible.

译 该公司表示，搬迁的成本可以忽略不计。

---

95 remake

['riːmeɪk]

义 *v.* 重制；翻新，改造；修改；重新摄制

例 They argue that only private capitalists can remake Poland's economy.

译 他们认为只有私人资本家才能重塑波兰经济。

---

96 remarkably

[rɪˈmɑːkəblɪ]

义 *adv.* 显著突出地，非常地

例 The cool water that tills the mine that is below the city of Bonne Terre is remarkably clean and clear.

译 在邦特尔市下面的矿井中，凉爽的水非常干净和清澈。

---

97 remediation

[rɪˌmiːdɪˈeɪʃn]

义 *n.* 补救，修复；矫正；补习

例 Remediation is a challenging and time-consuming task.

译 修复是一项具有挑战性且耗时的任务。

---

98 reminisce

[ˌremɪˈnɪs]

义 *v.* 追忆，缅怀

例 She likes to reminisce about her childhood.

译 她喜欢回忆她的童年。

---

99 remodeling

[rɪˈmɑːdlɪŋ]

义 *n.* 重新塑造，改型，重作

例 If it is not combined with the remodeling of the town's transportion system, it does not cure it.

译 如果不结合城镇交通系统的改造，就无法解决这个问题。

---

100 remorse

[rɪˈmɔːrs]

义 *n.* 懊悔，悔恨

例 I felt guilty and full of remorse.

译 我感到内疚，充满悔恨。

List 14

1　remoteness

[rɪ'məʊtnəs]

义　*n.* 远离，远隔

例　His remoteness made her feel unloved.

译　他的疏远使她觉得他不爱她。

2　rendition

[ren'dɪʃn]

义　*n.* 演奏；解释

例　The musicians burst into a rousing rendition of Paddy Casey's *Reel*.

译　这些音乐家激情演奏了帕迪·凯西的《里尔舞曲》。

3　renegade

['renɪɡeɪd]

义　*n.* 叛徒；变节者；叛党者

例　He was stereotyped by some as a renegade.

译　他被一些人定型为叛徒。

4　renege

[rɪ'niːɡ]

义　*v.* 背信，违约

例　He reneged on a promise to leave his wife.

译　他背弃了诺言，离开了他的妻子。

5　renovation

[ˌrenə'veɪʃn]

义　*n.* 革新，整修

例　There will be extensive renovations to the hospital.

译　这家医院将进行大规模整修。

6　repeatable

[rɪ'piːtəbl]

义　*adj.* 可重复的

例　It's pointless unless there is a repeatable process in place to turn inspiration into financial performance.

译　除非有一个可重复的过程将灵感转化为财务业绩，否则这是毫无意义的。

7　repellent

[rɪ'pelənt]

义　*adj.* 令人讨厌的；防……的；排斥的

例　Their political ideas are repellent to most people.

译　他们的政治思想使大多数人反感。

8　replant

[riː'plɑːnt]

义　*v.* 改种；移植

例　They have to replant the seedbeds as soon as possible.

译　他们必须尽快在苗床上重新培育上新苗。

9　replete

[rɪ'pliːt]

义　*adj.* 充满的；饱食的

例　The harbor was replete with boats.

| 译 | 港口里满是船只。 |

10 repopulate
['riː'pɑːpjʊleɪt]

义 *v.* 重新使定居；再次填充

例 We saw a need to really repopulate this movement with the younger folks.

译 我们看到了让年轻人重新参与这项运动的必要。

11 reprieve
[rɪ'priːv]

义 *v.* 暂缓处刑；暂时缓解

例 A man awaiting death by lethal injection has been saved by a last-minute reprieve.

译 一名等待注射死刑的男子在最后一刻得到了缓刑。

12 reprimand
['reprɪmænd]

义 *n.* 训斥；谴责　*v.* 谴责

例 He whapped his fist in it a few times and then locked it with both hands and bent it back and forth as if to reprimand it for the affectation of its deep pocket.

译 他用拳头打了它几下，然后用双手把它锁上，把它前后弯曲，好像在谴责它那装得很厚的口袋。

13 reputable
['repjətəbl]

义 *adj.* 声誉好的；规范的

例 You are well advised to buy your car through a reputable dealer.

译 建议你通过信誉好的经销商购买汽车。

14 requisite
['rekwɪzɪt]

义 *adj.* 必要的；需要的　*n.* 必需品；必要条件

例 An understanding of accounting techniques is a requisite for the work of the analysts.

译 熟悉会计技术是分析员工作的必要条件。

15 resemblance
[rɪ'zembləns]

义 *n.* 相像，相似

例 Despite these superficial resemblances, this is a darker work than her earlier novels.

译 尽管表面上有这些相似之处，但这部作品比她早期的小说更黑暗。

16 resentful
[rɪ'zentfl]

义 *adj.* 不满的，怨恨的

例 They seemed to be resentful of our presence there.

译 他们似乎对我们出现在那里感到不满。

17 resettle
[ˌriː'setl]

义 *v.* 重新定居，再安顿

例 They resettle themselves in Australia.

译 他们在澳大利亚重新定居下来。

18　reshaping

[riːˈʃeɪpɪŋ]

义　*n.* 整形，重塑

例　This thesis led to a radical reshaping of Democratic policies.

译　这篇论文导致了民主党政策的彻底改变。

19　resound

[rɪˈzaʊnd]

义　*v.* (使) 回响；驰名

例　Laughter resounded through the house.

译　笑声在屋里回荡。

20　resourceful

[rɪˈsɔːrsfl]

义　*adj.* 资源丰富的；足智多谋的

例　When Gerald Martin, around the middle of his rich and resourceful biography of Garcia Marquez, starts to tell this story, the reader may be a little surprised, even disappointed.

译　当杰拉德·马丁在其内容丰富的加西亚·马尔克斯传记中开始讲述这个故事时，读者可能会有点惊讶，甚至失望。

21　resourcefulness

[rɪˈsɔːrsflnəs]

义　*n.* 足智多谋

例　Because of his adventures, he is a person of far greater experience and resourcefulness.

译　由于他的冒险经历，他是一个经验丰富、足智多谋的人。

22　respectively

[rɪˈspektɪvlɪ]

义　*adv.* 分别地，各自地

例　Their sons were three and six respectively.

译　他们的儿子分别是 3 岁和 6 岁。

23　responsive

[rɪˈspɑːnsɪv]

义　*adj.* 应答的；易感应的

例　It is vitally important that the patch developer is responsive during this period.

译　在这段时间内，补丁开发者的反应是非常重要的。

24　restatement

[ˌriːˈsteɪtmənt]

义　*n.* 再声明，重述

例　The amounts of cash involved are too small to require a restatement of earnings.

译　因所涉及现金数额太小，不能要求收益重述。

25　restful

[ˈrestfl]

义　*adj.* 益于休息的；平静的，安静的

例　I live in Mentone, a quiet, simple, restful place, where the rich never come.

译　我住在芒通，一个安静、简单、宁静的地方，富人从不来这里。

26　restlessness

义　*n.* 辗转不安，烦躁不安；不安定

['restləsnəs]　　　例 Karen complained of hyperactivity and restlessness.

译 凯伦抱怨自己过度活跃和不安。

---

27 resultant

[rɪ'zʌltənt]

义 *adj.* 作为结果的；合成的

例 At least a quarter of a million people have died in the fighting and the resultant famines.

译 至少有 25 万人死于战斗和由其造成的饥荒。

---

28 resurgence

[rɪ'sɜːrdʒəns]

义 *n.* 再起；复活；再现

例 Police say drugs traffickers are behind the resurgence of violence.

译 警方说毒贩是暴力活动重新抬头的罪魁祸首。

---

29 resurrect

[ˌrezə'rekt]

义 *v.* 使复活；复兴；挖出

例 Attempts to resurrect the ceasefire have already failed once.

译 为再次停火做出的努力已经失败了一次。

---

30 resurrection

[ˌrezə'rekʃn]

义 *n.* 复活；复兴；恢复

例 The name Anastasia is derived from a Greek word meaning "of the resurrection".

译 安娜斯塔西娅这个名字来自一个希腊单词，意思是 "复活"。

---

31 reticent

['retɪsnt]

义 *adj.* 寡言少语的；沉默的

例 She was morose, pale, and reticent.

译 她郁郁寡欢，面色苍白，沉默寡言。

---

32 retinue

['retənuː]

义 *n.* 随行人员，随员

例 Mind trainers are now part of a tennis star's retinue.

译 如今，网球明星的随行人员中有心理培训师。

---

33 retract

[rɪ'trækt]

义 *v.* 缩回；收回；撤销

例 They tried to persuade me to retract my words.

译 他们试图说服我收回我的话。

---

34 retrain

[ˌriː'treɪn]

义 *v.* 重新培训

例 I had to retrain my fingers to make smaller movements in order to shape the chords.

译 为了形成和弦，我不得不重新训练手指做更小的动作。

---

35 retriever

义 *n.* 能寻回猎物的犬；复得者

[rɪ'triːvər]　例 For a labrador retriever, this turns out to be 4.3 Hz.

译 对于拉布拉多寻回犬来说，这个频率是 4.3 赫兹。

36 retro
['retrəʊ']
义 *adj.*（时装或化妆）重新流行的
例 Its neon displays have a retro feel and saxophone jazz eases from the speakers.
译 它的霓虹灯给人一种复古的感觉，萨克斯爵士乐从扬声器里舒缓地传出。

37 revel
['revl]
义 *v.* 狂欢作乐；陶醉
例 The foreign guests reveled in the scenery of the lake.
译 外宾们陶醉在湖边的景色中。

38 reverend
['revərənd]
义 *n.* 神职人员，牧师
例 The service was led by the Reverend Jim Simons.
译 这次礼拜仪式由吉姆·西蒙斯牧师大人主持。

39 reverent
['revərənt]
义 *adj.* 恭敬的；虔诚的
例 Airport personnel stand in reverent stillness.
译 机场工作人员肃静地站着。

40 rhapsodize
['ræpsədaɪz]
义 *v.* 过分赞美；狂热地写或说
例 And it's easy for the experts to rhapsodize about gratitude.
译 专家们很容易就能对感恩过分赞美。

41 rhetorically
[rɪ'tɔːrɪklɪ]
义 *adv.* 在修辞学上；讲究修辞地
例 Suddenly, the narrator speaks in his most rhetorically elevated mode.
译 突然，讲述者以其措辞最华丽的方式讲起来。

42 rhyme
[raɪm]
义 *n.* 韵，押韵　*v.* 押韵
例 I prefer poems that rhyme.
译 我喜欢句尾押韵的诗。

43 rhythmic
['rɪðmɪk]
义 *adj.* 有节奏的，有韵律的
例 Good breathing is slow, rhythmic and deep.
译 良好的呼吸缓慢、有节奏并且深沉。

44 ribbon
['rɪbən]
义 *n.* 缎带；带状物
例 The road was a ribbon of moonlight.

> **译** 那条路在月光照映下像条缎带。

---

45 richly

['rɪtʃlɪ]

义 *adv.* 理所当然地；完全地；浓厚地

例 He achieved the success he so richly deserved.

译 他获得了他当之无愧的成功。

---

46 rickety

['rɪkətɪ]

义 *adj.* 摇晃的；患软骨病的

例 Mona climbed the rickety wooden stairs.

译 莫娜爬上摇摇晃晃的木楼梯。

---

47 riddance

['rɪdns]

义 *n.* 摆脱；除去

例 He's gone back to Cleveland in a huff, and good riddance.

译 他气呼呼地回克利夫兰去了，总算解脱了。

---

48 ridership

['raɪdəʃɪp]

义 *n.* 客运量

例 Five years ago we discontinued train service between Lamberton and its suburbs because low ridership caused total fares collected to be substantially lower than the cost of operating the service.

译 五年前，我们停止了兰博顿和郊区之间的火车服务，因为低载客量导致总票价远远低于运营成本。

---

49 ridiculously

[rɪ'dɪkjələslɪ]

义 *adv.* 可笑地；荒谬地

例 Will their hard-won brand luster be forever cheapened, especially for items whose allure depends on their being ridiculously priced?

译 他们来之不易的品牌光彩是否会永远贬值，尤其是那些依赖于可笑价格的商品？

---

50 rifle

['raɪfl]

义 *n.* 步枪

例 When he appeared again, he was aiming the rifle at Wade.

译 他再次出现时，正拿步枪瞄准韦德。

---

51 righteousness

['raɪtʃəsnəs]

义 *n.* 正当；正义；正直

例 All my righteousness is like filthy rags.

译 我所有的正义都像肮脏的破布。

---

52 rigidity

[rɪ'dʒɪdətɪ]

义 *n.* 刚性，硬度

例 The amount of force needed is inversely proportional to the rigidity of the material.

译 所需的力与材料的硬度成反比。

53　rigor

['rɪɡə]

义　*n.* 严格，严厉

例　Schools acknowledge the rigor of European secondary training, and will give up to a year's credit to foreigners who have passed their high school exams.

译　学校承认欧洲中等教育的严格性，并将给予通过高中考试的外国学生高至一年的学分。

54　ringside

['rɪŋsaɪd]

义　*n.* 马戏团；拳击场

例　Most of the top trainers were at the ringside.

译　大多数顶级教练都在擂台边。

55　riot

['raɪət]

义　*n.* 暴乱；喧闹

例　Cars and buses were set ablaze during the riot.

译　暴乱中，小汽车和公共汽车被点燃了。

56　riparian

[raɪ'perɪən]

义　*adj.* 河岸的；生于河岸的

例　Riparian zone is an important component of forested watershed.

译　河岸带是森林流域的重要组成部分。

57　ripeness

[raɪpnəs]

义　*n.* 成熟；完成

例　The hot sun enables the grapes to reach optimum ripeness.

译　炎热的阳光使葡萄达到最佳成熟度。

58　riposte

[rɪ'pəʊst]

义　*n.* 还击；机敏的回答

例　The US delivered an early riposte to the air attack.

译　美国对空袭很快做出了反应。

59　riser

['raɪzər]

义　*n.* 海底取油管；起义者

例　When the rig sank, the riser broke near the top while remaining attached to the blowout preventer at the bottom.

译　当钻井平台沉没时，海底取油管在顶部附近断裂，但仍与底部的防喷器相连。

60　risky

['rɪskɪ]

义　*adj.* 危险的；冒险的；大胆的

例　Horse breeding is indeed a risky enterprise.

译　养马的确是一项冒险的事业。

61　rive

[raɪv]

义　*v.* 撕开；使沮丧

例　The four provinces are riven by deep family and tribal conflicts.

译 这四个省被严重的家族和部族纷争弄得四分五裂。

---

62 riverbank

['rɪvəbæŋk]

义 *n.* 河堤，河岸

例 As we travel south, the countryside begins to undulate as the rolling hills sweep down to the riverbanks.

译 当我们向南旅行时，随着起伏的山峦向河岸延伸，乡村开始起伏。

---

63 riverboat

['rɪvə‚bəʊt]

义 *n.* 内河船

例 This river was only recently made accessible to riverboat traffic by a new series of dams and locks.

译 这条河建造了一系列新的河堤和水闸，最近才有内河客轮通航。

---

64 riverfront

['rɪvərfrʌnt]

义 *n.*（城镇的）河边地区；河边陆地

例 New apartment blocks and office towers are rising along the riverfront.

译 新公寓住宅区和办公大楼纷纷沿着河边耸立起来。

---

65 rivet

['rɪvɪt]

义 *n.* 铆钉

例 Each rivet only takes a minute or two to do.

译 每颗铆钉只需一两分钟即可完成。

---

66 roadside

['rəʊdsaɪd]

义 *n.* 路边

例 The snow was banked up along the roadside.

译 路边积起了雪。

---

67 roadway

['rəʊdweɪ]

义 *n.* 车行道

例 Workers have erected scaffolding around the base of the tower below the roadway.

译 工人们已经在车行道下方的塔底周围搭起了脚手架。

---

68 rogue

[rəʊg]

义 *n.* 流氓；调皮鬼

例 Tell me, impudent little rogue, does your story end here?

译 告诉我，无耻的小流氓，你的故事到此为止了吗？

---

69 rollicking

['rɑːlɪkɪŋ]

义 *adj.* 喧闹而欢乐的　*n.* 申斥；责骂

例 He gave us both a rollicking.

译 他把我们俩都骂了一番。

---

70 rookie

['rʊkɪ]

义 *n.* 新手

例 I don't want to have another rookie to train.

译 我不想再训练一个菜鸟了。

---

71 roost
['ru:st']

义 *n.* 栖木；鸟窝；栖息处　*v.* 栖息

例 Birds roost in the canopy.

译 鸟儿栖息在树冠上。

---

72 roseate
['rəʊzɪət]

义 *adj.* 玫瑰色的，粉红的；乐观的

例 One of the Roseate Tern is ringed!

译 其中一只玫瑰燕鸥戴了环！

---

73 rover
['rəʊvər]

义 *n.* 漫游者

例 The discoveries of the two rovers answered some old questions, but they also brought up many new ones.

译 两个漫游者的发现回答了一些老问题，但也带来了许多新的问题。

---

74 rower
['rəʊər]

义 *n.* 划船手，桨手

例 Now they had one senior manager, six management consultants and one rower.

译 现在在他们有了一个高级舵手、六个舵手顾问、一个划船员。

---

75 royalty
['rɔɪəltɪ]

义 *n.* 皇家，皇族

例 The gala evening was attended by royalty and politicians.

译 王室成员和政治家参加了这个晚会。

---

76 rubb
['rʌb]

义 *v.* 摩擦

例 It sounded like two pieces of wood rubbing together.

译 它听起来就像两块木头摩擦在一起。

---

77 ruckus
['rʌkəs]

义 *n.* 喧闹；骚动

例 This caused such a ruckus all over Japan that they had to change their mind.

译 这在全日本引起了相当大的骚动，以至于他们不得不改变主意。

---

78 rudder
['rʌdər]

义 *n.* 方向舵；指导原则

例 You're out in the world, adrift, a ship without a rudder.

译 你在外面的世界里，随波逐流，就像一艘没有舵的船。

---

79 rugged
['rʌgɪd]

义 *adj.* 高低不平的；崎岖的

例 We left the rough track and bumped our way over a rugged mountainous terrain.

译 我们离开了崎岖不平的小路，又在崎岖不平的山地上颠簸前行。

---

80 ruggedness

['rʌgɪdnəs]

义 *n.* 强度；崎岖

例 On the life path equally also can have the roughness, and the ruggedness.

译 人生的道路上同样也会有坎坷和崎岖。

---

81 rumble

['rʌmbl]

义 *n.* 隆隆声，辘辘声

例 Inside, the noise of the traffic was reduced to a distant rumble.

译 在里面，来往车辆的嘈杂声减弱为远处的隆隆声。

---

82 rumor

['ru:mə]

义 *n.* 谣言；传闻

例 Sharing the latest rumor can make a person feel important because he or she knows something that others don't.

译 分享最新的谣言会让人觉得自己很重要，因为他或她知道一些别人不知道的事情。

---

83 runaway

['rʌnəweɪ]

义 *n.* 逃跑者；逃亡

例 Two runaways travel down the river in search of better lives.

译 两个离家出走的人沿河而下去寻找更好的生活。

---

84 ruse

[ru:z]

义 *n.* 策略，谋略；诡计

例 I saw through your little ruse from the start.

译 我从一开始就看穿了你的小计谋。

---

85 russet

['rʌsɪt]

义 *adj.* 红褐色的　*n.* 红褐色，黄褐色

例 The maple trees were in their autumn glory of russets, reds and browns.

译 正值秋季，红褐色、红色和棕色的枫树绚烂夺目。

---

86 rustle

['rʌsl]

义 *v.* 发出沙沙声　*n.* 沙沙声

例 You can see what was making the rustle in the undergrowth.

译 你可以看到是什么在灌木丛中发出沙沙声。

---

87 rusty

['rʌstɪ]

义 *adj.* 生锈的；荒废的

例 The bike is rusty but usable.

译 这辆自行车生锈了，但还能用。

---

88 rut

[rʌt]

义 *n.* 陈旧不变的一套，常规

例 I gave up my job because I felt I was stuck in a rut.

译 我放弃了我的工作，因为我觉得我的工作是一成不变的。

---

89 rutted

['rʌtɪd]

义 *adj.* 有车辙的

例 The car growls along rutted streets.

译 汽车在有车辙的街道上隆隆行驶。

---

90 sabbath

['sæbəθ]

义 *n.* 安息日

例 The retail shops were mixed in with the banks and law offices and cafés, all closed for the Sabbath.

译 零售商店与银行、律师事务所和咖啡馆混杂在一起，在安息日这天全部歇业。

---

91 sabotage

['sæbətɑ:ʒ]

义 *n.* 怠工；破坏　*v.* 破坏；妨碍

例 The main pipeline supplying water was sabotaged by rebels.

译 主要的供水管道被叛乱分子破坏了。

---

92 sacrosanct

['sækrəʊsæŋkt]

义 *adj.* 神圣不可侵犯的

例 Freedom of the press is sacrosanct.

译 出版自由是神圣不可侵犯的。

---

93 saddle

['sædl]

义 *n.* 鞍

例 Why don't we saddle a couple of horses and go for a ride?

译 为什么我们不给几匹马配上鞍，然后骑着去转转呢？

---

94 saga

['sɑ:gə]

义 *n.* 长篇故事，长篇记叙

例 The saga of this family continues.

译 这个家族的故事还在继续。

---

95 sage

[seɪdʒ]

义 *n.* 圣人，哲人

例 The sage gave advice to his friends.

译 那位圣贤给他的朋友提出忠告。

---

96 sailboat

['seɪlbəʊt]

义 *n.* (比赛、休闲用的)帆船

例 The sailboat skimmed the water.

| 译 | 帆船掠过水面。 |

---

97 salamander

['sæləmændər]

义 *n.* 蝾螈，火蜥蜴

例 A salamander embryo can attract algae inside its tissues and cells.

译 蝾螈胚胎可以吸引藻类进入其组织和细胞。

---

98 saloon

[sə'lu:n]

义 *n.* 大厅；沙龙；酒吧

例 How did it look in the furthest saloon?

译 最远的酒馆里是什么样子的？

---

99 saltwater

['sɔ:ltwɔ:tər]

义 *adj.* 盐水的；海产的　　*n.* 盐水，咸水

例 The main reason was that steel cables degrade very, very quickly in contact with saltwater.

译 主要原因是钢缆在与盐水接触时降解得非常非常快。

---

100 salutary

['sæljətərɪ]

义 *adj.* 有益的；有用的；有益健康的

例 It was a salutary experience to be in the minority.

译 做少数派是一种有益的经历。

List 15

1 salvage
['sælvɪdʒ]

义 *n.* 打捞，救援
例 The salvage operation went on.
译 打捞工作继续进行。

2 sanction
['sæŋkʃn]

义 *n.* 批准；约束力；处罚 *v.* 认可，准许；处罚
例 He may now be ready to sanction the use of force.
译 他可能现在正准备批准使用武力。

3 sandalwood
['sændlwʊd]

义 *n.* 檀香木
例 Theirs is a beautiful reddish color, made from sandalwood and powder.
译 它们的颜色是美丽的红色，由檀香和粉末制成。

4 sander
['sændər]

义 *n.* 打磨机；喷沙装置
例 I used my belt sander to do that.
译 我使用我的打磨机来做这个。

5 sandpiper
['sændpaɪpər]

义 *n.* 矶鹬
例 My mama says sandpipers come to bring us joy.
译 我妈妈说矶鹬会给我们带来欢乐。

6 sanitarium
[ˌsænə'terɪəm]

义 *n.* 疗养院
例 We must get him away to the sanitarium.
译 我们得把他送去疗养院。

7 sanitary
['sænəterɪ]

义 *adj.* 卫生的；干净的
例 Sanitary conditions are appalling.
译 卫生条件非常恶劣。

8 sanity
['sænətɪ]

义 *n.* 神智健全；头脑清楚
例 His behavior was so strange that I began to doubt his sanity.
译 他的行为如此奇怪，我开始怀疑他是否神志正常。

9 sapiens
['seɪpɪənz]

义 *adj.* 智人的
例 What distinguishes Homo sapiens from every other living creature is the mind.
译 智人与其他所有生物的区别在于思维。

10 sapling

['sæplɪŋ]

义 *n.* 树苗，小树

例 It becomes a weak, frail sapling.

译 它变成了一棵虚弱的树苗。

---

11 sapphire

['sæfaɪər]

义 *n.* 蓝宝石；深蓝色

例 She had the sapphire set in a gold ring.

译 她让人把蓝宝石镶在金戒指上。

---

12 sarcastic

[sɑːrˈkæstɪk]

义 *adj.* 讽刺的

例 She poked fun at people's shortcomings with sarcastic remarks.

译 她冷嘲热讽，取笑别人的缺点。

---

13 sassy

['sæsɪ]

义 *adj.* 无礼的；充满活力的；时髦的

例 Orenstein talks about the marketing that focuses little girls on pink, pretty, sexy and sassy.

译 奥伦斯坦谈到了将女孩的注意力集中在粉色、漂亮、性感和时髦上的市场营销。

---

14 sate

[seɪt]

义 *v.* 使心满意足；过分地给予

例 Some luxury labels hope that connecting the artisan to the aroma will sate buyers' desires for the authentic and the handcrafted.

译 一些奢侈品品牌将工匠与香气联系起来，可以满足买家对正品和手工制品的渴望。

---

15 satiety

[səˈtaɪətɪ]

义 *n.* 饱足；满足

例 Heat is a satiety signal.

译 温暖是饱腹的信号。

---

16 saturation

[ˌsætʃəˈreɪʃn]

义 *n.* 饱和；浸透

例 The concept of saturation marketing makes perfect sense.

译 饱和营销的概念非常有道理。

---

17 savant

[sæˈvɑːnt]

义 *n.* 学者；专家

例 In fact, the savants are considered sacrosanct and cannot be touched by anyone except with their expressed permission.

译 事实上，学者们被认为是神圣不可侵犯的，除非得到他们明确的许可，否则任何人都不能触碰他们。

---

18 savior

['seɪvjə]

义 *n.* 救助者；救世主

例 After all he was your savior.

译 毕竟他救了你。

19　savor

['seɪvə]

义 *v.* 尽情享受；使有风味

例 I went out to savor the loveliness of the grassland landscape.

译 我走出屋外来欣赏草原的美景。

20　savory

['seɪvərɪ]

义 *adj.* 美味可口的；香辣的

例 The scent of that crispy brown turkey, fluffy mashed potatoes, savory stuffing, and assorted vegetables made my mouth water.

译 酥脆的棕色火鸡、松软的土豆泥、美味的馅料和什锦蔬菜的香味让我流口水。

21　savviest

['sævi:st]

义 *adj.* 最精明老练的

例 The *Financial Times* has been the savviest newspaper at balancing free and paid.

译 《金融时报》在平衡免费和付费方面一直是最精明的报纸。

22　savvy

['sævɪ]

义 *n.* 悟性；理解能力　*adj.* 聪慧的

例 He is known for his political savvy and strong management skills.

译 他以政治头脑和高超的管理技巧而闻名。

23　saxophone

['sæksəfəun]

义 *n.* 萨克斯管

例 He started his career in show business by playing the saxophone and singing.

译 他以演奏萨克斯管和唱歌开始他的演艺生涯。

24　saxophonist

['sæksəfəunɪst]

义 *n.* 萨克斯管吹奏者

例 The saxophonist doubled the drum in the band.

译 这位萨克斯管吹奏者在乐队中还兼任鼓手。

25　scallop

['skæləp]

义 *n.* 扇贝壳；扇形饰边

例 The rays, in turn, decimated the bay scallop populations around North Carolina.

译 反过来，这些鳐鱼大量猎捕了北卡罗来纳州附近的海湾扇贝。

26　scalp

[skælp]

义 *n.* 头皮；胜利品

例 He smoothed his hair back over his scalp.

译 他把头发向后梳到头皮上。

27　scalpel

义 *n.* 手术刀，解剖刀

['skælpəl]   例 This is the scalpel which Norman Bethune used in those days.

译 这就是诺尔曼·白求恩当年用的那把手术刀。

---

28 scaly

['skeɪlɪ]

义 *adj.* 有鳞的；剥落的

例 The reptile's skin is tough and scaly.

译 这种爬行动物的皮肤坚韧且有鳞。

---

29 scandal

['skændl]

义 *n.* 丑闻；反感；耻辱；中伤

例 The only genuine public excitement for even the very first modern, Olympic literary contest was focused on the scandal surrounding the winning poem.

译 即使是在第一次现代奥林匹克文学比赛中，唯一真正让公众兴奋的是围绕获奖诗歌的丑闻。

---

30 scarab

['skærəb]

义 *n.* 圣甲虫

例 The unique design of the vehicle largely draws inspiration from the shape of the scarab.

译 该车辆的独特设计主要是从圣甲虫的形状汲取了灵感。

---

31 scatter

['skætər]

义 *n.* 散落   *v.* 撒，播撒；使散开

例 They've been scattering toys everywhere.

译 他们把玩具扔得到处都是。

---

32 scavenge

['skævɪndʒ]

义 *v.* 到处觅食；（在废物中）寻觅

例 Children scavenge through rubbish.

译 孩子们在垃圾中寻找东西。

---

33 schema

['ski:mə]

义 *n.* 图解；模式

例 This reduces the effort to write and maintain the schema, as well as ensures that no complex type is accidentally left inextensible.

译 这减少了编写和维护模式的工作量，还确保了不会有某个复杂类型被偶然遗漏而不能扩展。

---

34 schoolhouse

['sku:lhaʊs]

义 *n.* 校舍

例 McCreary lives in a converted schoolhouse outside Charlottesville.

译 麦克里住在夏洛茨维尔郊外一所改造过的校舍里。

---

35 schoolmaster

['sku:lmæstər]

义 *n.* 教师；男教员；校长

例 The new schoolmaster has some build!

译 新校长身材不错！

36 schoolmate

['sku:lmeɪt]

义 *n.* 同学；校友

例 He started the magazine with a schoolmate.

译 他和一个同学创办了这本杂志。

---

37 schooner

['sku:nər]

义 *n.* 纵帆船；大篷车

例 The schooner sailed coastward.

译 纵帆船向海岸航行。

---

38 scissor

['sɪzər]

义 *n.* 剪刀 *adj.* 剪刀的，剪刀似的

例 The legs move in a scissor action.

译 双腿像剪刀似地移动。

---

39 scoff

[skɔ:f]

义 *v./n.* 嘲笑，愚弄

例 Traditionalists may scoff.

译 传统人士可能会嘲笑。

---

40 scold

[skəʊld]

义 *v.* 责骂，叱责

例 Parents shouldn't keep scolding their child for his unintentional mistakes.

译 父母不应因孩子的无心错误而一直责备他。

---

41 scorch

[skɔ:rtʃ]

义 *v.* (使)烧焦，变焦

例 The leaves are inclined to scorch in hot sunshine.

译 树叶在烈日下容易晒焦。

---

42 scorecard

['skɔ:rkɑ:rd]

义 *n.* 记分卡

例 By enhancing communication, the scorecard also led to qualitative benefits.

译 通过加强沟通，记分卡还带来了质量效益。

---

43 scorn

[skɔ:rn]

义 *n.* 蔑视；轻视 *v.* 鄙视，嘲笑；拒绝；批评，抨击

例 Several leading officers have quite openly scorned the peace talks.

译 几名主要官员曾相当公开地蔑视和平谈判。

---

44 scorpion

['skɔ:rpɪən]

义 *n.* 蝎子；心黑的人

例 The scorpion has a sting in its tail.

译 蝎子的尾巴上有螫针。

45 scraggly

['skræglɪ]

义 *adj.* 散乱的；锯齿状的；凸凹不平的

例 There are only scraggly bushes.

译 那里只有乱蓬蓬的灌木丛。

---

46 scramble

['skræmbl]

义 *n.* 混乱；争夺

例 There was an undignified scramble for the best seats.

译 人们争抢最好的座位，很不体面。

---

47 scrapbook

['skræpbʊk]

义 *n.* 剪贴簿

例 He pasted the pictures into his scrapbook.

译 他把照片贴在他的剪贴簿上。

---

48 screech

[skriːtʃ]

义 *v.* 尖叫；发出尖锐的声音   *n.* 刺耳的尖叫，尖利刺耳的声音

例 The figure gave a screech.

译 黑影尖叫了一声。

---

49 scribble

['skrɪbl]

义 *v.* 潦草地书写；乱写   *n.* 潦草的书写；乱涂乱画的东西

例 I'm sorry what I wrote was such a scribble.

译 很抱歉我写的东西太潦草了。

---

50 scrim

[skrɪm]

义 *n.* 平纹棉麻织物；纱幕；薄纱

例 The windows were nearly opaque, with a scrim of some sort of pale fluff or dander.

译 窗户几乎是不透明的，上面有一层薄棉布，带着某种苍白的绒毛或皮屑。

---

51 scripted

['skrɪptɪd]

义 *adj.* 照原稿宣读的

例 He had prepared scripted answers.

译 他已事先写好了答案。

---

52 scripture

['skrɪptʃər]

义 *n.* 经文

例 They have lots of scripture.

译 他们有很多经文。

---

53 scrubland

['skrʌblənd]

义 *n.* 灌木丛林地

例 About two million acres of native forest and scrubland remain intact, according to the Nature Conservancy, and a quarter of them are managed by federal or state.

译 根据美国自然保护协会的数据，大约有 200 万英亩的原始森林和灌木丛仍然完好无损，其中四分之一由联邦政府或州政府管理。

54　scruffily

['skrʌfɪlɪ]

义　*adv.* 不整洁地；邋遢地

例　She was too scruffily dressed for such a formal occasion.

译　对于这样一个正规场合，她穿戴得太马虎了。

55　scruffy

['skrʌfɪ]

义　*adj.* 邋遢的；肮脏的

例　He looked a little scruffy.

译　他看着有点邋遢。

56　scuba

['skjuːbə]

义　*n.* 水中呼吸器　*adj.* 使用水肺的，有水下呼吸器的（=Self-Contained Underwater Breathing Apparatus）

例　The company offers scuba-diving as an add-on to the basic holiday price.

译　这家公司提供水肺潜水活动，不包括在基本度假费用以内。

57　scuff

[skʌf]

义　*v.* 磨损；拖着脚走

例　Constant wheelchair use will scuff almost any floor surface.

译　经常有轮椅在地板上移动的话，几乎任何地板都会有所磨损。

58　sculptural

['skʌlptʃərəl]

义　*adj.* 雕刻的；雕刻般的

例　He enjoyed working with clay as a sculptural form.

译　他喜欢把黏土做成雕塑。

59　scumming

['skʌmɪŋ]

义　*n.* 撇渣（吐渣，浮渣）

例　This paper analyzes the essential scumming reasons for magnesite product and every kind of modified measures and results used normally now.

译　这篇论文分析了镁产品产生浮渣的根本原因及目前常用的各种改进措施和效果。

60　scurry

['skɜːrɪ]

义　*v.* 小步疾走；急赶

例　He saw the cockroach scurry under it with the gecko far behind struggling to go under.

译　他看见蟑螂从它下面快速跑过去，壁虎在后面，挣扎着要钻过去。

61　seafarer

['siːferər]

义　*n.* 船员；航海家

例　The Estonians have always been seafarers.

译　爱沙尼亚人总是在海上漂泊。

62　seamlessly

['siːmləslɪ]

义　*adv.* 无缝地

例　For the first time in his life he saw himself as part of some whole, some whole world to which his own being was seamlessly connected.

译 他有生以来第一次把自己看作一个整体——一个他的存在与之无缝相连的整个世界中的一部分。

---

63 sear

['sɪr']

义 **v.** 使……干枯，烤焦；用强烈的感情影响

例 I distinctly felt the heat start to sear my throat.

译 我清楚地感觉到喉咙开始烧得难受。

---

64 searcher

['sɜ:rtʃər]

义 **n.** 搜索者；检察官

例 The searchers spread out to cover the area faster.

译 搜寻人员迅速展开搜索，以覆盖该地区。

---

65 searchlight

['sɜ:rtʃlaɪt]

义 **n.** 探照灯；探照灯光；手电

例 If a searchlight catches us, alarms will go off.

译 如果探照灯照到我们，警报就会响起来。

---

66 seashell

['si:ʃel]

义 **n.** 海贝，贝壳

例 The blue specks are likely naturally occurring seashell particles or minerals.

译 这些蓝色斑点很可能是自然产生的贝壳颗粒或矿物质。

---

67 seasonally

['si:zənəlɪ]

义 **adv.** 季节性地

例 The seasonally adjusted unemployment figures show a rise of twelve-hundred.

译 季节性调整的数字显示失业人数增加了 1 200 人。

---

68 seatmate

['si:tmeɪt]

义 **n.** （汽车、火车、飞机等上的）同座乘客

例 Her kinetic passion, her chatty-seatmate prose, and her detail-heckling made her a pop-culture oracle in an era that desperately needed one.

译 她那充满活力的激情、她那邻座健谈似的散文和她对细节的质疑，使她成为那个时代急需的流行文化权威。

---

69 seaworthy

['si:wɜ:rðɪ]

义 **adj.** 适于航海的；经得起风浪的

例 The ship was completely seaworthy.

译 这艘轮船完全适合在海上航行。

---

70 seclude

[sɪ'klu:d]

义 **v.** 隔离，隔绝

例 She would seclude herself from the world forever.

译 她将永远与这个世界隔绝。

---

71 secrecy

['si:krəsɪ]

义 *n.* 秘密，保密

例 The trial was conducted under a blanket of secrecy.

译 审讯在高度保密下进行。

---

72 secretariat

[ˌsekrə'terɪət]

义 *n.* 秘书处；书记处

例 Students tried to barge into the secretariat buildings.

译 学生们试图闯入秘书处大楼。

---

73 sectional

['sekʃənl]

义 *adj.* 部分的；小团体的，群体的

例 Voters elected him to represent them, rather than narrow sectional interests.

译 选民选他是为了代表他们，而不是为了狭隘的小团体利益。

---

74 sedate

[sɪ'deɪt]

义 *adj.* 安静的，镇静的

例 Her life was sedate, almost mundane.

译 她的生活平静，几乎平淡无奇。

---

75 sedge

[sedʒ]

义 *n.* 莎草；苔草

例 Sedge grows in marshes or near water.

译 苔草生长在沼泽或水边。

---

76 seditious

[sɪ'dɪʃəs]

义 *adj.* 煽动性的

例 The letter was declared seditious.

译 这封信被宣告具布煽动性。

---

77 seductive

[sɪ'dʌktɪv]

义 *adj.* 诱惑的；引人注意的；有魅力的

例 The idea of retiring to the south of France is highly seductive.

译 退休后到法国南方去，这个主意令人心驰神往。

---

78 seeker

['si:kər]

义 *n.* 寻找者，探求者

例 They campaigned on behalf of asylum seekers.

译 他们代表寻求庇护者开展活动。

---

79 segmented

['segməntɪd]

义 *adj.* 分段的

例 However, segmented blades have disadvantages.

译 不过，分段刀片有缺点。

---

80 segregate

义 *v.* 分离；隔离；分凝

['segrɪgeɪt]

例 A large detachment of police was used to segregate the two rival camps of protesters.

译 一支庞大的警察分遣队被调来隔离两个对立的抗议者阵营。

---

81 segue

['segweɪ]

义 *v.* 切换；转到

例 He then segued into a discussion of atheism.

译 然后他转而讨论无神论。

---

82 semantic

[sɪ'mæntɪk]

义 *adj.* 语义的

例 He did not want to enter into a semantic debate.

译 他不想卷入语义辩论。

---

83 semantically

[sɪ'mæntɪklɪ]

义 *adv.* 语义上地

例 There are two methods of classifying words semantically.

译 对词进行语义分类，通常有两类做法。

---

84 semicircle

['semɪsɜːrkl]

义 *n.* 半圆，半圆形，半圆物

例 We sat in a semicircle round the fire.

译 我们坐在炉火前，围成一个半圆形。

---

85 senseless

['sensləs]

义 *adj.* 无意识的；不省人事的

例 She drank herself senseless.

译 她喝得不省人事。

---

86 sentience

['senʃɪəns]

义 *n.* 感觉性；感觉能力

例 Some people believe in the sentience of flowers.

译 有些人相信花有知觉。

---

87 sentient

['senʃɪənt]

义 *adj.* 有知觉的；有感情的

例 Man is a sentient being.

译 人是有感觉的生物。

---

88 sentinel

['sentɪnl]

义 *n.* 哨兵

例 We gave the watchword, and the sentinel let us pass.

译 我们说出口令，哨兵就让我们过去了。

---

89 serenity

[sə'renətɪ]

义 *n.* 宁静；沉着

例 This serenity arose in part from Rachel's religious beliefs.

> **译** 这种平静在一定程度上源于雷切尔的宗教信仰。

---

90 serpent
['sɜːrpənt]

义 *n.* 蛇；狡猾的人

例 Serpents cast their skin once a year.

译 蛇每年蜕一次皮。

---

91 serpentine
['sɜːrpəntiːn]

义 *adj.* 蛇形的；弯曲的；阴险的

例 The serpentine lakeshore is 128 km long.

译 那个蜿蜒的湖岸长 128 公里。

---

92 servile
['sɜːrvl]

义 *adj.* 屈从的；奴隶的；不自由的

例 He was subservient and servile.

译 他卑躬屈膝。

---

93 servitude
['sɜːrvətuːd]

义 *n.* 奴役；徒刑

例 In the 19th century it was called indentured servitude.

译 在 19 世纪，它被称作劳役。

---

94 setup
['setˌʌp]

义 *n.* 组织，机构；安排，结构；计划，方案

例 This setup would require the players to throw the ball in an arc to make a goal.

译 这种设置需要球员将球投成弧形，才能进球。

---

95 sexism
['seksɪzəm]

义 *n.* 性别歧视

例 It's got nothing to do with sexism.

译 这跟性别歧视一点关系都没有。

---

96 sexually
['sekʃəlɪ]

义 *adv.* 性别地；两性之间地

例 She finds him sexually attractive.

译 她觉得他性感迷人。

---

97 shack
[ʃæk]

义 *n.* 棚房，窝棚

例 They lived in a shack with a dirt floor.

译 他们住在一间地板肮脏的棚屋里。

---

98 shad
[ʃæd]

义 *n.* 鲱鱼类

例 We have filet of sole, flounder, and baked shad.

译 我们有上等鳎目鱼排、比目鱼，还有烤鲱鱼。

---

99 shadowy

['ʃædəʊɪ]

义 *adj.* 阴暗的；朦胧的；鲜为人知的

例 Someone was waiting in the shadowy doorway.

译 有人守候在昏暗的门口。

---

100 shaky

['ʃeɪkɪ]

义 *adj.* 不稳固的，摇晃的

例 That ladder looks a little shaky.

译 这梯子看起来不大稳固。

List 16

1 shamelessness

['ʃeɪmləsnəs]

义 *n.* 无耻

例 Of course, not all rich man has a trait of shamelessness.

译 当然，并不是所有的有钱人都有无耻的特点。

2 shanty

['ʃæntɪ]

义 *n.* 简陋小屋；（水手唱的）劳动号子

例 In the shanty towns there are very poor living standards.

译 棚户区的生活水平很低。

3 shantytown

['ʃæntɪˌtaʊn]

义 *n.* 贫民区（以临时搭盖的陋屋为主的地区）

例 However, the core zone in the city shantytowns gradually disappears.

译 然而，城市核心地带的棚户区逐渐消失。

4 shapely

['ʃeɪplɪ]

义 *adj.*（女性）体形好看的，匀称的

例 She is a shapely young woman.

译 她是个身材好的年轻女子。

5 shard

[ʃɑːrd]

义 *n.* 碎片；一小片或一部分

例 All records in an atomic unit are stored in the same shard.

译 原子单元中的所有记录都会存储在相同的分片上。

6 shareholder

['ʃerhəʊldər]

义 *n.* 股东

例 As boards scrutinize succession plans in response to shareholder pressure, executives who don't get the nod also may wish to move on.

译 由于董事会迫于股东们的压力而严格审查公司的接任方案，那些未获得许可的高管们也可能会想辞职。

7 sharpener

['ʃɑːrpnər]

义 *n.* 卷笔刀；研磨者；研磨工具

例 I have a sharpener. It is red.

译 我有一个卷笔刀。它是红色的。

8 sheaf

[ʃiːf]

义 *n.* 束；捆；扎

例 She moved the sheaf of papers into position.

译 她把那捆文件搬到合适的位置。

9 sheepishly

['ʃiːpɪʃlɪ]

义 *adv.* 窘迫地；不好意思地

例 John nodded sheepishly in agreement.

译 约翰羞怯地点头同意。

10 shenanigan

[ʃɪ'nænɪgən]

义 *n.* 恶作剧；胡闹；诈骗

例 Laugh silly, shy, without a word, are actually quite shenanigans.

译 傻笑、害羞、一言不发，其实都是恶作剧。

---

11 shifter

['ʃɪftər]

义 *n.* 移动装置；搬移东西者

例 Full-decoder circuit structure is used in Barrel Shifter design.

译 桶形移位器的设计采用全译码电路结构。

---

12 shimmer

['ʃɪmər]

义 *n.* 微光；摇曳的光 *v.* 闪烁；发闪烁的微光

例 Everything seemed to shimmer in the heat.

译 在炎热中，一切似乎都在闪闪发光。

---

13 shin

[ʃɪn]

义 *n.* 胫骨

例 An operation finally cured his shin injury.

译 一次手术终于治好了他胫骨的伤。

---

14 shipbuilder

['ʃɪpbɪldər]

义 *n.* 造船商；造船工程师

例 Austal, an Australian shipbuilder, came to the city in 1999 and has been expanding.

译 澳大利亚造船商奥斯塔尔于 1999 年来到这座城市，并一直在扩张。

---

15 shipbuilding

['ʃɪpbɪldɪŋ]

义 *n.* 造船；造船业

例 This shipyard is at the cutting edge of world shipbuilding technology.

译 这家造船厂的造船技术位于世界前沿。

---

16 shipworm

['ʃɪp,wɜːrm]

义 *n.* 船蛆

例 To defend the region's well-preserved wrecks from shipworms, researchers have suggested draping submerged vessels in polypropylene covers or covering ships with seabed sediments and sandbags.

译 为了保护该地区保存完好的沉船不受船蛆侵害，研究人员建议用聚丙烯覆盖物或者用海底沉积物和沙袋覆盖沉没的船只。

---

17 shipyard

['ʃɪpjɑːrd]

义 *n.* 造船厂

例 George was a fitter at the shipyard.

译 乔治是造船厂的装配工。

---

18 shirk

[ʃɜːrk]

义 *v.* 逃避，躲避

例 A determined burglar will not shirk from breaking a window to gain entry.

译 一个下定决心的窃贼会不惜破窗而入。

19 shoddy

['ʃɑ:dɪ]

义 *adj.* 劣质的

例 This is a shoddy piece of work.

译 这是一件劣质作品。

---

20 shorebird

['ʃɔ:bɜ:rd]

义 *n.* 滨鸟

例 Certain shorebirds depend on these eggs for food during their annual spring migration to their northern breeding grounds.

译 某些滨鸟每年春季迁徙到北部繁殖地时，都以这些蛋为食。

---

21 shortcake

['ʃɔ:rtkeɪk]

义 *n.* 水果酥饼

例 I made strawberry shortcake.

译 我做了草莓酥饼。

---

22 shortstop

['ʃɔ:t‚stɑ:p]

义 *n.* (棒球) 游击手；游击手的位置

例 The shortstop was batting when the rain began.

译 正轮到游击手击球时，天下起雨来。

---

23 shovel

['ʃʌvl]

义 *v.* 铲除；用铲挖

例 He has to get out and shovel snow.

译 他必须出去铲雪。

---

24 showbiz

['ʃəʊbɪz]

义 *n.* 娱乐性行业；娱乐界

例 She gives showbiz parties a wide berth.

译 她对演艺圈的聚会敬而远之。

---

25 showcase

['ʃəʊkeɪs]

义 *n.* (玻璃) 陈列柜；显示优点的东西 *v.* 展示，展现

例 Toyota this week showcased a smaller, cheaper version of the Prius called the FT-CH concept.

译 丰田本周展示了一款更小、更便宜的普锐斯车型，名为 FT-CH 概念车。

---

26 showgirl

['ʃəʊgɜ:rl]

义 *n.* 歌舞女郎，广告女郎

例 Sandy tells Jeffrey about the case may be related to a nightclub showgirl.

译 桑迪告诉杰弗里案子可能与一名夜总会歌女有关。

---

27 shred

[ʃred]

义 *v.* 撕成碎片

例 They may be shredding documents.

译 他们也许正在粉碎那些文件。

28 shrimp

['ʃrɪmp]

义 *n.* 虾；瘦小的人（物） *v.* 捕虾

例 They will go shrimping this afternoon.

译 他们今天下午要去捕虾。

29 shrivel

['ʃrɪvl]

义 *v.*（使）枯萎，（使）干枯

例 The hot sun shriveled (up) the leaves.

译 炎热的太阳把树叶晒干了。

30 shrubbery

['ʃrʌbərɪ]

义 *n.* 灌木，灌木林

例 After she was gone Mary turned down the walk which led to the door in the shrubbery.

译 她走后，玛丽沿着通向灌木丛中的那扇门的小路走去。

31 shutter

['ʃʌtər]

义 *n.* 百叶窗；快门

例 There are a few things you should check before pressing the shutter release.

译 在按下快门之前，有几件事你应该检查一下。

32 shuttered

['ʃʌtərd]

义 *adj.* 关上（或装有）百叶窗的

例 I opened a shuttered window.

译 我打开了一扇紧闭的百叶窗户。

33 shyly

[ʃaɪlɪ]

义 *adv.* 畏缩地；羞怯地

例 He shyly nodded his head.

译 他害羞地点了点头。

34 sickle

['sɪkl]

义 *n.* 镰刀

例 Sickle-cell anaemia is passed on through a recessive gene.

译 镰状细胞贫血是通过隐性基因遗传的。

35 sickroom

['sɪkru:m]

义 *n.* 病房

例 Close friends were allowed into the sickroom.

译 允许亲密的朋友进入病房。

36 sidelong

['saɪdlɔ:ŋ]

义 *adj.* 斜着眼看的；向旁边的；侧面的 *adv.* 倾斜地；向横；向侧面

例 She gave him a quick sidelong glance.

译 她飞快地斜看了他一眼。

37 sideman

义 *n.* 伴奏者

['saɪdˌmæn]

例 He first recorded with Paul Howard's *Quality Serenaders*, and later as a sideman with the Les Hite Band.

译 他先为保罗·霍华德的《优质小夜曲》录音，后来为莱斯·海特乐队伴奏。

38　sidestep

['saɪdstep]

义 *v.* 向旁侧避让，回避

例 You will be able to sidestep problems, but you'll need to stay alert to do so.

译 你可以回避问题；但你需要保持警惕。

39　sidewalk

['saɪdwɔːk]

义 *n.* 人行道

例 Glass from broken bottles litters the sidewalk.

译 人行道上到处都是破瓶子里的玻璃。

40　siege

[siːdʒ]

义 *n.* 包围；围攻

例 The siege has ended peacefully.

译 围攻已经和平结束。

41　sift

[sɪft]

义 *v.* 筛下，筛分；详察

例 Sift out the wheat from the chaff.

译 把小麦从谷壳中筛出来。

42　signal

['sɪgnəl]

义 *n.* 信号，标志　*v.* 发信号，示意；标志，预示；表示

例 The policeman signaled the traffic to move forward slowly.

译 警察向车辆发出缓慢前进的信号。

43　silhouette

[ˌsɪlʊˈet]

义 *n.* 轮廓；侧影

例 The mountains stood out in silhouette.

译 群山的轮廓清晰可见。

44　silica

['sɪlɪkə]

义 *n.* 硅石，矽土

例 The basic ingredients in glass, including silica sand and soda ash, are found almost everywhere.

译 玻璃的基本成分，包括硅砂和苏打灰，几乎随处可见。

45　silken

['sɪlkən]

义 *adj.* 丝绸的，绸制的；柔软的

例 He mounted the picture upon silken cloth.

译 他把那幅画裱在丝绸上。

---

46 silky

['sɪlkɪ]

义 *adj.* 丝制的；温和的

例 He spoke in a silky tone.

译 他说话柔声细语的。

---

47 sill

[sɪl]

义 *n.* 窗台

例 Whitlock was perched on the sill of the room's only window.

译 惠特洛克坐在房间里唯一一扇窗户的窗台上。

---

48 silverware

['sɪlvərwer]

义 *n.* 银器；银餐具

例 He has his own silverware at home.

译 他家里有自己的银餐具。

---

49 silvery

['sɪlvərɪ]

义 *adj.* 含银的；银色光泽的

例 The carpet had a silvery sheen to it.

译 地毯有银色的光泽。

---

50 simile

['sɪmәlɪ]

义 *n.* 直喻；明喻

例 The simile is there ostensibly to compare Satan with the great sea beast, leviathan.

译 这个比喻表面上是要把撒旦和巨大的海兽利维坦相提并论。

---

51 sin

[sɪn]

义 *n.* 罪，罪恶

例 Treachery was the ultimate sin.

译 背叛曾是弥天大罪。

---

52 sinful

['sɪnfl]

义 *adj.* 有罪的，罪恶的

例 It's sinful to waste good food!

译 浪费好食物是罪恶的！

---

53 singularly

['sɪŋgjәlәrlɪ]

义 *adv.* 异常地；非常地

例 Control is what the Wright Brothers so ably and singularly demonstrated.

译 控制是莱特兄弟如此干练和独特的表现。

---

54 sinister

['sɪnɪstər]

义 *adj.* 邪恶的；灾难性的

例 He was a sinister and crafty speculator.

译 他是一个阴险狡诈的投机商。

55　sinuous

['sɪnjʊəs]

义 *adj.* 弯弯曲曲的；蜿蜒的

例 In most fish they contract successively to throw the body into sinuous waves, which propel it forward.

译 大多数鱼类会连续收缩，把身体抛入弯曲的波浪中，推动身体向前。

56　siphon

['saɪfn]

义 *v.* 用虹吸管吸出；抽取

例 He siphoned $1.2 billion from his companies to prop up his crumbling media empire.

译 他从自己的公司中抽走了 12 亿美元来支撑他摇摇欲坠的媒体帝国。

57　situational

[ˌsɪtʃʊ'eɪʃənl]

义 *adj.* 环境形成的

例 Improve soldiers' mobility and situational awareness in all lighting conditions and battlefield conditions.

译 提高士兵在所有光照条件和战场条件下的行动能力和态势感知能力。

58　skater

['skeɪtər]

义 *n.* 滑冰者

例 The spinning ice skater attracted her attention.

译 那位做旋转动作的滑冰者吸引了她的注意力。

59　skein

[skeɪn]

义 *n.* 一束（线或纱）；一群

例 She passed me a skein of wool.

译 她递给我一绞毛线。

60　skeptically

['skeptɪkəlɪ]

义 *adv.* 怀疑地

例 I looked at him skeptically.

译 我怀疑地看着他。

61　sketchbook

['sketʃbʊk]

义 *n.* 写生簿

例 Guys, have you seen my sketchbook?

译 伙计们，你们看到我的素描本了吗？

62　skillet

['skɪlɪt]

义 *n.* 煎锅

例 Heat butter in a skillet until melted.

译 黄油入锅，加热至融化。

63　skillfully

[ˌskɪlfəlɪ]

义 *adv.* 巧妙地；技术好地

例 Taxes must be restructured to increase revenue, but skillfully so as to not inhibit growth.

译 必须调整税收结构以增加收入，但要巧妙地避免抑制增长。

---

64 skydiver

['skaɪdaɪvə(r)]

义 *n.* 做空中造型动作的跳伞运动员

例 As well as being a world-class mountain climber, Erik is also a good skier and skydiver.

译 埃里克不仅是一名世界级的登山者，还是一名优秀的滑雪和跳伞运动员。

---

65 skyrocket

['skaɪrɑːkɪt]

义 *v.* (价格) 飞涨，猛涨

例 Income taxes skyrocketed and tax allowances were lowered.

译 所得税飞涨，税收减免降低。

---

66 skyward

['skaɪwəd]

义 *adv.* 向天空地；向上地

例 Meanwhile, global population is ticking skyward.

译 同时，全球人口剧增。

---

67 slack

[slæk]

义 *adj.* 松弛的；懈怠的；萧条的

例 Discipline in the classroom is very slack.

译 教室里纪律很松弛。

---

68 slacken

['slækən]

义 *v.* 使松弛；使缓慢；变弱

例 Redouble your efforts and not slacken off.

译 要加倍努力，不要懈怠。

---

69 slake

[sleɪk]

义 *v.* 消除；满足

例 Nothing but his death can slake my anger.

译 只有他的死才能平息我的怒气。

---

70 slang

[slæŋ]

义 *n.* 俚语；行话

例 "Old man" is a slang term for "father".

译 old man 为俚语，指父亲。

---

71 slap

[slæp]

义 *n.* 侮辱；掴；拍击声

例 She gave him a slap across the face.

译 她给了他一记耳光。

---

72 slapstick

['slæpstɪk]

义 *n.* 打闹剧 (演员用击板相互追打发出声响得名)

例 Slapstick humor works best around these days.

译 最近闹剧式的幽默最起作用。

73　slate

[sleɪt]

义 *n.* 板岩；石板

例 The sea was the color of slate.

译 大海是石板色的。

74　slaughter

['slɔːtər]

义 *n.* 屠杀；屠宰

例 The animals are stunned before slaughter.

译 这些动物在屠宰前被击昏。

75　sled

[sled]

义 *n.* 雪橇

例 We can see a sled in the store.

译 我们可以在商店里看到一个雪橇。

76　sleuth

[sluːθ]

义 *n.* 警犬

例 He pursued the problem like the sleuth-hound that he was.

译 他像一条侦探猎犬一样追查这个问题。

77　slick

[slɪk]

义 *adj.* 光滑的；顺利的；（指人）圆滑的

例 They are also covered with a slick, transparent lid that reduces drag.

译 它们还被光滑透明的盖子覆盖，以减少阻力。

78　slime

[slaɪm]

义 *n.* 烂泥；黏液

例 He swam down and retrieved his glasses from the muck and slime at the bottom of the pond.

译 他游下去，从池塘底部的淤泥和黏液中取出他的眼镜。

79　slimness

[slɪmnəs]

义 *n.* 细长；苗条；微薄

例 The girl wears the slimness of her mother.

译 这个女孩和她母亲一样苗条。

80　slimy

['slaɪmɪ]

义 *adj.* 黏滑的；卑劣的

例 His feet slipped in the slimy mud.

译 他的脚在泥泞中滑倒了。

81　sling

[slɪŋ]

义 *v.* 投掷；吊起　*n.* 吊索；投石器；抛掷

例 The engine was lifted in a sling of steel rope.

译 发动机是用钢索吊起来的。

---

82 slink

[slɪŋk]

义 *v.* 溜走；早产；潜逃

例 John was trying to slink into the house by the back door.

译 约翰试图从后门溜进房子。

83 slit

[slɪt]

义 *n.* 裂缝；狭长的切口

例 She watched them through a slit in the curtains.

译 她透过窗帘上的一条缝看着他们。

84 slither

['slɪðər]

义 *v.* (使)滑行，(使)滑动

例 A titanic snake has been identified as the top predator to walk, or at least slither, the land when the dinosaurs disappeared.

译 一条巨蟒被认为是恐龙消失后在陆地上行走或至少滑行的顶级捕食者。

85 slog

[slɑ:g]

义 *v.* 艰难行进；猛击　*n.* 一段时间的艰苦努力；猛击；长途跋涉

例 Writing the book took ten months of hard slog.

译 写这本书花了十个月的艰苦努力。

86 sloop

[slu:p]

义 *n.* 小帆船，单桅纵帆船

例 A sloop has only one central pole.

译 单桅帆船只有一根中央桅杆。

87 slop

[slɑ:p]

义 *v.* 涂上

例 The good news is that a combination of sunscreen and covering up can reduce melanoma rates, as shown by Australian figures from their slip slop-slap-campaign.

译 好消息是，根据澳大利亚的日光浴防晒大赛的结果，结合使用防晒霜和遮盖物可以降低黑色素瘤的发病率。

88 slosh

[slɑ:ʃ]

义 *v.* 泼溅；搅动

例 The children were sloshing water everywhere.

译 孩子们把水撒得四处都是。

89 slouch

[slaʊtʃ]

义 *n.* 没精打采的样子；下垂；笨人

例 She's no slouch on the guitar.

译 她弹吉他弹得很好。

90 slovenly

['slʌvnlɪ]

义 *adj.* 不修边幅的；邋遢的

例 He grew lazy and slovenly in his habits.

译 他养成了懒惰和邋遢的习惯。

91　slowdown

['sləʊdaʊn]

义 *n.* 降低速度，减速

例 There has been a sharp slowdown in economic growth.

译 经济增长急剧放缓。

92　slowness

[sləʊnəs]

义 *n.* 缓慢；迟钝

例 The elderly woman moved with her deliberate slowness back to her daughter.

译 老妇人慢条斯理地走回她女儿身边。

93　sluggishly

['slʌgɪʃlɪ]

义 *adv.* 懒怠地；慢吞吞地

例 The river is silted up and the water flows sluggishly.

译 河水淤塞，水流缓慢。

94　slump

[slʌmp]

义 *v.* 大幅度下跌；使倒下　*n.* 突然下跌；不景气；萧条

例 The toy industry is in a slump.

译 玩具业陷入了萧条。

95　slur

[slɜ:r]

义 *n.* 诽谤；耻辱

例 She had dared to cast a slur on his character.

译 她竟敢诋毁他的人格。

96　slurp

[slɜ:rp]

义 *v.* 出声地吃或喝　*n.* 吃的声音；啜食者

例 She took a slurp from her mug.

译 她从杯子里啜了一口。

97　slushy

['slʌʃɪ]

义 *adj.* 融雪的；泥泞的；无聊的

例 Here and there a drift across the road was wet and slushy.

译 路上不时有雪堆，又湿又泥泞。

98　smack

[smæk]

义 *v.* 用巴掌打，掴；猛击，重撞　*n.* 掌击声；打

例 I think it's wrong to smack children.

译 我认为打孩子是不对的。

99　smattering

['smætərɪŋ]

义 *n.* 一知半解；一点点

例 He only has a smattering of French.

译 他只懂一点法语。

List 17

1 smear
[smɪr]

义 *v.* 涂抹；弄脏
例 The children had smeared mud on the walls.
译 那几个孩子往墙上涂抹泥巴。

2 smelly
['smelɪ]

义 *adj.* 难闻的，臭的
例 Some plants pump out smelly chemicals to keep insects away.
译 有些植物释放难闻的化学物质以驱赶昆虫。

3 smite
[smaɪt]

义 *v.* 重击；折磨；迷惑
例 The heroic leader charged into battle, ready to smite the enemy.
译 这位英勇的领袖冲上战场，准备痛击敌人。

4 smoothness
[smuːðnəs]

义 *n.* 柔滑；平滑；平坦
例 They admired the smoothness and efficiency with which the business was run.
译 他们钦佩企业经营的顺利和高效。

5 smuggler
['smʌɡlər]

义 *n.* 走私者
例 The smuggler shrugged to the bugler hugging the bug in the tugboat.
译 走私者对拖船中和臭虫挤在一起的号手耸耸肩膀。

6 snacking
[snækɪŋ]

义 *n.* 小吃，点心
例 The Italians know a thing or two about healthy snacking.
译 意大利人懂得如何健康吃零食。

7 snag
[snæɡ]

义 *n.* (隐伏的) 障碍，困难
例 There is one big snag.
译 有一个很大的障碍。

8 snapshot
['snæpʃɑːt]

义 *n.* 快照
例 Let me take a snapshot of you guys.
译 让我给大家拍张快照。

9 snare
[sner]

义 *n.* 陷阱；诱惑
例 I felt like an animal caught in a snare.
译 我觉得自己像一只困在陷阱里的动物。

10 snarl

[snɑ:rl]

义 *v.* 嚎叫；咆哮 *n.* 低吼；嚎叫

例 Her mouth was contorted in a snarl.

译 她的嘴扭曲着发出咆哮。

---

11 snazzy

['snæzɪ]

义 *adj.* 时髦的；华丽的

例 That's a snazzy necktie you have.

译 你的领带真时髦。

---

12 snide

[snaɪd]

义 *adj.* 卑鄙的；恶意的

例 When their period in history is mentioned, many hasten to attach a snide disclaimer or a wised-up dismissal.

译 当他们所处的那一段历史被提起时，很多人都会立刻附上鄙夷的论断，或是故作聪明的批评。

---

13 snob

[snɑ:b]

义 *n.* 势利小人；自命不凡的人

例 She's such a snob!

译 她真是个势利小人！

---

14 snobbish

['snɑ:bɪʃ]

义 *adj.* 势利的，自命不凡的

例 They had a snobbish dislike for their intellectual and social inferiors.

译 他们势利地讨厌智力和社会地位不如自己的人。

---

15 snorkel

['snɔ:rkl]

义 *n.* 水下通气管，通气管 *v.* 用水下通气管潜水

例 We snorkelled and did some waterskiing.

译 我们戴潜水通气管潜泳，并玩了一些水橇运动。

---

16 snout

[snaʊt]

义 *n.* 鼻口部

例 Fossils show how the nostrils of ancestral whales moved from the tip of the snout to the top of the head.

译 化石展现了鲸鱼的祖先的鼻孔是如何一步步地从嘴巴前端跑到头顶上去的。

---

17 snowboarder

['snəʊbɔ:rd]

义 *n.* 滑雪运动员，滑雪者

例 Shaun White is still one of the best snowboarders in the world.

译 肖恩·怀特仍然是全世界最优秀的滑雪运动员之一。

---

18 snowbound

['snəʊbaʊnd]

义 *adj.* 被雪困住的

例 The farm became snowbound.

译 农场被雪封住了。

19 snowfall

['snəʊfɔːl]

义 *n.* 降雪；降雪量

例 The heaviest snowfalls today are expected in the south east.

译 今天最大的降雪预计将出现在东南部地区。

---

20 snowmelt

['snəʊ,melt]

义 *n.* 融雪水

例 Marc fires up the stove for fresh water from snowmelt.

译 马克点燃炉子，从融雪中取水。

---

21 snowmobile

['snəʊməʊbiːl]

义 *n.* 履带式雪上汽车

例 Snowmobiles may use this road.

译 雪地摩托可以走这条路。

---

22 snowpack

['snəʊ,pæk]

义 *n.* (发电用的)积雪场

例 Rain in winter can have serious impacts when it falls on an existing snowpack or on frozen ground.

译 当冬天的雨水落在现有的积雪场或冻土上时，会产生严重的影响。

---

23 snowshoe

['snəʊʃuː]

义 *n.* 雪鞋

例 To move over the snow, Inuit people wore special snowshoes on their feet.

译 为了在雪地上移动，因纽特人穿上了特制的雪鞋。

---

24 snub

[snʌb]

义 *v.* 冷落；斥责   *n.* 冷落；止住

例 Ryan took it as a snub.

译 瑞安认为这是一种冷落。

---

25 snug

[snʌg]

义 *adj.* 温暖舒适的；合身的；安全的

例 Each has a snug mezzanine area and an antler-fenced balcony about eight meters above ground.

译 每个房间都有一个舒适的夹层和一个离地约 8 米高的鹿角栅栏阳台。

---

26 snuggle

['snʌgl]

义 *v.* 依偎；舒服地蜷伏

例 I love to snuggle and cuddle with you.

译 我喜欢偎依着你，拥抱着你。

---

27 socialization

[,səʊʃələ'zeɪʃn]

义 *n.* 适应社会生活；社会(主义)化

例 Female socialization emphasizes getting along with others.

译 女性的社会化强调与他人相处。

28 sociological

['səʊsɪə'lɑ:dʒɪkl]

义 *adj.* 社会学的；社会的

例 Psychological and sociological studies were emphasizing the importance of the family.

译 心理学和社会学研究强调家庭的重要性。

29 sociopolitical

[ˌsəʊsɪəʊpə'lɪtɪkl]

义 *adj.* 社会政治的

例 He was influenced by the sociopolitical cliquism in late Ming Dynasty.

译 他受到晚明社会政治派系的影响。

30 softball

['sɔ:ftbɔ:l]

义 *n.* 垒球

例 The softball is solid.

译 垒球是实心的。

31 soggy

['sɑ:gɪ]

义 *adj.* 湿而软的，潮湿的

例 We squelched over the soggy ground.

译 我们咯吱咯吱地走过泥泞的土地。

32 sojourner

['sʌdʒɜ:rnər]

义 *n.* 逗留者；旅居者

例 I am a sojourner of that village.

译 我在那个村庄旅居。

33 solicit

[sə'lɪsɪt]

义 *v.* 恳求；征求；勾引

例 They were planning to solicit funds from a number of organizations.

译 他们正计划向一些组织募款。

34 solo

['səʊləʊ]

义 *v.* 独奏，独唱

例 He appeared quite nervous the first time he soloed before a large audience.

译 他第一次在大庭广众面前独唱时显得很紧张。

35 soloist

['səʊləʊɪst]

义 *n.* 独奏者，独唱者

例 Every group also has a few soloist performers.

译 每个团体中也会有一些独奏演员。

36 solstice

['sɑ:lstəs]

义 *n.* 至，至点，至日

例 The total lunar eclipse coincided with the date of the December Solstice.

译 这次月全食正好与冬至日重合。

37 solver

['sɑːlvər]

义 *n.* 解算机；求解程序；解决者

例 I'm a sequential problem solver.

译 我是一个循序渐进的问题解决者。

---

38 somber

['sɑːmbə]

义 *adj.* 阴暗的；忧郁的

例 There were the two somber figures still following him, though their black sacks were drenched and dripping with water.

译 那两个阴森的人影仍然跟在他后面，虽然他们的黑麻袋已经湿透了，而且还在滴水。

---

39 songwriter

['sɔːŋraɪtər]

义 *n.* 歌曲作家；歌曲作者

例 Sheriden was already known to Hiller as a songwriter.

译 希勒已经知道谢里登是一位作曲家。

---

40 songwriting

['sɔːŋraɪtɪŋ]

义 *n.* 作词

例 Taking up songwriting, he wrote "Brother, Can You Spare a Dime?"

译 开始写歌时，他写道："兄弟，能给我一毛钱吗？"

---

41 sonic

['sɑːnɪk]

义 *adj.* 音波的；音速的

例 He activated the door with the miniature sonic transmitter.

译 他用微型声波发射器开启了门。

---

42 sooty

['sʊtɪ]

义 *adj.* 煤烟熏黑了的；乌黑的

例 Their uniforms are torn and sooty.

译 他们的制服破破烂烂并沾满了烟灰。

---

43 sort

[sɔːrt]

义 *n.* 种类；某一种人

例 He's a reasonable sort of person.

译 他是个通情达理的人。

---

44 soulful

['səʊlfl]

义 *adj.* 深情的；充满感情的

例 There is something undeniably soulful about the eerie whine of the highland bagpipes.

译 不可否认，高地风笛的怪诞哀鸣有着深情的一面。

---

45 soundly

['saʊndlɪ]

义 *adv.* 完全地；坚牢地

例 These houses are soundly built.

译 这些房子建得很牢固。

46　soundness

['saʊndnəs]

义　*n.* 健康；完好

例　If you're taking part in a debate you need to persuade the listeners of the soundness of your argument.

译　如果你参加辩论，你需要让听众相信你的论点是正确的。

47　soundproof

['saʊndpru:f]

义　*adj.* 隔音的

例　The studio isn't soundproof.

译　录音室不隔音。

48　southbound

['saʊθbaʊnd]

义　*adj.* 向南行驶的

例　He heard a whistle, a train coming toward him, southbound from Columbia.

译　他听到了汽笛声，一列火车从哥伦比亚向南驶来。

49　southernmost

['sʌðərnməʊst]

义　*adj.* 最南的

例　The ancient province of Satsuma lies in the southernmost part of the Japanese island of Kyushu.

译　古老的萨摩省位于日本九州岛的最南端。

50　southwestern

[ˌsaʊθ'westən]

义　*adj.* 西南的

例　The first German village in southwestern Siberia was founded a century ago by settlers from the Volga region.

译　一个世纪前，来自伏尔加地区的定居者在西伯利亚西南部建立了第一个德国村庄。

51　spaciousness

['speɪʃəsnəs]

义　*n.* 开阔；宽广

例　The spaciousness of this land reigns and pushes against the borders of self-censorship and hesitation.

译　这片土地的广阔支配并推动着自我审查和犹豫的边界。

52　spade

[speɪd]

义　*n.* 铲子，铁锹

例　The spade jarred on something metal.

译　铁锹在某种金属上发出刺耳的响声。

53　spaniel

['spænjəl]

义　*n.* 西班牙猎犬

例　The dog was similar in general appearance to a spaniel.

译　这只狗的外表和西班牙猎犬很相似。

54　sparingly

['speərɪŋlɪ]

义　*adv.* 节俭地；保守地

例　Medication is used sparingly.

译　谨慎用药。

55 sparkle

['spɑ:rkl]

义 *n.* 闪耀；火花

例 The performance lacked sparkle.

译 该表演缺乏亮点。

---

56 sparsely

[spɑ:slɪ]

义 *adv.* 稀疏地；贫乏地

例 There are also sparsely distributed, highly nutritious fruits, and Bell found that only the Thomson's gazelles eat much of these.

译 这里还有一些分布稀疏、营养丰富的水果，贝尔发现只有汤氏瞪羚才会大量食用这些水果。

---

57 spasm

['spæzəm]

义 *n.* 抽筋；痉挛；一阵发作

例 I knew by instinct, by the spasm of my tendons and the ache in my bones, before I ever turned toward the clock or heard my coach scream, that I had made it.

译 凭借着直觉、我的肌腱痉挛和骨头的疼痛，在我转向时钟或听到我的教练尖叫之前，我知道我成功了。

---

58 spatially

['speɪʃəlɪ]

义 *adv.* 空间地；存在于空间地

例 The last dimension, how everything relates, is implied spatially.

译 最后一个维度，即事物之间的关系，是空间上隐含的。

---

59 spatter

['spætər]

义 *n.* 少量；洒

例 It gets nice and cool after a spatter of rain.

译 下了一阵雨后，天气凉快多了。

---

60 spearhead

['spɪrhed]

义 *n.* 突击队的先遣队；攻击的最前线

例 This spearhead raises many questions.

译 这个先锋队提出了许多问题。

---

61 specialization

[ˌspeʃəlaɪ'zeɪʃn]

义 *n.* 专门化；特殊化

例 A caste system consists of ranked groups, each with a different economic specialization.

译 种姓制度由有等级的群体组成，每个群体都有不同的经济分工。

---

62 specialty

['speʃəltɪ]

义 *n.* 专长；特性

例 Her specialty is taxation law.

译 她的专长是税法。

---

63 speck

[spek]

义 *n.* 斑点；少量

例 The ship was now just a speck in the distance.

译 那艘船现在只是远处的一个小点。

64　spectral

['spektrəl]

义 *adj.* 幽灵的；光谱的

例 So how do we know which spectral patterns match up with which elements?

译 那么，我们如何知道哪些光谱模式与哪些元素相匹配呢？

65　spectroscope

['spektrəskəʊp]

义 *n.* 分光镜

例 We put an infrared microscope—a spectroscope—on tiny tiny bits of paint.

译 我们把红外线显微镜——一个分光镜——放在很少很少的颜料上。

66　speechless

['spi:tʃləs]

义 *adj.* 说不出话的；不会说话的

例 Alex was almost speechless with rage and despair.

译 亚历克斯因愤怒和绝望几乎说不出话来。

67　sperm

[spɜ:rm]

义 *n.* 精液；精子

例 The male sperm fertilizes the female egg.

译 雄性的精子使雌性的卵子受精。

68　spew

[spju:]

义 *v.* 喷出，涌出

例 Europa, too, may spew out water on occasion.

译 木卫二也同样时不时地有水流喷涌而出。

69　spiderweb

[s'paɪdəweb]

义 *n.* 蜘蛛网

例 The trees became covered in a cocoon of spiderwebs.

译 树上结满了蜘蛛网。

70　spidery

['spaɪdərɪ]

义 *adj.* 细长的；蜘蛛一般的；蜘蛛网一般的

例 Writing his computations in a spidery script, with a quill dipped in the ink of oak galls, Newton correctly concluded that the nearest stars are about 100,000 times the distance from Earth to the Sun, about 10 trillion miles away.

译 牛顿用蜘蛛网般的笔迹写下了他的计算，用一支羽毛笔蘸上橡树的墨水，他正确地得出结论：最近的恒星大约是地球到太阳距离的 10 万倍，大约 10 万亿英里远。

71　spike

[spaɪk]

义 *n.* 尖状物；峰值

例 During some lightning storms, a bolt can send a 500-volt spike through the nearest utility pole.

译 在一些雷暴中，一道闪电可以通过最近的电线杆发出 500 伏特的尖峰电压。

---

72 spinal

['spaɪnl]

义 *adj.* 脊骨的；尖刺的

例 This movement lengthens your spine and tones the spinal nerves.

译 这一动作舒展脊椎，使脊神经更加强健。

---

73 spindly

['spɪndlɪ]

义 *adj.* 细长的；纤弱的

例 I did have rather spindly legs.

译 我的腿确实比较瘦长。

---

74 spiraling

['spaɪrəlɪŋ]

义 *adj.* 盘旋的；螺旋形的

例 In her works, the spiraling spindle represented the beginning of chaos.

译 在她的作品中，螺旋形的纺锤代表了混乱的开始。

---

75 spire

['spaɪər]

义 *n.* (教堂的) 尖塔，尖顶，螺旋

例 No one would dream of straightening out the church's knobbly spire.

译 没人会想到要把教堂那凹凸不平的尖顶弄直。

---

76 splash

[splæʃ]

义 *n.* 溅泼 (声)；溅污的斑点

例 There was a splash, and then silence.

译 先是哗啦一声，接着一片寂静。

---

77 splatter

['splætər]

义 *v.* 使水等飞溅；叽叽喳喳讲个不停

例 Coffee had splattered across the front of his shirt.

译 他的衬衣前襟上洒了一大片咖啡。

---

78 splay

[spleɪ]

义 *v.* 展开；张开　*n.* 展开；斜面

例 I love polka dots and this pattern has a more random splay of dots and almost looks like a hazy animal print from a distance.

译 我喜欢波尔卡圆点，这种布料上有更加随意展开的圆点，从远处看几乎就像模糊的动物花纹。

---

79 splice

[splaɪs]

义 *v.* 拼接，接合　*n.* 接合；衔接

例 He taught me to edit and splice film.

译 他教我剪辑电影。

80　splurge

[splɜːrdʒ]

义　*v./n.* 挥霍；炫耀

例　But we had agreed ahead of time to splurge on one night in a castle.

译　但我们已经提前商定在城堡里挥霍一晚。

81　spoilsport

['spɔɪlspɔːrt]

义　*n.* 损坏他人快乐的人，扫兴者

例　This will be a fun trip. Don't be a spoilsport.

译　这趟旅行会很好玩的。不要扫兴。

82　spokesperson

['spəʊkspɜːrsn]

义　*n.* 代言人，发言人

例　A spokesperson for the food industry said the TV program was alarmist.

译　食品工业的发言人说那个电视节目是危言耸听。

83　spoof

[spuːf]

义　*n.* 滑稽模仿；诓骗；愚弄

例　It's a spoof on horror movies.

译　这是对恐怖电影的恶搞。

84　spool

[spuːl]

义　*n.* 线轴；缠线用的卷盘

例　This time I'll do it right with a spool of thread.

译　这次我要用一卷线把它做好。

85　sportscaster

['spɔːrtskæstər]

义　*n.* 担任比赛实况转播或说明的广播员

例　In an interview with a sportscaster last month, he said, "I don't know if I would join some champion team in the future."

译　在上个月接受体育节目主持人的采访时，他说："我不知道将来是否会加入冠军队伍。"

86　sportsmanship

['spɔːrtsmənʃɪp]

义　*n.* 体育精神，运动员精神

例　Schools should foster children's interest in sports to instill into them the values of teamwork and sportsmanship.

译　学校应该培养孩子们对体育的兴趣，向他们灌输团队合作的价值观和体育精神。

87　spotter

['spɑːtər]

义　*n.* 观察员

例　I was a devoted train spotter.

译　我是个酷爱看火车的人。

88　sprawl

[sprɔːl]

义　*v.* 伸开四肢坐（或躺）；蔓延；扩展，延伸

例　The town sprawled along the side of the lake.

| | 译 | 小镇顺着湖的边缘扩展。 |

89 springboard
['sprɪŋbɔːrd]

义	*n.* 跳板；出发点
例	The 1981 budget was the springboard for an economic miracle.
译	1981 年的预算是经济奇迹的跳板。

90 springtime
['sprɪŋtaɪm]

义	*n.* 春季；青春期；初期
例	Springtime is coming.
译	春天来了。

91 sprint
[sprɪnt]

义	*v.* 全力奔跑；冲刺　*n.* 冲刺，快跑；短跑比赛
例	She won in a sprint finish.
译	她在冲刺中获胜。

92 sprite
[spraɪt]

义	*n.* 精灵
例	Once upon a time there was a wicked sprite, and he was the most mischievous of all sprites.
译	从前有一个邪恶的精灵，他是所有精灵中最淘气的一个。

93 sputter
['spʌtər]

义	*v.* 喷溅；发噼啪声
例	In 1874, Felix du Temple, a French naval officer, watched the steam-powered plane he devised speed down a ski-jump-like ramp and sputter through the air with a young sailor at the helm.
译	1874 年，法国海军军官费利克斯·杜·坦普尔看着他设计的蒸汽动力飞机在一个年轻水手的驾驶下，从一个类似跳台滑雪的坡道上快速下降，并在空中噼啪作响。

94 squarely
['skwerlɪ]

义	*adv.* 直接地
例	She looked at me squarely in the eye.
译	她直视着我的眼睛。

95 squat
[skwɑːt]

义	*v.* 蹲下，蹲坐；擅自占地　*n.* 蹲坐，蹲下
例	He bent to a squat and gathered the puppies on his lap.
译	他弯下腰蹲下来，把小狗们抱在腿上。

96 squeaky
['skwiːkɪ]

义	*adj.* 短促尖声的
例	He had a squeaky voice.
译	他的声音很尖。

97 squirm

| 义 | *v.* (因不舒适、羞愧或紧张而) 蠕动，扭动 |

[skwɜːrm]

例 He gave a feeble shrug and tried to squirm free.

译 他无力地耸耸肩，想扭动身子挣脱。

98　stabbing

['stæbɪŋ]

义 ***adj.*** (疼痛) 突然而剧烈的　***n.*** 持刀伤人事件

例 The stabbing was reported in the local press.

译 当地媒体报道了持刀伤人事件。

99　stagecoach

['steɪdʒkəʊtʃ]

义 ***n.*** 驿马车；公共马车

例 He invented the famous trick of sliding under a moving stagecoach.

译 他发明了在移动的公共马车下滑行的著名把戏。

100　stagnant

['stægnənt]

义 ***adj.*** 不流动的；不景气的

例 They have stagnant or shrinking markets for goods and services.

译 他们的商品和服务市场停滞或萎缩了。

List 18

1	**stainless** ['steɪnlɪs]	义 *adj.* 无瑕疵的；不锈的 例 The modern glass, marble, stainless steel, and concrete structure stands in striking contrast to the ancient monuments, such as the Parthenon, on the nearby hill of the Acropolis. 译 现代的玻璃、大理石、不锈钢和混凝土结构与雅典卫城附近山上的帕特农神庙等古代遗迹形成了鲜明的对比。
2	**stampede** [stæm'piːd]	义 *n.* (人群的)蜂拥 例 A stampede broke out when the doors opened. 译 门打开时发生了踩踏事件。
3	**standby** ['stændbaɪ]	义 *n.* 备用；待命者 例 Five ambulances are on standby at the port. 译 五辆救护车在那个港口待命。
4	**starburst** ['stɑːrbɜːrst]	义 *n.* 星暴 例 Starbursts may have more subtle effects as well. 译 星暴可能还有更微妙的影响。
5	**stargazer** ['stɑːrgeɪzər]	义 *n.* 占星师；天文学家 例 An amateur stargazer in Australia spotted the impression last Sunday. 译 来自澳大利亚的一名天文爱好者已于上周日观测到此现象。
6	**starkly** [stɑːrklɪ]	义 *adv.* 严酷地；明显地 例 The interior is starkly simple. 译 室内设计明显很简单。
7	**starlight** ['stɑːrlaɪt]	义 *n.* 星光 例 He stopped to try to adjust his vision to the faint starlight. 译 他停下来，试着使眼睛适应昏暗的星光。
8	**starry** ['stɑːrɪ]	义 *adj.* 星光照耀的；闪亮的 例 She stared up at the starry sky. 译 她抬头仰望繁星点点的天空。
9	**starship** ['stɑːrʃɪp]	义 *n.* 星际飞船 例 Starships can only be produced at bases which have built shipyards.

译 星际飞船只能在建造造船厂的基地生产。

---

10 starstruck

['stɑːrˌstrək]

义 *adj.* 崇拜明星的；一心想当明星的

例 At first I was a bit starstruck but then I realized they were just doing their job, same as me.

译 一开始我有点被明星迷住了，但后来我意识到他们只是在做他们的工作，就像我一样。

---

11 starter

['stɑːrtər]

义 *n.* 起动机；开胃菜

例 She made a salad of crisp vegetables for a starter.

译 她做了一份脆蔬菜沙拉作为开胃菜。

---

12 starvation

[stɑːr'veɪʃn]

义 *n.* 饿死，饥饿

例 If supplies ran short during a long voyage, and no fish or rainwater replenished them, then starvation became a possibility.

译 如果在长途航行中补给不足，又没有鱼和雨水补充，那么（人）就可能挨饿。

---

13 stately

['steɪtlɪ]

义 *adj.* 庄严的；堂皇的；高贵的

例 The building rose before him, tall and stately.

译 那栋大楼耸立在他面前，高大而又雄伟。

---

14 statewide

['steɪtwaɪd]

义 *adj.* 全州范围的

例 He argues that we need statewide uniformity.

译 他认为我们需要全州统一。

---

15 stationery

['steɪʃənerɪ]

义 *n.* 文具；信笺

例 They sell stationery and stuff like that.

译 他们卖文具之类的东西。

---

16 steadfast

['stedfæst]

义 *adj.* 坚定的；毫不动摇的

例 He remained steadfast in his belief that he had done the right thing.

译 他始终坚信自己做了正确的事。

---

17 steadily

['stedəlɪ]

义 *adv.* 稳定地；逐步地

例 The company's exports have been increasing steadily.

译 这家公司的出口量一直在稳步增长。

---

18 stealth

义 *n.* 秘密行动；鬼祟

[stelθ]

例 Lions rely on stealth when hunting.

译 狮子捕食全凭偷袭。

---

19 steamboat

['sti:mbəʊt]

义 *n.* 汽艇

例 Tom went on whitewashing the fence—paid no attention to the steamboat.

译 汤姆继续刷着栅栏——没有注意到那艘汽船。

---

20 steamy

['sti:mɪ]

义 *adj.* 蒸汽多的；色情的

例 He puffed out his fat cheeks and let out a lungful of steamy breath.

译 他鼓起胖乎乎的腮帮子，呼出了一大口热气。

---

21 stench

[stentʃ]

义 *n.* 臭气；恶臭

例 The stench of burning rubber was overpowering.

译 燃烧的橡胶散发出令人窒息的恶臭。

---

22 stepchild

['steptʃaɪld]

义 *n.* 继子

例 Aging is the neglected stepchild of the human life cycle.

译 衰老是人类生命周期中被忽视的继子。

---

23 stereotypical

['sterɪətɪpɪkl]

义 *adj.* 刻板印象的，类型化的

例 These are men whose masculinity does not conform to stereotypical images of the unfeeling male.

译 这些男人的阳刚之气并不符合刻板印象中的冷酷无情的男性形象。

---

24 stern

[stɜ:rn]

义 *adj.* 严厉的，苛刻的

例 He cast a stern glance at the two men.

译 他严厉地看了那两个人一眼。

---

25 steward

['stu:ərd]

义 *n.* 乘务员；管家

例 They also claim that the security team elbowed aside a steward.

译 他们还声称，安保团队把一名乘务员挤到了一边。

---

26 stewardess

['stu:ərdəs]

义 *n.* 女乘务员；女管家

例 Some people think a girl who wants to be a stewardess must be pretty and helpful.

译 有些人认为一个想成为空姐的女孩必须漂亮而且乐于助人。

---

27 stewardship

['stu:ərdʃɪp]

义 *n.* 管理员、服务员等的职位和职责

例 The organization certainly prospered under his stewardship.

译 这个组织在他的领导下确实兴旺起来了。

---

28 stickler

['stɪklər]

义 *n.* 坚持……的人；难题

例 He was a stickler for punctuality and precision, for looking and sounding sharp, for taking the job seriously.

译 他是一个守时、讲究精确的人，因为他看起来和听起来都很犀利，对待工作很认真。

---

29 stifle

['staɪfl]

义 *v.* 扼杀；扑灭

例 The technology industry was coming under the sway of a dominant behemoth, one that had the potential to stifle innovation and squash its competitors.

译 科技行业正受到一个占据主导地位的庞然大物的支配，这个庞然大物有可能扼杀创新性，压垮竞争对手。

---

30 stigma

['stɪgmə]

义 *n.* 耻辱，污名

例 There is still a stigma attached to cancer.

译 癌症仍被人看作是一种耻辱的事。

---

31 stilted

['stɪltɪd]

义 *adj.* 踩高跷的；生硬的

例 We made polite, stilted conversation.

译 我们进行了礼貌而生硬的谈话。

---

32 stingray

['stɪŋreɪ]

义 *n.* 黄貂鱼，刺鳐

例 The giant freshwater Mekong River stingray is just one of many mega fish species that could be threatened by dam-building plans in the Mekong River Basin.

译 巨大的湄公河淡水黄貂鱼只是众多巨型鱼类中的一种，它们可能会受到湄公河流域大坝建设计划的威胁。

---

33 stint

[stɪnt]

义 *v.* 节省；限制；＜古＞停止

例 We don't need to stint ourselves—have some more!

译 我们不需要节制自己——再多吃一点！

---

34 stipulate

['stɪpjʊleɪt]

义 *v.* 规定，保证

例 Some laws also stipulate in explicit terms that citizens have obligations to take care of parents and raise children.

译 一些法律还明确规定，公民有照顾父母和抚养孩子的义务。

---

35 stirring

['stɜːrɪŋ]

义 *n.* 搅动

例 Then came stirring and molding, drying and carving.

译 然后是搅拌、成型、干燥和雕刻。

---

36 stirrup

['stɪrəp]

义 *n.* 镫形具；马镫，【建】(抗剪的)箍筋

例 It is about the size of a grain of rice and is called the stirrup.

译 它大约有一粒米那么大，被称为马镫。

---

37 stockpile

['stɑːkpaɪl]

义 *v.* 贮存；储蓄；积累　*n.* 贮藏堆；积蓄

例 An unprecedented number of unsold cars in Japan have forced Toyota to stockpile them in the parking lots of Fuji Speedway.

译 日本未售出的汽车数量空前之多，迫使丰田公司在富士高速公路的停车场囤车。

---

38 stocky

['stɑːkɪ]

义 *adj.* 矮胖的，健壮结实的

例 He is stocky though not chubby.

译 他长得敦实，可并不发胖。

---

39 stoke

[stəʊk]

义 *v.* 煽动

例 These demands are helping to stoke fears of civil war.

译 这些要求激起了对内战的恐惧。

---

40 stolid

['stɑːlɪd]

义 *adj.* 不易激动的；冷漠的；神经麻木的

例 He glanced furtively at the stolid faces of the two detectives.

译 他偷偷地瞄了一下两名侦探面无表情的脸。

---

41 stonewashed

['stəʊnwɔːʃt]

义 *adj.* 石磨的；砂洗的(服装)

例 The Foodys ended up selling enzymes to clarify apple juice, whiten paper, and give blue jeans that stonewashed look, without the stones.

译 Foodys 最终出售酶来澄清苹果汁、漂白纸，并使蓝色牛仔裤看起来像石磨水洗的，(实际上)并没有用到石头。

---

42 stony

['stəʊnɪ]

义 *adj.* 石头的，多石的

例 I mean, it's easier to find an iron meteorite or a stony iron.

译 我的意思是，铁陨石或石铁更容易找到。

---

43 stopover

['stɑːpəʊvər]

义 *n.* 中途停留

例 The Sunday flights will make a stopover in Paris.

译 星期天的航班将在巴黎作中途停留。

---

44 storefront

义 *n.* 店头，店面

['stɔːrfrʌnt]

例 They run their business from a small storefront.

译 他们在一个店面里做生意。

---

45 **storeroom**

['stɔːruːm]

义 *n.* 储藏室；库房

例 It became possible to have a café because the building has been extended, and we've now got a new office and storeroom area.

译 我们可以拥有咖啡厅，因为大楼扩建了，我们现在有了一个新的办公室和储藏室。

---

46 **storyboard**

['stɔːrɪbɔːrd]

义 *n.* (电影、电视节目或商业广告等的)情节串联图板

例 Identify further storyboard themes.

译 确定进一步故事板的主题。

---

47 **storyline**

['stɔːrɪlaɪn]

义 *n.* 故事情节

例 The storyline is deceptively simple.

译 故事情节看似简单。

---

48 **stovepipe**

['stəʊvˌpaɪp]

义 *n.* 火炉的烟囱；大礼帽

例 It required military discipline to get us out of bed in a chamber warmed only by the stovepipe, to draw on icy socks and frosty boots and go to milking cows.

译 我们需要军纪把我们从只靠烟囱取暖的房间里叫起来，穿上冰冷的袜子和冰冻的靴子，去挤牛奶。

---

49 **straddle**

['strædl]

义 *v.* 跨坐；把两腿叉开；观望

例 The mountains straddle the French-Swiss border.

译 这些山脉横跨法国和瑞士的边界。

---

50 **strainer**

['streɪnər]

义 *n.* 过滤器；拉紧者；松紧装置

例 We need to put potatoes into the small dish by the strainer.

译 我们需要把土豆放在滤网旁边的小盘子里。

---

51 **strap**

[stræp]

义 *n.* 皮带，带子

例 He looped the strap over his shoulder.

译 他把带子绕了一个圈挎在肩上。

---

52 **stray**

[streɪ]

义 *v.* 走失，迷路；入歧途，犯错误 *n.* 走失的家畜；浪子

例 The problem is that many have strayed.

译 问题是许多人已经误入歧途。

---

53 streak

[striːk]

义 *n.* 条纹；倾向

例 He had a reckless, self-destructive streak.

译 他个性鲁莽，有自我毁灭的倾向。

---

54 streamer

['striːmər]

义 *n.* 横幅；流光

例 Streamer is a new approach to captioning, note-taking and translation.

译 横幅是一种用于配字幕、记笔记和翻译的新方法。

---

55 streetlight

['striːtˌlaɪt]

义 *n.* 路灯，街灯

例 The windows misted, blurring the stark streetlight.

译 窗户蒙上了一层薄雾，使昏暗的街灯模糊不清。

---

56 strep

[strep]

义 *n.* 链球菌

例 Nicola got her prescription for strep.

译 尼古拉拿到了治疗链球菌的处方。

---

57 stretchy

['stretʃɪ]

义 *adj.* 有弹性的；容易伸长的

例 For tracksuits you need stretchy material fabric.

译 做田径服需要用有弹性的料子。

---

58 strew

[struː]

义 *v.* 散播；撒满

例 The racoons knock over the rubbish bins in search of food, and strew the contents all over the ground.

译 浣熊们翻翻垃圾箱寻找食物，并把里面的东西撒得满地都是。

---

59 stricture

['strɪktʃər]

义 *n.* 苛评；【医】狭窄

例 If stricture develops, bouginage will be needed.

译 如果出现狭窄，则需用探条扩张术。

---

60 stride

[straɪd]

义 *n.* 大步走；进步　*v.* 大步走；阔步走；跨越，跨过

例 They were joined by a newcomer who came striding across a field.

译 他们中又来了个新人，那人穿过一块田地大步走过来。

---

61 stringed

[strɪŋd]

义 *adj.* 有弦的，由弦乐器产生的

例 A symphony orchestra is composed of a variety of brass, woodwind, percussion and stringed instruments.

译 交响乐团是由各种铜管乐器、木管乐器、打击乐器和弦乐器组成的。

62　strive

[straɪv]

义 *v.* 努力，力求

例 Newspaper editors all strive to be first with a story.

译 报纸编辑都力争率先报道。

63　strobe

[strəʊb]

义 *n.* 频闪闪光灯

例 The gigantic strikes flash around us like a giant strobe.

译 巨大的撞击像巨大的闪光灯在我们周围闪烁。

64　stroller

['strəʊlər]

义 *n.* 婴儿车

例 A woman pushes a stroller down the sidewalk in front of us.

译 一个女人推着婴儿车走在我们前面的人行道上。

65　struction

['strʌkʃn]

义 *n.* 教育；结构式

例 The query and inspection system struction of multimedia image data is introduced.

译 介绍了多媒体图像数据查询与检测系统的结构。

66　stubbornly

['stʌbənlɪ]

义 *adv.* 顽固地，倔强地

例 Unemployment remains stubbornly high.

译 失业率居高不下。

67　stud

[stʌd]

义 *n.* 饰钉，钉状首饰

例 You can see studs on lots of front doors.

译 你能看到许多人家的大门上都装有饰钉。

68　studded

['stʌdɪd]

义 *adj.* 布满装饰钉的；镶嵌珠宝的

例 She insisted on wearing the heavy studded boots.

译 她坚持要穿带防滑钉的厚重靴子。

69　stumble

['stʌmbl]

义 *v.* 绊倒；犯错误

例 I hope you don't stumble over any event during the holiday.

译 我希望你在假期不要碰上任何事情。

70　stump

[stʌmp]

义 *n.* 树桩；残余部分

例 If you have a tree stump, check it for fungus.

译 如果你有一个树桩，可以在上面找找菌类。

71 stunningly

['stʌnɪŋlɪ]

义 *adv.* 惊人地；令人目瞪口呆地

例 She looked stunningly beautiful that night.

译 那天晚上她看起来美极了。

---

72 stupor

['stuːpər]

义 *n.* 昏迷，麻木，不省人事

例 The pain roused him from his drunken stupor.

译 疼痛把他从酒醉的昏迷中唤醒。

---

73 stylist

['staɪlɪst]

义 *n.* 设计师；造型师；文体家

例 She is now a writer and fashion stylist.

译 她现在是一名作家和时装设计师。

---

74 stylistic

[staɪ'lɪstɪk]

义 *adj.* 风格上的；文体上的

例 There are some stylistic elements in the statue that just don't make sense.

译 这尊雕像的有些风格元素是没有意义的。

---

75 stymie

['staɪmɪ]

义 *v.* 使……处于困难境地；妨碍

例 You'll encounter obstacles that might stymie some individuals.

译 你将会遇到可能让人停步不前的障碍。

---

76 subcategory

['sʌbˌkætɪˌɡɔːrɪ]

义 *n.* 子范畴；亚类

例 Think of the category and subcategory problems.

译 想想类别和子类别的问题。

---

77 subculture

['sʌbkʌltʃər]

义 *n.* 亚文化群

例 Anime subculture has a distinctive effect on juvenile delinquency.

译 动漫亚文化对青少年犯罪的影响极为显著。

---

78 subdivision

[ˌsʌbdɪ'vɪʒn]

义 *n.* 细分，分部；再分的部分

例 Months are a conventional subdivision of the year.

译 月是一年的常规划分。

---

79 subdue

[səb'duː]

义 *v.* 使服从；压制；减弱

例 Troops were called in to subdue the rebels.

译 军队被调来镇压叛乱分子。

---

80 subfreezing

义 *adj.* 低于冰点的

[sʌbˈfriːzɪŋ]

例 She saw them in the subfreezing cold on Thursday morning.

译 周四早上，她在严寒中看到了他们。

81 subgroup

[ˈsʌbgruːp]

义 *n.* 子群；隶属组织

例 However, the country is just a subgroup of the world.

译 然而国家只是世界的一个子群体。

82 subhuman

[ˌsʌbˈhjuːmən]

义 *adj.* 近似人类的；低于人类的

例 They were living in subhuman conditions.

译 他们生活在非人的条件下。

83 sublime

[səbˈlaɪm]

义 *v.* 升华

例 Though I didn't stay long in this distinctive and amazing area, my spirit had sublimed.

译 我在这风光奇异的地方待的时间不长，但我的心灵得到了升华。

84 submersible

[səbˈmɜːrsəbl]

义 *adj.* 能潜水的（=submergible）

例 Submersible pumps of different sizes have different scope.

译 不同规格的潜水电泵有不同的使用范围。

85 subservient

[səbˈsɜːrvɪənt]

义 *adj.* 屈从的；奉承的

例 He was subservient and servile.

译 他卑躬屈膝。

86 substantially

[səbˈstænʃəlɪ]

义 *adv.* 大量地，可观地；大体上，基本上

例 The costs have increased substantially.

译 费用已大幅增加。

87 subtitle

[ˈsʌbtaɪtl]

义 *n.* 副标题（书本中的）；说明或对白的字幕

例 I hope the book's subtitle conveys that information.

译 我希望这本书的副标题传达出这一信息。

88 subtly

[ˈsʌtlɪ]

义 *adv.* 巧妙地；精细地

例 The truth is subtly different.

译 事实却略有不同。

89 subversively

义 *adv.* 颠覆性地；破坏性地

[səb'vɜ:rsɪvlɪ]

例 The movie is a fine, terrifying tragic poem that is also, at times, subversively funny: the women who like Brandon seem to want the feminine as well as the masculine in a lover.

译 这部电影是一首优美、恐怖的悲剧性诗歌，有时也非常有趣：喜欢布兰登的女性似乎既想要情人的女性气质，也想要情人的男性气质。

---

90 successively

[sək'sesɪvlɪ]

义 *adv.* 一个接一个地

例 In most fish they contract successively to throw the body into sinuous waves, which propel it forward.

译 大多数鱼类会连续收缩，把身体猛推入波浪中，推动身体向前。

---

91 succulence

['sʌkjələns]

义 *n.* 鲜美多汁，青饲料

例 In order to endure salinity, salt-dilution halophyte, the Suaeda salsa took the most important measures of succulence of some organs.

译 为了耐盐，稀释盐的盐生植物盐蓬采取了对某些器官采取了最重要的肉质化措施。

---

92 sucker

['sʌkər]

义 *n.* 傻瓜；吸管

例 I'm such a sucker for romance.

译 我对浪漫情有独钟。

---

93 suction

['sʌkʃn]

义 *v.* 吸；抽吸；吸出　*n.* 吸；吸入；吸水管

例 Michael was showing the nurse how to suction his saliva.

译 迈克尔正演示给护士看如何吸出他的唾液。

---

94 suffrage

['sʌfrɪdʒ]

义 *n.* 投票；选举权；参政权

例 The economic development theory is inadequate to explain certain historical facts about the implementation of women's suffrage.

译 经济发展理论不足以解释实施妇女选举权的某些历史事实。

---

95 sugarcane

['ʃʊgəˌkeɪn]

义 *n.* 甘蔗

例 Sugarcane needs less land than maize.

译 甘蔗需要的土地比玉米少。

---

96 suitability

[ˌsjuːtə'bɪlətɪ]

义 *n.* 适当，适合

例 His suitability for the job is open to question.

译 他是否适合这项工作还有待商榷。

---

97 suitor

['suːtər]

义 *n.* 求购公司；买主

例 The company was making little progress in trying to find a suitor.

译 该公司在寻找一家买主方面进展甚微。

98　sulky

['sʌlkɪ]

义 *adj.* 生气的；阴沉的

例 Sarah had looked sulky all morning.

译 萨拉整个上午都闷闷不乐。

99　sully

['sʌlɪ]

义 *v.* 玷污；弄脏

例 I felt loath to sully the gleaming brass knocker by handling it.

译 我不愿意用手去抓那个闪亮的黄铜门环以免把它弄脏。

100　sumac

['ʃuːmæk]

义 *n.* 漆树；漆树木料

例 There was the smell of sumac, orange and eucalyptus.

译 空气里有漆树、橙树和桉树的味道。

List 19

1	**sump** [sʌmp]	义 *n.* 污水坑；机油箱
		例 Excess oil is returned to a sump for re-use.
		译 多余的油被回收到机油箱中重复使用。

2	**sumptuous** ['sʌmptʃʊəs]	义 *adj.* 华丽的；奢侈的
		例 He lay down upon a sumptuous divan, and proceeded to instruct himself with honest zeal.
		译 他在一张豪华的长沙发上躺下，开始以真诚的热情自学。

3	**sunbather** ['sʌnbeɪðə]	义 *n.* 沐日光浴者
		例 As any sunbather will attest, too much of a good thing can be bad.
		译 正如每位日光浴者都能证明的那样，有益的事，做过头了也不好。

4	**sundown** ['sʌndaʊn]	义 *n.* 日落时分
		例 The fighting broke out about two hours after sundown.
		译 战斗在日落两小时后爆发。

5	**sundry** ['sʌndrɪ]	义 *adj.* 各种各样的；杂七杂八的
		例 She was known to all and sundry as Bella.
		译 大家都叫她贝拉。

6	**sunlike** ['sʌnlaɪk]	义 *adj.* 太阳似的
		例 According to observations of young sunlike stars, our Sun may have lost as much as six percent of its initial mass.
		译 根据对年轻的类太阳恒星的观察，我们的太阳可能损失了其初始质量的 6%。

7	**sunray** ['sʌnreɪ]	义 *n.* 太阳光线
		例 I would sit against the rock and feel the pleasure of the sunrays trapped in the rock warming my back.
		译 我会坐在岩石上，感受被困在岩石中的阳光温暖我的背部的乐趣。

8	**sunscreen** ['sʌnskriːn]	义 *n.* (防晒油中的)遮光剂；防晒霜
		例 Reapply sunscreen hourly and after swimming.
		译 每小时和游泳后重新涂抹防晒霜。

9	**superbly** [suː'pɜːrblɪ]	义 *adv.* 壮丽地；极度地
		例 The orchestra played superbly.

译 管弦乐队演奏得棒极了。

---

10 supercomputer

['suːpərkəmpjuːtər]

义 *n.* 【计】巨型计算机，超级计算机

例 Supercomputers are big-ticket items.

译 超级计算机是高价商品。

---

11 supercomputing

[suːpərkəm'pjuːtɪŋ]

义 *n.* 超级计算

例 But first, some background on the supercomputing cluster.

译 但首先，让我们了解一些超级计算集群的背景知识。

---

12 superimpose

[ˌsuːpərɪm'pəʊz]

义 *v.* 置于某物之上；添加

例 She has tried to superimpose her own attitudes onto this ancient story.

译 她试图把自己的态度强加在这个古老的故事上。

---

13 supernova

[ˌsjuːpə'nəʊvə]

义 *n.* 超新星（复数形式为 supernovae）

例 Smaller light echoes have been seen around supernovae.

译 可在超新星附近看见规模较小的光回音。

---

14 superstar

['suːpərstɑːr]

义 *n.* 超级明星

例 She rose from being a nobody to become a superstar.

译 她从无名小卒一跃成为超级明星。

---

15 superstore

['suːpərstɔːr]

义 *n.* 大型超级市场

例 Superstores are roughly 200,000 square feet, and parking lots are about four times that.

译 超市大约有 20 万平方英尺，停车场大约是这个面积的四倍。

---

16 supervision

[ˌsjuːpə'vɪʒn]

义 *n.* 监督；管理

例 The old man's will was executed under the personal supervision of the lawyer.

译 那位老人的遗嘱是在律师的亲自监督下执行的。

---

17 supplemental

[ˌsʌplɪ'mentl]

义 *adj.* 补充的，增补的；追加的

例 Do we really need all this supplemental protein?

译 我们真的需要这些补充蛋白质吗？

---

18 supplementation

[ˌsʌplɪmen'teɪʃn]

义 *n.* 增补；追加

例 The product provided inadequate vitamin and mineral supplementation.

译 该产品提供的维生素和矿物质补充不足。

---

19 surfer

['sɜːrfər]

义 *n.* 冲浪者

例 Sea seems to be his home for a surfer.

译 对于冲浪者来说大海就像他们的家。

---

20 surreal

[sə'riːəl]

义 *adj.* 超现实的，离奇的

例 They are just too surreal.

译 它们太离奇了。

---

21 surrogate

['sɜːrəgət]

义 *n.* 代理人；代用品；代孕者

例 She saw him as a sort of surrogate father.

译 在她心目中，他仿佛是能替代父亲角色的人。

---

22 susceptibility

[sə,septə'bɪlətɪ]

义 *n.* 敏感性；感受性；磁化率

例 Stress reactions can reduce the disease fighting effectiveness of the body's immune system, thereby increasing susceptibility to illnesses ranging from colds to cancer.

译 应激反应会降低人体免疫系统对抗疾病的能力，从而提高患从感冒到癌症等各种疾病的概率。

---

23 suspension

[sə'spenʃn]

义 *n.* 暂停；悬浮；悬架，减震装置

例 The car's improved suspension gives you a smoother ride.

译 这辆汽车改进后的悬架使得行驶更加平稳。

---

24 suture

['suːtʃər]

义 *n.* 缝合；缝合处；缝合用的线

例 Sutures or stitches that hold a wound or cut together don't always work well and can lead to infections.

译 用来缝合伤口的缝合针或缝合线并不总是有效，而且可能会导致感染。

---

25 swaddle

['swɑːdl]

义 *v.* 束缚；用襁褓包

例 Swaddle your newborn baby so that she feels secure.

译 用襁褓包住你刚出生的婴儿，使她感到安全。

---

26 swampy

['swɑːmpɪ]

义 *adj.* 沼泽似的，沼泽地的

例 Malaria is still rampant in some swampy regions.

译 疟疾在一些沼泽地区仍然猖獗。

---

27 swash

义 *v.* 冲洗；泼

['swɔːʃ]

例 I like to live by the sea and hear the waves swashing.

译 我喜欢住在海边，听海浪拍打（礁石）。

---

28 sweaty

['swetɪ]

义 *adj.* 汗流浃背的，出汗的

例 The wet heat smacked him in the face like a big sweaty hand.

译 湿热就像一只汗流浃背的大手拍打在他的脸上。

---

29 sweetheart

['swiːthɑːrt]

义 *n.* 心上人；甜心

例 Do you want a drink, sweetheart?

译 你想喝点什么吗，亲爱的？

---

30 sweetness

['swiːtnəs]

义 *n.* 美味；芳香；甜美

例 Florida oranges have a natural sweetness.

译 佛罗里达的橙子有一种天然的甜味。

---

31 swelling

['swelɪŋ]

义 *n.* 肿胀物；膨胀

例 You may notice redness and swelling after the injection.

译 注射后你可能会注意到发红和肿胀。

---

32 swelter

['sweltər]

义 *v.* 中暑；热得难受 *n.* 闷热的天气；热得难受

例 He often works in a swelter.

译 他经常在酷热的天气里工作。

---

33 swinger

['swɪŋər]

义 *n.* 赶时髦的人

例 That girl is not a swinger.

译 那个女孩不是一个赶时髦的人。

---

34 swipe

[swaɪp]

义 *v.* 在解码器上刷（信用卡等卡）

例 I could actually swipe a card and generate an electronic receipt via email and then send it out to a person.

译 我可以刷卡，通过电子邮件生成电子收据，然后发送给某个人。

---

35 swiveling

['swɪvlɪŋ]

义 *adj.* 旋转的

例 The coral is made up of swiveling sections.

译 珊瑚是由可旋转的部分组成的。

---

36 swoop

[swuːp]

义 *v.* 俯冲；突然袭击

例 The hawk poised in mid-air ready to swoop.

译 鹰在半空中盘旋准备俯冲。

---

37 sword

[sɔːrd]

义 *n.* 剑，刀

例 Fame can be a two-edged sword.

译 名声可能是一把双刃剑。

---

38 symphonic

[sɪmˈfɑːnɪk]

义 *adj.* 交响乐的；和音的

例 Berlioz's 1830 symphonic composition comes down to us shot through with impetuous passion.

译 柏辽兹 1830 年的交响乐作品带着激昂的激情传向我们。

---

39 symphonie

[ˈsɪmfənɪ]

义 *n.* 交响乐

例 But two weeks later the *Symphonie Parhetique* was performed in all its glory and those who listened bowed their heads and wept.

译 但是两星期后《悲怆交响曲》极为成功地演出了，听到的人都低下头来哭泣了。

---

40 synapse

[ˈsaɪnæps]

义 *n.*【解】突触，神经键

例 At the side of a synapse that belongs to the transmitting neuron, an electrical signal arrives and releases packets of chemicals.

译 电信号到达传递神经元的突触附近后，释放化学物质泡。

---

41 synaptic

[sɪˈnæptɪk]

义 *adj.* 突触的

例 In general, action potentials that reach the synaptic knobs cause a neurotransmitter to be released into the synaptic cleft.

译 一般来说，动作电位到达突触节会导致神经递质释放到突触间隙。

---

42 synchrony

[ˈsɪŋkrənɪ]

义 *n.* 同步性；同时发生

例 Another aspect of synchrony is that people often try to validate their opinions to those of others.

译 同步性的另一个方面是，人们经常试图验证别人的观点。

---

43 syntactic

[sɪnˈtæktɪk]

义 *adj.* 句法的

例 The writing displays accurate but limited range of syntactic structures and vocabulary.

译 这篇文章的句法结构和词汇准确，但范围有限。

---

44 syntax

[ˈsɪntæks]

义 *n.* 句法

例 Each computer language has its own syntax and vocabulary.

译 每种计算机语言都有自己的语法和词汇。

---

45 synthetically

[sɪn'θetɪklɪ]

义 *adv.* 综合地；合成地

例 It can synthetically measure external signal.

译 它可以对外界信号进行综合测量。

---

46 syrupy

['sɪrəpɪ]

义 *adj.* 糖浆的；糖浆状的

例 Meanwhile, in a small saucepan over medium-low heat, reduce the marinade to a syrupy consistency.

译 同时，把腌料放在平底锅里用中低火小煮至成浓浆状。

---

47 tableau

['tæbləʊ]

义 *n.* 画面；活人画（舞台上活人扮的静态画面）

例 The procession included a tableau of the Battle of Hastings.

译 游行队伍中包括黑斯廷斯战役的人物造型。

---

48 tablecloth

['teɪblklɔ:θ]

义 *n.* 桌布，台布

例 If you soak the tablecloth before you wash it, the stains should come out.

译 如果你在洗台布之前把它浸湿，就能洗掉污迹。

---

49 tabletop

['teɪbltɑ:p]

义 *n.* 桌面，台面

例 The toys, floors, tabletops and bathrooms should be clean.

译 玩具、地板、桌面和浴室要干净。

---

50 taboo

[tə'bu:]

义 *n.* 禁忌；禁止接近；禁止使用

例 The topic of addiction remains something of a taboo in our family.

译 上瘾的话题在我们家仍然是一个禁忌。

---

51 taco

['tɑ:kəʊ]

义 *n.* 墨西哥煎玉米卷

例 He serves tilapia at his restaurant, like fish tacos.

译 他的餐厅供应罗非鱼，比如鱼肉玉米饼。

---

52 tactile

['tæktl]

义 *adj.* 触觉的，有触觉的；能触知的

例 It brings you a cozy feeling with soft tactile sensors.

译 它带给你惬意的感觉和柔软的触感。

---

53 taffeta

['tæfɪtə]

义 *n.* 塔夫绸，平纹皱丝织品

例 We also need taffeta or shantung or organdy with flocking.

译 我们还需要塔夫绸、山东绸或带植绒的蝉翼纱。

---

54 tailback

['teɪlbæk]

义 *n.* 堵车，车子排长队

例 There was a seven-mile tailback on the motorway.

译 高速公路上排起了七英里长的长队。

---

55 taint

[teɪnt]

义 *n.* 污点，耻辱；感染

例 Her government never really shook off the taint of corruption.

译 她的政府从未真正摆脱腐败的污点。

---

56 takeover

['teɪkəʊvər]

义 *n.* 收购；接管

例 He lost his job in a corporate takeover.

译 他在一次公司兼并中丢掉了工作。

---

57 talkie

['tɔːkɪ]

义 *n.* 有声电影

例 From now on the talkie is born.

译 从现在起，有声电影就诞生了。

---

58 tally

['tælɪ]

义 *n.* 账；记分

例 Keep a tally of how much you spend while you're away.

译 记下你不在的时候花了多少钱。

---

59 tamp

[tæmp]

义 *v.* 夯实；减少

例 Then I tamp down the soil with the back of a rake.

译 然后我用耙子的背面把土压实。

---

60 tangerine

['tændʒəriːn]

义 *n.* 橘子；橘子树

例 Is this tangerine sweet?

译 这橘子甜吗？

---

61 tango

['tæŋgəʊ]

义 *n.* 探戈舞

例 Arthur Murray taught the foxtrot, the tango and the waltz.

译 亚瑟·默里教狐步舞、探戈和华尔兹。

---

62 tapestry

['tæpəstrɪ]

义 *n.* 挂毯

例 The walls were covered with tapestry with a forest scene embroidered on it.

译 墙上挂着绣有森林景色的挂毯。

---

63 tar

义 *n.* 焦油，柏油

[tɑːr]　例 The oil has hardened to tar.

译 油已硬化成焦油。

64　tare

[ter]

义 **n.** 皮重；包装重量

例 Please tell me the tare and the size of the cargo.

译 请告诉我货物的包装皮重和尺寸。

65　tarmac

['tɑːrmæk]

义 **n.** 柏油碎石路面

例 Standing on the tarmac were two American planes.

译 停机坪上停着两架美国飞机。

66　tarnish

['tɑːrnɪʃ]

义 **n.** 晦暗；污渍　**v.** 使失去光泽，使变暗淡；玷污

例 The affair could tarnish the reputation of the senator.

译 这件事可能会损害参议员的名誉。

67　taro

['tɑːrəʊ]

义 **n.** 芋头

例 I look down at my toes in the cool, black mud of the taro patch.

译 我低头看了看自己的脚趾头，脚趾头浸在凉爽的、黑色的芋头泥里。

68　tarp

[tɑːrp]

义 **n.** 柏油帆布；防水布

例 When the elk got up, the tarp slid off.

译 当麋鹿站起来时，防水布滑了下来。

69　tarpaulin

[tɑːrˈpɔːlɪn]

义 **n.** 放水油布；油布帽

例 He turned to face a chandelier covered with tarpaulin.

译 他转过身来，面对着一个用防水油布覆盖的枝形吊灯。

70　tarry

['tærɪ]

义 **v.** 耽搁；逗留

例 Hugo did not tarry for the miracle.

译 雨果没有等待奇迹的出现。

71　tassel

['tæsl]

义 **n.** 流苏；穗

例 The curtains were held back by tassels.

译 窗帘用穗子拢了起来。

72　tattoo

[tæˈtuː]

义 **v./n.** 文身

例 The first time I heard about tattoo, I was still a little girl.

译 第一次听说文身的时候，我还是个小女孩。

---

73 taut

[tɔːt]

义 *adj.* 绷紧的；紧张的

例 She began to hear her own taut, shallow breathing.

译 她开始听到自己急促、微弱的呼吸。

---

74 tautness

['tɔːtnəs]

义 *n.* 绷紧，拉紧

例 For a string of specified length, tautness and density only certain note can be generated.

译 一根特定长度、紧度和密度的弦只能发出特定的音。

---

75 taxonomic

[ˌtæksə'nɑːmɪk]

义 *adj.* 分类学的

例 It falls outside the scope of the formal taxonomic categories.

译 它不属于正规的分类阶元的范畴。

---

76 taxonomy

[tæk'sɑːnəmɪ]

义 *n.* (动植物的)分类学

例 Anthropologists were the first to recognize that taxonomy might be more than the science officially founded by Carl Linnaeus, the Swedish botanist, in the 1700s.

译 人类学家首先认识到，分类学可能不仅仅是瑞典植物学家卡尔·林奈在 18 世纪正式创立的一门科学。

---

77 taxpayer

['tækspeɪər]

义 *n.* 纳税人

例 Once again it will be the taxpayer who has to foot the bill.

译 买单的还是纳税人。

---

78 teammate

['tiːmmeɪt]

义 *n.* 队友

例 All summer long my teammates and I swam under an open sky.

译 整个夏天，我和队友们都在开阔的天空下游泳。

---

79 tearful

['tɪrfl]

义 *adj.* 含泪的；悲伤的；使人流泪的

例 John gently disengaged himself from his sister's tearful embrace.

译 约翰轻轻地从他含泪的姐姐的怀抱中挣脱出来。

---

80 teat

[tiːt]

义 *n.* 奶嘴；奶头；乳头状物

例 This top fits over the bottle and keeps the teat sterile.

译 将这个盖子盖在瓶子上，保持奶嘴无菌。

---

81 technologically

义 *adv.* 技术上地

[ˌteknəˈlɑːdʒɪklɪ]

例 "The dialogue is changing from what is technologically possible to what is technologically meaningful." said economist Shawn DuBravac.

译 经济学家肖恩·杜布拉瓦克 (Shawn DuBravac) 表示："双方的对话正在从技术可行性转向技术意义。"

---

82 technologist

[tekˈnɑːlədʒɪst]

义 *n.* 技术专家

例 These seem to be some of the ways in which a successful scientist or technologist thinks and acts.

译 这些似乎是一个成功的科学家或技术专家思考和行动的一些方式。

---

83 teem

[tiːm]

义 *v.* 充满，富于

例 Fish teem in the Chinese waters.

译 中国水域鱼类丰富。

---

84 teeny

[ˈtiːnɪ]

义 *adj.* 极小的，微小的；青少年的

例 I'll tackle that teeny, tiny problem in my column next week.

译 我将在下周的专栏中解决这个小问题。

---

85 telegram

[ˈtelɪɡræm]

义 *n.* 电报

例 The president received a briefing by telegram.

译 总统收到一份电报简报。

---

86 televise

[ˈtelɪvaɪz]

义 *v.* 用电视放映

例 The BBC plans to televise all Shakespear's plays.

译 英国广播公司计划播放莎士比亚的所有戏剧。

---

87 temperance

[ˈtempərəns]

义 *n.* 禁酒；节制

例 The age of hedonism is being ushered out by a new era of temperance.

译 享乐主义的时代正被节制的新时代所引领。

---

88 tempestuous

[temˈpestʃʊəs]

义 *adj.* 有暴风雨的；剧烈的

例 Now we recognize the medium as a tempestuous mixture with an extreme diversity of density, temperature and ionization.

译 现在我们认识到，介质是一种剧烈混合物，有着不同的密度、温度和电离度。

---

89 tempo

[ˈtempəʊ]

义 *n.* 节奏；速率

例 It's a difficult piece, with numerous changes of tempo.

译 这是一首难度很大的曲子，节奏变化很多。

---

90 tender

['tendər]

义 *adj.* 温柔的，亲切的

例 Her voice was tender, full of pity.

译 她的声音温柔，充满怜悯。

---

91 tendon

['tendən]

义 *n.* 腱

例 Peggy hurt an elbow tendon while batting.

译 佩吉在击球时伤到了肘部肌腱。

---

92 tendril

['tendrəl]

义 *n.* 蔓；卷须状物

例 The morning glory climbs the trunk with its tendril.

译 牵牛花用藤蔓爬上树干。

---

93 tenet

['tenɪt]

义 *n.* 教义；原则；宗旨

例 This view has become the tenet of the modern linguistic approach to grammatical analysis.

译 这一观点已成为现代语言学研究语法分析的宗旨。

---

94 tenon

['tenən]

义 *n.* 榫

例 The structure was made in the traditional manner using mortise and tenon joints secured with oak pegs.

译 这栋建筑物是按传统风格建造的，采用了橡木钉固定卯和榫头。

---

95 tenor

['tenər]

义 *n.* 男高音

例 He's generally considered to have the finest tenor voice in the country.

译 普遍认为他是全国最佳男高音歌手。

---

96 tentatively

['tentətɪvlɪ]

义 *adv.* 试验性地；暂时地

例 The next round of talks is tentatively scheduled to begin October 21st in Washington.

译 下一轮会谈暂定于 10 月 21 日在华盛顿开始。

---

97 tenuous

['tenjʊəs]

义 *adj.* 脆弱的；稀薄的

例 He did not speculate on the future of his tenuous career.

译 他没有考虑他那脆弱的事业的前途。

---

98 tern

义 *n.* 燕鸥

[tɜːrn]
例 While local gulls will dive voraciously for such handouts, the tern flies on.

译 当地的海鸥会贪婪地扑向这些施舍的食物，而燕鸥会继续飞行。

99　terrazzo

[teˈrɑːtsəʊ]

义 *n.* 水磨石，水磨石地面

例 Other stools have an artificial blue and purple terrazzo surface applied.

译 其他的凳子有蓝色和紫色的人造水磨石表面。

100　terrifically

[təˈrɪfɪklɪ]

义 *adv.* 非常地；极端地

例 They work terrifically fast.

译 他们工作非常快。

List 20

1 testament
['testəmənt]

义 *n.* 【律】遗嘱；确实的证明

例 The new model is a testament to the skill and dedication of the workforce.

译 这种新型产品证明了全体员工的技术水平和敬业精神。

2 tether
['teðər]

义 *n.* (能力、财力、忍耐等的)极限

例 She was jealous, humiliated, and emotionally at the end of her tether.

译 她觉得又嫉妒又屈辱，情绪低落至极。

3 tetra
['tetrə]

义 *n.* 脂鲤(南美产的热带鱼)

例 Researchers studied three populations of Mexican tetra in the lab.

译 研究人员在实验室研究了三种墨西哥脂鲤种群。

4 textured
['tekstʃərd]

义 *adj.* 有织纹的；质地不平的

例 The shoe's sole had a slightly textured surface.

译 鞋底表面有较浅的纹理。

5 thankful
['θæŋkfl]

义 *adj.* 感谢的，感激的

例 The man is thankful to the woman for her assistance.

译 男人感谢女人的帮助。

6 Thanksgiving
[ˌθæŋks'gɪvɪŋ]

义 *n.* 感恩节

例 Are you going home for Thanksgiving?

译 你回家过感恩节吗？

7 theatergoer
[θɪətə'gəʊər]

义 *n.* 戏迷；戏剧家

例 The theatergoer met with each of the twelve actors individually for a series of "mini-dates".

译 观众与 12 位演员分别单独进行了一系列的"迷你约会"。

8 thematic
[θɪ'mætɪk]

义 *adj.* 主题的；【语】词干的；【音】主旋律的

例 Swedish art academies claimed that the contest, with its thematic focus on sport, lacked purpose.

译 瑞典的艺术学院称，这项以体育为主题的比赛缺乏目的性。

9 thenceforth
[ˌðens'fɔːrθ]

义 *adv.* 从那时，其后

例 My life was totally different thenceforth.

译 从那以后，我的生活就完全不同了。

---

10 theology

[θɪˈɑːlədʒɪ]

义 *n.* 神学

例 Annalisa Gennaro is a 21-year-old theology student.

译 安娜莉萨·吉纳罗是 21 岁的神学学生。

---

11 theorem

[ˈθiːərəm]

义 *n.* 定理

例 The theorem that alternativity can replace associativity is true.

译 可选性能代替结合性的定理是正确的。

---

12 thermodynamic

[ˌθɜːməʊdaɪˈnæmɪk]

义 *adj.* 热力的，热力学的

例 Under the thermodynamic framework we've been working with all term.

译 在热力学的框架下，我们已经研究了所有的项。

---

13 thermos

[ˈθɜːrməs]

义 *n.* 热水瓶

例 It's handy to have the thermos here.

译 把保温瓶放在这儿比较方便。

---

14 thesaurus

[θɪˈsɔːrəs]

义 *n.* 辞典；（知识）宝库

例 Still stumped, she browses an online thesaurus.

译 她还是被难住了，于是浏览了在线词典。

---

15 thicket

[ˈθɪkɪt]

义 *n.* 灌木丛，树丛

例 In front of the door he observed a bird which had caught itself in the thicket.

译 在门前，他看到一只困在灌木丛中的鸟。

---

16 thickly

[ˈθɪklɪ]

义 *adv.* 厚厚地；浓密地，声音沙哑地

例 Buildings old and new are thickly covered with graffiti.

译 老建筑和新建筑上都满是涂鸦。

---

17 thigh

[θaɪ]

义 *n.* 大腿

例 He tore a muscle in his right thigh.

译 他右大腿肌肉拉伤。

---

18 thimble

[ˈθɪmbl]

义 *n.* 顶针；嵌环；套管

例 Now shall I give you a thimble?

译 现在我要给你一个顶针吗?

---

19 thorn

[θɔːrn]

义 *n.* 刺;荆棘

例 Nightingale pressed closer against the thorn, and the thorn touched her heart, and a fierce pang of pain shot through her.

译 夜莺紧靠着荆棘,刺碰到了她的心,一阵剧痛穿透了她的全身。

---

20 thoroughbred

['θɜːrəʊbred]

义 *n.* 纯种动物(尤指马);有教养的人

例 I have the oldest thoroughbred blood in the world.

译 我有世界上最古老的纯种血统。

---

21 thoughtfulness

['θɔːtflnəs]

义 *n.* 体贴,关切;认真思考

例 I am writing to show my appreciation of your thoughtfulness.

译 我写这封信是为了感谢您的体贴。

---

22 thoughtless

['θɔːtləs]

义 *adj.* 没有考虑的;轻率的

例 I seem to be in evil case—and all for an innocent and thoughtless pleasantry.

译 我似乎陷入了不幸的境地——而这一切都是为了一句天真而轻率的玩笑。

---

23 threadlike

['θred,laɪk]

义 *adj.* 丝状的,像丝的;细长的

例 Aromatic threadlike foliage of the dill plant is used as seasoning.

译 莳萝植物的芳香的丝状叶子被用作调味品。

---

24 throaty

['θrəʊtɪ]

义 *adj.* 声音低沉的,沙哑的

例 He has a wonderfully throaty voice.

译 他的声音低沉洪亮。

---

25 throne

[θrəʊn]

义 *n.* 王位,君主

例 The country acknowledged his claim to the throne.

译 这个国家承认了他继承王位的权利。

---

26 throwaway

['θrəʊəweɪ]

义 *adj.* 用后即扔的;浪费的

例 We should not turn the most luxuriant forests into throwaway paper products.

译 我们不应该把最茂密的森林变成各种一次性的纸制品。

---

27 thrum

义 *n.* 嗡嗡声

[θrʌm]

例 My head was going thrum.

译 我的脑袋嗡嗡嗡地响着。

28 thud

[θʌd]

义 *n.* 重击声，砰的一声

例 There was silence, broken only by the thud of falling debris.

译 四周一片寂静，只有碎片落地的撞击声打破了寂静。

29 thumbnail

['θʌmneɪl]

义 *n.* 拇指的指甲；极小之物；小图片

例 For this miniscule chameleon is so small that it can sit on a human thumbnail with room to spare.

译 因为这种微小的变色龙太小了，它坐在人类的指甲上还有多余的空间。

30 thump

[θʌmp]

义 *v.* 怦怦跳；猛击　*n.* 重击，捶击；重击声；心脏怦怦跳动声

例 Outside the car, Susan heard a shriek, a loud thump, and a strange gurgling noise.

译 在车外，苏珊听到一声尖叫，一声巨响，还有一种奇怪的咯咯声。

31 thunderbolt

['θʌndərbəʊlt]

义 *n.* 雷电；晴天霹雳

例 The news came as a thunderbolt. I could hardly believe my ears.

译 这消息犹如晴天霹雳。我简直不敢相信自己的耳朵。

32 thunderous

['θʌndərəs]

义 *adj.* 打雷的；雷鸣般的

例 They greeted him with thunderous applause.

译 他们以雷鸣般的掌声欢迎他。

33 thunk

[θʌŋk]

义 *n.* 沉闷空洞的声响

例 The tapping on each point should be rapid little "thunks".

译 在每个点上轻敲应该是快速的"咚"声。

34 thymus

['θaɪməs]

义 *n.* 胸腺

例 Part of the involutive thymus was replaced by myoid cells.

译 一部分胸腺组织已被肌样细胞代替。

35 ticker

['tɪkər]

义 *n.* 滴答响的东西；钟表

例 That watch sure is a fine loud ticker.

译 那是个会滴答响的怀表。

36 tickle

['tɪkl]

义 *v.* 使发痒；逗乐

例 The final question for anybody interested in laughter is, "Why can't we tickle ourselves?"

| 译 | 对任何对笑感兴趣的人来说，最后一个问题是，"为什么我们不能给自己挠痒？" |

37 tidiness

['taɪdɪnəs]

义 *n.* 整齐，整洁

例 The authors are witheringly contemptuous of the bogus equation of tidiness and morality.

译 两位作者对把整洁和道德等同起来的说法不屑一顾。

38 timbre

['tæmbər]

义 *n.* 音色，音质

例 His voice had a deep timbre.

译 他的嗓音深沉。

39 timeless

['taɪmləs]

义 *adj.* 永恒的；不受时间影响的

例 Elves, goblins, and trolls seem to be the timeless creations of the distant past, but gremlins were born in the 20th century.

译 精灵、小妖精和巨魔似乎是遥远过去的永恒产物，但小妖精诞生于 20 世纪。

40 timely

['taɪmlɪ]

义 *adj.* 及时的，适时的

例 The incident served as a timely reminder of just how dangerous mountaineering can be.

译 这一事件及时地提醒人们登山是多么危险。

41 timepiece

['taɪmpiːs]

义 *n.* 钟，表，计时器

例 This cool timepiece was inspired by Salvador Dalí's creative art.

译 这款很酷的手表的灵感来自萨尔瓦多·达利的创意艺术。

42 timer

['taɪmər]

义 *n.* 计时器，定时器；计时员

例 Set the kitchen timer going.

译 启动厨房定时器。

43 tin

[tɪn]

义 *n.* 罐头

例 Hide items such as tins of food, tubes of toothpaste, toys, shoes, etc. around your house and let your kids find them.

译 把罐头食品、牙膏、玩具、鞋子等藏在房子周围，让你的孩子去找。

44 tine

[taɪn]

义 *n.* 齿；叉；鹿角尖

例 Has deep-tine aerification been tried?

译 是否试过深度通气的方法？

45 tinge

[tɪndʒ]

义 *n.* 淡色；些微气味（常与 with 连用）；一丝痕迹

例 His skin had an unhealthy greyish tinge.

译 他的皮肤有一种不健康的淡灰色。

---

46 tingle

['tɪŋgl]

义 *n.* 刺痛；使激动　*v.* 感到刺痛；使激动

例 The cold air made her face tingle.

译 冷空气使她的脸发麻。

---

47 tinkerer

['tɪŋkərər]

义 *n.* 喜欢捣鼓小器具、小发明的人

例 Evolution is a tinkerer, and its products are not necessarily neat or elegant.

译 进化是一个修补匠，它的产品不一定整洁或优雅。

---

48 tinny

['tɪnɪ]

义 *adj.*（声音）尖细刺耳；弱小或瘦的

例 He could hear the tinny sound of a radio playing a pop song.

译 他能听到收音机里播放流行歌曲的尖细而刺耳的声音。

---

49 tinsel

['tɪnsl]

义 *n.* 闪亮的金属片；俗丽的东西

例 Until it could be shipped to restoration experts, Lewis's masterpiece was stored—alongside paper turkeys, tinsel streamers, and half—empty cans of paint—in a back room somewhere.

译 在被运到修复专家那里之前，路易斯的这幅杰作一直被保存在后面的某个房间里，旁边还有纸火鸡、金属丝彩带和半空的油漆罐。

---

50 tint

[tɪnt]

义 *n.* 色彩；浅色；染发剂

例 Its large leaves often show a delicate purple tint.

译 它的大叶子常现出一种柔和的淡紫色。

---

51 tireless

['taɪərləs]

义 *adj.* 不知疲倦的，孜孜不倦的

例 Where the tiller is tireless, the land is fertile.

译 人勤地不懒。

---

52 tizzy

['tɪzɪ]

义 *n.* 慌乱；紧张；兴奋

例 She was in a real tizzy before the meeting.

译 她在会议前感到心慌意乱。

---

53 toaster

['təʊstər]

义 *n.* 烤面包机；烤面包的人；祝酒人

例 When you pop a frozen waffle into the toaster, electrical energy turns into heat energy.

译 当你取出一块冷冻华夫饼放进烤面包机时，电能转化成了热能。

54 tomboy

['tɑ:mbɔɪ]

义 *n.* 行为似男孩的顽皮姑娘，假小子

例 She was considered a tomboy and belly flopped downhill on sleds, climbed trees, and hunted.

译 人们认为她是个假小子，她趴在雪橇上下坡、爬树、打猎。

55 toned

[təʊnd]

义 *adj.* 年久变色的；有声调的，具有……音质的

例 As she played with skill, and had a toned voice, it was not disagreeble to listen to her.

译 由于她演奏技巧娴熟、声音柔和所以听她演奏并没有什么不愉快的。

56 tonnage

['tʌnɪdʒ]

义 *n.* 吨位；吨数

例 Right now we only allow the passage of vessels above a tonnage of 1,500.

译 现在我们只允许 1 500 吨以上的船只通过。

57 toothpick

['tu:θpɪk]

义 *n.* 牙签

例 Never microwave a whole egg without pricking the yolk with a toothpick to break the outer membrane.

译 用微波炉加热整个鸡蛋时，一定要用牙签刺破蛋黄的外膜。

58 topaz

['təʊpæz]

义 *n.* 黄晶，黄玉，托帕石

例 There are five options for the gemstone: blue topaz, opalite, onyx, sapphire and ruby.

译 有五种宝石可供选择：蓝色托帕石、蛋白石、缟玛瑙、蓝宝石和红宝石。

59 topical

['tɑ:pɪkl]

义 *adj.* 有关时事的

例 The newscast covers topical events and entertainment.

译 新闻广播包括时事和娱乐节目。

60 torch

[tɔ:rtʃ]

义 *n.* 手电筒；火炬，火把

例 Edward tossed his clothes into the air and waved a torch.

译 爱德华把衣服抛向空中，挥舞着手电筒。

61 torrid

['tɔ:rɪd]

义 *adj.* 酷热的；热情的

例 She almost can tolerate any kind of torrid days.

译 她几乎能忍受任何炎热的天气。

62 torture

['tɔ:rtʃər]

义 *n.* 拷问，酷刑逼供；折磨，煎熬；变形

例 Many of the refugees have suffered torture.

译 许多难民都遭受过酷刑。

63 toss

[tɔːs]

义 *n.* 投掷；掷硬币决定

例 She won the toss and chose to receive.

译 她猜中了掷币结果，选择接发球。

---

64 tote

[təʊt]

义 *v.* 手提；搬运

例 We arrived, toting our bags and suitcases.

译 我们提着包拎着衣箱到达了那里。

---

65 totter

['tɑːtər]

义 *v.* 蹒跚；摇摇欲坠

例 The property market is tottering.

译 房地产市场摇摇欲坠。

---

66 tow

[təʊ]

义 *v.* 拖，拉

例 They threatened to tow away my car.

译 他们威胁着要拖走我的车。

---

67 townspeople

['taʊnzpiːpl]

义 *n.* 市民，镇民

例 Some townspeople made no effort to hide their hostility.

译 有些城镇居民毫不掩饰他们的敌意。

---

68 toxicity

[tɑːkˈsɪsəti]

义 *n.* 毒性，毒效

例 A gene that helps neutralize aluminum toxicity in rice has been identified.

译 一种有助于中和水稻中铝毒性的基因已经被鉴定出来。

---

69 trace

['treɪs]

义 *v.* 查出，发现，追踪；描绘，记述；画

例 The research effort has focused on tracing the effects of growing levels of five compounds.

译 这项研究的重点是追踪五种化合物水平不断上升的影响。

---

70 traceable

['treɪsəbl]

义 *adj.* 可追踪的；起源于

例 Most telephone calls are traceable.

译 大多数电话都可查出是从哪里打来的。

---

71 trachea

['treɪkɪə]

义 *n.* 气管；导管

例 Radical surgical resection is recommended for all cartilaginous tumors of the trachea.

译 外科切除术是所有气管软骨类肿瘤的首选治疗方式。

72 trademark

['treɪdmɑːrk]

义 *n.* 商标；特点

例 Upon registration, a trademark is usually granted for a period of ten years.

译 商标注册后，通常授予期限为十年。

73 tragically

['trædʒɪklɪ]

义 *adv.* 悲剧地，悲惨地

例 Tragically, Larsson did not live to enjoy his success.

译 不幸的是，拉尔森没能活着享受他的成功。

74 trail

[treɪl]

义 *v.* (在游戏、比赛中)落后

例 He left a host of other riders trailing in his slipstream.

译 他把一群其他的骑手甩在他的尾流后面。

75 trailblazer

['treɪlbleɪzər]

义 *n.* 开拓者；先驱者

例 This removes much of the doubt and discomfort experienced by a trailblazer.

译 这就消除了先驱者所经历的许多疑虑和不适。

76 trail

[treɪl]

义 *v.* 拖，拉

例 The bride's dress trailed behind her.

译 新娘的礼服拖在身后。

77 trajectory

[trə'dʒektərɪ]

义 *n.* 轨道

例 Let's follow a typical trajectory.

译 让我们遵循一个典型的轨迹。

78 trance

[træns]

义 *n.* 昏睡状态；恍惚出神，发呆

例 Lozanov experimented with teaching by direct suggestion during sleep, hypnosis and trance states, but found such procedures unnecessary.

译 拉扎诺夫在睡眠、催眠和恍惚状态下实验了直接暗示的教学法，但发现这些步骤是不必要的。

79 tranquility

[træŋ'kwɪlətɪ]

义 *n.* 宁静，平静；稳定

例 The hotel is a haven of peace and tranquility.

译 这家旅馆是一处安宁的天堂。

80 transatlantic

[trænzət'læntɪk]

义 *adj.* 横渡大西洋的；大西洋彼岸的

例 The transatlantic deal, by contrast, is all about complementarity.

译 相比之下，跨大西洋协议完全是补充性的。

81 transfiguration

[ˌtrænsˌfɪɡə'reɪʃn]

义 *n.* 变形；美化

例 She considers other forms of magic to be somewhat less elegant and more simplistic than transfiguration.

译 她认为其他形式的魔法似乎没有变形术那样复杂和巧妙。

82 transmitter

[træns'mɪtər]

义 *n.* 传播者；发射台

例 Emphasis was placed on the school as a transmitter of moral values.

译 人们强调学校为道德价值观的传输者。

83 transmutation

[ˌtrænsmju:'teɪʃn]

义 *n.* 变化

例 Boyle developed the theory of transmutation after watching plants soak up water and grow leaves, flowers, and berries.

译 波义耳在观察植物吸收水分并长出叶子、花朵和浆果后，提出了嬗变理论。

84 transmute

[trænz'mju:t]

义 *v.* 使……变形

例 Lavoisier hypothesized that boiled water would transmute into a new clement.

译 拉瓦锡假设煮沸的水会变成一种新的液体。

85 transpiration

[ˌtrænspɪ'reɪʃn]

义 *n.* 植物的蒸腾（作用）；蒸发

例 Plants release water through their leaves by transpiration.

译 植物通过蒸腾作用从叶片中释放水分。

86 transpire

[træn'spaɪər]

义 *v.* 蒸发；泄露

例 The plants transpire to give off more water vapor.

译 植物通过蒸腾释放出更多的水蒸气。

87 transposition

[ˌtrænspə'zɪʃn]

义 *n.* 调换；移项

例 Transposition was not protective in this analysis.

译 本研究中转位并没有保护作用。

88 trapdoor

['træpdɔ:r]

义 *n.* 活板门；活盖

例 Old medieval dungeons had trapdoors laid underneath stones.

译 古老的中世纪地牢在石头下面设有活板门。

89 trapezium

义 *n.* 梯形；大多角骨

[trə'pi:zɪəm] 　例 This will be slightly more difficult because of their trapezium shape.

译 这有点困难，因为它们是梯形的。

90　trappings

['træpɪŋz]

义 *n.* 服饰；装饰；外部标志

例 The family ruled for several generations and evidently loved the trappings of power.

译 这个家族统治了几代人，显然喜欢权力的外衣。

91　traumatic

[traʊ'mætɪk]

义 *adj.* 创伤的；外伤的

例 Divorce can be traumatic for everyone involved.

译 离婚对所有相关的人都会造成痛苦。

92　treacherous

['tretʃərəs]

义 *adj.* 背信弃义的，背叛的；有潜在危险的

例 She tried to go away, but her feet were treacherous, and carried her to the group instead.

译 她试图走开，但她的脚不听话，反而把她带到了人群中。

93　treatise

['tri:tɪs]

义 *n.* 论文；论述

例 In 1839, in the first scientific treatise on the sperm whale, Thomas Beale, a surgeon aboard a whaler, wrote that it was "one of the most noiseless of marine animals".

译 1839 年，在第一篇关于抹香鲸的科学论文中，捕鲸船上的外科医生托马斯·比尔写道，抹香鲸是"海洋中最无声的动物之一"。

94　treble

['trebl]

义 *adj.* 三倍的

例 Capital expenditure was treble the 2002 level.

译 资本支出是 2002 年的三倍。

95　trek

[trek]

义 *v.* 长途跋涉　　*n.* 一段路程；长途艰苦旅行

例 He is on a trek through the South Gobi desert.

译 他正徒步穿越南戈壁沙漠。

96　trellis

['trelɪs]

义 *n.* 棚；框架

例 The vine wound about the trellis.

译 葡萄藤缠绕在棚架上。

97　trespass

['trespəs]

义 *n.* 非法侵入；罪过；【律】侵害诉讼

例 You could be prosecuted for trespass.

译 你可能会被起诉非法侵入。

98　tress

[tres]

义 *n.* 一绺头发

例 They like to run their fingers through heavy tresses.

译 他们喜欢将手指穿进厚实的发丝。

99　trestle

['tresl]

义 *n.* 架柱，支架

例 Plywood was also used to create a simple trestle-legged table where customers and staff can sit and read.

译 用胶合木来打造了一张简单的支架式桌子，供顾客和员工休息和阅读。

100　tribal

['traɪbl]

义 *adj.* 部落的

例 They would go back to their tribal lands.

译 他们会回到自己部族的地盘上。

List 21

1 trickster

['trɪkstər]

义 *n.* 骗子；魔术师；狡猾的人

例 He is the great trickster.

译 他是个大骗子。

2 tricycle

['traɪsɪkl]

义 *n.* 三轮车

例 He shrugged his shoulders and began to heave bags from his tricycle on to the scales.

译 他耸了耸肩，开始把袋子从三轮车上搬到秤上。

3 trill

[trɪl]

义 *n.* 颤声；颤音；啭声 *v.* 用颤音唱；用颤音说

例 Some birds trill their songs.

译 有些鸟用颤音唱歌。

4 trillion

['trɪljən]

义 *n.* 大量；万亿

例 Between July 1st and October 1st, the central bank printed over 2 trillion roubles.

译 在 7 月 1 日至 10 月 1 日之间，中央银行印发了逾两万亿卢布。

5 trilogy

['trɪlədʒɪ]

义 *n.* 三部曲

例 The Hungarian director has completed her powerful diary trilogy, set against the background of events in her country.

译 这名匈牙利导演已经完成了她震撼人心的"日记三部曲"，故事以发生在她本国的事件为背景。

6 trimming

['trɪmɪŋ]

义 *n.* 修剪；边角料

例 Hair that's thick and luxuriant needs regular trimming.

译 浓密的头发需要定期修剪。

7 trio

['triːəʊ]

义 *n.* 三个一组；三重唱（奏）

例 She chose to be backed by a classy trio of acoustic guitar, bass and congas.

译 她选择了由原声吉他、贝斯和康加鼓组成的古典三重奏伴奏。

8 tripod

['traɪpɑːd]

义 *n.*（摄影机的）三脚架

例 Klimas attaches his camera to a tripod and positions the camera so it is level with the paint puddle.

译 克里马斯将他的相机安装在三脚架上，并将相机放置在与油漆坑持平的位置。

9 troll

[trəʊl]

义 *v.* 设法得到；搜索

例 Both candidates have been trolling for votes.

译 两个候选人一直都在拉票。

---

10 trombonist

[trɑːmˈbəʊnɪst]

义 *n.* 长号手，低音大喇叭手

例 It is also why a keen-eared virtuoso like Jack Teagarden, the greatest jazz trombonist of his generation, found it impossible to enjoy the Ellington band.

译 这也是为什么像杰克·蒂加登（他那一代最伟大的爵士长号手）这样敏锐的艺术大师发现无法享受艾灵顿乐团（的音乐）的原因。

---

11 trophy

[ˈtrəʊfɪ]

义 *n.* 奖品，战利品

例 He lifted the trophy up and kissed it.

译 他把奖杯举起来吻了吻。

---

12 trot

[trɑːt]

义 *n.* 快步走；小跑

例 Her horse broke into a trot.

译 她的马突然小跑起来。

---

13 troublemaking

[ˈtrʌblˌmeɪkɪŋ]

义 *n.* 捣乱的行为 *adj.* 捣乱的，惹是生非的

例 To drive troublemaking spirits away, friends would visit each other on their birthdays.

译 为了把招致麻烦的恶灵赶走，朋友们会在生日时互相拜访。

---

14 troupe

[truːp]

义 *n.* （演出的）一团，一班

例 The dancing troupe will give three performances at the Century Theater.

译 这个舞蹈团将在世纪剧院演出三场。

---

15 trudge

[trʌdʒ]

义 *v.* 缓慢或吃力地走 *n.* 长途跋涉；艰难的步行

例 We were reluctant to start the long trudge home.

译 我们不愿开始长途跋涉回家。

---

16 truism

[ˈtruːɪzəm]

义 *n.* 自明之理；老生常谈

例 It is a truism that both brevity and readability are good.

译 简洁和可读性都是好的，这是一个不言自明的事实。

---

17 trumpeter

[ˈtrʌmpɪtər]

义 *n.* 小号手；号兵；鹤形鸟

例 A trumpeter swan glides across the surface of the Yellowstone River.

译 一只黑嘴天鹅（号声天鹅）滑过黄石河河面。

18 trustee

[trʌ'stiː]

义 *n.* 受托人；理事

例 If the sale isn't completed by then, the trustee would have 12 months to sell the stake.

译 如果到那时还没有完成出售，受托人将有 12 个月的时间出售股份。

---

19 tuft

[tʌft]

义 *v.* 丛生

例 Stems often tufted.

译 茎通常丛生。

---

20 tuition

[tʊ'ɪʃn]

义 *n.* 学费；教学

例 Your parents will have to cover your tuition fees.

译 你的父母必须支付你的学费。

---

21 tulip

['tuːlɪp]

义 *n.* 郁金香

例 We called that craze "tulip mania".

译 我们称这种狂热为"郁金香狂热"。

---

22 tun

[tʌn]

义 *n.* 酒桶；发酵桶

例 One drop of poison infects the whole tun of wine.

译 一滴毒药会感染整桶酒。

---

23 tuner

['tuːnər]

义 *n.* 调音者；调谐器

例 It looks more like a small TV set than a computer and, in fact, comes with a built-in TV tuner.

译 它看上去更像一台小电视而非电脑，而它实际上也带有内置的电视调谐器。

---

24 tunnel

['tʌnl]

义 *n.* 隧道，地道；洞穴

例 The company is planning to place surveillance equipment at both ends of the tunnel.

译 该公司计划在隧道的两端安装监视装备。

---

25 turban

['tɜːrbən]

义 *n.* 女用（头巾帽）

例 She was dressed all in white except for his red turban.

译 除了那项红色的头巾，她还穿了一身白的。

---

26 turbine

['tɜːrbaɪn]

义 *n.* 涡轮

例 If we can make a turbine, it's sold.

译 如果我们能造出一个涡轮机，它就卖出去了。

27 turbulent

['tɜːrbjələnt]

义 *adj.* 骚动的；汹涌的

例 I had to have a boat that could handle turbulent seas.

译 我必须有一艘能应付汹涌大海的船。

28 turmoil

['tɜːrmɔɪl]

义 *n.* 混乱，骚动

例 She lived through the turmoil of the French Revolution.

译 她经历过法国大革命的动乱。

29 turnip

['tɜːrnɪp]

义 *n.* 萝卜，芜菁

例 A turnip is another root vegetable.

译 萝卜是另一种根茎类蔬菜。

30 turret

['tɜːrət]

义 *n.* 小塔，角楼

例 Archaeologists have found Chinese-style tiles and turret decorations that probably adorned the roofs of buildings.

译 考古学家已发现了可能是作为建筑物顶部装饰用的中国风格的瓦片和角楼。

31 tweezer

['twiːzə]

义 *n.* 镊子

例 I used a little tweezer which I made from a hair clip.

译 我用的是一把由小发卡改造成的镊子。

32 twilight

['twaɪlaɪt]

义 *n.* 黄昏，微光

例 They returned at twilight.

译 他们在黄昏时回来了。

33 twine

[twaɪn]

义 *v.* 捻，搓，结

例 The stories twine together in obscure ways, some successful, some less so.

译 故事晦涩地交织在一起，有些写得很成功，有些就稍逊一筹。

34 twinge

[twɪndʒ]

义 *n.*（生理，心理上的）剧痛，刺痛

例 He felt a twinge in his knee.

译 他感到膝盖一阵剧痛。

35 twinkle

['twɪŋkl]

义 *v.* 闪烁；眨眼

例 At night, lights twinkle in distant cabins across the valleys.

译 夜晚，山谷那边远处的小木屋里灯光闪烁。

36 twirl

[twɜːrl]

义 *v.* 快速转动，扭转

例 When I twirl this around, it produces a particular tone.

译 当我旋转它时，它会发出一种特殊的音调。

---

37 twitch

[twɪtʃ]

义 *v.* 急拉，抽动　　*n.* (肌肉的) 抽搐，颤动；猛的一拉，一动

例 She has a twitch in her left eye.

译 她左眼跳了一下。

---

38 typesetter

['taɪpsetər]

义 *n.* 排字工人；排字机

例 For a number of years I worked as a typesetter.

译 我做了几年排字工人。

---

39 typographical

[ˌtaɪpə'ɡræfɪkl]

义 *adj.* 排字上的；印刷上的

例 It is a mere typographical error.

译 这是单纯的印刷错误。

---

40 tyrannical

[tɪ'rænɪkl]

义 *adj.* 暴虐的；压制的；残暴的

例 What bothered me was the tyrannical influence of the tourist trade.

译 令我烦恼的是旅游业的专横影响。

---

41 ukulele

[ˌjuːkə'leɪlɪ]

义 *n.* 尤克里里琴

例 As soon as I could, I bought a ukulele of my own.

译 一有机会，我就自己买了一个尤克里里。

---

42 ultimately

['ʌltɪmətlɪ]

义 *adv.* 最后，最终

例 The divorce ultimately led to his ruin.

译 离婚最终使得他一贫如洗。

---

43 ultraconservative

[ˌʌltrəkən'sɜːvətɪv]

义 *adj.* 极端保守主义的

例 He's a feisty ultraconservative who has managed, seemingly on purpose, to make enemies of all the other casino owners, a pretty friendly group.

译 他是一个活跃而又超级保守的人，他成功地，也似乎是故意地把其他赌场大亨的敌人们变成了一个友好的小团体。

---

44 ultrafiltration

[ˌʌltrəfɪl'treɪʃən]

义 *n.* 超过滤作用

例 Each mangrove has an ultrafiltration system to keep much of the salt out and a complex root system that allows it to survive in the intertidal zone.

译 每个红树林都有一个超滤系统，可以将大部分盐分过滤出去，还有一个复杂的根系，可以让它们在潮间带生存。

---

45 ululate

['ʌljʊleɪt]

义 *v.* 哀叫，哀鸣

例 A widow is ululating in sorrow.

译 一名寡妇在悲伤地呻吟。

---

46 unaccompanied

[ˌʌnə'kʌmpənɪd]

义 *adj.* 不伴随的；无伴奏的

例 Many of those unaccompanied children are orphans.

译 那些无人陪伴的孩子里有许多是孤儿。

---

47 unaccounted

[ˌʌnə'kaʊntɪd]

义 *adj.* 未说明的；未解释的；未计入的

例 5,000 American servicemen who fought in Korea are still unaccounted for.

译 5 000 名在朝鲜作战的美国军人仍然下落不明。

---

48 unaccustomed

[ˌʌnə'kʌstəmd]

义 *adj.* 异乎惯例的；不习惯的

例 He was unaccustomed to hard work.

译 他不习惯于艰苦的工作。

---

49 unadvertized

[ˌʌn'ædvətaɪzd]

义 *adj.* 未公开的，未登广告的

例 The next day, Sunday, I drove with my mother to the far side of Houston where a time trial was being held—an informal, unadvertized event thrown together at the last minute.

译 第二天，也就是周日，我和母亲开车来到休斯敦的另一边，那里正在举行一场计时赛——这是一场非正式的、未经宣传、临时举办的比赛。

---

50 unaltered

[ʌn'ɔːltərd]

义 *adj.* 未被改变的；不变的；依然如此的

例 The rest of the apartment had fortunately remained unaltered since that time.

译 幸运的是，公寓的其他部分从那时起就没有改变过。

---

51 unanimous

[jʊ'nænɪməs]

义 *adj.* 全体一致的；一致同意的

例 The decision was not unanimous.

译 这个决定没有得到一致同意。

---

52 unanswered

[ʌn'ænsərd]

义 *adj.* 未予答复的；无响应的

例 Some of the most important questions remain unanswered.

译 一些最重要的问题仍然没有答案。

---

53 unappreciated

[ˌʌnəˈpriːʃieɪtɪd]

义 *adj.* 未得到欣赏的

例 He was in a job where he felt unappreciated and undervalued.

译 他觉得自己的工作不受赏识，不被重视。

---

54 unattainable

[ˌʌnəˈteɪnəbl]

义 *adj.* 难到达的；难得到的

例 There are those who argue that true independent advice is unattainable.

译 有些人认为真正的独立建议是不可能得到的。

---

55 unbalance

[ˌʌnˈbæləns]

义 *v.* 使失衡；使精神紊乱

例 Tax cuts may unbalance the budget.

译 减税可能使预算不平衡。

---

56 unbroken

[ʌnˈbrəʊkən]

义 *adj.* 不间断的；未破的

例 We've had ten days of almost unbroken sunshine.

译 我们已经有了十天几乎不间断的阳光。

---

57 uncapped

[ˈʌnkæpt]

义 *adj.* 开盖的（未封管壳的）；无上限的

例 There are two types of partition modes—capped and uncapped.

译 分区模式有两种类型：有上限的和无上限的。

---

58 uncaring

[ʌnˈkeərɪŋ]

义 *adj.* 不关注的，不注意的

例 In the article she was misrepresented as an uncaring mother.

译 在这篇文章中，她被歪曲成一个冷漠的母亲。

---

59 uncharacteristic

[ˌʌnˌkærəktəˈrɪstɪk]

义 *adj.* 不典型的；无典型特征的

例 It was uncharacteristic of her father to disappear like this.

译 她父亲这样消失是不寻常的。

---

60 unclipped

[ʌnˈklɪpt]

义 *adj.* 未剪短的

例 Last year we hired a crane to lift some giant unclipped bays over a house because they were physically impossible to move by hand.

译 去年我们曾雇了一辆起重机，将一些巨大的未经修剪的月桂树吊过房顶，因为它们实在无法用手搬动。

---

61 uncluttered

[ˌʌnˈklʌtərd]

义 *adj.* 整齐的；整洁的

例 Ever since I removed those collages, I realized that I actually prefer to see clean, uncluttered walls.

译　自从我拿掉那些拼贴画后，我意识到我其实更喜欢看到干净整洁的墙壁。

---

62 **uncoated**

[ʌnˈkəʊtɪd]

义　*adj.* 无覆盖的；无涂层的

例　The hardness of the tools to be coated should not be less than that of uncoated tools.

译　涂层的工具硬度应不低于不涂层的工具硬度。

---

63 **uncompromising**

[ʌnˈkɑːmprəmaɪzɪŋ]

义　*adj.* 不让步的；强硬的

例　On stage she seems hard, brash and uncompromising.

译　在舞台上，她显得生硬、鲁莽、毫不妥协。

---

64 **unconditioned**

[ˌʌnkənˈdɪʃnd]

义　*adj.* 无条件的

例　When Pavlov put food powder in the dog's mouth, and saliva was generated. That's an unconditioned stimulus giving rise to an unconditioned response.

译　当巴甫洛夫把食物粉放进狗嘴里时，狗就会分泌唾液。这是一个无条件刺激引起的无条件反应。

---

65 **unconsciously**

[ʌnˈkɑːnʃəslɪ]

义　*adv.* 无意识地，不知不觉地

例　Perhaps, unconsciously, I've done something to offend her.

译　我也许无意中做了什么得罪她的事。

---

66 **unconventional**

[ˌʌnkənˈvenʃənl]

义　*adj.* 非传统的；非常规的

例　The vaccine had been produced by an unconventional technique.

译　这种疫苗是用非常规技术生产的。

---

67 **unconvinced**

[ˌʌnkənˈvɪnst]

义　*adj.* 不信服的

例　I remain unconvinced of the need for change.

译　我仍然不相信变革的必要性。

---

68 **undaunted**

[ˌʌnˈdɔːntɪd]

义　*adj.* 不屈不挠的，无畏的

例　He seemed undaunted by all the opposition to his idea.

译　尽管他的想法屡遭非难，但他似乎仍然百折不挠。

---

69 **undefined**

[ˌʌndɪˈfaɪnd]

义　*adj.* 未定义的；不明确的

例　The money was lent for an undefined period of time.

译　这笔钱借出的时间没有规定。

70 undeniable

[ˌʌndɪˈnaɪəbl]

义 *adj.* 不可否认的，无可辩驳的

例 It is an undeniable fact that crime is increasing.

译 犯罪在增多是无可争辩的事实。

---

71 undependable

[ˌʌndɪˈpendəbəl]

义 *adj.* 不可靠的，靠不住的，不可信赖的

例 Would you like to have an undependable person as one of your best friends?

译 你愿意一个不可靠的人来做你最好的朋友吗？

---

72 underbelly

[ˈʌndərbelɪ]

义 *n.* 下腹部；易受攻击的地带

例 Many people are shocked to learn that, just as in human life, there's an incredible, dark and even lascivious underbelly to the animal world.

译 许多人震惊地发现，就像人类生活一样，动物世界也有令人难以置信、黑暗甚至淫荡的弱点。

---

73 underdog

[ˈʌndərdɔːg]

义 *n.* 处于劣势的一方；牺牲者

例 Most of the crowd were cheering for the underdog to win just this one time.

译 大多数观众都在为处于劣势一方的这一次胜利欢呼。

---

74 underfoot

[ˌʌndərˈfʊt]

义 *adv.* 在脚下面；踩着地；碍手碍脚地

例 Morgan dropped his cigarette and crushed it underfoot.

译 摩根把香烟掉在地上，用脚踩碎了。

---

75 underling

[ˈʌndərlɪŋ]

义 *n.* 部下，下属

例 There had just been a head cashier and an underling cashier, both women.

译 刚刚有一名收银主管和一名下属收银员在这，都是女性。

---

76 understate

[ˌʌndərˈsteɪt]

义 *v.* 轻描淡写地说，少说

例 It would be a mistake to understate the seriousness of the problem.

译 低估问题的严重性是错误的。

---

77 underused

[ˌʌndərˈjuːzd]

义 *adj.* 未充分利用的

例 Currently many schools' sports grounds are grossly underused.

译 目前，许多学校的操场都未得到充分使用。

---

78 underworld

[ˈʌndərwɜːrld]

义 *n.* 黑社会；下层社会；阴间

例 Some claim that she still has connections to the criminal underworld.

译 一些人声称她仍与犯罪的黑社会有联系。

---

79 undetectable

[ˌʌndɪˈtektəbl]

义 *adj.* 察觉不到的，发现不了的

例 Worse still, such ploys are often undetectable.

译 更糟糕的是，这样的伎俩往往是察觉不到的。

---

80 undetermined

[ˌʌndɪˈtɜːmɪnd]

义 *adj.* 未确定的，待定的

例 The source of infection was undetermined.

译 感染源尚未确定。

---

81 undeterred

[ˌʌndɪˈtɜːrd]

义 *adj.* 未受阻的，未受挫折的

例 He was undeterred by these disasters.

译 他没有被这些灾难吓倒。

---

82 undifferentiated

[ˌʌndɪfəˈrenʃɪeɪtɪd]

义 *adj.* 无差别的，未显出差别的

例 We realize that they are all fused in an undifferentiated continuum.

译 我们意识到它们都融合在一个无差别的连续体中。

---

83 undiluted

[ˌʌndaɪˈluːtɪd]

义 *adj.* 未稀释的，未冲淡的

例 I will look back at this one with undiluted pleasure.

译 我会带着无比的快乐回顾这一段。

---

84 undisturbed

[ˌʌndɪˈstɜːrbd]

义 *adj.* 未受干扰的；安静的，镇定的

例 The desk looked undisturbed.

译 这张桌子看上去没有被动过。

---

85 uneasily

[ʌnˈiːzɪlɪ]

义 *adv.* 不安地，局促地

例 Meg shifted uneasily on her chair.

译 麦格在椅子上不安地挪动着。

---

86 unenforceable

[ˈʌnɪnˈfɔːsəbl]

义 *adj.* 不能强制执行的

例 Such rules would probably be unenforceable anyway.

译 无论如何，这样的规则很可能无法执行。

---

87 unequivocally

[ˌʌnɪˈkwɪvəklɪ]

义 *adv.* 明确地，不含糊地

例 He stated unequivocally that the forces were ready to go to war.

译 他明确表示部队已经做好准备去打仗。

88 unessential

[ˌʌnə'senʃəl]

义 *adj.* 非本质上的；非必要的

例 There are many ways to achieve ease of use, and simplicity—the reduction of the unessential—is just one of them.

译 有很多种方法可以实现易用性，但简约（也就是剔除不必要功能）只是其中的一种方式。

---

89 unethical

[ʌn'eθɪkl]

义 *adj.* 不道德的；缺乏职业道德的

例 Your teacher's grading system may be unwise, but it is not unethical.

译 你的老师的评分系统可能是不明智的，但它并非是不道德的。

---

90 unfavorably

[ʌn'feɪvərəblɪ]

义 *adv.* 不利地；反对地；令人不快地

例 Your price compare unfavorably with your competitor's.

译 你们的价格与你们竞争对手的相比，实在不占优势。

---

91 unfilled

[ʌn'fɪld]

义 *adj.* 空的；未填充的

例 Unfilled positions number several million countrywide.

译 全国有几百万个空缺职位。

---

92 unfinished

[ʌn'fɪnɪʃt]

义 *adj.* 未完成的

例 They are unfinished designs.

译 它们是未完成的设计。

---

93 unfired

[ʌn'faɪəd]

义 *adj.* 未燃烧的；未点着的

例 The unfired pots were missing.

译 没有烧制的罐子不见了。

---

94 unfocused

[ʌn'fəʊkəst]

义 *adj.* 未聚焦的，无焦点的；不专心的

例 But for now, she is in the grip of a blind, unfocused anger.

译 但现在，她被一种盲目的、无法集中的愤怒所控制。

---

95 unforgiving

[ˌʌnfər'gɪvɪŋ]

义 *adj.* 不原谅的；不可宽恕的

例 He was an unforgiving man who never forgot a slight.

译 他是一个从不原谅别人的人，从不会忘记任何小事。

---

96 unforgotten

[ʌnfə'gɑːtən]

义 *adj.* 不被遗忘的；牢记的

例 His literature's style is unique, which has the unforgotten value in the literary history.

译 他的文学风格独树一帜，在文学史上具有不可磨灭的价值。

97　unfulfilled

[ˌʌnfʊlˈfɪld]

义　*adj.* 没有成就感的；未完成的

例　Do you have any unfulfilled ambitions?

译　你有未实现的抱负吗？

98　ungainly

[ʌnˈɡeɪnlɪ]

义　*adj.* 笨拙的；难看的；不雅的

例　I thought him terribly ungainly when he danced.

译　他跳舞时我觉得他非常笨拙。

99　ungenerous

[ʌnˈdʒenərəs]

义　*adj.* 心胸狭窄的；吝啬的

例　This was a typically ungenerous response.

译　这是一个典型的吝啬回应。

100　unhook

[ʌnˈhʊk]

义　*v.* 从取下；解开

例　Some officials claimed to unhook connections with the companies but still maintained close ties on the sly.

译　一些官员声称已与公司脱钩，但暗地里仍保持着密切联系。

List 22

1	**unhurried** [ʌn'hɜːrɪd]	**义** *adj.* 不慌不忙的；从容不迫的 **例** The unhurried way in which he spoke and the gentle smile on his lips reminded you of an unaffected young girl. **译** 他那慢条斯理的样子和款款浅笑的神情，像个质朴敦厚的大姑娘。
2	**unidentified** [ˌʌnaɪ'dentɪfaɪd]	**义** *adj.* 未确认的；无法识别的 **例** The painting was sold to an unidentified American dealer. **译** 这幅画卖给了一名未披露姓名的美国商人。
3	**uniformly** ['juːnɪfɔːmlɪ]	**义** *adv.* 均匀地；一致地 **例** Pressure must be uniformly distributed over the whole surface. **译** 压力必须均匀地分布在整个表面。
4	**uninformed** [ˌʌnɪn'fɔːrmd]	**义** *adj.* 未得到通知的；知识贫乏的 **例** The public is generally uninformed about these diseases. **译** 公众通常不了解这些疾病。
5	**uninhibited** [ˌʌnɪn'hɪbɪtɪd]	**义** *adj.* 不受禁止的；无拘无束的 **例** The dancing is uninhibited and as frenzied as an aerobics class. **译** 舞蹈是不受限制的，就像有氧运动课一样疯狂。
6	**uninitiated** [ˌʌnɪ'nɪʃɪeɪtɪd]	**义** *adj.* 缺乏某种特定知识和经验的；不谙此道的 **例** To the uninitiated the system seems too complicated. **译** 对于外行来说，这个系统似乎太复杂了。
7	**uninviting** [ˌʌnɪn'vaɪtɪŋ]	**义** *adj.* 不能吸引人的；讨厌的 **例** The actual house is just as uninviting as the house in. **译** 真正的房子和里面的房子一样不招人喜欢。
8	**uniquely** [ju'niːklɪ]	**义** *adv.* 独特地，唯一地 **例** The problem isn't uniquely American. **译** 这个问题并不是美国独有的。
9	**uniqueness** [ju'niːknəs]	**义** *n.* 唯一性，独特性 **例** The author stresses the uniqueness of the individual. **译** 作者强调个人的独特性。

10 universally

[ˌjuːnɪˈvɜːrsəlɪ]

义 *adv.* 普遍地

例 The disadvantage is that it is not universally available.

译 缺点在于它并不是随处都可获得。

---

11 unjustly

[ˌʌnˈdʒʌstlɪ]

义 *adv.* 不公正，不法地

例 She was unjustly accused of stealing money, and then fired.

译 她被冤枉偷钱，然后被解雇了。

---

12 unkempt

[ˌʌnˈkempt]

义 *adj.* 乱蓬蓬的，不整洁的

例 His hair was unkempt and filthy.

译 他的头发又乱又脏。

---

13 unknowingly

[ʌnˈnəʊɪŋlɪ]

义 *adv.* 不知不觉地

例 Other birds unknowingly carry seeds that cling to them for the ride.

译 另一些鸟在不知不觉中携带了附着在它们身上的种子。

---

14 unlatch

[ʌnˈlætʃ]

义 *v.* 打开（门闩）

例 Stop your horse at the gate and unlatch it.

译 在门的前面停下你的马，然后拔掉门闩。

---

15 unlit

[ˌʌnˈlɪt]

义 *adj.* 不发光的；未点燃的

例 As soon as I walked in the restaurant, I saw him sitting by himself at a table, twirling an unlit cigarette through his fingers like a miniature baton.

译 我一走进餐厅，就看见他一个人坐在桌旁，手指间捻着一根没有点燃的香烟，就像捻着一根迷你警棍。

---

16 unmanned

[ˌʌnˈmænd]

义 *adj.* 无人操纵的；难以自持的

例 Unmanned post offices meant millions of letters went unsorted.

译 邮局无人工作意味着许多信件无人分拣。

---

17 unmatched

[ʌnˈmætʃt]

义 *adj.* 无配偶的；无匹敌的

例 He had a talent unmatched by any other politician of this century.

译 他的才华是本世纪其他政坛人物所望尘莫及的。

---

18 unmistakably

[ʌnmɪˈsteɪkəblɪ]

义 *adv.* 明白地，显然地

例 Like historians, we were unmistakably on the side of what had actually happened.

译 和历史学家一样，我们显然站在实际发生的事情的那边。

19 unmoved

[ˌʌn'muːvd]

义 *adj.* 无动于衷的；坚定的

例 She pleaded with him but he remained unmoved.

译 她恳求他，但他不为所动。

20 unnamed

[ˌʌn'neɪmd]

义 *adj.* 未命名的；不知名的

例 Two casualties, as yet unnamed, are still in the local hospital.

译 两名未透露姓名的伤者仍在当地医院。

21 unnerve

[ˌʌn'nɜːrv]

义 *v.* 使气馁；使焦躁

例 The high house price unnerves ordinary residents.

译 高房价使普通居民不安。

22 unnervingly

[ˌʌn'nɜːrvɪŋlɪ]

义 *adv.* 令人担心地，使人紧张不安地

例 His tone is unnervingly mild, and she squeezes open one eye to look at him.

译 他的语气温和得令人不安，她微睁一只眼睛偷偷地看着他。

23 unobserved

[ˌʌnəb'zɜːrvd]

义 *adj.* 未被注意的

例 Looking around to make sure he was unobserved, he slipped through the door.

译 他环顾四周，以确保没有人注意到他，然后溜进了门。

24 unobstructed

[ˌʌnəb'strʌktɪd]

义 *adj.* 无阻碍的，没有阻挡的

例 It results in a stream of home-going ants passing unobstructed through the center of a crowd of out-going ants.

译 它导致了一群回家的蚂蚁畅通无阻地穿过一群外出的蚂蚁的中心。

25 unoccupied

[ˌʌn'ɑːkjʊpaɪd]

义 *adj.* 空闲的；没人住的

例 The house was unoccupied at the time of the explosion.

译 爆炸发生时，这所房子无人居住。

26 unofficial

[ˌʌnə'fɪʃl]

义 *adj.* 非官方的，非正式的

例 Unofficial estimates put the figure at over two million.

译 非官方估计数字超过 200 万。

27 unpalatable

[ʌn'pælətəbl]

义 *adj.* 不可口的；让人不快的，难以接受的

例 Only then did I learn the unpalatable truth.

译 直到那时我才得知令人难以接受的真相。

28 unpolluted

义 *adj.* 未受污染的；清洁的

[ˌʌnpəˈluːtɪd]

例 I envy you your peace of mind, your clean conscience and your unpolluted memory.

译 我羡慕你平静的心灵，清白的良心和纯洁的记忆。

---

29 unpredictability

[ˌʌnprɪˌdɪktəˈbɪlətɪ]

义 **n. 不可预测性**

例 There is also the same exuberance and unpredictability in sudden fad switches.

译 在突然的时尚转变中，也有同样的活力和不可预测性。

---

30 unprepared

[ˌʌnprɪˈperd]

义 **adj. 无准备的；还没有准备好的**

例 Our enemies were caught unprepared and we disposed of them without firing a single shot.

译 我们的敌人措手不及，我们一枪未发就把他们干掉了。

---

31 unprofessional

[ˌʌnprəˈfeʃənl]

义 **adj. 违反职业道德的**

例 She was found guilty of unprofessional conduct.

译 她被判犯有违反职业道德的行为。

---

32 unquestioned

[ʌnˈkwestʃənd]

义 **adj. 无可争议的**

例 This unquestioned assumption shaped how France's early experimentation approached airplane design, and it cost them dearly.

译 这个毋庸置疑的假设影响了法国早期的飞机设计实验，并使他们付出了高昂的代价。

---

33 unravel

[ʌnˈrævl]

义 **v. 解散；阐明**

例 Yet today, these markets are unraveling.

译 但是现在，市场正在解体。

---

34 unreal

[ʌnˈriːəl]

义 **adj. 不真实的，虚幻的**

例 The violence in those films was too unreal.

译 那些电影中的暴力太不真实了。

---

35 unrealized

[ˌʌnˈriːəlaɪzd]

义 **adj. 没有实现的；未被察觉的**

例 Many a mother tries to act out her unrealized dreams through her daughter.

译 许多母亲都试图通过女儿实现她们未能实现的梦想。

---

36 unrecognizable

[ˌʌnrekəgˈnaɪzəbl]

义 **adj. 无法认出的，无法识别的**

例 Today that same hotel is almost unrecognizable.

译 今天，同一家酒店几乎认不出来了。

---

37 unrelenting

义 **adj. 不屈不挠的；不松懈的**

[ˌʌnrɪˈlentɪŋ]

例 He was unrelenting in his search for the truth about his father.

译 他不顾一切地搜集有关他父亲的事实真相。

---

38 unreliability

[ˌʌnrɪˌlaɪəˈbɪlətɪ]

义 *n.* 不可靠性；不安全性

例 Downtime of an application due to bugs in the software is called the unreliability factor.

译 软件中的错误导致的应用程序宕机被称为不可靠性因素。

---

39 unrivaled

[ʌnˈraɪvəld]

义 *adj.* 无比的；无敌的

例 Berry showcases his unrivaled ability to play a solo that blends into the background.

译 贝瑞展示了他无与伦比的独奏能力，他的独奏融入了背景。

---

40 unruly

[ʌnˈruːlɪ]

义 *adj.* 难控制的；不同寻常的

例 The man had remarkably black, unruly hair.

译 那个男子有一头不同寻常的乱蓬蓬的黑发。

---

41 unsaid

[ʌnˈsed]

义 *adj.* 未说出口的；收回的

例 Some things are better left unsaid.

译 有些事情还是不说为好。

---

42 unscathed

[ʌnˈskeɪðd]

义 *adj.* 没有受伤的；未受损害的

例 East Los Angeles was left relatively unscathed by the riots.

译 相对来说，东洛杉矶没有受到骚乱的影响。

---

43 unseasonal

[ʌnˈsiːzənl]

义 *adj.* 非季节性的

例 We lurch between terrible drought and unseasonal flood.

译 我们徘徊在可怕的干旱和非季节性的洪水之间。

---

44 unselfconscious

[ˌʌnselfˈkɑːnʃəs]

义 *adj.* 自然的；不装腔作势的

例 The best psychological place from which to speak is an unselfconscious self-consciousness, providing the illusion of being natural.

译 最好的心理表达方式是一种无意识的自我意识，提供一种自然的幻觉。

---

45 unskilled

[ˌʌnˈskɪld]

义 *adj.* 不熟练的；未成熟的；拙劣的

例 He worked as an unskilled laborer.

译 他是一个不熟练的工人。

---

46 unsolved

[ˌʌnˈsɑːlvd]

义 *adj.* 未解决的

例 The mystery is likely to remain unsolved until better technology is invented.

译 在发明更好的技术之前，这个谜可能仍未能解开。

---

47 unsophisticated

[ˌʌnsəˈfɪstɪkeɪtɪd]

义 *adj.* 不谙世故的；不复杂的

例 It was music which unsophisticated audiences enjoyed listening to.

译 这是那些不懂世故的听众喜欢听的音乐。

---

48 unspeakable

[ʌnˈspiːkəbl]

义 *adj.* 不能以言语表达的；坏透了的

例 The pain is unspeakable.

译 这种痛苦是无法形容的。

---

49 unsullied

[ʌnˈsʌlɪd]

义 *adj.* 没弄脏的；清白的；纯洁的

例 She had the combined talents of toughness, intellect, experience and unsullied reputation.

译 她兼具坚韧、才智、经验和清白的名声。

---

50 unsurpassed

[ˌʌnsərˈpæst]

义 *adj.* 非常卓越的；未被超越的

例 They showed unsurpassed bravery in battle.

译 在战斗中他们表现得无比英勇。

---

51 unsurprising

[ˌʌnsərˈpraɪzɪŋ]

义 *adj.* 不令人吃惊的

例 His choice was unsurprising.

译 他的选择并不出人意料。

---

52 unsuspecting

[ˌʌnsəˈspektɪŋ]

义 *adj.* 无疑心的；未料到的

例 He had crept up on his unsuspecting victim from behind.

译 他从后面悄悄接近那个毫无防备的受害者。

---

53 untie

[ʌnˈtaɪ]

义 *v.* 解开，松开

例 Please untie the safe belt.

译 请解开安全带。

---

54 untold

[ˌʌnˈtəʊld]

义 *adj.* 数不清的；没有说到的

例 That simple act, a Jack Foley classic, cut the movie's budget by untold thousands of dollars.

译 这个简单的动作，杰克·福利 (Jack Foley) 的经典动作，让这部电影的预算减少了数千美元。

---

55 untreated

[ˌʌnˈtriːtɪd]

义 *adj.* 未经处理的；未经治疗的

例 All the bedding is made of simple, untreated cotton.

译 所有的床上用品都是由简单的未经处理的棉花制作的。

---

56 untruth

[ˌʌnˈtruːθ]

义 *n.* 不真实；谎言

例 There is truth, and there is untruth.

译 有真理，也有谎言。

---

57 untutored

[ʌnˈtuːtərd]

义 *adj.* 未受教导的；未经训练的

例 This untutored mathematician had an obsession with numbers.

译 这位未接受正规教育的数学家对数字很痴迷。

---

58 untypical

[ʌnˈtɪpɪkl]

义 *adj.* 非典型的

例 Schools in this area are quite untypical of schools in the rest of the country.

译 这个地区的学校与这个国家其他地方的学校很不一样。

---

59 unwise

[ˌʌnˈwaɪz]

义 *adj.* 不明智的；愚笨的

例 I think this is extremely unwise.

译 我认为这是非常不明智的。

---

60 unwittingly

[ʌnˈwɪtɪŋlɪ]

义 *adv.* 不知不觉地；无意地

例 He was unwittingly caught up in the confrontation.

译 他无意中陷入了这场冲突。

---

61 unworkable

[ʌnˈwɜːrkəbl]

义 *adj.* 难运转的；不能实行的

例 There is the strong possibility that such cooperation will prove unworkable.

译 这种合作很有可能行不通。

---

62 unworthiness

[ʌnˈwɜːrðɪnəs]

义 *n.* 不值得；无价值

例 Does your own guilt or unworthiness stop you from receiving?

译 你的内疚感和无价值感是否阻碍了你去接受呢？

---

63 upbeat

[ˈʌpbiːt]

义 *adj.* 乐观的，积极向上的

例 The Defense Secretary gave an upbeat assessment of the war so far.

译 国防部长对迄今为止的战争进行了乐观的评估。

---

64 upend

[ʌpˈend]

义 *v.* 竖立；颠覆

例 To do so again could upend bond markets.

译 再次这样做可能会颠覆债券市场。

---

65 upkeep

['ʌpkiːp]

义 *n.* 检修；维护

例 Tenants are responsible for the upkeep of rented property.

译 承租人负责维护租赁财产。

---

66 uppermost

['ʌpərməʊst]

义 *adj.* 最高的，最重要的

例 These thoughts were uppermost in my mind.

译 这些事是我心里最重要的。

---

67 upriver

[ˌʌp'rɪvər]

义 *adj.* 上游的；向水源的　**adv.** 在上游；朝上游地

例 Heavy goods could be brought upriver in barges.

译 重型货物可以用驳船往上游运。

---

68 upscale

[ˌʌp'skeɪl]

义 *adj.* 高消费的；高端的

例 She browsed in an upscale antiques shop.

译 她逛了一家高档古玩店。

---

69 upstage

[ˌʌp'steɪdʒ]

义 *adj.* 自负的

例 He is too upstage for us recently.

译 他们近来对我们太傲慢了。

---

70 upstart

['ʌpstɑːrt]

义 *n.* 暴发户；傲慢自负之人

例 Many prefer a familiar authority figure to a young upstart.

译 许多人更喜欢熟悉的权威人物而不喜欢自命不凡的年轻新贵。

---

71 uptown

[ˌʌp'taʊn]

义 *n.* 住宅区　**adv.** 在市郊，非商业区　**adj.** 市郊住宅区的

例 They live in an apartment uptown.

译 他们住在市郊的一套公寓。

---

72 upturned

[ˌʌp'tɜːrnd]

义 *adj.* 仰着的；向上翘的；翻过来的

例 She looked down at the sea of upturned faces.

译 她低头看着无数张仰起的脸。

---

73 upwelling

[ʌp'welɪŋ]

义 *n.* 喷出；上升流

例 The mantle upwelling is originated from core-mantle boundary and mostly presents in the middle mantle and lower part of upper mantle.

译 地幔上升流起源于核幔边界，主要表现在地幔中部和上地幔下部。

---

74 urbanize

['ɜːbəˌnaɪz]

义 *v.* 使都市化，使城市化

例 Is this necessary to urbanize a rural country?

	译 这是农村城市化的必要条件吗？

75 usher
['ʌʃər]

义 *n.* 招待员

例 He did part-time work as an usher in a theater.

译 他在一家剧院做招待员的兼职工作。

76 utility
[juːˈtɪlətɪ]

义 *n.* 效用，实用

例 We can greatly enhance the utility of green space through designs that provide a range of different uses in a confined space.

译 我们可以通过在密闭空间中提供一系列不同用途的设计，大大提高绿地的利用率。

77 utterance
['ʌtərəns]

义 *n.* 说话；发表；说话的方式

例 They lack the kind of structure that enables us to divide a human utterance into words.

译 它们缺乏一种结构，使我们能够将人类的话语分成单词。

78 vacationer
[vəˈkeɪʃnər]

义 *n.* 度假者，休假者

例 Vacationers can also add on a week in Florida before or after the cruise.

译 度假者也可以在游船前后在佛罗里达待上一周。

79 vagabond
['vægəbɑːnd]

义 *n.* 流浪汉；无业游民 *adj.* 流浪的；流浪者的

例 These were strange words to the vagabond boy's ears, and the pleasantest he had ever heard.

译 这些话在这个流浪儿的耳朵里是陌生的，也是他有生以来听到的最愉快的话。

80 vaguely
['veɪglɪ]

义 *adv.* 含糊地，模糊地；茫然地

例 "I'm not sure," Liz said vaguely.

译 莉斯含糊地说，"我不确定。"

81 vane
[veɪn]

义 *n.* 风向标

例 There is a vane on top of the building.

译 楼顶上有一个风向标。

82 vanguard
['vængɑːrd]

义 *n.* 先锋，先驱

例 The company is proud to be in the vanguard of scientific progress.

译 这家公司为走在科学进步的前列而自豪。

83 variance

['veɪrɪəns]

义 *n.* 不同差异；【律】(诉讼中)两步骤间的不一致，诉状与证据的不符；分歧，争论，不合；【统】方差

例 Many of his statements were at variance with the facts.

译 他的许多陈述都与事实相矛盾。

---

84 variegated

['veɪrɪɡeɪtɪd]

义 *adj.* 杂色的；斑驳的

例 The leaves are a variegated red.

译 这些树叶呈斑驳的红色。

---

85 varmint

['vɑːrmɪnt]

义 *n.* 流氓，恶棍

例 I think you like me because I am a varmint.

译 我觉得你喜欢我是因为我是个流氓。

---

86 vastly

['væstlɪ]

义 *adv.* 极大地，广大地，巨大地

例 Like most of my contemporaries, I grew up in a vastly different world.

译 像我同时代的大多数人一样，我在一个非常不同的世界里长大。

---

87 vastness

['væstnəs]

义 *n.* 广阔，广袤

例 The vastness of space really boggles the mind.

译 浩瀚的太空真让人难以置信。

---

88 vat

[væt]

义 *n.* 大桶，大盆，缸

例 Turn the vat upside down.

译 把缸扣过来。

---

89 vaudeville

['vɔːdəvɪl]

义 *n.* 杂耍；轻歌舞剧

例 For the next fifteen years she sang and danced in both Broadway and vaudeville shows.

译 在接下来的 15 年里，她在百老汇和杂耍表演中载歌载舞。

---

90 vault

[vɔːlt]

义 *v.* 撑竿跳过；跳跃

例 He could easily vault the wall.

译 他能轻而易举地越过那堵墙。

---

91 veer

[vɪr]

义 *v.* 转向；改变观点

例 He is unlikely to veer from his boss's strongly held views.

译 他不太可能改变他老板的强硬立场。

92 vegetarianism

['vedʒə'teərɪənɪzəm]

义 *n.* 素食主义

例 Vegetarianism has been mainstreamed.

译 素食主义已经成为主流。

---

93 vehement

['vi:əmənt]

义 *adj.* 感情强烈的，猛烈的

例 He had been vehement in his opposition to the idea.

译 他曾强烈反对这个想法。

---

94 veil

[veɪl]

义 *n.* 面纱；面罩；掩饰物

例 The veil she was wearing obscured her features.

译 她戴的面纱遮住了她的容貌。

---

95 veined

[veɪnd]

义 *adj.* 有脉纹的；有叶脉的

例 Helen's hands were thin and veined.

译 海伦的手很细，布满了青筋。

---

96 vellum

['veləm]

义 *n.* 上等皮纸，精制皮纸

例 Very special books are still occasionally produced on vellum, but they are one-of-a-kind show pieces.

译 非常特别的书仍然会偶尔用羊皮纸制作，但它们是独一无二的展览品。

---

97 vend

[vend]

义 *v.* 叫卖，出售

例 Do you vend magazines here?

译 你们这儿卖杂志吗？

---

98 venerate

['venəreɪt]

义 *v.* 尊敬，尊崇，崇拜

例 They venerate the old man's memory.

译 他们崇拜这位老人的记忆力。

---

99 venous

['vi:nəs]

义 *adj.* 静脉的；有脉纹的

例 A venous reflux occurring in congestive heart failure.

译 静脉回流出现在充血性心力衰竭。

---

100 ventilate

['ventɪleɪt]

义 *v.* 使……空气流通，通风

例 Ventilate the area thoroughly.

译 给该区域彻底通风。

List 23

1 ventilation

[ˌventɪˈleɪʃn]

义 *n.* 通风；通风设备

例 Make sure that there is adequate ventilation in the room before using the paint.

译 在使用油漆之前，要确保房间足够通风。

2 venue

[ˈvenjuː]

义 *n.* 审判地；场所

例 We're still trying to decide on a venue.

译 我们还在决定地点。

3 veranda

[vəˈrændə]

义 *n.* 阳台；游廊

例 After dinner, we sat talking on the veranda.

译 晚饭后，我们坐在阳台上聊天。

4 verbalize

[ˈvɜːrbəlaɪz]

义 *v.* 用语言表达；赘述

例 Feelings are often very difficult for you to verbalize.

译 你常常很难用语言表达自己的感受。

5 verbena

[vɜːrˈbiːnə]

义 *n.* 马鞭草；美女樱

例 I could see bright pink sand verbenas blooming in the distance.

译 我可以看到粉红色的沙马鞭草在远处盛开。

6 verdict

[ˈvɜːrdɪkt]

义 *n.* 裁决；定论

例 The jury's verdict went against him.

译 陪审团的裁决对他不利。

7 verge

[vɜːrdʒ]

义 *n.* 边缘；绿地

例 He seemed to be on the verge of total derangement.

译 他似乎处于完全错乱的边缘。

8 vermin

[ˈvɜːrmɪn]

义 *n.* 害兽；害鸟；害虫

例 On farms the fox is considered vermin and treated as such.

译 在农场里，狐狸被视为害兽，并被当作害兽对待。

9 verse

[vɜːrs]

义 *n.* 诗，韵文

例 He used to declaim French verse to us.

译 他过去常给我们朗诵法语诗歌。

10 vested

['vestɪd]

义 *adj.* 穿好衣服的；【律】既定的

例 The administration has no vested interest in proving public schools good or bad.

译 行政部门在证明公立学校是好是坏方面没有既得利益。

---

11 vestige

['vestɪdʒ]

义 *n.* 丝毫；遗迹

例 There's not a vestige of truth in the rumor.

译 谣言中没有一点真实性。

---

12 veteran

['vetərən]

义 *adj.* 老练的

例 He is a veteran parliamentarian whose views enjoy widespread respect.

译 他是一位经验丰富的国会议员，他的观点广受尊重。

---

13 veterinarian

[ˌvetərɪ'nerɪən]

义 *n.* 兽医

例 If you're a veterinarian, you're out of luck.

译 如果你是一名兽医，那你就倒霉了。

---

14 viability

[ˌvaɪə'bɪlətɪ]

义 *n.* 生存能力；发育能力；可行性

例 That is exactly why a more sensible preservation strategy would be to assist the farmers to modernize their farms to the extent needed to maintain viability.

译 这就是为什么一个更明智的保存策略应该是帮助农民使他们的农场现代化到能保持生存能力的程度。

---

15 viaduct

['vaɪədʌkt]

义 *n.* 高架桥

例 They recommended that the viaduct be replaced rather than quake-proofed.

译 他们建议更换这座高架桥，而不要对其做抗震处理。

---

16 vibe

[vaɪb]

义 *n.* 感应；氛围；气氛

例 The vibe in the restaurant is pretty laid back, not like ritzier restaurants in Beverly Hills.

译 这家餐厅的氛围相当悠闲，不像比弗利山庄的豪华餐厅。

---

17 vibraphone

['vaɪbrəfəʊn]

义 *n.* 电颤琴

例 Mounted on a roof, one of the systems looks vaguely like a giant vibraphone.

译 安装在屋顶上的其中一个系统看上去隐约像一个巨大的颤音琴。

---

18 vibrato

[vɪ'brɑːtəʊ]

义 *n.* 振动音，颤音

例 I encourage oboe and clarinet players to use plenty of vibrato.

译 我鼓励双簧管和单簧管的演奏者使用大量的颤音。

---

19 vibrio

['vɪbrɪˌəʊ]

义 *n.*（微生物）弧菌（一种 S 形霍乱菌）

例 This event of vibrio parahaemolyticus food poisoning was due to the food pollution in residents' home dinner.

译 本次副溶血性弧菌食物中毒事件是居民家庭晚餐食物污染引起的。

---

20 victorious

[vɪk'tɔ:rɪəs]

义 *adj.* 胜利的，得胜的

例 In 1978 he played for the victorious Argentinian side in the World Cup.

译 1978 年，他为赢得世界杯的阿根廷队效力。

---

21 victual

['vɪtl]

义 *n.* 食物；食物供应

例 I can't abide to see good victuals go to waste.

译 我不能眼睁睁地看着好的食物白白浪费掉。

---

22 vide

['vi:deɪ]

义 *v.* 请见，参阅

例 The "excessive entanglement" test was added (vide supra).

译 添加了"过度纠缠"测试（见上）。

---

23 video

['vɪdɪəʊ]

义 *n.* 录像；视频

例 If your kid gets hooked on video games, turn that addiction into a bargaining chip.

译 如果你的孩子沉迷于电子游戏，那就把这种上瘾变成讨价还价的筹码。

---

24 videotape

['vɪdɪəʊteɪp]

义 *v.* 将……录到录像带上

例 She videotaped the entire trip.

译 她录下了整个旅程。

---

25 vie

[vaɪ]

义 *v.* 竞争

例 The two are vying for the support of New York voters.

译 两人正在争夺纽约选民的支持。

---

26 viewable

['vju:əbəl]

义 *adj.* 看得见的；值得一看的

例 The Bilys wanted the clocks to be viewable by the public.

译 比利夫妇希望公众能够看到这些时钟。

---

27 vigil

['vɪdʒɪl]

义 *n.* 守夜，值夜；监视

例 Outside the building people continue their vigil, huddling around bonfires.

| 译 | 大楼外的人们继续守夜，挤在篝火旁。 |

---

28 vigilant

['vɪdʒɪlənt]

义 *adj.* 警戒的；警惕的

例 However, a different explanation is necessary in cases where the vigilant behavior is not directed at predators.

译 然而，当警觉的行为不是针对捕食者时，就需要另一种解释了。

---

29 vigorously

['vɪgərəslɪ]

义 *adv.* 有力地；健壮地

例 He shook his head vigorously.

译 他用力地摇了摇头。

---

30 vilify

['vɪlɪfaɪ]

义 *v.* 诽谤，中伤

例 The agency has been vilified by some doctors for being unnecessarily slow to approve life-saving drugs.

译 一些医生指责该机构在批准救命药物方面过于迟缓。

---

31 violator

['vaɪəleɪtə(r)]

义 *n.* 违反者；违背者；妨害者

例 It then punishes violators of the rules and regulations.

译 然后它对违反规章制度的人进行处罚。

---

32 violinist

[ˌvaɪə'lɪnɪst]

义 *n.* 小提琴手

例 Did you know then that you would become a professional violinist?

译 那时候你知道你会成为一名职业小提琴家吗？

---

33 viral

['vaɪrəl]

义 *adj.* 病毒的

例 Nuclear polyhedrosis viral infection is one factor these disparate species share.

译 核多角体病毒感染是这些不同物种共有的一个因素。

---

34 virtuoso

[ˌvɜːrtʃʊ'əʊsəʊ]

义 *n.* 艺术能手；演艺精湛的人

例 The team gave a virtuoso performance.

译 这个团队举办了一场名家表演。

---

35 virtuous

['vɜːrtʃʊəs]

义 *adj.* 有品德的；贞洁的

例 Louis was shown as an intelligent, courageous and virtuous family man.

译 路易斯被认为是一个聪明、勇敢、有道德的顾家男人。

---

36 viscosity

义 *n.* 黏度；黏性

[vɪ'skɑːsətɪ]

例 Magnetic fields reduce blood viscosity.

译 磁场可以降低血液黏度。

37　viscous

['vɪskəs]

义 *adj.* 黏的，黏性的

例 Although the hot rock of the mantle is a solid, under the tremendous pressure of the crust and overlying rock of the mantle, it flows like a viscous liquid.

译 尽管地幔的热岩石是固体，但在地壳和地幔上的岩石的巨大压力下，它像黏性液体一样流动。

38　visibility

[ˌvɪzə'bɪlətɪ]

义 *n.* 能见度；可见性

例 Fog severely restricted visibility.

译 雾严重限制能见度。

39　visionary

['vɪʒənerɪ]

义 *adj.* 幻想的；有远见卓识的　　*n.* 有远见的人

例 He sees himself as a visionary.

译 他认为自己是一个有远见的人。

40　visitation

[ˌvɪzɪ'teɪʃn]

义 *n.* 访问；探视

例 She is seeking more liberal visitation with her daughter.

译 她正在寻求对女儿更自由的探视权。

41　visualization

[ˌvɪʒʊəlaɪ'zeɪʃn]

义 *n.* 可视化，形象化

例 Net-language is characterized as pidginization, visualization, popularization and personalization etc.

译 网络语言具有混杂化、视觉化、时尚化与个性化等特点。

42　visualize

['vɪʒʊəlaɪz]

义 *v.* 使……看得见；设想

例 He could not visualize her as old.

译 他无法想象她年老时的样子。

43　visually

['vɪʒʊəlɪ]

义 *adv.* 看得见地，视觉上地

例 Consumers like being able to visually examine the color of the milk.

译 消费者喜欢能够直观地检查牛奶的颜色。

44　vitro

['viːtrəʊ]

义 *adj.* 体外的

例 Many of these deaths could be prevented through the development of in vitro models of human cells and tissues that better mimic in vivo environments.

译 通过建立能够更好地模拟体内环境的人体细胞和组织的体外模型，许多此类死亡是可以避免的。

45　vocalist

['vəʊkəlɪst]

义 *n.* 声乐家；歌手

例 The band is breaking in a new backing vocalist, who sounds great.

译 该乐队在让一名听上去很棒的新伴奏歌手适应。

46　vocalize

['vəʊkəlaɪz]

义 *v.* 发声

例 Your baby will begin to vocalize long before she can talk.

译 你的宝宝在会说话前很早就开始咿呀发声了。

47　vocation

[vəʊ'keɪʃn]

义 *n.* 职业；使命

例 Her vocation is her work as an actress.

译 她的职业是当演员。

48　voltmeter

['vəʊltmiːtər]

义 *n.* 伏特计，电压表

例 We believe that the design of digital voltmeter would be used abroad in future.

译 相信这个设计会在未来的电压表中广泛应用。

49　voluntarily

[ˌvɑːlən'terəli]

义 *adv.* 自动地；以自由意志

例 Four people who sought refuge in the Italian embassy have left voluntarily.

译 四名在意大利大使馆寻求庇护的人已经自愿离开。

50　voraciously

[və'reɪʃəsli]

义 *adv.* 贪吃地；贪婪地

例 All I can say for myself is that I read voraciously and draw fairly well.

译 我能说的就是，我经常读书，画画也画得也不错。

51　vow

[vaʊ]

义 *n.* 誓约

例 I made a silent vow to be more careful in the future.

译 我默默发誓今后要更加小心。

52　voyager

['vɔɪɪdʒər]

义 *n.* 航行者

例 Its spaceship was engineered by Bert Rutan, renowned for designing the Voyager.

译 它的宇宙飞船是由伯特·鲁坦设计的，他以设计旅行者号而闻名。

53 voyeur

[vwɑːˈjɜːr]

义 *n.* 窥淫狂者，窥隐私者

例 The media has made unfeeling voyeurs of all of us.

译 媒体把我们所有人都变成了无情的偷窥狂。

54 vulgar

[ˈvʌlgər]

义 *adj.* 通俗的；粗俗的

例 He was a vulgar old man, but he never swore in front of a woman.

译 他是个粗俗的老头，但他从不在女人面前骂人。

55 vulture

[ˈvʌltʃər]

义 *n.* 秃鹰，兀鹰；贪婪的人

例 The Turkey Vulture could scent up to 10 miles.

译 土耳其秃鹰，能够闻到 10 英里以外的气味。

56 wader

[ˈweɪdər]

义 *n.* 跋涉者；（钓鱼用的）防水长靴

例 My dad always wears his wader and fishing vest when he goes fishing.

译 我爸爸去钓鱼时都会穿他的防水长靴和钓鱼背心。

57 wag

[wæg]

义 *v.* （狗）摇摆（尾巴）

例 Dogs wag their tails when they are pleased.

译 狗高兴时就摇尾巴。

58 wager

[ˈweɪdʒər]

义 *n.* 赌注；赌博　*v.* 打赌

例 I'll wager that she knows more about it than she's saying.

译 我敢打赌她知道的比她说的要多。

59 wail

[weɪl]

义 *v.* 痛哭，悲叹　*n.* 恸哭，号啕大哭

例 I joined my wail to theirs, loud and bitter.

译 我和他们一起大声痛哭。

60 walleye

[ˈwɔːˌlaɪ]

义 *n.* 斜视；碧古鱼

例 The Lake Superior National Marine Conservation Area offers unparalleled waters for trout, whitefish, lake herring, and walleye.

译 苏必利尔湖国家海洋保护区为鳟鱼、白鱼、湖鲱鱼和碧古鱼提供了无与伦比的水域。

61 wallpaper

[ˈwɔːlpeɪpər]

义 *n.* 壁纸，墙纸；电脑屏幕图案

例 Wallpaper is sold in rolls.

译 墙纸是成卷出售的。

62 wand

[wɑːnd]

义 *n.* 棒，棍，杖

例 Visitors can expect to be searched with a metal-detecting wand.

译 游客可能会被一根金属探测棒搜身。

---

63 warbler

['wɔːrblər]

义 *n.* 莺，啭鸟

例 A reed warbler is feeding a baby cuckoo.

译 一只苇莺正在喂养小杜鹃。

---

64 warm-blooded

['wɔːrm'blʌdɪd]

义 *adj.* 热血的

例 Those finds are critical to understanding how warm-blooded creatures evolved.

译 这些发现对于了解温血动物是如何进化的至关重要。

---

65 warmer

['wɔːrmər]

义 *n.* 取暖器   *adj.* 更温暖的

例 Warmer and drier weather leads to dangerous fire conditions.

译 更温暖干燥的天气导致了危险的火灾情况。

---

66 warmongering

['wɔːrmɑːŋɡərɪŋ]

义 *adj.* 好战者的

例 The warmongering orcs depicted in *The Lord of the Rings* trilogy are evil, unpleasant creatures that leave death and destruction in their wake.

译 在《指环王》三部曲中，好战的兽人是一种邪恶的、令人讨厌的生物，他们留下了死亡和毁灭。

---

67 warranty

['wɔːrəntɪ]

义 *n.* (商品的)保修单；保修期

例 Is the car still under warranty?

译 这辆车还在保修期内吗?

---

68 warship

['wɔːrʃɪp]

义 *n.* 军舰，战舰

例 The navy is to launch a new warship today.

译 海军今天有一艘新军舰要下水。

---

69 wasteland

['weɪstlænd]

义 *n.* 荒地；未开垦地

例 If everyone lets their goats graze in the commons, it turns into a devastated wasteland with no grass left for anyone.

译 如果每个人都让他们的山羊在共有地吃草，共有地就会变成一片荒芜的荒地，没有草留给大家了。

---

70 wastewater

['weɪstwɔːtər]

义 *n.* 废水，污水

例 Treating wastewater is a good way to provide fresh water for us.

译 处理废水是为我们提供淡水的一种好方法。

---

71 watchmaker

['wɑːtʃmeɪkər]

义 *n.* 钟表匠

例 The watchmaker is near-sighted.

译 这位钟表匠是个近视眼。

---

72 watercolor

['wɔːtəkʌlə]

义 *n.* 水彩颜料；水彩画（法）

例 Capturing moments such as this in a watercolor still life has become the life.

译 在水彩静物中捕捉这样的瞬间就成了生活。

---

73 watercraft

['wɔːtəˌkrɑːft]

义 *n.* 船，水运工具

例 The paper analyzes the factors that influence the reliability of fire alarm system in watercraft.

译 文章分析了船舶火灾报警系统中影响可靠性的因素。

---

74 waterfowl

['wɔːtərfaʊl]

义 *n.* 水鸟，水禽

例 The salt marshes and mud flats attract large numbers of waterfowl.

译 盐碱地和淤泥滩吸引来大量水鸟。

---

75 waterline

['wɔːtərlaɪn]

义 *n.* 吃水线，水印横线

例 Boot Topping is the black paint used at the waterline of many warships.

译 水线带是许多战舰水线上使用的黑色油漆。

---

76 wavy

['weɪvi]

义 *adj.* 波浪形的；起伏的

例 Curly or wavy hair is a must.

译 卷发是必须的。

---

77 waxy

['wæksi]

义 *adj.* 像蜡的；蜡色的；苍白的

例 Symptoms can include catatonic stupor and waxy flexibility.

译 症状包括紧张性麻木和蜡像屈曲。

---

78 weariness

['wɪərɪnəs]

义 *n.* 疲倦，疲劳；厌倦

例 He returned home as wet as a rag, and tired out from weariness and hunger.

译 他回到家里，浑身湿透，又累又饿。

---

79 weary

['wɪri]

义 *adj.* 疲倦的；厌烦的

例 Rachel looked pale and weary.

译 雷切尔看上去脸色苍白，疲惫不堪。

80　weeklong

['wiːkˌlɔːŋ]

义 *adj.* 为时一周的

例 You only pass by one village on the entire weeklong trip.

译 在为期一整周的旅程中，你只会经过一个村庄。

81　weft

[weft]

义 *n.* 纬，纬纱；织物；信号旗

例 The term weft is taken from weaving terminology.

译 纬纱这一术语是来自机织工艺。

82　weld

[weld]

义 *v.* 焊接；使结合

例 The car has had a new wing welded on.

译 这辆汽车焊上了一块新挡泥板。

83　werewolf

['werwʊlf]

义 *n.* 狼人；凶人

例 The werewolf and vampire are similar in many ways.

译 狼人和吸血鬼在很多方面都很相似。

84　westbound

['westbaʊnd]

义 *adj.* 向西行的

例 He leaned against the sill of the ticket window and said, "when's the next westbound train?".

译 他靠在售票窗口的窗台上说："下一班西行的火车是什么时候？"

85　westerner

['westərnər]

义 *n.* 西方人；（美国的）西部人

例 For most Westerners, Chinese characters are hard to learn well.

译 对多数西方人来说，汉字很难学好。

86　wettest

['wetɪst]

义 *adj.* 湿的；多雨的

例 Last summer was the wettest on record.

译 去年夏天是有记录以来最潮湿的夏天。

87　whaler

['weɪlər]

义 *n.* 捕鲸者；捕鲸船

例 Jill and I did take the boat—a large, underpowered whaler—for a cruise to an amazing snorkeling spot.

译 吉尔和我确实乘坐了这艘船———一艘动力不足的大型捕鲸船——到一个令人惊叹的浮潜地点巡航。

88　wheeze

[wiːz]

义 *v.* 喘息；呼哧呼哧地响

例 Do you wheeze sometimes?

译 你会有时喘息吗？

---

89 whelk

[welk]

义 *n.* 海螺

例 Moon snail is one of the relatives of whelk living in the shallow Yellow sea.

译 月亮蜗牛是一种生活在黄海浅海处的海螺近亲。

---

90 whereabouts

['weərəˌbaʊts]

义 *adv.* 哪里，在哪一带   *n.* 行踪；下落

例 The police are anxious to hear from anyone who may know the whereabouts of the firearms.

译 警方急于听取任何可能知道枪支下落的人的消息。

---

91 whet

[wet]

义 *v.* 刺激；促进

例 The book will whet your appetite for more of her work.

译 这本书会激起你对她更多作品的兴趣。

---

92 whiff

[wɪf]

义 *n.* 一阵香气

例 He caught a whiff of her perfume.

译 他闻到一股她的香水味。

---

93 whim

[wɪm]

义 *n.* 一时的兴致，奇想

例 He was forced to pander to her every whim.

译 他被迫迎合她的每一个怪念头。

---

94 whimsy

['wɪmzɪ]

义 *n.* 怪念头；异想天开

例 The papers are not bereft of whimsy, but it is confined to footnotes and asides.

译 这些论文并非没有奇思妙想，但仅限于脚注和旁注。

---

95 whine

[waɪn]

义 *n.* 闹声；抱怨，牢骚

例 There is something undeniably soulful about the eerie whine of the highland bagpipes.

译 不可否认，高地风笛怪异的哀鸣充满了深情。

---

96 whip

[wɪp]

义 *n.* 鞭子；鞭打

例 At his belt he carried a rawhide whip.

译 他腰间挎着一根生皮鞭。

---

97 whir

[wɜːr]

义 *n.* 呼呼声

例 He could hear the whir of a vacuum cleaner.

译 他能听到吸尘器的嗡嗡声。

98 whirl

[wɜːrl]

义 *v.* 使……旋转，回旋

例 To free electrons, something has to make them whirl fast enough to break away from their nuclei.

译 为了释放电子，必须让它们旋转得足够快，才能脱离原子核。

99 whisk

[wɪsk]

义 *n.* 毛掸子；搅拌器　*v.* 拂，掸；搅动；匆匆带走

例 Whisk the batter with a wire whisk or hand beater until it is smooth and light.

译 用电动打蛋器或手动打蛋器搅拌面糊，直到它变得轻薄丝滑。

100 whit

[wɪt]

义 *n.* 些微，一点点

例 He cared not a whit for the social, political or moral aspects of literature.

译 他完全不在乎文学的社会、政治或道德层面。

List 24

1 whiteness

[waɪtnəs]

义 *n.* 白；苍白；洁白

例 Even his ivory whiteness seemed to change.

译 甚至他象牙白色的皮肤似乎也变了。

2 whiz

[wɪz]

义 *n.* 飕飕掠过；奇才　*v.* 飕飕作声

例 They heard bullets continue to whiz over their heads.

译 他们听到子弹不断在他们头顶上嗖嗖飞过。

3 wholeheartedly

[ˌhəʊl'hɑːrtɪdlɪ]

义 *adv.* 尽力；全心全意地

例 Most obviously, the rest of Europe (wrongly) failed to liberalize wholeheartedly too.

译 最明显的是，欧洲其他国家（错误地）也未能全心全意地实现自由化。

4 wholesale

['həʊlseɪl]

义 *adj.* 批发的；大规模的

例 Twenty years later, scientists observing metamorphosis in flies, ants, and beetles noted in the changing muscles and glands the wholesale death of cells.

译 20 年后，科学家们在观察苍蝇、蚂蚁和甲虫的变形时，注意到肌肉和腺体的变化导致了细胞的大规模死亡。

5 wholesaler

['həʊlseɪlər]

义 *n.* 批发商

例 My wholesaler gives me a really good price.

译 我的批发商给了我一个很好的价格。

6 wholesomeness

['həʊlsəmnəs]

义 *n.* 有益于身心健康；增进健康

例 To maintain consistent high quality and to ensure wholesomeness, we must be able to measure, check and take action!

译 为了保持一贯的高质量和确保健康，我们必须能够测量、检查和采取行动！

7 wicked

['wɪkɪd]

义 *adj.* 坏的；邪恶的；缺德的

例 She described the shooting as a wicked attack.

译 她把那次射击描述成一次邪恶的攻击。

8 wildflower

['waɪldˌflaʊə]

义 *n.* 野花

例 This spring, I started a wildflower garden in our yard.

译 今年春天，我在院子里开辟了一个野花园。

9 wile

义 *v.* 欺骗，诱骗；消遣

[waɪl]	例 The teahouse is a great place to wile away an evening.
	译 茶馆是消磨夜晚的好去处。

10 will

[wɪl]

义 *n.* 遗嘱；愿望

例 Our solicitor holds our wills.

译 律师保存着我们的遗嘱。

11 willful

['wɪlfəl]

义 *adj.* 任性的；故意的，有意的

例 They swear, they are ill-mannered and aggressive, willful as two-years-olds and utterly selfish.

译 他们骂人、举止粗鲁、好斗，像两岁小孩一样任性，非常自私。

12 winch

[wɪntʃ]

义 *n.* 绞车

例 The platoon tried to use a winch and a hook to pull the truck back onto the road, but it was too heavy.

译 部队试图用绞车和钩子把卡车拽回路上，但它太重了。

13 windchill

['wɪndtʃɪl]

义 *n.* 吹风冷却

例 The mercury reads 12 degrees outside, but it feels like minus 2 with the windchill.

译 水银温度计显示屋外 12℃，可是寒风袭人，感觉就像零下 2℃一样。

14 winder

['waɪndər]

义 *n.* 卷线机；上发条的转柄

例 The winder will consist of an air expanded winding mandrel.

译 卷线机由气动涨缩卷筒组成。

15 windmill

['wɪndmɪl]

义 *n.* 风车

例 He would look at a simple church or a windmill and notice its beauty.

译 他会看着一座简朴的教堂或一个风车，注意到它的美。

16 wingless

['wɪŋləs]

义 *adj.* 无翼的，没有翅膀的

例 Flea Markets get their name from small, wingless insects called fleas.

译 跳蚤市场是因叫跳蚤的没有翅膀的小虫子而得名。

17 wirelessly

['waɪərləslɪ]

义 *adv.* 以无线的方式

例 It includes plans for breaking up satellites into smaller components that communicate wirelessly.

译 该计划包括将卫星分解成更小的无线通信组件。

18 wiry

['waɪərɪ]

义 *adj.* 金属丝的；坚硬的；瘦而结实的

例 His body is wiry and athletic.

译 他的身体精瘦结实而且健壮。

---

19 wishful

['wɪʃfəl]

义 *adj.* 渴望的；一厢情愿的

例 It is wishful thinking to expect deeper change under his leadership.

译 期望在他的领导下进行更深层次的变革是一厢情愿的想法。

---

20 wisp

[wɪsp]

义 *n.* 小束；一缕；瘦小的人

例 She's just a little bitty wisp of a girl.

译 她只是个小女孩。

---

21 wistful

['wɪstfl]

义 *adj.* 渴望的；忧思的；留恋的

例 I can't help feeling slightly wistful about the perks I'm giving up.

译 对于我将要放弃的津贴，我不禁有点伤感。

---

22 witty

['wɪtɪ]

义 *adj.* 机智的，诙谐的

例 His plays were very good, very witty.

译 他的那些剧作非常好，非常诙谐。

---

23 wizard

['wɪzərd]

义 *n.* 男巫；奇才

例 The wizard recited a spell.

译 巫师念了一个咒语。

---

24 wobbly

['wɑ:blɪ]

义 *adj.* 摆动的

例 I was sitting on a wobbly plastic chair.

译 我当时正坐在一把摇摇晃晃的塑料椅子上。

---

25 wonderland

['wʌndərlænd]

义 *n.* 仙境，奇境

例 It tells the story of a girl named Alice who falls down a rabbit hole into a wonderland.

译 它讲述了一个名叫爱丽丝的女孩掉进兔子洞，进入仙境的故事。

---

26 wonderment

['wʌndərmənt]

义 *n.* 惊奇；惊叹；奇异的事

例 His big blue eyes opened wide in wonderment.

译 他那双蓝色的大眼睛惊奇地睁得大大的。

27 woodcarver

[ˈwʊdkɑ:vər]

义 *n.* 木雕艺人，木雕家

例 Woodcarvers were a very important group of artists.

译 木雕师是一个非常重要的艺术家群体。

---

28 woodchuck

[ˈwʊdtʃʌk]

义 *n.* 土拨鼠

例 Unlike squirrels, woodchucks, and many other woodland animals, bears do not actually hibernate.

译 与松鼠、旱獭和其他林地动物不同，熊并不是真正的冬眠动物。

---

29 woodworking

[ˈwʊdˌwɜːrkɪŋ]

义 *n.* 木工活，木工艺

例 Painting, woodworking, sculpting, programming or blogging are all great starts.

译 绘画、木工、雕刻、编程或写博客都是很好的开始。

---

30 woolen

[ˈwʊlɪn]

义 *adj.* 羊毛的；羊毛制的 *n.* 毛制品

例 I want some woolen yarn.

译 我想要一些毛线。

---

31 wordplay

[ˈwɜːrdpleɪ]

义 *n.* 双关语；文字游戏

例 Puns are a form of wordplay that exists in all languages.

译 双关语是所有语言里都存在的一种文字游戏。

---

32 workmanship

[ˈwɜːrkmənʃɪp]

义 *n.* 手艺，技巧；工艺品

例 The problem may be due to poor workmanship.

译 这个问题可能是工艺不好造成的。

---

33 workplace

[ˈwɜːrkpleɪs]

义 *n.* 工作场所

例 Non-smoking is now the norm in most workplaces.

译 现在禁烟已成为大多数工作场所的规范。

---

34 workweek

[ˈwɜːrkwiːk]

义 *n.* 一星期工作时间

例 Finally, the option of a four-day workweek would be better for individual employees.

译 最后，这种一周四天工作日的选择对于员工个人来说也是有利的。

---

35 worldliness

[ˈwɜːrldlɪnəs]

义 *n.* 俗气；世故

例 He was the embodiment of the Master's ideal of life in the world, unstained by worldliness.

译 他是大师理想生活在人间的化身，不被世俗所玷污。

36 worldview

['wɜːrldvjuː]

义 *n.* 世界观

例 This new worldview will provide a major revelation for sustainable development.

译 这种新的世界观对于实施可持续发展有重大启示意义。

---

37 worshipful

['wɜːrʃɪpfl]

义 *adj.* 崇拜的，虔敬的

例 It is generally regarded as benevolent, powerful, worshipful and lucky.

译 它通常被认为是仁慈的、强大的、值得崇拜的和幸运的。

---

38 worthiness

['wɜːrðɪnəs]

义 *n.* 值得；相当；有价值

例 Equuleus is only produced in exceptional vintages and is notable for its age worthiness and concentration.

译 天马星座葡萄酒只能在特定的时期酿造，它以时期性和集中的时间性体现独特的价值。

---

39 wrapping

['ræpɪŋ]

义 *n.* 包装材料

例 Foil wrapping paper is beautiful but difficult to use.

译 锡箔包装纸很漂亮，但使用起来很困难。

---

40 wreathe

[riːð]

义 *v.* 环绕，盘绕；作成花圈

例 The postures of these dragons have different characteristics during various ages. Some dragons curve and wreathe, some curvet through the clouds, some march forward leisurely and some are poised.

译 这些龙的姿态各具时代特色，有的曲体盘绕，有的穿云腾越，有的信步前行，有的蓄力待发。

---

41 wreckage

['rekɪdʒ]

义 *n.* 破坏；残骸

例 They stared unseeingly at the wreckage.

译 他们茫然地盯着残骸。

---

42 wrench

[rentʃ]

义 *n.* 扳钳，扳手

例 I ran to several stores before I found the wrench.

译 我跑了好几家商店，才找到这个扳手。

---

43 wrestle

['resl]

义 *v.* 摔跤；奋力对付

例 Armed guards wrestled with the intruder.

译 武装警卫和闯入者扭打起来。

---

44 wring

[rɪŋ]

义 *v.* 拧

例 He turned away to wring out the wet shirt.

译 他转过身去拧湿衬衣。

---

45 wrinkle

['rɪŋkl]

义 *n.* 皱纹；皱褶

例 Ben brushed smooth a wrinkle in his trousers.

译 本用刷子把裤子上的皱褶刷平。

---

46 yarmulke

['jɑ:rmʊlkə]

义 *n.* 圆顶小帽

例 Even though I'm an atheist, I still wear my yarmulke as it keeps my brain warm.

译 虽然我是个无神论者，但我仍然戴着圆顶小帽来取暖。

---

47 yarn

[jɑ:rn]

义 *n.* 纱，线

例 Before entering the stadium, I bought homespun yarn from a huge knitting supply booth, set up by a local shop owner, right outside the ball park.

译 在进入体育场之前，我从一个巨大的针织供应摊位上买了土布纱线，这个摊位是当地一家商店的老板在球场外面设立的。

---

48 yellowish

['jeləʊɪʃ]

义 *adj.* 微黄色的

例 Loess is fine yellowish mineral stuff, rock pulverized by glaciers over the 150 millennia of the last ice age and carried south by rivers.

译 黄土是微细的淡黄色矿物，是在上一个冰期的 15 万年里被冰川磨碎的岩石，并被河流冲入南方。

---

49 yew

[ju:]

义 *n.* 紫杉

例 All parts of the yew tree are poisonous, including the berries.

译 紫杉树的所有部分都有毒，包括浆果。

---

50 zeal

[zi:l]

义 *n.* 热情，热忱

例 His reforming zeal was boundless.

译 他的改革热情是无穷的。

第二部分
数学词汇

List 1

1 add

[æd]

义 *v.* 加

例 An integer, *n*, is added to 4.

译 将整数 *n* 加到 4 上。

---

2 addition

[ə'dɪʃn]

义 *n.* 加法

例 This service is a simple math calculation service, providing addition and subtraction operations.

译 该服务是一项简单的算术计算服务，提供了加法和减法运算。

---

3 arithmetic operation

义 算术运算

例 This arithmetic operation of the general interual numbers has wide applicants.

译 广义区间数的算术运算有着广泛的应用。

---

4 calculator

['kælkjʊleɪtər]

义 *n.* 计算器

例 A calculator has a regular price of $58.95 before taxes. It goes on sale at 20% below the regular price.

译 计算器的正常价格是税前 58.95 美元。它以比原价低 20% 的价格出售。

---

5 digit

['dɪdʒɪt]

义 *n.* 数字

例 Note: The overbar notation shows that the digits under the bar will repeat.

译 注意：横线表示法提示横线下面的数字将重复。

---

6 divide

[dɪ'vaɪd]

义 *v.* 除，除以

例 While doing a problem on his calculator, Tom meant to divide a number by 2, but instead he accidentally multiplied the number by 2.

译 在用计算器做一道题时，汤姆本想把一个数除以 2，但却不小心把这个数乘以了 2。

---

7 divisible

[dɪ'vɪzəbl]

义 *adj.* 可除尽的

例 If *x* is any positive integer, then the sum of 8*x* and 13*x* is always divisible by which of the following?

译 如果 *x* 是任意正整数，那么 8*x* 和 13*x* 的和总能被下列哪个数整除？

---

8 division

[dɪ'vɪʒn]

义 *n.* 除法

例 There will be simple tests in addition, subtraction, multiplication and division.

译 会有对加、减、乘、除运算的简单测试。

9 equal

['iːkwəl]

义 *v.* 等于

例 50% of 8 is equal to 25% of what number?

译 8 的 50% 等于哪个数的 25%？

---

10 estimate

['estɪmət]

义 *n.* 估计值

例 Which of the following values is closest to this estimate?

译 下面哪个值最接近这个估计值？

---

11 greatest common factor

义 最大公因数

例 If the positive integers x and y are relatively prime (their greatest common factor is 1) and, $\frac{1}{2} + \frac{1}{3} \times \frac{1}{4} \div \frac{1}{5} = \frac{x}{y}$, then $x + y = ?$

译 如果正整数 x 和 y 是相对质数（它们的最大公因数是 1），且 $\frac{1}{2} + \frac{1}{3} \times \frac{1}{4} \div \frac{1}{5} = \frac{x}{y}$，那么 $x + y = ?$

---

12 multiply

['mʌltɪplaɪ]

义 *v.* 乘

例 When $(x-6)(x-5)(x-4)(x-3)(x-2)$ is multiplied out and all like terms are combined, the resulting expression is written so that powers of x are ordered from greatest to least.

译 将 $(x-6)(x-5)(x-4)(x-3)(x-2)$ 乘起来所得的相似项都结合后，得出的表达式写成 x 的幂从大到小排序形式。

---

13 perfect square

义 完全平方

例 The sum of a sequence of consecutive odd numbers, where the smallest term is 1, is always a perfect square.

译 一个连续的奇数序列的和，其中最小的项是 1，总是一个完全平方。

---

14 root

[ruːt]

义 *n.* 根

例 Which of the following equations given in factored form has roots at $\frac{1}{2}$, $\frac{3}{4}$, i, and $-i$?

译 以下哪一个以因子形式给出的方程的根在 $\frac{1}{2}$，$\frac{3}{4}$，i 和 $-i$？

---

15 scientific notation

义 科学计数法

例 Decimals and scientific notation are permissible for numeric values.

译 数值可用小数形式和科学计数法形式表示。

---

16 simplified form

义 简化式

例 Which of the following is a simplified form of $\sqrt{20} - \sqrt{45}$?

译 下列哪项是 $\sqrt{20} - \sqrt{45}$ 的简化式？

17 square

[skwer]

义 *n.* 正方形；平方

例 The square of a number is the number produced when you multiply that number by itself. For example, the square of 3 is 9.

译 一个数的平方是当你将这个数乘以它本身时产生的数。例如，3 的平方是 9。

---

18 square root

义 平方根

例 What are the two positive integers such that the square root of their sum is 5 and the square root of their product is 12?

译 哪两个正整数的和的平方根是 5，且它们乘积的平方根是 12？

---

19 statement

['steɪtmənt]

义 *n.* 表述

例 Which of the following statements gives the real number values of x for which $x^2 < x$ is true?

译 以下哪项表述给出了使 $x^2 < x$ 为真的 x 的实数值？

---

20 subtraction

[səb'trækʃn]

义 *n.* 减法

例 What is the result of the subtraction problem below?

译 下面这道减法题的结果是什么？

---

21 sum

[sʌm]

义 *n.* 总数，总和

例 In $\triangle ABC$, the sum of the measures of $\angle A$ and $\angle B$ is 68°. What is the measure of $\angle C$?

译 $\triangle ABC$ 中$\angle A$ 和$\angle B$ 的测量值总和为 68°。那么$\angle C$ 的大小是多少？

---

22 the greatest common factor

义 最大公因数

例 The greatest common factor of two whole numbers is 10.

译 两个整数的最大公因数是 10。

---

23 the least common multiple (LCM)

义 最小公倍数

例 The least common multiple (LCM) of two numbers is 108.

译 两个数字的最小公倍数是 108。

---

24 value

['væljuː]

义 *n.* 数值

例 What is the value of $3 \times 2 - 5x$, when $x = -2$?

译 当 $x = -2$ 时，$3 \times 2 - 5x$ 的值是多少？

List 2

1　absolute value

义 绝对值

例 The absolute value of which of the following numbers is the greatest?

译 下列哪个数的绝对值最大？

2　common multiple

义 公倍数

例 What is the least common multiple of the numbers 1, 2, 3, 4, 5, and 6?

译 1，2，3，4，5，6 的最小公倍数是多少？

3　complex number

义 复数

例 For the complex number i and an integer x, which of the following is a possible value of ix?

译 对于复数 i 和整数 x，下列哪一个可能是 ix 的值？

4　consecutive integer

义 连续整数

例 For two consecutive integers, the result of adding the smaller integer and triple the larger integer is 79.

译 对于两个连续的整数，较小的整数加上较大的大整数的三倍，得到的结果是 79。

5　consecutive odd integer

义 连续奇数

例 What is the sum of three consecutive odd integers whose mean is 27?

译 三个平均值为 27 的连续奇整数的和是多少？

6　data set

义 数据集

例 The median of the third data set is 50. What is the median of the first data set?

译 第三个数据集的中位数是 50。第一个数据集的中位数是多少？

7　decimal

['desɪml]

义 *adj.* 十进位的；小数的

例 The figure is accurate to two decimal places.

译 这个数精确到小数点后两位。

8　decimal number

义 十进制数；小数

例 When $\dfrac{n}{200}$ is written as a decimal number, what is the minimum number of digits to the right of the decimal point?

译 当将 $\dfrac{n}{200}$ 写成小数时，小数点右边的最小一位数是多少？

9　decimal point

义　小数点

例　A decimal point, followed by 92 zeros, then the digits 3 and 9.

译　一个小数点，后面有 92 个零，然后是数字 3 和 9。

10　denominator

['dɪ'nɑ:mɪneɪtər]

义　*n.* 分母

例　In order for the sum to be in lowest terms, its numerator and denominator must be reduced by a factor of which of the following?

译　为了使这个和是最简分数，它的分子和分母必须被下列哪个项的一个因数化简？

11　even integer

义　偶数

例　If you add up six consecutive even integers that are each greater than 25, what is the smallest possible sum?

译　如果你把 6 个大于 25 的连续偶数相加，最小的和可能是多少？

12　even number

义　偶数

例　Erin had six slips of paper, numbered 1 through 6. Erik renumbers them once by adding 3 to each odd number and subtracting 1 from each even number.

译　艾琳有六张纸条，从 1 到 6 编号。埃里克给它们重新编号，每个奇数加 3，每个偶数减 1。

13　factor

['fæktər]

义　*n.* 因数

例　If *x* is a factor of 35 and *y* is a factor of 16, the product of *x* and *y* could NOT be which of the following?

译　如果 *x* 是 35 的因数，*y* 是 16 的因数，*x* 和 *y* 的乘积不可能是下列哪个？

14　fraction

['frækʃn]

义　*n.* 分数

例　The students had a grasp of decimals, percentages and fractions.

译　学生们掌握了小数、百分数和分数。

15　imaginary number

义　虚数

例　The imaginary number comes in physical world along with physical evolution.

译　随着当代物理学的发展，虚数进入物理世界。

16　improper fraction

义　假分数，可约分数

例　When $5\frac{4}{9}$ is written as an improper fraction in lowest terms, the numerator of the fraction is 49.

译　当 $5\frac{4}{9}$ 写成最简假分数时，分子是 49。

17　infinite number

义　无穷数

例　For what value of *a* would the following system of equations have an infinite number of solutions?

译　对于 *a* 的什么值，下列方程组有无穷多个解？

18　integer

['ɪntɪdʒər]

义　*n.* 整数

例　The integer 239 is in which of these sets?

译　整数 239 在哪个集合中？

19　irrational number

义　无理数

例　The square root of 2 is an irrational number.

译　2 的平方根是一个无理数。

20　least common multiple

义　最小公倍数

例　What is the least common multiple of 4, 6, and 8?

译　4，6 和 8 的最小公倍数是多少？

21　negative number

义　负数

例　The exponent is a fraction or negative number.

译　指数是一个分数或负数。

22　negative real number

义　负实数

例　Both are negative real numbers.

译　两者都是负实数。

23　negative value

义　负值

例　Whenever $(x+4)(x-3)<0$, which of the following expressions always has a negative value?

译　当 $(x+4)(x-3)<0$ 时，下列哪个表达式总是负的值？

24　numerator

['nu:məreɪtər]

义　*n.* 分子

例　In order for the sum to be in lowest terms, its numerator and denominator must be reduced by a factor of which of the following?

译　为了使这个和是最简分数，它的分子和分母必须被下列哪个项的一个因数化简？

25　odd integer

义　奇整数

例　The lengths of the sides of a triangle are three consecutive odd integers.

译 三角形的边长是三个连续的奇整数。

---

26 odd number

义 奇数

例 The sum of two positive prime numbers is a prime number, and three times that sum is an odd number.

译 两个正质数的和是质数，和的 3 倍是奇数。

---

27 positive integer

义 正整数

例 What are the real solutions for x, if any, to the equation $(|x| - a)(|x| - b) = 0$ if a and b are positive integers?

译 如果 a 和 b 是正整数，那么方程 $(|x| - a)(|x| - b) = 0$ 的实数解是什么？

---

28 positive number

义 正数

例 The period of this function $f(x)$ is the smallest positive number p such that $f(x + p) = f(x)$ for every real number x.

译 该函数的周期 $f(x)$ 是最小的正数 p，因此对于每个实数 x，$f(x + p) = f(x)$。

---

29 positive prime number

义 正质数

例 Let a and b be positive prime numbers. Which of the following numbers must be a factor of both a and b?

译 假设 a 和 b 是正质数。下列哪个数一定是 a 和 b 共同的因数？

---

30 positive rational number

义 正有理数

例 If x and a are positive rational numbers such that $x^{2a} = 3$, then $x^{6a} = ?$

译 如果 x 和 a 是正有理数，使 $x^{2a} = 3$，那么 $x^{6a} = ?$

---

31 positive real number

义 正实数

例 If a and b are positive real numbers, which of the following is equivalent to $(2a^{-1}\sqrt{b})^4/ab^{-3}$?

译 如果 a 和 b 都是正实数，下列哪项等于 $(2a^{-1}\sqrt{b})^4/ab^{-3}$？

---

32 prime factor

义 质因数

例 How many positive prime factors does the number 30 have?

译 数字 30 有多少个正质因数？

---

33 prime factorization

义 分解质因数

例 The number 1,001 is the product of the prime numbers 7,11, and 13. Knowing this, what is the prime factorization of 30,030?

译 数字 1 001 是质数 7，11 和 13 的乘积。知道了这个，那数字 30 030 的质因数是多少？

34 prime number

义 质数

例 Which of the following prime numbers must be one of the original prime numbers?

译 下列哪个质数一定是原始质数之一?

---

35 quarter

['kwɔːrtər]

义 *n.* 四分之一

例 The diagram below shows a quarter of each of two circles both having point *C* as their center.

译 下图显示了以 *C* 点为中心的两个圆的四分之一。

---

36 rational number

义 有理数

例 What rational number is halfway between $\frac{1}{5}$ and $\frac{1}{3}$?

译 $\frac{1}{5}$ 和 $\frac{1}{3}$ 之间的有理数是什么?

---

37 real number

义 实数

例 If *p* is a positive real number and $2\sin x = 2\sin(x + p)$ for every real value of *x*, what is the smallest possible value for *p*, in degrees?

译 如果 *p* 是一个正实数,对于每一个 *x* 的实数都有 $2\sin x = 2\sin(x + p)$,那么 *p* 的最小度数是多少?

---

38 real number line

义 实数线

例 The difference $\frac{3}{5} - \frac{1}{3}$ lies in which of the following intervals graphed on the real number line?

译 $\frac{3}{5} - \frac{1}{3}$ 的差在实数线以下哪个区间上?

---

39 reciprocal

[rɪ'sɪprəkl]

义 *n.* 倒数

例 What positive number when divided by its reciprocal has a result of $\frac{4}{25}$?

译 哪个正数除以它的倒数结果是 $\frac{4}{25}$?

---

40 set

[set]

义 *n.* 集合

例 A function that is defined by the set of ordered pairs {(2, 1), (4, 2), (6, 3)} has domain {2, 4, 6}.

译 由有序对 {(2, 1), (4, 2), (6, 3)} 集合定义的函数具有 {2, 4, 6} 域。

---

41 solution set

义 解集

例 Which of the following number line graphs shows the solution set of $3(x + 2) + 1 < 4x + 15$?

译 下面哪个数轴图体现了 $3(x + 2) + 1 < 4x + 15$ 的解集?

42 **subset**

['sʌbset]

义 *n.* 子集

例 Consider sets *A*, *B*, *C*, and *D* such that *B* is a subset of *A*, *C* is a subset of *B*, and *Z* is a subset of *C*.

译 思考集合 *A*、*B*、*C* 和 *D*，使 *B* 是 *A* 的子集，*C* 是 *B* 的子集，*Z* 是 *C* 的子集。

---

43 **the least common denominator**

义 最小公分母

例 What is the least common denominator for adding the fractions $\frac{4}{35}$, $\frac{1}{56}$, and $\frac{35}{16}$?

译 分数 $\frac{4}{35}$，$\frac{1}{56}$ 和 $\frac{35}{16}$ 相加的最小公分母是多少?

---

44 **whole number**

义 整数

例 Each of 20 students in a class took a test and received a whole number score.

译 一个班中的 20 名学生中的每个人都参加了一项测试，并得到了一个整数的分数。

List 3

1　arithmetic mean

义 算术平均数；等差中项

例 One should therefore take the arithmetic mean as the sum.

译 必须取算术平均数作为和。

2　arithmetic progression

义 等差数列

例 The nth term of an arithmetic progression is given by the formula $a_n = a_1 + (n-1)d$, where d is the common difference and a_1 is the first term.

译 等差数列的第 n 项由公式 $a_n = a_1 + (n-1)d$ 给出，其中 d 是公差，a_1 是第一项。

3　arithmetic sequence

义 等差数列

例 The degree measure of the interior angles of $\triangle ABC$ form an arithmetic sequence with common difference 30°.

译 $\triangle ABC$ 各内角的度数形成一个公差为 30° 的等差数列。

4　common difference

义 公差

例 Consecutive terms of a certain arithmetic sequence have a positive common difference.

译 某等差数列的连续项有正的公差。

5　common ratio

义 公比

例 The sum of an infinite geometric series with first term a and common ratio $r < 1$ is given by $\frac{a}{1-r}$.

译 首项为 a，公比为 r 且 $r < 1$ 的无穷等比数列的和为 $\frac{a}{1-r}$。

6　consecutive terms

义 连续项

例 In an arithmetic sequence, consecutive terms differ by the same amount.

译 在等差序列中，连续项的差值相同。

7　explicit formula

义 显式公式

例 Which of the following equations is an explicit formula for this sequence?

译 下面哪个方程是这个序列的显式公式?

8　finite arithmetic sequence

义 有穷等差序列

例 A finite arithmetic sequence has seven terms, and the first term is 34.

译 有穷等差序列有 7 项，第一项是 34。

9 geometric mean

义 几何平均数，等比中项

例 What is the geometric mean of 12 and 48?

译 12 和 48 的几何平均数是多少？

---

10 geometric sequence

义 等比数列

例 The 1st term in the geometric sequence below is -4. If it can be determined, what is the 6th term?

译 下面等比数列的第一项是 -4。如果可以确定，第六项是什么？

---

11 number sequence

义 数字数列

例 In a certain number sequence, each element after the 1st element is the result of multiplying the previous element by 3 and adding 2 to that product.

译 在某个数字数列中，第 1 个元素之后的每个元素都是前一个元素乘以 3，然后再加上 2 的结果。

---

12 recursive formula

义 递归公式

例 The recursive formula for a sequence is given below, where a_n, is the value of the nth term.

译 下面给出了一个序列的递归公式，其中 a_n 是第 n 项的值。

---

13 sequence

['siːkwəns]

义 *n.* 数列

例 We shall study a very particular kind of sequences, called convergent sequences.

译 我们将学习一类很特别的数列，叫作收敛数列。

List 4

1　acute angle

义 锐角

例 In the right triangle shown below, a leg is 2 meters long and its adjacent acute angle measures 53°.

译 在下图的直角三角形中，一条边有 2 米长，它相邻的锐角为 53°。

2　acute triangle

义 锐角三角形

例 The sides of an acute triangle measure 14 cm, 18 cm and 20 cm, respectively.

译 锐角三角形的边长分别为 14 厘米、18 厘米和 20 厘米。

3　adjacent angle

义 邻角

例 The noncommon rays of two adjacent angles form a straight angle.

译 两个相邻角的非共射线构成一个平角。

4　angle
['æŋgl]

义 *n.* 角度，角

例 What is the measure of the angle indicated with a question mark?

译 问号表示的角度是多少？

5　angle of depression

义 俯角

例 The instrument is 60 feet above sea level and indicates an angle of depression of 53° to the rowboat.

译 该仪器位于海平面以上 60 英尺的地方，指向划艇的俯角为 53 度。

6　angle of inclination

义 倾斜角，倾角

例 Which of the following expressions gives the angle of inclination of the ramp?

译 下面哪个表达式体现了斜面的倾斜角？

7　Angle-Side-Angle (ASA) property

义 角边角性质

例 One of the following angle congruences completes what is needed to prove as directly as possible that △*ABE* is congruent to △*DCE* by applying the Angle-Side-Angle (ASA) property. Which one?

译 利用下列全等角的一个角就可以运用角边角（ASA）性质，尽可能直接地证明△*ABE* 全等于△*DCE*。是哪一个？

8　arc
[ɑːrk]

义 *n.* 弧

例 The length of arc *AB* of a circle is equal to 1/5 of the circumference of the circle.

译 圆的弧 *AB* 的长度等于圆周长的 1/5。

9 area

['erɪə]

义 *n.* 面积

例 What is the area, in square inches of △*ABC* below?

译 下图的△*ABC* 面积是多少平方英寸?

---

10 bisector

[baɪ'sektə]

义 *n.* 二等分物，二等分线，角平分线

例 In △*ABC* below, the measure of ∠*ABD* is 70°, the measure of ∠*ACB* is 32°, *D* is on *BC*, and *AD* is a bisector of ∠*BAC*. What is the measure of ∠*ADB*?

译 在下图的△*ABC* 中，∠*ABD* 的测量值为 70°，∠*ACB* 的测量值为 32°，*D* 在 *BC* 上，*AD* 是∠*BAC* 的角平分线。∠*ADB* 的测量值是多少?

---

11 central angle

义 圆心角

例 A central angle with measure 18° intercepts minor arc *AB*.

译 从测量值为 18° 的圆心角截取小弧 *AB*。

---

12 chord

[kɔ:rd]

义 *n.* 弦

例 The figure below shows a circle with a radius of 5 cm and a chord of the circle.

译 下图显示了一个半径为 5 厘米的圆和其中一条弦。

---

13 circle

['sɜ:rkl]

义 *n.* 圆 (圈)

例 The chord is 3 cm from the center of the circle.

译 弦距圆心 3 厘米。

---

14 circumference

[sər'kʌmfərəns]

义 *n.* 圆周，周长

例 The seven congruent circles shown in the figure below are centered at points *A* through *G*, and each circle has a circumference of 24π cm.

译 下图所示的 7 个全等圆的圆心位于 *A* 到 *G* 的点上，每个圆的周长为 24π cm。

---

15 collinear

[kə'lɪnɪə]

义 *adj.* 同线的，共轴的

例 Points *A*, *B*, *C*, and *D* are collinear such that *A* is between *C* and *B*, and *D* is between *A* and *B*. Which of the following statements about the distances between these points must be true?

译 点 *A*、*B*、*C* 和 *D* 共线，因此 *A* 在 *C* 和 *B* 之间，而 *D* 在 *A* 和 *B* 之间，关于这些点之间的距离，下列哪个说法一定是正确的?

---

16 collinear point

义 共线点

例 Points *A*, *B*, and *C* are vertices of an equilateral triangle. Points *A*, *B*, and *D* are collinear points, with *B* between *A* and *D*.

译 点 *A*、*B* 和 *C* 是一个等边三角形的顶点。点 *A*、*B*、*D* 共线，点 *B* 在点 *A* 和点 *D* 之间。

17 column

['kɑ:ləm]

义 *n.* 圆柱；纵行

例 The table below shows the numbers of rows and columns in each of five matrices.

译 下表显示了 5 个矩阵中每个矩阵的行数和列数。

---

18 concentric circle

义 同心圆

例 Two concentric circles have radius of 5 centimeters and 6 centimeters, respectively.

译 两个同心圆的半径分别为 5 厘米和 6 厘米。

---

19 cone

[kəʊn]

义 *n.* 圆锥体

例 Cones *A* and *B* are both right circular cones.

译 锥 *A* 和锥 *B* 都是正圆锥体。

---

20 congruent

['kɑ:ŋgrʊənt]

义 *adj.* 全等的

例 The interior angles that are not right angles are congruent.

译 不是直角的内角是全等的。

---

21 congruent trapezoid

义 全等梯形

例 As shown below, $\overline{BE}$ divides rectangle *ACDF* into two congruent trapezoids.

译 如下图所示，$\overline{BE}$ 将矩形 *ACDF* 分成两个全等的梯形。

---

22 convex polygon

义 凸面多角形

例 The sum of the measures of the interior angles of a convex polygon with t sides is $180(t-2)$ degrees.

译 一个有 t 条边的凸多边形的内角之和是 $180(t-2)$ 度。

---

23 corresponding side

义 对应边

例 One pair of corresponding sides of two similar triangles are 3 and 8 inches long, respectively.

译 2 个相似三角形的一对对应边长度分别为 3 英寸和 8 英寸。

---

24 coterminal

[kəʊ'təmɪnəl]

义 *adj.* 共终端的

例 What is the measure of the smallest negative angle that is coterminal with 110°?

译 与 110° 角共端点的最小负角是多少度？

---

25 cube

[kju:b]

义 *n.* 立方体

例 A large cube consists of eight small cubes as shown below.

译 如下图所示一个大立方体由 8 个小立方体组成。

---

26 cylinder

['sɪlɪndər]

义 *n.* 圆柱体

例 A formula for the volume, *V*, of a right circular cylinder in terms of its radius, *r*, and its height, *h*, is $V = \pi r^2 h$.

译 正圆柱体的体积 *V* 用半径 *r* 和高度 *h* 表示的公式是：$V = \pi r^2 h$。

---

27 degree

[dɪ'griː]

义 *n.* 度数

例 Through how many degrees does a wheel rotate in 1.5 minutes at 45 revolutions per minute?

译 一个轮子在 1.5 分钟内以每分钟 45 转的速度旋转了多少度？

---

28 diagonal

[daɪ'ægənl]

义 *adj.* 对角线的

例 In the figure below, *AC* is the longer diagonal of rhombus *ABCD* and *E* is on *AD*.

译 下图中，*AC* 是菱形 *ABCD* 较长的对角线，*E* 在 *AD* 上。

---

29 diameter

[daɪ'æmɪtər]

义 *n.* 直径

例 A circle with a diameter of 8 inches is inscribed in square *ABCD*, as shown below.

译 一个直径为 8 英寸的圆内嵌在正方形 *ABCD* 中，如下图所示。

---

30 ellipse

[ɪ'lɪps]

义 *n.* 椭圆，椭圆形

例 The area of an ellipse may be found by using the expression π*ab*, where *a* is 12 the length of the major axis and *b* is 12 the length of the minor axis.

译 椭圆的面积可用表达式 π*ab* 求得，其中 *a* 为长轴长度的 12 倍，*b* 为短轴长度的 12 倍。

---

31 endpoint

['end,pɔɪnt]

义 *n.* 端点

例 What is the length, in coordinate units, of the line segment with endpoints ($-$8, 4) and (4, 9) in the standard (*x, y*) coordinate plane?

译 在标准 (*x, y*) 坐标平面上，端点为 ($-$8, 4) 和 (4, 9) 的线段，用坐标单位表示的长度是多少？

---

32 equilateral

[,iːkwɪ'lætərəl]

义 *adj.* 等边的，等面的

例 In the figure below, $\triangle QRS$ is equilateral, side *QR* is bisected by *T*, and side *QS* is bisected by *U*.

译 下图中 $\triangle QRS$ 为等边三角形，边 *QR* 被 *T* 平分，边 *QS* 被 *U* 平分。

---

33 equilateral triangle

义 等边三角形

例 The figure below is composed of square *BCDE* and equilateral triangle △*ABE*. The length of *CD* is 6 inches.

译 下图由正方形 *BCDE* 和等边三角形△*ABE* 组成。*CD* 的长度是 6 英寸。

34　exterior angle

义 外角

例 Given the triangle shown below with exterior angles that measure $x°$, $y°$, and $z°$ as shown, what is the sum of x, y, and z?

译 给定下面这个三角形的外角是 $x°$，$y°$ 和 $z°$，那么 x，y，z 的和是多少？

35　height

[haɪt]

义 *n.* 高度

例 What is the height, in centimeters, of a right circular cylinder that has a volume of 270π cubic centimeters and a radius of 3 centimeters?

译 体积为 270π 立方厘米，当单位为厘米时，半径为 3 厘米的正圆柱的高度是多少？

36　heptagon

['heptəgɑːn]

义 *n.* 七角形，七边形

例 In the regular heptagon shown below, what is the sum of the measures of the seven interior angles?

译 在下面的正七边形中，7 个内角之和是多少？

37　hexagon

['heksəgɑːn]

义 *n.* 六角形

例 The hexagon shown below has 6 sides of equal length. What is the sum of the measures of the interior angles in this hexagon?

译 下面所示的六边形有六个等长的边。这个六边形的内角之和是多少？

38　horizontal line

义 水平线

例 The pattern has both a horizontal line and a vertical line of symmetry.

译 这个图案有一条对称的水平线和一条对称的垂直线。

39　horizontal line segment

义 水平线段

例 The first horizontal line segment end points are (2, 5) and (2, 7) with length 3.

译 第一条水平线段端点为 (2, 5) 和 (2, 7)，长度为 3。

40　hypotenuse

[haɪ'pɑːtənuːs]

义 *n.*（直角三角形的）斜边

例 The hypotenuse of a right triangle is 12 cm long.

译 一个直角三角形的斜边长 12 厘米。

41　icosahedron

[ˌaɪkəʊsə'hiːdrən]

义 *n.* 二十面体

例 A regular icosahedron is a solid that has 20 congruent faces, each of which is an equilateral triangle.

译 正二十面体是一个有 20 个全等面的实心体，每个面都是一个等边三角形。

---

42 initial side

义 始边

例 Angle *B* has the same initial side and terminal side as Angle *A*.

译 角 *B* 与角 *A* 有相同的起始边和终点边。

---

43 interior angle

义 内角

例 The interior angles of a quadrilateral are in the ratio 1:2:3:4. What is the measure of the largest interior angle?

译 一个四边形的内角度数的比例是 1:2:3:4。其最大的内角度数是多少？

---

44 intersect

[ˌɪntər'sekt]

义 *v.* 相交

例 At how many values of *x* in this interval does the graph of *y* = 2sin*bx* intersect the *x*-axis?

译 在这个区间内，*y* = 2sin*bx* 的图像与 *x* 轴相交的 *x* 值有多少？

---

45 intersection

[ˌɪntər'sekʃn]

义 *n.* 交点

例 In isosceles trapezoid *ABCD* below, *E* is the intersection of the diagonals.

译 在下面的等腰梯形 *ABCD* 中，*E* 是对角线的交点。

---

46 isosceles

[aɪ'sɑːsəliːz]

义 *adj.*（三角形）二等边的，等腰的

例 Triangles △*ABC* and △*DBC*, shown below, are isosceles with base *BC*.

译 三角形△*ABC* 和△*DBC*，如下所示，是以 *BC* 为底边的等腰三角形。

---

47 isosceles right triangle

义 等腰直角三角形

例 In the figure below, small isosceles right triangles are congruent.

译 在下图中，小等腰直角三角形全等。

---

48 isosceles trapezoid

义 等腰梯形

例 An isosceles trapezoid is graphed in the standard (*x*, *y*) coordinate plane below.

译 在下面的标准 (*x*, *y*) 坐标平面上画出等腰梯形。

---

49 isosceles triangle

义 等腰三角形

例 In a certain isosceles triangle, the measure of each of the base angles is twice the measure of the vertex angle.

译 在一个等腰三角形中，每个底角的度数是顶角的两倍。

50　lateral surface area

义　侧表面积

例　Note: For a right circular cylinder with radius r and height h, the lateral surface area is $2\pi rh$ and the volume is $\pi r^2 h$.

译　注意：对于一个半径为 r、高度为 h 的正圆柱体，侧面积是 $2\pi rh$，体积是 $\pi r^2 h$。

51　length

[leŋθ]

义　*n.* 长度

例　What are the lengths, in inches, of the bases of the trapezoid?

译　梯形底边的长度（单位是英寸）是多少？

52　line segment

义　线段

例　What is the midpoint of the line segment with endpoints (3, 5) and (−1, 3) in the standard (x, y) coordinate plane?

译　在标准 (x, y) 坐标平面中，端点为 (3, 5) 和 (−1, 3) 的线段的中点是什么？

53　measure

['meʒər]

义　*v.* 测量，量度为　*n.* 量度；尺寸

例　Each edge of a cube measures 3 inches. What is the volume, in cubic inches, of the cube?

译　立方体的每条边长测量为 3 英寸。以立方英寸为单位，这个立方体的体积是多少？

54　midpoint

['mɪdˌpɔɪnt]

义　*n.* 中点

例　What is the x-coordinate of the midpoint of JK?

译　线段 JK 的中点的 x 坐标是多少？

55　minor arc

义　劣弧

例　What is the measure of minor arc DE?

译　劣弧 DE 的弧长是多少？

56　obtuse triangle

义　钝角三角形

例　Note: An obtuse triangle is a triangle that has an angle with a measure greater than 90° but less than 180°.

译　注：钝角三角形是一个有一个大于 90° 但小于 180° 的角的三角形。

57　opposite angle

义　对角

例　Note: The Law of Sines states that the lengths of the sides of a triangle are proportional to the sines of the opposite angles.

译　注：正弦定理指出三角形边的长度与对角的正弦成正比。

58　parallel

['pærəlel]

义　*adj.* 平行的

例　What is the slope of any line parallel to the line $6x + 5y = 7$?

译　平行于直线 $6x + 5y = 7$ 的直线斜率是多少？

59　parallel line

义　平行线

例　Parallel lines will never meet no matter how far extended.

译　平行线不管延伸多长，都永不相交。

60　parallelogram

[ˌpærə'leləgræm]

义　*n.* 平行四边形

例　What is the area, in square coordinate units, of the parallelogram with vertices as shown in the standard (x, y) coordinate plane below?

译　下面这个标准 (x, y) 坐标平面中顶点平行四边形的面积（以平方坐标单位表示）是多少？

61　pentagon

['pentəgɑ:n]

义　*n.* 五边形

例　A regular pentagon, $P1$, has a perimeter of 25 inches, while another regular pentagon, $P2$, has a perimeter that is 15 inches greater than the perimeter of $P1$.

译　一个正五边形 $P1$ 的周长是 25 英寸，而另一个正五边形 $P2$ 的周长比 $P1$ 的周长大 15 英寸。

62　pentagonal

[pen'tægənl]

义　*adj.* 五角的，五边形的

例　How many 1-quart containers of paint will Marcie need in order to cover the 1 pentagonal wall of the playhouse?

译　玛茜需要多少容量是一夸脱的颜料才能涂满游戏室的一面五角形的墙？

63　perimeter

[pə'rɪmɪtər]

义　*n.* 周长

例　In the standard (x, y) coordinate plane, what is the perimeter, in coordinate units, of an isosceles triangle having vertices $A(-2, -1)$, $B(3, 11)$, and $C(8, -1)$?

译　在标准 (x, y) 坐标平面中，已知顶点坐标为 $A(-2, -1)$，$B(3, 11)$，$C(8, -1)$ 的一个等腰三角形，它的周长是多少？

64　polygon

['pɑ:ligɑ:n]

义　*n.* 多边形

例　In polygon $ABCDE$ shown below, the angles at A, B, and E are right angles.

译　在下图所示的多边形 $ABCDE$ 中，A、B 和 E 处的角度为直角。

65　prism

['prɪzəm]

义　*n.* 棱柱

例　What is the total surface area, in square meters, of all six faces of the prism?

译 以平方米为单位，棱柱所有的六个面的总面积是多少？

---

66 pyramid

['pɪrəmɪd]

义 *n.* 棱锥体，金字塔

例 What is the total length of all eight edges of the pyramid?

译 金字塔所有 8 条边的总长度是多少？

---

67 quadrilateral

[ˌkwɑːdrɪˈlætərəl]

义 *n.* 四边形

例 A quadrilateral has diagonals that do NOT bisect each other. Which of the following types of quadrilaterals could it be?

译 四边形的对角线互不等分。它可能是下列哪一种四边形？

---

68 radian

['reɪdɪən]

义 *n.* 弧度

例 What is the degree measure of an angle that measures $\frac{5}{12}\pi$ radians?

译 $\frac{5}{12}\pi$ 弧度对应的角的度数是多少？

---

69 radius

['reɪdɪəs]

义 *n.* 半径

例 If the radius of the circle is 2 feet. How long is a side of the rhombus, in feet?

译 如果圆的半径是 2 英尺。以英尺为单位，菱形的一边是多长？

---

70 rectangle

['rektæŋgl]

义 *n.* 长方形，矩形

例 A rectangle has an area of 48 square meters and a width of 6 meters. What is the perimeter, in meters, of the rectangle?

译 长方形的面积是 48 平方米，宽是 6 米。以米为单位，这个长方形的周长是多少？

---

71 rectangular

[rek'tæŋgjələ(r)]

义 *adj.* 矩形的，长方形的；直角的

例 If 12 identical cylindrical cans are packed into an 18×24 rectangular carton, as shown below, what is the approximate radius, in inches, of each of the cans?

译 如果将 12 个相同的圆柱形罐子装到一个 18 英寸 ×24 英寸的长方形盒子里，如下所示，每个罐子的半径（单位为英寸）大约是多少？

---

72 rectangular prism

义 长方柱

例 The plans for a diving pool call for a rectangular prism that has a length of 30 meters, a width of 25 meters, and a depth of 5 meters.

译 跳水池的设计需要一个长 30 米、宽 25 米、深 5 米的长方柱。

---

73 regular polygon

义 正多边形

例 Suppose that equally spaced dots are marked on each side of a regular polygon, with a dot at each vertex, and that the distance between consecutive dots is the same for all sides.

译	假设正多边形的每边都有等距的点，每个顶点都有一个点，并且连续点之间的距离对于所有边都是相同的。

74 rhombus

['rɑːmbəs]

义 *n.* 菱形，斜方形

例 Point *A* is at the center of the circle, rectangle, and rhombus in the figure below.

译 点 *A* 位于下图中圆形、矩形和菱形的中心。

75 right angle

义 直角

例 In △*ABC* below, ∠*B* is a right angle, the measure of ∠*C* is 30°, and *AC* is 4 inches long. What is the length, in inches, of *BC*?

译 在下图的△*ABC* 里，∠*B* 是直角，∠*C* 的度数为 30°，边 *AC* 的长度为 4 英寸。*BC* 的长度（单位是英寸）是多少？

76 right circular cone

义 正圆锥体

例 A formula for the volume of a right circular cone is $V = \frac{1}{3}\pi r^2 h$, where *r* is the radius of the base and *h* is the height of the cone.

译 正圆椎体的体积公式为 $V = \frac{1}{3}\pi r^2 h$，其中 *r* 为底面的半径，*h* 为圆锥的高度。

77 right circular cylinder

义 正圆柱

例 The solid shown below is composed of a right circular cylinder and a right circular cone with base diameters and heights given in centimeters.

译 下图所示的正多面体是由一个正圆柱体和一个正圆锥体组成，其底部直径和高度以厘米为单位。

78 right prism

义 直棱柱

例 A right prism with triangular bases and with dimensions given in inches is shown below.

译 下面显示的是一个以三角为底面、以英寸为尺寸单位的直棱柱。

79 right triangle

义 直角三角形

例 For right triangle △*KLM* below, what is sin∠*M*?

译 对于下面的直角三角形△*KLM*，sin∠*M* 的值是多少？

80 scale

[skeɪl]

义 *n.* 比例

例 Gerry is building a dollhouse that is to be a scale model of a house that is 36 feet high, 84 feet long, and 48 feet wide.

译 格里正在建造一个玩具屋，这是一个 36 英尺高、84 英尺长、48 英尺宽的房子的等比例模型。

81 sector

['sektər]

义 *n.* 扇形

例 The length of the arc of the unshaded sector is 7π decimeters.

译 无阴影扇形的弧长为 7π 分米。

82　semicircle

['semɪsɜːrkl]

义 *n.* 半圆

例 The figure shown below is composed of a rectangle and a semicircle.

译 下图由一个矩形和一个半圆组成。

83　side

[saɪd]

义 *n.* 边

例 Each small square on the grid shown below has a side length of 1 cm.

译 下图显示的网格上的每个小正方形的边长为 1 厘米。

84　side length

义 边长

例 The triangle below has side lengths given in meters.

译 下图的三角形边长以米为单位。

85　similar triangle

义 相似三角形

例 Shown below are similar triangles △*ABC* and △*DEF* with ∠*A* = ∠*D* and ∠*B* = ∠*E*.

译 下图所示的相似三角形分别为 △*ABC* 和 △*DEF*，且∠*A* = ∠*D*，∠*B* = ∠*E*。

86　solid

['sɑːlɪd]

义 *n.* 正多面体

例 If one small cube is removed, how does the surface area, in square inches, of the original large cube compare to that of the remaining solid?

译 如果一个小立方体被移走，以平方英寸为单位，原始大立方体的表面积和剩余的正多面体的对比如何？

87　spaced dot

义 间隔点

例 The figure below shows four equally spaced dots per side, including a dot at each vertex, for an equilateral triangle.

译 下图显示了等边三角形每边的 4 个间隔点，包括每个顶点上的一个点。

88　sphere

[sfɪr]

义 *n.* 球体

例 The volume of a sphere is $\frac{4}{3}\pi r^3$, where r is the radius of the sphere.

译 球面的体积是 $\frac{4}{3}\pi r^3$，其中 r 是球的半径。

89　supplementary angle

义 补角

例 Suppose that the measure of the larger of two supplementary angles is five times the measure of the smaller angle.

译 假设两个补角中较大的角是较小的角的 5 倍。

---

90 surface area

义 表面积

例 The original cube has the same surface area as the remaining solid.

译 原来的立方体和剩下的正多面体有相同的表面积。

---

91 symmetric

[sɪ'metrɪk]

义 *adj.* 对称的，匀称的

例 The ends of the supports are connected with string to form a 4-sided figure that is symmetric with respect to the longer support.

译 支架的两端用绳子连接，形成一个相对于较长支架对称的四边形。

---

92 tangency

['tændʒənsɪ]

义 *n.* 相切

例 From point A outside a circle and in the same plane as the circle, two rays are drawn tangent to the circle with the points of tangency labeled B and C, respectively.

译 从圆外和圆在同一平面内的 A 点，分别画出两条与圆相切的线，切点分别为 B 和 C。

---

93 terminal side

义 终边

例 Two angles are coterminal if they have the same initial and terminal sides.

译 如果两个角的起始边和末端边相同，那么它们就是共终止角。

---

94 the Law of Cosines

义 余弦定律

例 Note: For $\triangle ABC$ with side of length a opposite $\angle A$, side of length b opposite $\angle B$, and side of length c opposite $\angle C$, the Law of Cosines states $c^2 = a^2 + b^2 - 2ab\cos\angle C$.

译 注：对于边长为 a 的 $\angle A$，边长为 b 的 $\angle B$，边长为 c 的 $\angle C$，余弦定理为：$c^2 = a^2 + b^2 - 2ab\cos\angle C$。

---

95 the Law of Sines

义 正弦定律

例 The Law of Sines states that for a triangle with sides of lengths a, b, and c opposite angles of measure α, β and γ, $\dfrac{a}{\sin\alpha} = \dfrac{b}{\sin\beta} = \dfrac{c}{\sin\gamma}$.

译 正弦定律表明，对于边长为 a, b, c 的三角形，测量所对的角 α, β 和 γ，$\dfrac{a}{\sin\alpha} = \dfrac{b}{\sin\beta} = \dfrac{c}{\sin\gamma}$。

---

96 transversal

[træns'vɜːsəl]

义 *n.* 截线

例 In the plane shown in the figure below, lines m and n are cut by transversal line t.

译 在下图所示的平面上，直线 m 和 n 被截线 t 切割。

---

97 trapezoid

义 *n.* 梯形，不等边四边形

['træpəzɔɪd]

例 The trapezoid below, with dimensions given in inches, has an area of 36 square inches.

译 下面的梯形，尺寸以英寸为单位，面积是 36 平方英寸。

---

98 triangle

['traɪæŋgl]

义 *n.* 三角（形）

例 How many triangles that have integer side lengths are similar to the triangle shown below?

译 有多少个有整数边长的三角形与下面的三角形相似？

---

99 trigonometry

[ˌtrɪgə'nɑːmətrɪ]

义 *n.* 三角学

例 In trigonometry, an angle of $-\frac{7}{6}\pi$ radians has the same sine and cosine as an angle that has which of the following degree measures?

译 在三角学中，弧度为 $-\frac{7}{6}\pi$ 的角与以下哪个度数的角具有相同的正弦值和余弦值？

---

100 vector

['vektər]

义 *n.* 向量

例 What will be the coordinates of the terminal point of the new vector?

译 新向量终点的坐标是多少？

---

101 vertex

['vɜːrteks]

义 *n.* 顶点；最高点

例 One vertex can only have one normal.

译 一个顶点只能有一条法线。

---

102 vertex angle

义 顶角

例 The point about which an angle is measured is called the angle's vertex, and the angle associated with a given vertex is called the vertex angle.

译 一个角的测量点称为该角的顶点，与给定顶点相关的角度称为顶角。

---

103 vertical line

义 垂直线

例 The pattern has only a vertical line of symmetry.

译 这种图案只有一条垂直的对称线。

---

104 vertical line segment

义 垂线段

例 The line segment connecting a point outside the straight line and the perpendicular foot is called the vertical line segment.

译 连接直线外一点与垂足形成的线段叫垂线段。

---

105 vertice

['vɜːrtɪsiː]

义 *n.* 顶点

例 The vertices of rectangle *BCDE* lie on the circle and the vertices of rhombus *FGHI* are the midpoints of the sides of rectangle *BCDE*.

译 矩形的顶点 *BCDE* 位于圆上，菱形 *FGHI* 的顶点是矩形 *BCDE* 各边的中点。

---

106 view

[vju:]

义 *n.* 视图

例 The figure below shows three different views of the same fair cube.

译 下图显示了同一个均匀立方体的 3 个不同视图。

---

107 volume

['vɑ:lju:m]

义 *n.* 体积

例 What is the ratio of the volume of the original cone to the volume of the new cone?

译 原锥体的体积和新锥体的体积之比是多少?

---

108 width

[wɪdθ]

义 *n.* 宽度

例 A rectangle with the same area as square *ABCD* has a length of 9 meters. What is the rectangle's width, in meters?

译 与正方形 *ABCD* 面积相同的矩形长为 9 米。矩形的宽 (单位是米) 是多少?

List 5

1 axis

['æksɪs']

义 *n.* 轴

例 What is the equation of the axis of symmetry of the parabola given by the equation $y = 6(x + 1)(x - 5)$?

译 抛物线方程 $y = 6(x + 1)(x - 5)$ 的对称轴方程是什么？

---

2 coordinate

[kəʊˈɔːrdɪneɪt]

义 *n.* 坐标

例 Sheila has broken the balloons at coordinates $(-4, 2)$ and $(-5, 1)$.

译 希拉打破了位于坐标 $(-4, 2)$ 和 $(-5, 1)$ 上的气球。

---

3 coordinate plane

义 坐标平面

例 The coordinates of the endpoints of JK, in the standard (x, y) coordinate plane, are $(-2, -6)$ and $(4, 6)$.

译 线段 JK 的端点在标准 (x, y) 坐标平面上的坐标为 $(-2, -6)$ 和 $(4, 6)$。

---

4 grid line

义 网格线，坐标线

例 Grid lines are shown at 1-unit intervals in the standard (x, y) coordinate plane below.

译 网格线在下面的标准 (x, y) 坐标平面上以 1 单位间隔显示。

---

5 horizontal axis

义 横轴

例 The (r, A) plane is the standard (x, y) coordinate plane with r along the horizontal axis and A along the vertical axis.

译 (r, A) 平面是标准的 (x, y) 坐标平面，r 沿水平轴，A 沿垂直轴。

---

6 number line

义 数轴

例 The number a is located at -2.5 on the number line below.

译 数字 a 位于下面数轴上的 -2.5 处。

---

7 ordered pair

义 有序数对

例 Which of the following ordered pairs in the standard (x, y) coordinate plane satisfies the system of inequalities below?

译 在标准 (x, y) 坐标系中下列哪个有序数对满足下面的不等式组？

---

8 origin

[ˈɔːrɪdʒɪn]

义 *n.* 原点

例 The vertex of CA is the origin of the standard (x, y) coordinate.

译 CA 的顶点是标准 (x, y) 坐标平面的原点。

---

9 perpendicular

义 *adj.* 垂直的

[ˌpɜːrpənˈdɪkjələr] 例 In the figure below, *AW* and *BY* are perpendicular at *X* and bisect each other.

译 在下图中，*AW* 和 *BY* 垂直于 *X*，并相互平分。

---

10 point

[pɔɪnt]

义 *n.*（坐标上的）点

例 What is the distance between the points with coordinates (3, 4) and (−2, 7) in the standard (*x*, *y*) coordinate plane?

译 在标准 (*x*, *y*) 坐标平面上坐标点 (3, 4) 和 (−2, 7) 之间的距离是多少？

---

11 quadrant

[ˈkwɑːdrənt]

义 *n.* 象限

例 In which quadrant, if it can be determined, is point *B*?

译 如果可以确定，那么 *B* 点在哪个象限？

---

12 rotate

[ˈrəʊteɪt]

义 *v.* 旋转

例 When is *D* rotated 180° about *E*?

译 何时 *D* 绕 *E* 旋转 180°？

---

13 rotation

[rəʊˈteɪʃn]

义 *n.* 旋转

例 The Ferris wheel at a state fair has a radius of 60 feet, rotates at a constant speed, and completes one rotation in 4 minutes.

译 州博览会上的摩天轮半径为 60 英尺，以恒定的速度旋转，4 分钟旋转一圈。

---

14 shift

[ʃɪft]

义 *v.* 移动

例 One of the following graphs in the standard (*x*, *y*) coordinate plane shows the result of shifting the function up 4 coordinate units.

译 下面的标准 (*x*, *y*) 坐标平面中的一张图显示了将函数向上移动 4 个坐标单位的结果。

---

15 symmetry

[ˈsɪmətrɪ]

义 *n.* 对称

例 The pattern has only a horizontal line of symmetry.

译 这个图案只有一条对称的水平线。

---

16 terminal point

义 终点

例 A vector from the origin to terminal point (2, 3) is shown in the standard (*x*, *y*) coordinate plane below.

译 下面的标准 (*x*, *y*) 坐标平面显示了从原点到终点 (2, 3) 的矢量。

---

17 transformation

[ˌtrænsfərˈmeɪʃn]

义 *n.* 变换

例 Which of the following transformations shifts all points graphed in the standard (*x*, *y*) coordinate plane down 5 coordinate units?

译 下面哪个变换将标 (*x*, *y*) 坐标平面上的所有点都向下平移 5 个坐标单位?

---

18 translation

[træns'leɪʃn]

义 *n.* 平移

例 The figure below shows △*ABC* and its translation image △*QRS* in the standard (*x*, *y*) coordinate plane, where *A* translates to *Q*, *B* translates to *R*, and *C* translates to *S*.

译 下图显示了标准 (*x*, *y*) 坐标平面上△*ABC* 及其平移图像△*QRS*,其中 *A* 点平移到 *Q* 点,*B* 点平移到 *R* 点,*C* 点平移到 *S* 点。

---

19 vertical axis

义 纵轴

例 The (*r*, *A*) plane is the standard (*x*, *y*) coordinate plane with *r* along the horizontal axis and *A* along the vertical axis.

译 (*r*, *A*) 平面是标准的 (*x*, *y*) 坐标平面,*r* 沿水平轴,*A* 沿垂直轴。

---

20 *x*-axis

义 *x* 轴

例 The unit of measurement for the *x*-axis is days.

译 *x* 轴的测量单位是天。

---

21 *x*-coordinate

义 *x* 坐标

例 The x-coordinates of points *A*, *B* are respectively *x* = 0 and *x* = 3.

译 点 *A*、*B* 的横坐标分别为 *x* = 0 和 *x* = 3。

---

22 *y*-axis

义 *y* 轴

例 Vertex *A* has coordinates (2, 0, 0), and 3 other vertices are at the origin, on the positive *y*-axis, and on the positive *z*-axis, respectively.

译 顶点 *A* 的坐标是 (2, 0, 0),另外 3 个顶点分别在正 *y* 轴和正 *z* 轴上。

---

23 *y*-intercept

义 *y* 截距

例 What is the *y*-intercept of line *s*?

译 直线 *s* 的 *y* 轴截距是多少?

List 6

1 algebra

['ældʒɪbrə]

义 *n.* 代数学

例 Coursework for this degree will include college algebra and calculus, technical writing, instrument calibration, and laboratory techniques.

译 此学位的课程将包括大学代数学和微积分、技术写作、仪器校准和实验室技术。

---

2 amplitude

['æmplɪtuːd]

义 *n.* 振幅

例 What is the amplitude of the function $f(x) = 12\cos(3x + \pi)$?

译 函数 $f(x) = 12\cos(3x + \pi)$ 的振幅是多少?

---

3 ascending order

义 升序

例 In which of the following are 12, 56 and 58 arranged in ascending order?

译 在以下哪一个选项中，12，56，58 是升序排列的?

---

4 asymptote

['æsɪmˌtəʊt]

义 *n.* 渐近线

例 At what point in the standard (x, y) coordinate plane do the asymptotes of the function $y = \dfrac{2x(x+2)}{x-3}$, graphed below, intersect?

译 函数 $y = \dfrac{2x(x+2)}{x-3}$ 的渐近线与标准 (x, y) 坐标平面的什么点相交?

---

5 binomial

[baɪ'nəʊmɪəl]

义 *n.* 二项式

例 One of the binomials is $x - 6$. Which of the following is the other binomial?

译 其中一个二项式是 $x - 6$。下面哪个是另一个二项式?

---

6 coefficient

[ˌkəʊɪ'fɪʃnt]

义 *n.* 系数

例 What is the coefficient of x^9 in the product of the two polynomials below?

译 下面两个多项式的乘积中 x^9 的系数是多少?

---

7 composite function

义 复合函数

例 Which of the following pairs of functions, $f(x)$ and $g(x)$, form the composite function $f(g(x)) = \sqrt{2x^2} + 3$?

译 下面哪对函数 $f(x)$ 和 $g(x)$ 构成复合函数 $f(g(x)) = \sqrt{2x^2} + 3$?

---

8 cosine

['kəʊsaɪn]

义 *n.* 余弦

例 What is the cosine of the triangle's smallest interior angle?

译 三角形最小内角的余弦值是多少?

9　curve

[kɜːrv]

义 *n.* 曲线

例 Which of the following points must also lie on that curve?

译 下面哪个点一定也在这条曲线上？

10　determinant

[dɪˈtɜːrmɪnənt]

义 *n.* 行列式

例 When the determinant is expanded, it produces a polynomial, called the characteristic polynomial.

译 当行列式展开后，得到一个多项式，叫作特征多项式。

11　determinant of the matrix

义 矩阵的行列式

例 What is the determinant of the matrix shown below?

译 下面这个矩阵的行列式是什么？

12　domain

[dəʊˈmeɪn]

义 *n.* 定义域

例 The domain of the function $y(x) = 3\cos(5x - 4) + 1$ is all real numbers.

译 函数 $y(x) = 3\cos(5x - 4) + 1$ 的定义域都是实数。

13　equation

[ɪˈkweɪʒn]

义 *n.* 方程式，等式

例 Which of the following describes the solutions to the equation $x^2 - 8x - 48 = 0$?

译 下面哪个选项描述了方程式 $x^2 - 8x - 48 = 0$ 的解？

14　equivalent algebraic expression

义 等价代数表达式

例 Which of the following inequalities is an equivalent algebraic expression for the statement below?

译 下面哪个不等式是下面陈述的等价代数表达式？

15　exponential equation

义 指数方程（式）

例 Consider the exponential equation $y = C^a$, where C and a are positive real constants and it is a positive real number.

译 思考指数方程 $y = C^a$，其中 C 和 a 是正实数常数，所以方程值是一个正实数。

16　expression

[ɪkˈspreʃn]

义 *n.* 表达式

例 What is the value of the expression $(x - 2y)(x + 2y)$ when $x = 4$ and $y = 12$?

译 当 $x = 4$，$y = 12$ 时，表达式 $(x - 2y)(x + 2y)$ 的值是多少？

17　factorization

[ˌdæktəraɪˈzeɪʃən]

义 *n.* 因式分解

例 Which of the following is a complete factorization of the expression $2x + 2xy + 6x^2y$?

译 下面哪个选项是 $2x + 2xy + 6x^2y$ 的完整因数分解？

---

18 formula

['fɔ:rmjələ]

义 *n.* 公式

例 A formula that gives m, the recommended maximum heart rate, in beats per minute, while exercising, for a person a years old is $m = 0.8(220 - a)$.

译 一个方程可以得出 m，它表示最大推荐心率（单位为每分钟跳动次数），当一个人运动时，一个年龄为 a 岁的人的心率可以表示为：$m = 0.8(220 - a)$。

---

19 function

['fʌŋkʃn]

义 *n.* 函数

例 One of the following equations defines the function $g(x)$.

译 下面的方程定义了函数 $g(x)$。

---

20 greatest

['greɪtɪst]

义 *adj.* 最大的

例 Given real numbers a, b, c, d, and e such that $c < d$, $e < c$, $e > b$, and $b > a$, which of these numbers is the greatest?

译 给定实数 a，b，c，d 和 e，使 $c < d$，$e < c$，$e > b$ 和 $b > a$，这些数中哪个最大？

---

21 greatest value

义 最大值

例 Which of the following expressions has the greatest value?

译 下列哪个表达式的值最大？

---

22 horizontal asymptote

义 水平渐近线

例 What is the horizontal asymptote?

译 水平渐近线是什么？

---

23 hyperbola

[haɪ'pɜ:rbələ]

义 *n.* 双曲线

例 A hyperbola that has vertices (1, 2) and (3, 2) and that passes through the origin is shown below in the standard (x, y) coordinate plane. The hyperbola has which of the following equations?

译 如下图所示，一个顶点为 (1, 2) 和 (3, 2) 并经过原点的双曲线在标准 (x, y) 坐标平面上。双曲线有下列哪个方程？

---

24 inequality

[ˌɪnɪ'kwɑ:lətɪ]

义 *n.* 不等式

例 Which of the following is equivalent to the inequality $-5 + m \leq -4 + 2m$?

译 下面哪个选项等价于不等式 $-5 + m \leq -4 + 2m$?

---

25 intercept

义 *n.* 截距

[ˌɪntər'sept]

例 Which of the following points is the *y*-intercept of the graph of $y = f(x)$?

译 以下哪一个点是 $y = f(x)$ 图像的 *y* 轴截距？

26　interval

['ɪntərvl]

义 *n.*（数学）区间

例 For a specific nonzero value of *b*, the graph of $y = \sin bx$ in the standard (x, y) coordinate plane intersects the *x*-axis at *k* values of *x* in the interval $0 \leqslant x \leqslant 2\pi$.

译 对于一个特定的非零值 *b*，在标准 (x, y) 坐标平面上 $y = \sin bx$ 的图形与 *x* 轴相交于 *x* 的 *k* 个值，区间为 $0 \leqslant x \leqslant 2\pi$。

27　inverse function

义 反函数

例 Suppose $f(x)$ and $g(x)$ are functions defined for all real numbers *x*, and $f(x)$ is the inverse function of $g(x)$.

译 假设 $f(x)$ 和 $g(x)$ 是为所有实数 *x* 定义的函数，而 $f(x)$ 是 $g(x)$ 的反函数。

28　linear equation

义 线性方程

例 The equations below are a system of linear equations where *a*, *b*, and *c* are positive integers.

译 下面的方程是一个线性方程组，其中 *a*，*b*，*c* 是正整数。

29　linear factor

义 线性因子

例 Which of the following are linear factors of $krx^2 + (kn + rm)x + mn$, a general quadratic expression in *x*?

译 下列哪个是 $krx^2 + (kn + rm)x + mn$（*x* 的一般二次表达式）的线性因子？

30　linear function

义 线性函数

例 The graph below depicts projections for the linear cost function, $C(x)$, and the linear revenue function, $R(x)$.

译 下图显示了线性成本函数 $C(x)$ 和线性收入函数 $R(x)$ 的投影。

31　linear relation

义 线性关系

例 One of the following is an equation of the linear relation shown in the standard (x, y) coordinate plane below. Which equation is it?

译 下面方程中的一个是在标准 (x, y) 坐标系下的线性关系方程。是哪个方程？

32　linear relationship

义 线性关系

例 She graphs the three weights and corresponding microwave defrost times in the standard (x, y) coordinate plane, as shown below, and notices a linear relationship between these 3 points.

译 如图所示，她在标准的 (x, y) 坐标平面上画出了 3 个重量和相应的微波解冻时间，并注意到了这 3 个点之间的线性关系。

---

33 mathematical expression

义 数学表达式

例 Which of the following mathematical expressions is equivalent to the verbal expression "A number, x, squared is 39 more than the product of 10 and x"?

译 下列哪个数学表达式与口头表达式 "一个数 x 的平方比 10 和 x 的乘积大 39" 等价？

---

34 matrix

['meɪtrɪks]

义 *n.* 矩阵

例 How do I multiply a matrix by a vector?

译 我怎么用一个矩阵乘以一个向量呢？

---

35 matrix equation

义 矩阵方程

例 Which of the following matrices, when substituted for T, satisfies the matrix equation below?

译 下面哪个矩阵，当用 T 代替时，满足下面的矩阵方程？

---

36 matrix product

义 矩阵乘积

例 What is the matrix product?

译 矩阵乘积是什么？

---

37 maximum

['mæksɪməm]

义 *n.* 最大值

例 If $2 \leqslant x \leqslant 5$ and $-4 \leqslant y \leqslant -3$, what is the maximum value of $|y - 2x|$?

译 如果 $2 \leqslant x \leqslant 5$，$-4 \leqslant y \leqslant -3$，$|y - 2x|$ 的最大值是多少？

---

38 maximum number

义 最大数量

例 What is the maximum number of bats that can be produced by the company for $15,000?

译 以 15 000 美元计，该公司可生产球拍的最大数量是多少？

---

39 maximum value

义 最大值

例 For what value of t does the equation $h = 3t^2$ have its maximum value for h?

译 当 t 的值是多少时方程 $h = 3t^2$ 对 h 有最大值？

40　minimum value

义　最小值

例　If x and y are real numbers such that $4 \leqslant x \leqslant 12$ and $2 \leqslant y \leqslant 4$, then the minimum value for $\dfrac{x}{y}$ is?

译　如果 x 和 y 是实数，且 $4 \leqslant x \leqslant 12$，$2 \leqslant y \leqslant 4$，则 $\dfrac{x}{y}$ 的最小值为多少？

41　monomial

[məˈnəʊmɪəl]

义　*adj.* 单项的　　*n.* 单项式

例　All of the following monomials are factors, over the integers of $18x^2y + 12x^2y^3 - 6x^3y$, EXCEPT?

译　以下所有单项式都是 $18x^2y + 12x^2y^3 - 6x^3y$ 整数上的因子，除了哪一个？

42　negative slope

义　负斜率

例　So it's got a negative slope.

译　因此它得到的是负斜率。

43　nonzero

[nɑːnˈzɪrəʊ]

义　*n.* 非零数

例　For all nonzero values of a, b, c, which of the following is the solution for x of the equation $ax + b = c$?

译　对于所有非零数 a，b，c，下面哪个是方程 $ax + b = c$ 中 x 的解？

44　nonzero value

义　非零值

例　The values of the polynomial $x^2 - x - 2 = 0$ are nonzero values.

译　多项式 $x^2 - x - 2 = 0$ 的值是非零值。

45　parabola

[pəˈræbələ]

义　*n.* 抛物线

例　The graph of one of the following equations is the parabola shown in the standard (x, y) coordinate plane below.

译　下面方程其中一个的图形是下面标准 (x, y) 坐标平面上的抛物线。

46　polynomial

[ˌpɑːlɪˈnəʊmɪəl]

义　*n.* 多项式

例　The polynomial $x^2 - kx - 3 = 0$ is the product of the binomial $(x + 5)$ and another binomial.

译　多项式 $x^2 - kx - 3 = 0$ 是二项式 $(x + 5)$ 和另一个二项式的乘积。

47　polynomial function

义　多项式函数

例　A polynomial function $P(x)$ has degree n.

译　多项式函数 $P(x)$ 为 n 次函数。

48　positive slope

义　正斜率

例	Line Q has a positive slope and a positive y-intercept.
译	直线 Q 有正斜率和正的 y 轴截距。

49 positive solution

义	正数解
例	What is the positive solution to the equation $16x^2 = 30$?
译	方程 $16x^2 = 30$ 的正数解是什么？

50 possible value

义	可能值
例	If $x + 9x = 19$, what are the possible values for x?
译	如果 $x + 9x = 19$，x 可能的值是多少？

51 projectile

[prə'dʒektl]

义	$n.$ 抛射物
例	The figure below shows the path of a certain projectile launched from the ground at an angle of θ.
译	下图显示了以 θ 角从地面发射的某一抛射物的路径。

52 quadratic equation

义	二次方程
例	Which of the following is a quadratic equation that has $-\dfrac{2}{3}$ as its only solution?
译	以下哪一个二次方程的唯一解是 $-\dfrac{2}{3}$？

53 quadratic expression

义	二次表达式
例	Given that $(x + 2)$ and $(x - 1)$ are factors of the quadratic expression below, what are the values of a and b?
译	已知 $(x + 2)$ 和 $(x - 1)$ 是下面二次表达式的因子，a 和 b 的值是多少？

54 quadratic formula

义	二次公式
例	Which of the following equations shows a correct use of the quadratic formula to solve $x^2 - 5x + 3 = 0$?
译	以下哪一个方程式体现了在求解 $x^2 - 5x + 3 = 0$ 时二次公式的正确使用？

55 quadratic function

义	二次函数
例	Each of the following (x, y) coordinate planes shows the graph of a quadratic function.
译	下面的每一个 (x, y) 坐标平面都体现了二次函数的图像。

56 rational function

义	有理函数
例	Consider the rational function $f(x) = \dfrac{x^2 - 9}{x - 7}$, whose graph is shown in the standard (x, y) coordinate plane below.

译 思考有理函数 $f(x) = \dfrac{x^2-9}{x-7}$，其图像如下面的标准 (x, y) 坐标平面所示。

---

57 real solution

义 实解

例 When solved for x, this equation will have exactly one real solution for which of the following values of k?

译 当为 x 求解时，对于以下哪个 k 值，该方程将有一个精确的实解？

---

58 secant

['si:kənt]

义 *n.* 割线，正割

例 For any circle with 2 secants drawn from P to the circle, as shown in the figure below, the lengths of the segments of the secants are determined by $a(a + b) = c(c + d)$.

译 对于任意从 P 到圆有 2 个正割的圆，如下图所示，正割部分的长度由 $a(a + b) = c(c + d)$ 决定。

---

59 sine

[saɪn]

义 *n.* 正弦

例 Which of the following expressions equals the sine of $\angle R$?

译 下面哪个表达式等于 $\sin\angle R$？

---

60 slope

[sləʊp]

义 *n.* 斜率

例 If the slope of the line is 2, what is the value of k?

译 如果直线的斜率是 2，k 的值是多少？

---

61 slope-intercept

[sləʊpˌɪntər'sept]

义 斜截式

例 One of the following equations, in slope-intercept form, is the equation of the line shown below in the standard (x, y) coordinate plane.

译 下面的其中一个斜截式方程是在标准 (x, y) 坐标平面上的直线方程。

---

62 slope-intercept equation

义 斜截式方程

例 The points $(-2, 3)$ and $(0, 1)$ lie on a straight line. What is the slope-intercept equation of the line?

译 点 $(-2, 3)$ 和 $(0, 1)$ 位于一条直线上。这条直线的斜截式方程是什么？

---

63 slope-intercept form

义 斜截式形式

例 What is the slope-intercept form of $6x - y - 2 = 0$?

译 $6x - y - 2 = 0$ 的斜截式形式是什么？

---

64 smallest possible value

义 最小可能值

例 Which of the following is the smallest possible value of x?

译 下面哪个是 x 最小可能值？

---

65 solution

['sə'luːʃn]

义 *n.* (数学中的)解

例 What is the sum of the two solutions of the equation $x^2 + 3x - 28 = 0$?

译 方程 $x^2 + 3x - 28 = 0$ 的两个解的和是多少？

---

66 system of equation

义 方程组

例 Consider the following system of equations in x and y, where the values of m and n are NOT the same.

译 考虑以下有 x 和 y 的方程组，其中 m 和 n 的值不相同。

---

67 tangent

['tændʒənt]

义 *adj.* 相切的

例 Which of the following is an equation of the line that is tangent to the circle at the point $(0, -2)$?

译 下面哪个选项是与圆在 $(0, -2)$ 点相切的直线的方程？

---

68 term

[tɜːrm]

义 *n.* 项

例 If 4 is the first term and 256 is the fourth term of a geometric progression, which of the following is the second term?

译 如果 4 是等比数列的第一项，256 是第四项，那么下列哪项是第二项？

---

69 the largest value

义 最大值

例 What is the largest value of x for which there exists a real value of y such that $x^2 + y^2 = 256$?

译 x 的最大值是多少，使得 y 的实数值满足 $x^2 + y^2 = 256$？

---

70 the least value

义 最小值

例 For the equation above, which of the following values of x gives the least value of y?

译 对于上面的方程，下列哪个 x 值给出的 y 值的最小值？

---

71 trigonometric function

义 三角函数

例 Which of the following trigonometric functions has an amplitude of 2?

译 下面哪个三角函数的振幅是 2？

---

72 variable

['veriəbl]

义 *n.* 变量

例 The variables a, b, and c are all integers and $a + b + c = 50$.

译 变量 a, b 和 c 都是整数，且 $a + b + c = 50$。

73 **vertical asymptote**

义 垂直渐近线

例 This function has no vertical asymptote.

译 这个函数没有垂直的渐近线。

---

74 **vertical axis of symmetry**

义 垂直对称轴

例 The parabola has vertex $(-3, -2)$, has a vertical axis of symmetry, and passes through $(-2, -1)$.

译 抛物线有顶点 $(-3, -2)$，有垂直对称轴，并通过点 $(-2, -1)$。

---

75 *x*-intercept

义 x 截距

例 The graph of $\dfrac{x^2}{36} + \dfrac{y^2}{64} = 1$ has an x-intercept at which of the following points?

译 $\dfrac{x^2}{36} + \dfrac{y^2}{64} = 1$ 的图像在以下哪个点有 x 截距？

List 7

1 bar graph

义 条形图

例 Which of the following bar graphs most accurately represents the data on the number of fat calories in a small order of french fries at the 9 fast food restaurants?

译 以下哪个条形图最准确地表示了 9 家快餐店小份薯条中脂肪热量的数据?

2 distance-versus-time graph

义 距离—时间图

例 The distance-versus-time graph below represents Barbara Jean's walk to school on Friday.

译 下面的距离—时间图代表了芭芭拉·简周五去学校的路程。

3 frequency chart

义 频数(分布)图表

例 The frequency chart below shows the cumulative number of Ms. Hernandez's science students whose test scores fell within certain score ranges.

译 下面的频数(分布)图表显示了埃尔南德斯女士的科学学生的考试分数落在某个分数范围内的累计人数。

4 frequency histogram

义 频率直方图

例 The frequency histogram below shows the distribution of the heights, in inches, of 11 basketball players.

译 下面的频率直方图显示了 11 名篮球运动员身高(以英寸为单位)的分布。

5 graph

[græf]

义 *n.* 图表;示意图

例 Which of the following number line graphs shows the solution set for x of $x^2 > 25$?

译 下列哪个数轴图显示了 $x^2 > 25$ 中 x 的解集?

6 histogram

['hɪstəgræm]

义 *n.* 直方图

例 The 20 responses are summarized by the histogram below.

译 下面的直方图总结了这 20 个回答。

7 image

['ɪmɪdʒ]

义 *n.* 图像

例 What will be the coordinates of the final image of *A* resulting from both transformations?

译 这两个变换得到的 *A* 的最终图像的坐标是什么?

8 pie chart

义 *n.* 饼形图,圆形分格统计图表

例 The pie chart is divided into two sections: covered and not covered.

译 饼图分为两个部分：已覆盖的和未覆盖的。

---

9 scatterplot

['skætərplɑːt]

义 散点图

例 The figure below shows a scatterplot for the data points in the table and five solid-line graphs that represent possible models for this data set.

译 下图显示了表中数据点的散点图和 5 个实线图，它们代表了该数据集的可能模型。

---

10 side view

义 侧视图

例 Shown below are the rectangular floor plan (left figure) and a side view of the cabin (right figure).

译 下图是矩形平面图（左图）和舱室的侧视图（右图）。

---

11 stem-and-leaf plot

义 茎叶图

例 The distances of one jump by each of the students are represented in the stem-and-leaf plot below.

译 每个学生跳跃一次的距离在下面的茎叶图中表示。

---

12 top view

义 俯视图

例 The figure below shows the top view of the Santana family's house and yard.

译 下图显示了桑塔纳家的房子和院子的俯视图。

List 8

1	**average**	义 *n.* 平均数　*adj.* 平均(数)的
	['ævərɪdʒ]	例 The average density of an object is defined as the object's average weight per unit volume.
		译 物体的平均密度的定义是物体每单位体积的平均重量。

2	**mean**	义 *n.* 平均数
	[miːn]	例 What is the difference between the mean and the median of the set {3, 8, 10, 15}?
		译 集合 {3,8,10,15} 的平均值和中位数的差值是多少?

3	**median**	义 *n.* 中值，中位数；中线
	['miːdɪən]	例 The first 10 World Series listed in the table (1980 through 1989) had a median length of how many games?
		译 表中列出的前 10 个世界大赛(1980 年到 1989 年)的中位数是多少场?

4	**mode**	义 *n.* 众数
	[məʊd]	例 For this data set, the mean, the median, and the mode are each equal to 10.
		译 这个数据集的平均值、中值和众数都等于 10。

5	**random sample**	义 随机样本，随机抽样
		例 Because this was a random sample, the percents in the sample are the most likely estimates for the corresponding percents among all the people at the mall today.
		译 因为这是一个随机样本，所以样本中的百分比是对今天购物中心所有人中相应百分比的最有可能的估计。

6	**range**	义 *n.* 值域；极差
	[reɪndʒ]	例 Given that the function f defined as $f(x) = 5 - 3x$ has domain $\{-1, 0, 2\}$, what is the range of f?
		译 定义为 $f(x) = 5 - 3x$ 的给定函数 f 有定义域 $\{-1, 0, 2\}$，f 的值域是什么?

7	**standard deviation**	义 标准差
		例 The percent of the data that falls within each standard deviation from the mean is given to the nearest 0.1%.
		译 在每个标准差范围内的数据百分比被给出到离平均值最近的 0.1%。

List 9

1 constant of proportionality

义　比例常数

例　Let k be a constant of proportionality and let w, x, y, and z be positive real number variables.

译　设 k 为比例常数，设 w，x，y，z 为正实数变量。

---

2 independent event

义　独立的事件

例　The probabilities that each of two independent events will occur are given in the table below.

译　下表给出了两个独立事件各自发生的概率。

---

3 normal distribution

义　正态分布

例　Which of the following percentages is closest to the percent of the data points that are within two standard deviations of the mean in any normal distribution?

译　下面哪个百分比最接近任何正态分布中离均值 2 个标准差范围内的数据点的百分比？

---

4 percent

[pə'sent]

义　*n.* 百分比

例　The National League, won about what percent of the 20 World Series listed in the table?

译　在表中所列出的 20 场世界大赛中国家队获取的百分比是多少？

---

5 percentage

[pər'sentɪdʒ]

义　*n.* 百分比

例　The table below gives the percentage of the audience that gave each of the ratings.

译　下表给出了每个收视率的观众百分比。

---

6 probability

[ˌprɑːbə'bɪlətɪ]

义　*n.* 概率

例　What is the probability that the student picked had earned an A on the book report?

译　被选中的学生在读书报告中获得 A 的概率是多少？

---

7 proportion

[prə'pɔːrʃn]

义　*n.* 比例

例　The basic ingredients are limestone and clay in the proportion 2︰1.

译　基本成分是石灰石和黏土，比例为 2︰1。

---

8 ratio

['reɪʃɪəʊ]

义　*n.* 比率，比例

例　The ratio of the width of the rectangle to its length is 1︰2.

译 该矩形的长宽比是 2：1。

---

9 the normal distribution curve

义 正态分布曲线

例 The graph below illustrates the normal distribution curve.

译 下图展示了正态分布曲线。

---

10 true

[tru:]

义 *adj.* 正确的；真的

例 If the statement "If a cat is tricolor, then it is a female" were true, which of the following statements would also have to be true?

译 如果 "如果一只猫是三色的，那么它就是雌性的" 这句话是正确的，那么下面哪句话也是正确的呢？

List 10

1 average speed

义 平均速度

例 During which second of its fall, if any, was the average speed of the flowerpot, in feet per second, the greatest?

译 如果有的话，花盆下落的哪一秒的平均速度（单位为英尺／秒）是最大的？

2 centimeter

['sentə͵mi:tə]

义 *n.* 厘米

例 The circle in the figure below has a radius of 8 centimeters.

译 下图中的圆半径为 8 厘米。

3 constant rate

义 恒定的速度

例 Students studying motion observed a cart rolling at a constant rate along a straight line.

译 研究运动的学生们观察到一辆小车沿着直线以恒定的速度滚动。

4 constant speed

义 恒速，等速

例 How many minutes would it take a car to travel 120 miles at a constant speed of 50 miles per hour?

译 一辆汽车以每小时 50 英里的恒速行驶 120 英里需要多少分钟？

5 coordinate unit

义 坐标单位

例 In quadrilateral *ABCD* shown in the standard (*x*, *y*) coordinate plane below, what is the distance, in coordinate units, from the midpoint of *AD* to the midpoint of *CD*?

译 在下列标准 (*x*, *y*) 坐标平面下的四边形 *ABCD* 中，从 *AD* 中点到 *CD* 中点的距离，用坐标单位表示是多少？

6 cubic centimeter

义 立方厘米

例 What is the volume, in cubic centimeters, of the solid?

译 以立方厘米为单位，固体的体积是多少？

7 gallon

['gælən]

义 *n.* 加仑（容量单位）

例 This car does 30 miles to the gallon.

译 这辆汽车每加仑汽油可行驶 30 英里。

8 inch

[ɪntʃ]

义 *n.* 英寸

例 The perimeter of a parallelogram is 80 inches, and the length of one side is 18 inches.

译 平行四边形的周长是 80 英寸，一条边的长度是 18 英寸。

9 maximum speed

义 最高速度

例 The car reached its maximum speed and began to slow down.

译 汽车达到了最高速度，然后开始减速。

---

10 meter

['mi:tər]

义 *n.* 公尺，米

例 The shortest side has an actual length of 410 meters.

译 最短的边实际长度为 410 米。

---

11 millimeter

['mɪləˌmi:tə]

义 *n.* 毫米

例 What is the area, in square millimeter, of the small circle?

译 以平方毫米为单位，这个小圆的面积是多少？

---

12 square centimeter

义 平方厘米

例 What is the area, in square centimeters, of △*DEF*?

译 △*DEF* 的面积是多少平方厘米？

---

13 square feet

义 平方英尺

例 What is the area, in square feet, of the portion of the floor that will NOT be covered by cabinets?

译 不被橱柜覆盖的地板面积（单位为平方英尺）是多少？

---

14 square meter

义 平方米 (m²)

例 The length of *AO* is 4 meters, and the area of the shaded sector is 6π square meters.

译 *AO* 的长度是 4 米，阴影部分的面积是 6π 平方米。

---

15 unit

['ju:nɪt]

义 *n.* 单位

例 What is the area of *ABCD*, in square units?

译 以平方为单位，*ABCD* 的面积是多少？

List 11

1　cost
[kɔ:st]

义 *n.* 费用；成本　*v.* 要价，需花费；估算……的费用

例 how much would the gasoline cost to drive the car 300 miles?

译 这车开 300 英里要消耗多少汽油?

2　deposit
[dɪ'pɑ:zɪt]

义 *n.* 存款

例 Lou does not make any further deposits or withdrawals.

译 卢不再进行任何存款或取款。

3　fixed cost

义 固定成本

例 Which of the following is the fixed cost?

译 下列哪项是固定成本?

4　interest rate

义 利率

例 According to this formula, which of the following is closest to the dollar value of $1,000 invested for two years at a 5% annual interest rate?

译 根据这个公式，下列哪项最接近 1 000 美元以 5% 年利率投资两年的利息?

5　maximum profit

义 最大利润

例 What is the maximum profit Marcia can earn from the picture frames she makes in one week?

译 马西娅在一周内能从她制作的相框中获得的最大利润是多少?

6　price
[praɪs]

义 *n.* 价格

例 Original price is $12.50.

译 原价是 12.50 美元。

7　profit
['prɑ:fɪt]

义 *n.* 利润

例 The actual profits are represented by the graph of the function *g*.

译 实际利润用函数 *g* 的图像表示。

8　revenue
['revənu:]

义 *n.* 收入

例 The store will adjust the price to maximize revenue.

译 商店会调整价格以使收入最大化。

9　tax
[tæks]

义 *n.* 税

例 Ignoring sales tax, what is the total amount of these purchases?

译 如果不考虑销售税，这些采购的总金额是多少？

10 total cost

义 **总成本**

例 Using the average fuel cost per gallon given in the fuel economy window sticker, which of the following dollar amounts is closest to the total cost for fuel over the 350 miles of highway driving?

译 使用燃油经济性车窗贴纸给出的每加仑平均燃油成本，下面哪一项最接近 350 英里高速公路行驶的燃油总成本？

第三部分
科学词汇

List 1

1 absorbed

['əb'sɔ:rbd]

义 *adj.* 吸收的

例 As the concentration of betacyanin in the solution increases, the amount of light absorbed increases.

译 随着溶液中甜菜红素浓度的增加，吸收的光量也增加。

2 acid

['æsɪd]

义 *n.* 酸；酸性物质

例 If no acid was produced, the solution remained red.

译 如果不产生酸，溶液仍将是红色的。

3 acidity

[ə'sɪdəti]

义 *n.* 酸性；酸度

例 One of the fermentation pathways produces CO_2 gas and increases the acidity (lowers the pH) of the solution.

译 其中一种发酵方式会产生二氧化碳气体，增加溶液的酸度（降低 pH 值）。

4 adenine

['ædənɪn]

义 *n.* 腺嘌呤

例 There are four types of bases in DNA: Adenine, Guanine, Cytosine, and Thymine.

译 DNA 中有四种碱基：腺嘌呤、鸟嘌呤、胞嘧啶和胸腺嘧啶。

5 aerobic

[e'rəʊbɪk]

义 *adj.* 需氧的

例 Aerobic bacteria, which require O_2, generate CO_2.

译 需要氧气的好氧细菌会产生二氧化碳。

6 agar

['eɪgɑ:r]

义 *n.* 琼脂；【微】琼脂培养基

例 Each fly was placed in a separate petri dish containing nutrient agar.

译 每只苍蝇被单独放置在一个含有营养琼脂的陪替氏培养皿中。

7 aggregate

['ægrɪgət]

义 *n.* 骨料

例 Each sample contained the same type and amount of aggregate.

译 每个样本含有相同类型和数量的骨料。

8 albinotic

[ælbaɪ'nɑ:tɪk]

义 *adj.* 白化的

例 Corn snakes can appear orange and black, all black, all orange, or albinotic (lacking in pigment).

译 玉米锦蛇可以呈现橙色和黑色、全黑色、全橙色或白化（缺乏色素）。

9 algae

义 *n.* 水藻，海藻

['ældʒiː]

> 例 Unlike P. caudatum and P. aurelia, P. bursaria harbor cells of photosynthetic algae, called Chlorella, in their cytoplasm.
>
> 译 与尾草履虫和双小核草履虫不同，绿草履虫的细胞质中含有光合藻类小球藻细胞。

---

10 allele

[ə'liːl]

> 义 *n.* 等位基因
>
> 例 A corn snake's coloration depends on the alleles (forms of a gene) it carries at these genes.
>
> 译 玉米锦蛇的颜色取决于它携带的等位基因（一种基因的形式）。

---

11 amino acid

> 义 氨基酸
>
> 例 Cells contain 20 different amino acids that can be arranged in a virtually infinite number of ways to make different proteins.
>
> 译 细胞里含有 20 种不同的氨基酸，它们可以以几乎无穷无尽的方式排列来制造不同的蛋白质。

---

12 amino sugar

> 义 【生化】氨基糖
>
> 例 A soil's amino sugar N (a naturally occurring N source different from soil test N) content can determine whether a soil will be responsive.
>
> 译 土壤氨基糖态氮（一种自然产生的氮源，不同于土壤试验氮）的量可以决定土壤是否具有反应性。

---

13 anaerobic

[ˌæne'rəʊbɪk]

> 义 *adj.* 厌氧的
>
> 例 Anaerobic bacteria, which require little or no O_2, generate CH_4.
>
> 译 厌氧细菌只需要很少的氧气或不需要氧气，就能产生甲烷（CH_4）。

---

14 arginine

['ɑːdʒəˌniːn]

> 义 *n.* 【生化】精氨酸
>
> 例 Citrullination is the process of posttranslational modification of arginine residues.
>
> 译 瓜氨酸化是精氨酸残基的翻译后修饰的过程。

---

15 backbone

['bækbəʊn]

> 义 *n.* 主链
>
> 例 Each polynucleotide is then fragmented along the length of the sugar-phosphate backbone into many short, single-stranded polynucleotide fragments.
>
> 译 然后，每个多核苷酸被沿着糖磷酸主链的长度分裂成许多短的单链多核苷酸片段。

---

16 bacterial

[bæk'tɪərɪəl]

> 义 *adj.* 细菌的
>
> 例 After the 24-hour period, researchers checked the samples for bacterial growth.
>
> 译 24 小时后，研究人员检查了样本中的细菌生长情况。

17 base

[beɪs]

义 *n.* 碱基，碱

例 Base pairs are connected together with hydrogen bonds.

译 碱基对通过氢键连接在一起。

18 beak

[bi:k]

义 *n.* 鸟嘴；喙

例 Birds with shallower beaks can efficiently crush and eat only small seeds.

译 喙较浅的鸟类只可以有效地粉碎和吃掉小种子。

19 beech

[bi:tʃ]

义 *n.* 山毛榉

例 The Indian beech tree produces oil-rich seeds.

译 印度山毛榉树产生富含油脂的种子。

20 biomarker

['baɪəʊˌmɑːrkər]

义 *n.* 生物标志物

例 Petroleum contains biomarkers, compounds that can be produced only through the breakdown of once-living matter.

译 石油含有生物标志物，这些化合物只能通过分解曾经有生命的物质来产生。

21 biosorption

[bi:əʊˈzɔːpʃn]

义 *n.* 生物吸附

例 Biosorption is a process that uses certain biological materials (biomass) to remove metal ions from a solution.

译 生物吸附是利用某些生物材料（生物量）从溶液中去除金属离子的过程。

22 caffeinated

['kæfɪneɪtɪd]

义 *adj.* 含咖啡因的

例 Two studies, one with humans and one with rats, examined the effect of caffeinated cola consumption on BMD.

译 两项研究，一项针对人类，一项针对老鼠，检验喝含咖啡因的可乐对骨密度的影响。

23 carbohydrate

[ˌkɑːrbəʊˈhaɪdreɪt]

义 *n.* 碳水化合物

例 Amylase is an enzyme that speeds up the breakdown of starch into smaller carbohydrates (such as maltose).

译 淀粉酶是一种能让淀粉加速分解成更小的碳水化合物（如麦芽糖）的酶。

24 carboxylic

[ˌkɑːrbɑːkˈsɪlɪk]

义 *adj.* 含羧基的

例 A carboxylic acid (CA) is a compound that contains a -COOR group.

译 羧酸（CA）是一种含有 -COOR 基团的化合物。

25 carburetor

['kɑːrbəˌreɪtər]

义 *n.* 化油器

例 The carburetors in gasoline engines have a constriction called a venturi, where gasoline and air are mixed.

译 汽油发动机的化油器有一个叫作喉管的收缩部分，汽油和空气在这里混合。

26 carnivorous

[kɑːrˈnɪvərəs]

义 *adj.* 食肉的

例 Dimetrodon is a large, extinct, cold-blooded, carnivorous reptile.

译 异齿龙是一种已灭绝的大型冷血食肉爬行动物。

27 casein

['keɪsiːn]

义 *n.* 酪蛋白

例 A sample of human milk was separated into three fractions: casein (a protein), lipids, and non-casein proteins.

译 母乳样本被分离成 3 个部分：酪蛋白（一种蛋白质）、脂类和非酪蛋白。

28 caterpillar

['kætərpɪlər]

义 *n.* 毛虫

例 Nemoria caterpillars that hatch in the spring mature into a yellow, ridged morph (body type).

译 内莫里亚毛虫在春天孵化，成熟后（体型）会变成黄色的脊状变体。

29 cellular

['seljələr]

义 *adj.* 细胞的

例 A student performed an experiment to determine how the pH of an aqueous solution is affected by the addition to the solution of an organism that is undergoing both photosynthesis and cellular respiration.

译 一名学生进行了一项实验，以确定在溶液中加入正在进行光合作用和细胞呼吸的生物是怎样对水溶液的 pH 值产生影响的。

30 chamber

['tʃeɪmbər]

义 *n.* 室，房

例 In the first trial 100 uninfected mosquitoes were released into the chamber.

译 在第一次试验中，将 100 只未感染的蚊子释放到室内。

31 chickpea

['tʃɪkpiː]

义 *n.* 鹰嘴豆

例 A sample of 50 dried chickpeas with similar sizes and masses was selected.

译 选择 50 个大小和质量相似的干鹰嘴豆样品。

32 chlorophyll

['klɔːrəfɪl]

义 *n.* 叶绿素

例 All plants in Population A produce chlorophyll.

译 种群 A 中的所有植物都产生叶绿素。

33 **chromosome**

['krəʊməsəʊm]

义 *n.* 染色体

例 These genes are on separate chromosomes.

译 这些基因位于不同的染色体上。

---

34 **clade**

[kleɪd]

义 *n.* 进化枝

例 A clade is a set of related species and their most recent common ancestor (MRCA).

译 进化枝是一组相关物种和它们最近的共同祖先。

---

35 **cladogram**

['klædə,græm]

义 *n.* 进化分枝图

例 A cladogram organizes species into clades based on descent from a common ancestor.

译 进化分枝图根据共同祖先的血统将物种分成进化枝。

---

36 **cleft**

[kleft]

义 *n.* 裂缝

例 Botulin is absorbed from the synaptic cleft by the synaptic terminal.

译 肉毒杆菌素从突触间隙被突触末端吸收。

---

37 **colony**

['kɑːlənɪ]

义 *n.* 菌落

例 E. coli levels that are above 100 colonies formed per 100 mL of water indicate reduced water quality.

译 大肠杆菌高于每 100 毫升水形成 100 个菌落的水平表明水质下降。

---

38 **conifer**

['kɑːnɪfər]

义 *n.* 针叶树

例 In the fall, Monarch butterflies (Danaus plexippus) in eastern North America migrate to Mexico, where they overwinter in high-altitude forests of oyamel fir (an evergreen conifer).

译 秋天，北美东部的帝王蝴蝶(学名：Danaus plexippus)迁徙到墨西哥，在那里的高海拔欧亚梅尔杉(一种常绿针叶树)森林中越冬。

---

39 **contractile**

[kən'træktaɪl]

义 *adj.* 可收缩的

例 Botulin then binds to and breaks down myosin, a protein that is an essential component of the contractile apparatus of a muscle fiber.

译 然后肉毒杆菌素结合并分解肌凝蛋白，肌凝蛋白是肌纤维收缩装置的重要组成部分。

---

40 **crab**

[kræb]

义 *n.* 蟹

例 Because snow crab are eaten by fish such as cod, the number of cod present in an area may affect snow crab populations.

译 因为鳕鱼等鱼类会以雪蟹为食，所以一个地区鳕鱼的数量可能会影响雪蟹的数量。

41　cricket

['krɪkɪt]

义　*n.* 蟋蟀

例　Small crickets were dyed either red, yellow, green, blue or brown when they drank water containing a dye.

译　当小蟋蟀喝了含有染料的水时，它们被染成红色、黄色、绿色、蓝色或棕色。

42　cross-pollinated

[krɔːsˈpɑːləneɪtɪd]

义　*adj.* 异花授粉的

例　The flowers can be self-pollinated (egg and pollen are from the same H. metallica plant) or cross-pollinated (egg and pollen are from different H.metallica plants).

译　这些花可以自花授粉（卵和花粉来自同一蝎尾蕉植物）或异花授粉（卵和花粉来自不同的蝎尾蕉植物）。

43　cytoplasm

['saɪtəuplæzəm]

义　*n.* 细胞质

例　DNA is found exclusively in the cell's nucleus, whereas proteins are found throughout the nucleus and cytoplasm.

译　DNA 只存在于细胞核中，而蛋白质则存在于细胞核和细胞质中。

44　decompose

[ˌdiːkəmˈpəʊz]

义　*v.* 分解，腐烂

例　The four containers were then left in a warm location for about a week to allow the materials to decompose.

译　然后，将这 4 个容器放在一个温暖的地方大约一周，以使材料分解。

45　defoliation

[ˌdiːˌfəʊlɪˈeɪʃn]

义　*n.* 落叶

例　Short-term effects include the disturbances directly associated with the action of the pest, which may cause the defoliation, loss of vigor, or death of trees.

译　短期影响包括与害虫行为直接相关的干扰，而这些干扰可能导致树木落叶、失去活力或死亡。

46　denature

[diːˈneɪtʃə]

义　*v.* 变性

例　When the DNA began to denature, the absorbance increased sharply.

译　当 DNA 开始变性时，吸光度急剧增加。

47　dialysis

[ˌdaɪˈæləsɪs]

义　*n.* 透析

例　A sealed bag made of dialysis tubing (a dialysis bag) containing the solution was submerged in a beaker containing the starch solution.

译　将装有溶液的由透析管制成的密封袋（透析袋）浸泡在含有淀粉溶液的烧杯中。

48　dietary

义　*adj.* 饮食的

['daɪətərɪ]

例 Scientists have determined that BMD (bone mineral density) is linked to dietary intake.

译 科学家们已经确定，骨密度（BMD）与饮食的摄入有关。

---

49 digestive

[daɪ'dʒestɪv]

义 *adj.* 消化的

例 The amoeba histolytica can infect the human digestive tract.

译 阿米巴原虫能感染人的消化道。

---

50 dimorphic

[daɪ'mɔːrfɪk]

义 *adj.* 双晶的；二态的

例 Both types of rice embryos have dimorphic cotyledons.

译 两种类型稻胚都具有二型子叶。

---

51 disinfectant

[ˌdɪsɪn'fektənt]

义 *adj.* 消毒的　　*n.* 消毒液，消毒剂

例 Researchers performed the following experiments to evaluate the effectiveness of a disinfectant (chemical) called NoGrow (NG) at stopping bacterial growth.

译 研究人员进行了以下实验，以评估一种名为 NoGrow(NG) 的消毒剂（化学物质）阻止细菌生长的有效性。

---

52 DNA

义 *abbr.* 脱氧核糖核酸（= deoxyribonucleic acid）

例 Thus, after replication, one DNA molecule is composed of parental DNA, and the other is composed of new DNA.

译 因此复制后，一个 DNA 分子由亲本 DNA 组成，另一个则是由新的 DNA 组成的。

---

53 dominant

['dɑːmɪnənt]

义 *adj.* 显性的

例 Gene G has two alleles: G, which is dominant, and g, which is recessive.

译 G 基因有两个等位基因：显性的 G 和隐性的 g。

---

54 double-stranded

['dʌbl'strændɪd]

义 *adj.* 双链的

例 When sense and anti-sense RNA molecules meet, they bind to each other and form double-stranded RNA.

译 当正义和反义 RNA 分子相遇的时候，它们结合在一起形成双链的 RNA。

---

55 ecosystem

['iːkəʊsɪstəm]

义 *n.* 生态系统

例 Gypsy moth larvae (caterpillars) eat tree leaves and have caused serious damage to forest ecosystems in the United States.

译 舞毒蛾幼虫（毛虫）以树叶为食，对美国的森林生态系统造成了严重破坏。

56 electrophoresis

[ɪˌlektrəʊfəˈriːsɪs]

义 *n.* 电泳

例 A DNA fingerprint can be analyzed using gel electrophoresis (a technique that uses an electric field to separate DNA fragments into bands based on size) along with various DNA visualization methods.

译 DNA 指纹可以通过凝胶电泳（一种根据大小利用电场将 DNA 片段分离成条带的技术）和各种 DNA 可视化方法进行分析。

---

57 embryo

[ˈembrɪəʊ]

义 *n.* 胚胎；萌芽

例 Ova with very large volumes tend to contain large amounts of nutrients that are used for growth by the embryo.

译 体积非常大的卵子往往含有大量的营养物质，这些物质可供胚胎生长使用。

---

58 endothermic

[ˌendəʊˈθɜːrmɪk]

义 *adj.* 吸热的；温血的

例 Fecal coliforms are bacteria found in the intestines of all endothermic animals.

译 粪便大肠菌群是在所有恒温动物的肠道中都发现的细菌。

---

59 enzyme

[ˈenzaɪm]

义 *n.* 酶

例 Each of these reactions is catalyzed by an enzyme.

译 这些反应都是由一种酶催化的。

---

60 ephippia

[ɪˈfipiːə]

义 *n.* 卵包（复数形式）

例 When Moina micrura (microscopic aquatic crustaceans) are exposed to unfavorable environmental conditions, they produce ephippia (specialized eggs that each contain a dormant embryo).

译 当微型裸腹溞（微小的水生甲壳动物）暴露在不利的环境条件下，它们会产生卵包（一种特殊的卵，每个卵都含有一个休眠的胚胎）。

---

61 Escherichia coli

义 大肠杆菌

例 Two measures of water quality are the number of Escherichia coli bacteria present and the biotic index, BI.

译 衡量水质的两种指标是现存大肠杆菌的数量和生物指数（BI）。

---

62 eucaryote

[juːˈkæriːəʊːət]

义 *n.*【生】真核细胞

例 Gene expression in eucaryotes is controlled by regulatory DNA sequences (RSs).

译 真核生物中的基因表达受调控 DNA 序列（RSs）控制。

---

63 evolutionary

[ˌiːvəˈluːʃənerɪ]

义 *adj.* 进化的

例 Dingle is an evolutionary biologist who studies insects.

译 丁格尔是一位研究昆虫的进化生物学家。

---

64 feces

['fi:si:z]

义 *n.* 排泄物

例 Two studies were done to examine how the proportion of vermicompost (feces from earthworms) in a particular potting soil affects the yield of each of two plant species: Solarium lycopersicum (a tomato plant) and Capsicum annuum (a pepper plant).

译 研究人员做了两项研究，以检验在特定的盆栽土壤中蚯蚓粪便的比例如何影响两种植物：番茄和辣椒的产量。

---

65 fermentation

[ˌfɜ:men'teɪʃn]

义 *n.* 发酵

例 Bacteria break down sugars by fermentation.

译 细菌通过发酵分解糖。

---

66 fiber

['faɪbə]

义 *n.* 纤维（物质）

例 Research now says adding fiber to the teen diet may help lower the risk of breast cancer.

译 现在的研究表明，在青少年饮食中添加纤维有助于降低患乳腺癌的风险。

---

67 fission

['fɪʃn]

义 *n.* 【核】裂变；【生】分裂，裂殖

例 Nuclear fission releases tremendous amounts of energy.

译 核裂变释放出巨大的能量。

---

68 forage

['fɔ:rɪdʒ]

义 *v.* 觅食

例 Wood mice (a species of mammal) typically forage for food at night.

译 木鼠（一种哺乳动物）通常在夜间觅食。

---

69 fruit fly

义 果蝇

例 Most fruit flies have red eyes; some have white eyes.

译 大多数果蝇的眼睛是红色的，有些则有白色的眼睛。

---

70 fungus

['fʌŋgəs]

义 *n.* 真菌，霉菌

例 If a competitor fungus—Fungus A—outcompetes Fungus M in the gallery, SPB larval development will be disrupted.

译 如果竞争对手真菌——真菌 A 超过在露台的真菌 M，南方松平幼虫的发育将受到干扰。

---

71 gamete

义 *n.* 【生】配子

['gæmi:t]

例 Gametes have half the amount of DNA as other cells in the body.

译 配子的 DNA 含量只有生物体内其他细胞的一半。

---

72 genetic

[dʒə'netɪk]

义 *adj.* 遗传的，基因的

例 In the 1940s, scientists thought all genetic material was contained in structures called chromosomes and that chromosomes had been found only in the nucleus of a cell.

译 20 世纪 40 年代，科学家们认为所有的遗传物质都包含在染色体结构中，而染色体只存在于细胞的细胞核中。

---

73 genetically

[dʒə'netɪklɪ]

义 *adv.* 遗传(基因)方面地

例 All plants in Population A are genetically identical, so they all have the ability to produce both pigments.

译 种群 A 中的所有植物在基因上都是相同的，所以它们都有能力产生两种色素。

---

74 genome

['dʒi:nəʊm]

义 *n.* 基因组

例 The human genome has now been sequenced.

译 人类基因组序列测定已完成。

---

75 genotype

['dʒenətaɪp]

义 *n.* 基因型

例 Genotype refers to the combination of alleles an individual has at a gene.

译 基因型是指个体在一个基因上的等位基因的组合。

---

76 germinate

['dʒɜ:rmɪneɪt]

义 *v.* 发芽

例 Some seed varieties germinate fast, so check every day or so.

译 有一些品种的种子发芽快，所以差不多每天都要察看一下。

List 2

1 GFP

义 绿色荧光蛋白（= green fluore scent protein）

例 GFP is a protein that emits green light when viewed with a certain microscope.

译 GFP 是一种在显微镜下观察时发出绿光的蛋白质。

---

2 globin

['gləʊbɪn]

义 *n.*【生化】球蛋白

例 Each Hb molecule contains four globin polypeptides—a pair of P-type globins and a pair of Q-type globins.

译 每个血红蛋白分子包含四个珠蛋白多肽——一对 P 型球蛋白和一对 Q 型球蛋白。

---

3 glucose

['glu:kəʊs]

义 *n.* 葡萄糖

例 In yeast, the genes that are expressed at a given time depend on environmental conditions, such as the glucose concentration in the environment.

译 在酵母中，在特定时间表达的基因取决于环境条件，如环境中的葡萄糖浓度。

---

4 glycerin

['glɪsərɪn]

义 *n.* 甘油

例 The clear layer is glycerin.

译 透明的那层是甘油。

---

5 gravid

['grævɪd]

义 *adj.* 怀孕的

例 Every gravid frog participated in six trials, each with a different alternative PRR.

译 每只怀孕的蛙参加了 6 个试验，每个试验都有不同的替代横式识别受体（PRR）。

---

6 gravitropism

['grævɪtrəʊpɪzəm]

义 *n.*【植】向地性

例 Response to gravity is gravitropism.

译 向地性是对重力作用所做出的反应。

---

7 hatch

[hætʃ]

义 *n./v.* 孵化

例 The embryos remain dormant until the ephippia are exposed to favorable environmental conditions that cause the ephippia to hatch.

译 胚胎一直处于休眠状态，直到卵包暴露在有利的环境条件下，才会孵化。

---

8 hemoglobin

[ˌhi:mə'gləʊbɪn]

义 *n.* 血红蛋白

例 In red blood cells (RBCs), the protein hemoglobin (Hb) carries oxygen.

译 在红细胞（RBC）中，血红蛋白（Hb）运输氧气。

---

9 herbaceous

[ɜːrˈbeɪʃəs]

义 *adj.* 草本植物的

例 The herbaceous layer in Plot Y was then killed using an herbicide.

译 然后用除草剂杀死 Y 地块的草本层。

---

10 hereditary

[həˈredɪterɪ]

义 *adj.* 遗传的

例 The number and arrangement of different amino acids within a protein form the codes that contain hereditary information.

译 蛋白质中不同氨基酸的数量和排列构成了包含遗传信息的密码。

---

11 heterogeneous

[ˌhetərəˈdʒiːnɪəs]

义 *adj.* 异质的

例 We wonder five seconds after the shaking, the contents of the test tube would have been better classified as a heterogeneous mixture or a homogeneous mixture.

译 我们想知道在摇晃五秒后，试管里的物质是属于异质混合物还是均质混合物。

---

12 histidine

[ˈhɪstɪˌdiːn]

义 *n.* 组氨酸

例 Strains of bacteria carrying a genetic mutation that prevents them from synthesizing the amino acid histidine are called His-.

译 细菌菌株携带的一种基因突变会阻止其合成氨基酸组氨酸，这种菌株被称为 His-。

---

13 homeothermic

[həʊmɪəʊˈθɜːrmɪk]

义 *adj.* 【动】恒温的

例 Homeothermic animals had body temperatures that remained relatively constant.

译 恒温动物的体温保持相对恒定。

---

14 homolog

[ˈhɑːməlɔːg]

义 *n.* 同系物（同系化合物、同系染色体等）

例 During meiosis, the two copies of a chromosome, or homologs, undergo DNA replication.

译 在减数分裂期间，染色体或同源物的两个副本会进行 DNA 复制。

---

15 homologous

[həʊˈmɑːləgəs]

义 *adj.* 【生】同源的

例 As a result, genes on homologous chromosomes recombine, forming new allele combinations along chromosomes.

译 因此，同源染色体上的基因重组，沿着染色体形成新的等位基因组合。

---

16 hypocotyl

[ˌhaɪpəʊˈkɑːtəl]

义 *n.* 【植】下胚轴

例 Hypocotyl was the best explant for rapid callus induction.

译 下胚轴是快速诱导愈伤组织的最佳外植体。

---

17 hypothetical

[ˌhaɪpəˈθetɪkl]

义 *adj.* 假设的，假定的

例 No doubt this hypothetical pattern did apply at times during the course of the recovery.

译 毫无疑问，在复苏的过程中，这种假设的模式确实适用于某些时候。

---

18 inedible

[ɪnˈedəbl]

义 *adj.* 不适合食用的

例 The oil is inedible, however, it can be converted to biodiesel fuel in a chemical reaction with methanol (a solvent) and a catalyst.

译 这种油是不可食用的，但它可以与甲醇（一种溶剂）和催化剂发生化学反应，转化为生物柴油燃料。

---

19 infiltrate

[ˈɪnfɪltreɪt]

义 *v.* (使)渗透

例 Water that infiltrates the soil or rock may increase the rate of mass movement.

译 渗入土壤或岩石的水可能会加快块体运动的速度。

---

20 infrequent

[ɪnˈfriːkwənt]

义 *adj.* 不频发的，不常见的

例 Wind pollination is infrequent because Zamia pollen is large and heavy.

译 风媒授粉是不常见的，因为泽米属植物的花粉又大又重。

---

21 inheritable

[ɪnˈherɪtəbl]

义 *adj.* 可遗传的

例 Finch beak depth is an inheritable trait (it can be passed from parents to offspring).

译 雀喙深度是一种可遗传的特征（它可以从父母遗传给后代）。

---

22 insect

[ˈɪnsekt]

义 *n.* 昆虫

例 In Zamia, 90% of ovule pollinations result from insect pollination; 10% result from wind pollination.

译 在泽米属植物中，90% 的胚珠授粉来自昆虫授粉，10% 来自风媒传粉。

---

23 lactose

[ˈlæktəʊs]

义 *n.* 乳糖

例 To study two fermentation pathways, researchers performed two experiments using broth that contained either the sugar sucrose or the sugar lactose.

译 为了研究两种发酵的过程，研究人员使用含有蔗糖或乳糖的培养液进行了两项实验。

---

24 ladderlike

['lædəlaɪk]

义 *adj.* 梯子状的

例 Nucleotides are joined in a ladderlike structure.

译 核苷酸以阶梯状结构连接。

---

25 larvae

['lɑːrviː]

义 *n.* 幼虫

例 As water quality improves, the number of stone fly larvae (a type of aquatic invertebrate) increases.

译 随着水质的改善，石蝇幼虫（一种水生无脊椎动物）的数量也会增加。

---

26 leach

[liːtʃ]

义 *v.* 过滤

例 In a lake, water leaches (dissolves out) soluble organic compounds from decaying tree leaves, producing dissolved organic carbon (DOC).

译 在一个湖泊中，水从腐烂的树叶中过滤（溶解）出可溶性有机化合物，产生溶解性有机碳（DOC）。

---

27 leachate

['liːtʃeɪt]

义 *n.* 浸出液，渗滤液

例 The resulting liquid (the leachate) was analyzed for DOC.

译 对产生的液体（渗滤液）进行了溶解性有机碳分析。

---

28 lipid

['lɪpɪd]

义 *n.* 脂质

例 The butterflies store (accumulate) body lipids to use as a source of energy at a later time.

译 蝴蝶储存（积聚）身体脂质，以便在以后将其用作能量的来源。

---

29 lizard

['lɪzərd]

义 *n.* 蜥蜴

例 Modern lizards change their skin color and pattern to attract a mate.

译 现代蜥蜴通过改变皮肤颜色和图案来吸引配偶。

---

30 lunge feeding

义 冲刺式进食法

例 Fin whales engulf and filter massive amounts of water and prey during an event called lunge feeding.

译 长须鲸吞噬并过滤大量的水和猎物，这一过程被称为冲刺进食。

---

31 mammal

['mæml]

义 *n.* 哺乳动物

例 Meerkats are mammals that typically live in groups of 2 to 30 individuals.

译 狐獴是一种哺乳动物，通常生活在 2 到 30 只的群体中。

32 mammalian

['mæ'meɪlɪən]

义 *adj.* 哺乳动物的

例 Urea is also a compound that is found in mammalian urine, so it must be soluble in water.

译 尿素也是一种在哺乳动物尿液中发现的化合物，所以它必须能溶于水。

33 marine

[mə'riːn]

义 *adj.* 海洋的

例 Threespine sticklebacks are fish that can live in marine (saltwater) and freshwater environments.

译 三刺鱼是一种既可以生活在海洋（咸水）又可以生活在淡水环境中的鱼。

34 matrix

['meɪtrɪks]

义 *n.* 基质

例 It shows the percent by mass of the matrix by particle size class.

译 它显示了按粒度分类的基质质量百分比。

35 maturity

[mə'tʃʊrətɪ]

义 *n.* 成熟期

例 Teenage is the period at which the body reaches maturity.

译 青少年是身体成熟期。

36 meiosis

[maɪ'əʊsɪs]

义 *n.*【生】减数分裂

例 During prophase of meiosis, homologous chromosomes frequently exchange segments in a process called crossing over.

译 在减数分裂的前期，同源染色体经常交换片段，这一过程称为交叉互换。

37 membrane

['membreɪn]

义 *n.* 薄膜，膜状物

例 In certain solutions, beet cells undergo membrane disruption, causing the cells to release betacyanin (a red pigment).

译 在某些溶液中，甜菜细胞的细胞膜会被破坏，导致细胞释放甜菜红素（一种红色色素）。

38 metabolism

[mə'tæbəlɪzəm]

义 *n.* 新陈代谢

例 The accumulation of DNA damage can be slowed by decreasing the rate of metabolism.

译 DNA 损伤的积累可以通过降低代谢速率来减缓。

39 metaphase

['metəˌfeɪz]

义 *n.*（细胞分裂）中期

例 Let's compare the number of onion root tip cells in telophase compare with the number of onion root tip cells in metaphase.

译 让我们比较一下末期洋葱根尖细胞的数量与中期洋葱根尖细胞的数量。

40 microscopic

[ˌmaɪkrəˈskɑːpɪk]

义 *adj.* 显微镜的；极小的

例 Microscopic examination of a cell's chromosomes can reveal the sex of the fetus.

译 利用显微镜检查细胞染色体可以查出胎儿的性别。

---

41 mitotic

[maɪˈtɑːtɪk]

义 *adj.*【生】有丝分裂的

例 Five hundred mitotic onion root tip cells were examined.

译 对 500 个有丝分裂的洋葱根尖细胞进行了观察。

---

42 moisten

[ˈmɔɪsn]

义 *v.* 使……湿润

例 During the week, the materials were stirred periodically and moistened with distilled water.

译 在一周内，这些材料被定期搅拌，并用蒸馏水湿润。

---

43 monomorphic

[mɒnəʊˈmɔːfɪk]

义 *adj.*【生】单态的，单型的，单形的

例 The nuclei are monomorphic with inconspicuous nucleoli.

译 细胞核形态单一，核仁不明显。

---

44 morphology

[mɔːrˈfɑːlədʒɪ]

义 *n.* 形态学

例 A researcher hypothesized that caterpillar morphology is influenced by three environmental factors: temperature, photoperiod, and diet.

译 一位研究人员假设，毛虫的形态会受 3 个环境因素的影响：温度、光周期和饮食。

---

45 mosquito

[məˈskiːtəʊ]

义 *n.* 蚊子

例 For the parasite to survive, mosquitoes must bite humans infected with gametocytes.

译 为了让这种寄生虫存活，蚊子必须叮咬受配子细胞感染的人类。

---

46 moth

[mɔːθ]

义 *n.* 蛾

例 The gypsy moth, which is native to Asia and Europe, was accidentally introduced to the northeastern United States in 1869.

译 舞毒蛾原产于亚洲和欧洲，1869 年偶然被引入美国东北部。

---

47 mutagen

[ˈmjuːtədʒən]

义 *n.* 突变原

例 Exposing His⁻ strains of bacteria to mutagens (substances that induce DNA mutations) can cause new mutations that restore the ability of some bacteria to synthesize histidine.

译 将 His⁻ 菌株暴露在突变原（引起 DNA 突变的物质）下可以导致新的突变，从而修复某些细菌合成组氨酸的能力。

48 mutagenic

[ˌmjuːtəˈdʒenɪk]

义 *adj.* 诱导有机体突变的

例 The number of His⁺ revertants in a population of bacteria can indicate the potential of a substance to be mutagenic in humans.

译 细菌群体中 His⁺ 逆转录因子的数量可以表明这种物质在人类中具有变异的潜力。

49 mutant

[ˈmjuːtənt]

义 *adj.* 突变的　*n.* 突变体

例 The normal form of this gene (S⁺) produces sleep factor protein; a mutant form (S⁻) does not produce the protein.

译 该基因的正常形式（S⁺）产生睡眠因子蛋白，突变型（S⁻）则不产生这种蛋白质。

50 mutation

[mjuːˈteɪʃn]

义 *n.* 突变，变异

例 This results in mutations that cause defects in proteins and in gene expression, leading to aging.

译 这引起突变，突变会导致蛋白质和基因表达的缺陷，最终导致衰老。

51 mutualistic

[ˈmjuːtʃuəlɪstɪk]

义 *adj.* 互利共生的

例 Zamia have mutualistic (mutually beneficial) relationships with insects.

译 泽米属植物与昆虫有着互惠互利的关系。

52 nectar

[ˈnektər]

义 *n.* 花蜜

例 To store lipids, monarch butterflies convert sugar from nectar they have consumed into lipids.

译 为了储存脂质，帝王蝴蝶将它们所吸食的花蜜中的糖转化为脂质。

53 negative tropism

义 负向性

例 Growth away from a stimulus is a negative tropism.

译 远离刺激的增长是一种负向性。

54 neuron

[ˈnʊrɑːn]

义 *n.* 神经元，神经细胞

例 Botulin then binds to and breaks down the neuron's docking proteins (proteins required for the fusion of synaptic vesicles with the neuron's plasma membrane).

译 然后肉毒杆菌素结合并分解神经元的对接蛋白质（突触囊泡与神经元的质膜融合所需的蛋白质）。

55 neurotransmitter

[ˈnʊrəʊtrænzmɪtər]

义 *n.* 神经递质

例 It is a neurotransmitter because it carries information from a muscle fiber to a synaptic terminal.

译 它是一种神经递质，因为它将信息从肌肉纤维传递到突触末端。

56 non-avian

[nɑːn ˈeɪvɪən]

义 *adj.* 非鸟类的

例 Two scientists discussed the evolution of three animal groups: crocodiles, non-avian dinosaurs (all dinosaurs except modern birds), and modern birds.

译 两位科学家讨论了三种动物的进化：鳄鱼、非鸟类恐龙（除了现代鸟类以外的所有恐龙）和现代鸟类。

---

57 nucleotide

[ˈnjuːklɪəˌtaɪd]

义 *n.* 核苷酸

例 A nucleotide is composed of a sugar, a phosphate group, and a base.

译 核苷酸由核糖、磷酸和碱基组成。

---

58 nucleus

[ˈnuːklɪəs]

义 *n.* 细胞核，原子核

例 The nucleus (core) of an atom contains protons (positively charged particles) and neutrons (uncharged particles).

译 原子核（核）包含质子（带正电荷的粒子）和中子（不带电荷的粒子）。

---

59 nutrient

[ˈnuːtrɪənt]

义 *adj.* 营养的　*n.* 营养

例 The nutrient solution was replaced every 5 days.

译 营养液每 5 天更换一次。

---

60 oak

[əʊk]

义 *n.* 橡树

例 A compound is found in oak leaves, but not found in catkins.

译 在橡树叶中发现一种化合物，但在柔荑花序中不存在。

---

61 osmosis

[ɑːzˈməʊsɪs]

义 *n.* 渗透

例 Osmosis is a process by which the molecules of a solvent pass from a solution of low concentration to a solution of high concentration through a semi-permeable membrane.

译 渗透是溶液分子通过半透膜从低浓度溶液扩散到高浓度溶液的过程。

---

62 ovule

[ˈəʊvjuːl]

义 *n.* 胚珠

例 The ovules then develop into seeds.

译 胚珠随后发育成种子。

---

63 parasite

[ˈpærəsaɪt]

义 *n.* 寄生虫

例 One of the ways the parasite spreads is through faecal matter.

译 寄生物传播的方式之一就是通过排泄物。

64 parental

[pəˈrentl]

义 *adj.* 亲本的

例 Each parental polynucleotide serves as a template for the synthesis of a new polynucleotide.

译 每个亲本多核苷酸都是合成新多核苷酸的模板。

65 pathway

[ˈpæθweɪ]

义 *n.* 路径

例 The pathway then shuts down at the reaction catalyzed by that enzyme.

译 然后，该途径在该酶催化的反应中关闭。

66 petri dish

义 陪替氏培养皿（实验室用于培养细菌等的有盖小玻璃盆）

例 It was necessary for the nutrient agar in the petri dishes to be sterile until the flies were placed in the dishes.

译 在苍蝇被放入陪替氏培养皿之前，培养皿中的营养琼脂必须是无菌的。

67 phenotype

[ˈfiːnətaɪp]

义 *n.* 表现型

例 The result is a cell with completely new traits: a new phenotype.

译 其结果就是形成一个具有全新特性的细胞，也就是一个新的表现型。

68 phosphate group

义 磷酸基

例 The sugars and phosphate groups form the sides of the ladder, or backbones, while pairs of bases form the rungs.

译 糖和磷酸基团构成了梯子的两侧，也就是主链，而成对的碱基构成了阶梯。

69 phosphorus

[ˈfɑːsfərəs]

义 *n.* 磷

例 If a plant receives enough phosphorus, it does not produce this purple pigment, so its stem is green.

译 如果植物吸收了足够多的磷，它就不会产生这种紫色的色素，所以它的茎是绿色的。

70 photoperiod

[ˌfəʊtəˈpɪriəd]

义 *n.* 光周期

例 Female caterpillars were raised at 25℃ with a 14-hour photoperiod on either catkins or oak leaves.

译 在 25℃、14 小时光周期条件下，在柳絮或橡树叶上饲养雌毛虫。

71 photosynthesis

[ˌfəʊtəʊˈsɪnθəsɪs]

义 *n.* 光合作用

例 Carbon dioxide (CO_2) is consumed during photosynthesis and produced during cellular respiration.

译 光合作用消耗二氧化碳（化学式为 CO_2），而细胞呼吸过程产生二氧化碳。

72 phototropism

[ˌfəʊtəʊˈtrəʊpɪzəm]

义 *n.* 向光性

例 Response to light is phototropism.

译 对光的反应就是向光性。

---

73 phytoplankton

[ˌfaɪtəʊˈplæŋktən]

义 *n.* 浮游生物

例 Nutrients in seawater are removed by phytoplankton and other marine organisms.

译 海水中的营养物质被浮游植物和其他海洋生物带走。

---

74 pigment

[ˈpɪgmənt]

义 *n.* 色素

例 Gene O determines whether orange pigment is produced.

译 基因 O 决定是否产生橙色色素。

---

75 pisum

[ˈpɪsʌm]

义 *n.* 豌豆属

例 Four genes were found in Pisum sativum (a garden pea).

译 在豌豆中发现了 4 个基因。

---

76 plate

[pleɪt]

义 *n.* 骨板

例 Marine sticklebacks and freshwater sticklebacks have plates (bony scales) that provide protection from predators, such as fish and birds.

译 海洋棘鱼和淡水棘鱼都有骨板（骨鳞），这可以保护它们免受捕食者的伤害，比如其他鱼和鸟。

---

77 pod

[pɑːd]

义 *n.* 豆荚

例 The cowpea crop growing at the base of the maize plants was infested with pod borers.

译 玉米底部周围种植的豇豆到处滋生着豇豆荚螟。

---

78 poikilothermic

[ˌpɔɪkələʊˈθəmɪk]

义 *adj.*【动】变温的

例 Poikilothermic animals had body temperatures that varied significantly.

译 变温动物的体温变化很大。

---

79 pollen

[ˈpɑːlən]

义 *n.* 花粉

例 In Zamia (a genus of seed plants), males have pollen-producing cones, and females have seed-producing cones.

译 在泽米属植物（种子植物的一个属）中，雄性有产生花粉的球果，雌性有产生种子的球果。

---

80 pollination

义 *n.* 授粉

[ˌpɑːlə'neɪʃn]

例 Pollination requires the movement of pollen from inside a male cone to inside a female cone, where multiple ovules are located and pollinated.

译 授粉需要花粉从雄球花内移动到雌球花内，在那里有多个胚珠进行授粉。

81 pollinator

['pɑːlɪneɪtə]

义 *n.* 【植】传粉者

例 Then, the flowers were covered with nylon bags to prevent the normal pollinators from pollinating the flowers.

译 然后，用尼龙袋覆盖住花，以防止正常的传粉者给花授粉。

82 polynucleotide

[ˌpɑːlɪ'njuːklɪəˌtaɪd]

义 *n.* 【生化】多（聚）核苷酸

例 Each single strand, or polynucleotide, is composed of repeating subunits called nucleotides.

译 每条单链或多核苷酸，是由叫作核苷酸的重复亚基组成的。

83 porous

['pɔːrəs]

义 *adj.* 可渗透的；多孔的

例 The bones of non-avian dinosaurs had a porous structure, no growth rings, and extensive vascularization (channels containing blood vessels).

译 非鸟类恐龙的骨骼有多孔结构，没有生长环，有广泛的血管组织（含血管的管道）。

84 positive tropism

义 正向性

例 Growth toward a stimulus is a positive tropism.

译 向着刺激生长是一种正向性。

List 3

1 precursor
[priːˈkɜːrsər]

义 *n.* 从中产生变化的产物母体，前身，前体

例 In the first reaction, acetylornithine is the precursor.

译 在第一个反应中，乙酰鸟氨酸是前体。

2 procedural memory

义 程序记忆

例 Scientists investigated whether sleep improves procedural memory (memory of skilled movements).

译 科学家们研究了睡眠是否能改善程序记忆（对熟练动作的记忆）。

3 prophase
[ˈprəʊˌfeɪz]

义 *n.*（细胞分裂）前期

例 The number of tillers was lower in prophase and higher in anaphase.

译 分蘖数前期较低，后期较高。

4 pup
[pʌp]

义 *n.* 幼畜

例 Some group members, called helpers, help parents care for their pups.

译 一些被称为助手的小组成员帮助父母照顾它们的幼崽。

5 pupation
[pjʊˈpeɪʃn]

义 *n.*【昆】化蛹

例 Pupation time in days, pupal weight, and number of offspring produced by female moths were recorded.

译 记录化蛹天数、蛹重和雌蛾产生的后代数。

6 radical
[ˈrædɪkl]

义 *n.* 自由基

例 Most DNA damage is caused by free oxygen radicals (oxygen species containing oxygen atoms with unpaired electrons) formed during metabolic processes.

译 大多数 DNA 损伤是由代谢过程中形成的氧自由基（含有未配对电子的氧原子的氧物种）引起的。

7 radicle
[ˈrædɪkl]

义 *n.*【植】胚根

例 The lower concentrations stimulated the growth of plumule and radicle.

译 低浓度促进了幼芽和胚根的生长。

8 radiocarbon
[ˌreɪdɪəʊˈkɑːrbən]

义 *n.* 放射性碳

例 A small piece of each shell was used to determine the shell's age by radiocarbon dating.

> **译** 从每个贝壳上取下一小块，通过放射性碳定年法测定贝壳的年龄。

---

9 rash

[ræʃ]

义 *n.* 疹子

例 The first sign of Lyme disease is often a bull's-eye rash on the skin.

译 莱姆病的第一个症状通常是皮肤上的牛眼状皮疹。

---

10 receptor

[rɪ'septər]

义 *n.* 受体

例 ACh (acetylcholine) then diffuses across the synaptic cleft and binds to ACh (acetylcholine) receptors (membrane proteins produced by the muscle fiber) in the motor endplate.

译 然后，ACh（乙酰胆碱）扩散到突触间隙，并与运动终板上的ACh（乙酰胆碱）受体（肌肉纤维产生的膜蛋白）结合。

---

11 recessive

[rɪ'sesɪv]

义 *adj.* 隐性的

例 Gene G has two alleles: G, which is dominant, and g, which is recessive.

译 G 基因有两个等位基因：显性的 G 和隐性的 g。

---

12 renature

[riː'neɪtʃə(r)]

义 *v.* (使)复性

例 When the DNA began to renature, the absorbance decreased sharply.

译 当 DNA 开始复性时，吸光度急剧下降。

---

13 respiration

[ˌrespə'reɪʃn]

义 *n.* 呼吸作用

例 In soil, CO_2 is produced through two processes—respiration in plant roots and bacterial decomposition of organic matter.

译 在土壤中，CO_2 是通过植物根的呼吸和有机物的细菌分解两个过程产生的。

---

14 respiratory

['respərətɔːrɪ]

义 *adj.* 呼吸的

例 The respiratory cycle for resting humans who are breathing normally has been studied by physiologists.

译 生理学家对休息时正常呼吸的人的呼吸周期进行了研究。

---

15 responsive

[rɪ'spɑːnsɪv]

义 *adj.* 反应积极的

例 In a responsive soil, the yield is greater when fertilizer N is added than when fertilizer N is not added.

译 在反应积极的土壤中，施用氮肥的土壤产量大于不施用氮肥的土壤产量。

---

16 resting metabolic rate

义 静息代谢率

例 The scientists characterized the animals in each group by their resting metabolic rate, RMR (the rate at which an animal uses caloric energy when at rest).

译 科学家们用静息代谢率——RMR（动物在静息时消耗能量的速率）来描述每一组动物。

---

17 rhizome

['raɪzəʊm]

义 *n.* 【植】根茎；地下茎

例 Both species spread by means of underground stems called rhizomes and by means of seeds.

译 这两种植物都是通过地下茎（称为根茎）和种子传播的。

---

18 ripen

['raɪpən]

义 *v.* （使）成熟

例 As an apple ripens, it undergoes changes in its firmness (the maximum force that can be applied to the apple without puncturing its skin) and in its production of volatile (readily vaporized) compounds.

译 随着苹果成熟，它的硬度（施加在苹果上但不刺破果皮的最大力量）和挥发性（易于转化为气态的）化合物的产生都会发生变化。

---

19 rock layer

义 岩层

例 Twenty complete fossil snail shells were randomly extracted from each rock layer on the island.

译 从岛上的每一岩层中随机提取了 20 个完整的蜗牛壳化石。

---

20 sail

[seɪl]

义 *n.* 背鳍

例 Two scientists discuss the sail's function.

译 两位科学家讨论背鳍的功能。

---

21 seedling

['siːdlɪŋ]

义 *n.* 幼苗

例 Fifty seedlings from each of the 4 lines were grown in 10 L of nutrient solution for 80 days.

译 从 4 个品系各取 50 株幼苗，在 10 升营养液中培养 80 天。

---

22 seedling emergence

义 出苗

例 The figure shows, for each tree species, the seedling emergence (average number of seedlings per square meter that emerged from the forest floor) for each plot.

译 图表显示了每种树种在每个地块上的出苗情况（每平方米森林地面出苗的平均数量）。

---

23 self-pollinated

[self'pɑːlɪneɪtɪd]

义 *adj.* 【植】自花授粉的

例 The flowers can be self-pollinated (egg and pollen are from the same plant) or cross-pollinated (egg and pollen are from different plants).

译 这些花可以自花授粉（卵细胞和花粉来自同一植物）或异花授粉（卵细胞和花粉来自不同的植物）。

24　semipermeable

[ˌsemɪˈpɜːrmɪəbəl]

义　*adj.* 半渗透性的

例　A semipermeable membrane, such as dialysis tubing, is a barrier with tiny pores that allow only molecules under a certain size, such as H_2O molecules, to pass through.

译　半透膜，如透析管，是一种带有微小孔的屏障，只允许一定尺寸以下的分子（如 H_2O 分子）通过。

25　shell

[ʃel]

义　*n.* 壳

例　Fossil snail shells, along with living snails' shells were studied to determine how the snails have changed over time.

译　研究人员对蜗牛壳化石和现存的蜗牛壳进行了研究，以确定蜗牛是如何随时间变化的。

26　shrink

[ʃrʌŋk]

义　*v.* 收缩

例　After one hour, the bag had shrunk.

译　1 小时后，袋子变小了。

27　shrub

[ʃrʌb]

义　*n.* 灌木

例　Each site consisted of adjacent plots of land: one covered only with grasses (grass plot) and one that had once been covered only with grasses but was now covered only with shrubs (shrub plot).

译　每个地点由相邻的地块组成：一个只被草覆盖的地块（草地块）和一个曾经只被草覆盖但现在只被灌木覆盖的地块（灌木地块）。

28　somatic

[səʊˈmætɪk]

义　*adj.* 身体的，肉体的

例　Aging is caused by random DNA damage that accumulates over the lifetime of somatic (non-reproductive) cells.

译　衰老是由体细胞（非生殖细胞）生命历程内积累的随机 DNA 损伤引起的。

29　spider

[ˈspaɪdər]

义　*n.* 蜘蛛

例　Jumping spiders prey on many types of small insects.

译　跳蛛以许多种小昆虫为食。

30　spore

[spɔːr]

义　*n.* 孢子

例　The function of meiosis is to divide a diploid cell into 4 haploid cells called spores.

译　减数分裂的功能是将一个二倍体细胞分裂成四个叫作孢子的单倍体细胞。

31　Staphylococcus epidermidis

义　【医】表皮葡萄球菌

例　Experiment one was repeated with the bacterium Staphylococcus epidermidis (S. epidermidis).

译 用表皮葡萄球菌重复实验一。

---

32 starch

[staːtʃ]

义 *n.* 淀粉

例 A starch solution, an amylase solution, and several buffer solutions (solutions that maintain a constant pH) were prepared.

译 一种淀粉溶液、一种淀粉酶溶液和几种缓冲溶液（保持恒定 pH 值的溶液）被制备出来了。

---

33 stem

[stem]

义 *n.* 茎

例 A plant could have a green stem or a purple stem.

译 植物的茎可能是绿色的，也可能是紫色的。

---

34 sterile

['sterəl]

义 *adj.* 无菌的

例 Four test tubes containing equal amounts of S. epidermidis and 1.0 mL of sterile water were subjected to different temperatures.

译 将 4 个装有等量的表皮葡萄球菌和 1.0 毫升无菌水的试管置于不同的温度下。

---

35 stomach

['stʌmək]

义 *n.* 胃

例 Sugar and starch are broken down in the stomach.

译 糖和淀粉在胃里被分解。

---

36 strain

[streɪn]

义 *n.* 品种

例 A scientist discovered the cells of a new strain of bacteria, Bacteria X.

译 一位科学家发现了一个新的细菌品种——细菌 X 的细胞。

---

37 subunit

['sʌbˌjuːnɪt]

义 *n.* 亚单位，亚基

例 Proteins are composed of subunits called amino acids.

译 蛋白质是由称为氨基酸的亚基组成的。

---

38 sucrose

['suːkrəʊs]

义 *n.* 蔗糖

例 Sucrose broth was added to 5 large test tubes.

译 将蔗糖培养液加入 5 个大试管中。

---

39 suspension

[sə'spenʃn]

义 *n.* 悬浮液

例 Drilling mud (DM) is a suspension of clay particles in water.

译 钻井泥浆（DM）是黏土颗粒在水中形成的悬浮液。

40 sweetgrass

['swi:tgræs]

义 *n.* 香草

例 Several sweetgrass plants were placed in a large Plexiglass chamber.

译 在一个大的有机玻璃房间里，放着几株香草。

---

41 synergism

['sɪnədʒɪzm]

义 *n.* 协同作用

例 Synergism occurs when 2 bacterial species act together to ferment a sugar by using a pathway that neither species can use alone.

译 当两种细菌种类通过一种各自无法单独使用的途径共同作用来发酵糖时，就会发生协同作用。

---

42 syringe

[sɪ'rɪndʒ]

义 *n.* 注射器

例 Each syringe contained 8 mL of air, and the total volume of air in the closed apparatus was 20 mL.

译 每个注射器含 8 毫升空气，封闭装置中空气的总量为 20 毫升。

---

43 tablet

['tæblət]

义 *n.* 药片

例 Multivitamin (MV) tablets often contain iron in the form of Fe^{2+}.

译 复合维生素片通常含有以亚铁离子形式存在的铁。

---

44 telomere

['teləˌmɪə]

义 *n.* 【生化】端粒（稳定染色体末端的结构）

例 Aging is caused by the shortening of telomeres, specialized DNA sequences at the ends of chromosomes.

译 衰老是由端粒缩短引起的，端粒是染色体末端的特殊 DNA 序列。

---

45 template

['templeɪt]

义 *n.* 模板

例 Each polynucleotide serves as a template for the synthesis of a new polynucleotide.

译 每个多核苷酸都是合成新多核苷酸的模板。

---

46 terminal

['tɜːrmɪnl]

义 *n.* 末端

例 The synaptic terminal contains synaptic vesicles: structures that contain the neurotransmitter acetylcholine(ACh).

译 突触末端包含突触囊泡——包含神经递质乙酰胆碱（ACh）的结构。

---

47 terrestrial

[tə'restrɪəl]

义 *adj.* 陆地的，陆生的

例 It's a gharial, perhaps the largest terrestrial carnivore ever to walk the earth, larger than T-Rex.

译 这是一条长吻鳄，可能是地球上有史以来最大的陆生食肉动物，比霸王龙还要大。

---

48 thrive

义 *v.* 繁荣；茁壮成长

[θraɪv]

例 Many freshwater fish species, including crappie, perch, and bass, require a minimum average DO concentration of 5 parts per million (ppm) to thrive.

译 许多淡水鱼品种，包括莓鲈、河鲈和巴斯鱼，都需要最低平均溶解氧浓度为百万分之五（ppm）才能茁壮成长。

---

49 thymine

['θaɪmiːn]

义 *n.* 胸腺嘧啶

例 Pairing between bases is specific: adenine always binds with thymine, and guanine always binds with cytosine.

译 碱基之间的配对是特定的：腺嘌呤总是与胸腺嘧啶结合，鸟嘌呤总是与胞嘧啶结合。

---

50 toxin

['tɑːksɪn]

义 *n.* 毒素

例 P. caudatum and P. bursaria were able to reach stable population densities because neither species can produce the toxin.

译 尾草履虫和绿草履虫的种群密度稳定，因为它们都不能产生毒素。

---

51 transcription

[træn'skrɪpʃn]

义 *n.* 转录

例 Each type of cell is thought to have a special set of transcription factors.

译 他们认为每类细胞都应该有一组特殊的转录因子。

---

52 transferrin

[træns'fɜːrɪn]

义 *n.* 【生化】转铁蛋白

例 Transferrin is a blood protein.

译 转铁蛋白是一种血液蛋白。

---

53 twitch

[twɪtʃ]

义 *v.* 痉挛，抽搐　　*n.* 抽搐，抽动

例 A muscle twitch (a stimulus-contraction-relaxation cycle) is divided into 3 phases (the latent period, the contraction phase, and the relaxation phase) based on the timing of the stimulus and changes in the force generated by the muscle.

译 肌肉抽搐（刺激—收缩—松弛周期）根据刺激的时间和肌肉产生的力的变化分为三个阶段（潜伏期、收缩期和松弛期）。

---

54 ultraviolet light

义 紫外线

例 The stripes on the fossil shells were not visible to the naked eye, but could be seen when the shells were viewed under ultraviolet light.

译 化石壳上的条纹用肉眼是看不见的，但在紫外线下可以看到。

---

55 understory

['ʌndəˌstɔːri]

义 *n.* 林下层

例 The understory is the area below the forest canopy.

> 译 林下层是指林冠层以下的区域。

---

56 vacuole

['vækjʊəʊl]

义 *n.*【生】液泡

例 The microspore lacks a large central vacuole.

译 小孢子缺中央大液泡。

---

57 vascularization

[væskjʊləraɪ'zeɪʃən]

义 *n.* 血管化

例 Extensive vascularization, which is also seen in modern birds, is evidence of an efficient circulatory system and a high RMR.

译 广泛血管化也见于现代鸟类，是有效循环系统和高静息代谢率（RMR）的证据。

---

58 vesicle

['vesɪkl]

义 *n.* 小囊，泡

例 Because the vesicles cannot fuse with the plasma membrane, they cannot release ACh (acetylcholine) into the synaptic cleft.

译 因为囊泡不能与质膜融合，它们不能释放 ACh（乙酰胆碱）到突触间隙。

---

59 vessel

['vesl]

义 *n.* 血管

例 Grooves on the sail's spines held large blood vessels.

译 背鳍上的刺的凹槽支撑着大血管。

---

60 virus

['vaɪrəs]

义 *n.* 病毒，病原体

例 To treat water for drinking, ozone (O_3) gas can be bubbled through the water to kill bacteria and viruses.

译 为了处理饮用水，可以将臭氧（O_3）气体注入水中来杀死细菌和病毒。

---

61 wetland

['wetlənd]

义 *n.* 湿地

例 When two types of bacteria found in the soil of a wetland (land having a high water table) break down organic matter, gases are generated.

译 当在湿地（地下水位高的土地）土壤中发现的两种细菌分解有机物时，气体就会产生。

---

62 whorl

[wɜːrl]

义 *n.* 螺纹

例 The number of whorls, the inner lip length, and the diameter of the shell were measured for each shell.

译 测量了每个壳的螺纹的数量、内唇的长度和壳的直径。

List 4

1　alternating current

义 交流电

例 Some students studied RC circuits containing a source of AC (alternating current) voltage.

译 一些学生研究了包含交流电压源的阻容电路。

2　altitude

['æltɪtuːd]

义 *n.* 高度

例 The aircraft had reached its cruising altitude of about 39,000 feet.

译 那架飞机已经达到了大约三万九千英尺的巡航高度。

3　ammeter

['æmiːtər]

义 *n.* 电流表

例 As soon as the ammeter indicated 0.80 amp, they measured the voltage, V, across the test wire.

译 当电流表显示 0.80 安培时，他们测量了测试导线上的电压（V）。

4　angular acceleration

义 角加速度

例 The angular acceleration, a, of the cylinder is the change of the cylinder's rotational speed over time.

译 圆柱体的角加速度（a）指圆柱体随时间变化的转速。

5　angular frequency

义 角频率

例 The angular frequency of the current is a measure of the number of times each second that the current reverses direction.

译 电流的角频率是每秒电流改变方向的次数。

6　angular separation

义 角距

例 The farther from Jupiter a moon appears to be, the greater its angular separation, θ.

译 离木星越远的卫星，其角距 θ 越大。

7　anode

['ænəʊd]

义 *n.* 阳极，正极

例 The anode and cathode are connected to a voltmeter.

译 阳极和阴极被连接到电压表上。

8　apparatus

[ˌæpə'rætəs]

义 *n.* 装置，仪器

例 This entire apparatus fits on a chip no larger than a few square millimeters.

译 这整个装置可以被安置在不超过几平方毫米的芯片上。

9　aquatic

[ə'kwætɪk]

义　*adj.* 水生的

例　That long skeletal structure suggests that it was aquatic.

译　这种长长的骨骼结构表明它是水生动物。

10　average speed

义　平均速率

例　Therefore, the average speed of Block A will be greater than the average speed of Block B, so Block A will reach the bottom of the incline first.

译　因此木块 A 的平均速率会大于木块 B 的平均速率，所以木块 A 会先到达斜坡的底部。

11　baryon

['bæriːɑn]

义　*n.* 重子

例　Three quarks bound together form a type of particle called a baryon.

译　由结合在一起的三个夸克组成的一种粒子称为重子。

12　bearing

['berɪŋ]

义　*n.* 轴承；支撑物

例　A solid cylinder is mounted on frictionless bearings.

译　实心圆柱被安装在无摩擦的轴承上。

13　boiling point

义　沸点

例　Students did the following experiments to study vapor pressures and boiling points.

译　学生们做了以下实验来研究蒸汽压和沸点。

14　buckle

['bʌkl]

义　*v.* 弯曲

例　Because excessive gas densities will cause the magnetic field to buckle, allowing the gas to escape confinement and to strike the walls of the containment vessel.

译　因为过高的气体密度会导致磁场发生弯曲，使气体逃脱束缚，撞击安全壳的壁。

15　buoyant force

义　浮力

例　The air exerted an upward buoyant force on the apparatus that was equal to the weight of the volume of air that was displaced by the apparatus.

译　空气对装置施加了向上的浮力，该浮力等于被装置排出的空气体积的重量。

16　capacitance

[kə'pæsɪtəns]

义　*n.* 电容

例　Capacitance is the amount of charge a capacitor can hold at a given voltage.

译 电容是电容器在给定电压下所能容纳的电荷量。

17　capacitor

[kəˈpæsɪtər]

义 *n.* 电容器

例 The students varied the frequency of the input voltage and measured the output voltage, the voltage across the resistor or the capacitor.

译 学生们改变输入电压的频率并测量输出电压，即电阻或电容器上的电压。

18　chromatography

[ˌkrəʊməˈtɑːgrəfɪ]

义 *n.* 层析法，色谱法

例 In liquid column chromatography, a mixture is carried by the flow of solvent through a glass column containing an adsorbent material.

译 在液柱色谱法中，溶剂通过含有吸附剂材料的玻璃柱流动，将混合物进行输送。

19　circuit

[ˈsɜːrkɪt]

义 *n.* 电路；回路

例 The solutions were connected with a salt bridge (which allows ions to flow between solutions) to complete the circuit.

译 这些溶液用盐桥连接（盐桥允许离子在溶液之间流动）来形成回路。

20　colorimeter

[ˌkʌləˈrɪmətə]

义 *n.* 色度计，比色计

例 Each experiment was done using a colorimeter.

译 每个实验都是用色度计完成的。

21　combustion

[kəmˈbʌstʃən]

义 *n.* 燃烧

例 The candle's flame results from a combustion reaction.

译 蜡烛的火焰是由燃烧反应产生的。

22　compressibility

[kəmˌpresəˈbɪlətɪ]

义 *n.* 压缩系数

例 The compressibility factor is a value that quantifies the deviation of a gas from ideal behavior.

译 压缩系数因子是一个数值，它量化了气体与理想状态的偏差。

23　compression

[kəmˈpreʃn]

义 *n.* 压缩；压力

例 The vertical compression needed to break the sample is called the compressive strength and is measured in kg/cm^3.

译 打破试样所需的垂直压力叫作抗压强度，以千克每立方厘米（kg/cm^3）为单位。

24　concentration

[ˌkɑːnsenˈtreɪʃən]

义 *n.* 浓度

例 Ocean color varies from green to blue, depending on the type and concentration of phytoplankton.

译 根据浮游植物的种类和浓度，海洋颜色从绿色到蓝色变化。

---

25 conduct

[kən'dʌkt]

义 *v.* 传导

例 The wire would conduct heat from Block A to Block B.

译 这根导线将热量从 A 块传导到 B 块。

---

26 conductivity

[ˌkɑːndʌk'tɪvətɪ]

义 *n.*【物】传导性，电导率

例 Conductivity is a measure of a substance's ability to conduct electricity.

译 电导率是衡量物质导电能力的指标。

---

27 conductor

[kən'dʌktər]

义 *n.* 导体

例 Each slide wire generator contained a U-shaped electrical conductor (USEC), a movable conducting rod of length L that connected the sides of the USEC, and an ammeter (A).

译 每个线滑发电机包含一根 U 形电导体（USEC），一根连接 U 形电导体两侧的长度为 L 的活动导体棒和一个电流表（A）。

---

28 confinement

[kən'faɪnmənt]

义 *n.* 限制

例 Two methods for confinement (preventing nuclei from colliding with vessel walls) and for producing nuclear fusion are discussed below.

译 下面讨论两种限制原子核与管壁碰撞和产生核聚变的方法。

---

29 conservation

[ˌkɑːnsər'veɪʃn]

义 *n.* 守恒

例 A group of students performed 2 experiments to investigate the conservation of total mechanical energy.

译 一组学生进行了两个实验来研究总机械能守恒。

---

30 constant

['kɑːnstənt]

义 *n.* 常数

例 First, a spring having a spring constant of k (a measure of the spring's stiffness) was attached to a block of mass Mb.

译 首先，一个弹簧的弹簧常数是 k（弹簧刚度的量度），它被连接到一个质量为 Mb 的物体上。

---

31 containment vessel

义 安全壳

例 Moreover, energy is consumed in preventing the nuclei from striking the walls of the containment vessel, where the nuclei would lose speed.

译 此外，消耗能量以防止原子核转机撞击安全壳壁，原子核在安全壳壁上会失去速度。

32　counterclockwise

[ˌkaʊntərˈklɑːkwaɪz]

义　*adj./adv.* 逆时针方向的（地）

例　It was positive when the current moved clockwise through the circuit and negative when the current moved counterclockwise through the circuit.

译　当电流顺时针通过电路时，电流是正的，当电流逆时针通过电路时，电流是负的。

33　cross section

义　横截面

例　You probably know that we can determine a tree's age by counting the rings on a cross section of its trunk.

译　你可能知道我们可以根据计算树干横截面的圈来确定一棵树的年龄。

34　current

[ˈkɜːrənt]

义　*n.* （水、气、电）流

例　When the currents were parallel, the field generated by one current attracted the charges in the other current.

译　当两种电流平行时，一种电流产生的电场吸引另一种电流中的电荷。

35　cylindrical

[səˈlɪndrɪkl]

义　*adj.* 圆柱形的

例　The strength of a cylindrical sample of concrete is measured.

译　测量圆柱形混凝土试样的强度。

36　density

[ˈdensətɪ]

义　*n.* 密度

例　Speed changes indicate a phase or density change of material inside Earth.

译　速度的变化表明地球内部物质的相位或密度的变化。

37　detector

[dɪˈtektər]

义　*n.* 探测器

例　To determine the amount of light absorbed by a solution, light is directed through a sample of the solution onto a detector.

译　为了确定溶液吸收的光量，引导光通过溶液样品照射到检测器上。

38　deuterium

[djuːˈtɪrɪəm]

义　*n.* 氘

例　A containment vessel holds a mixture of deuterium nuclei (containing 1 proton and 1 neutron) and tritium nuclei (containing 1 proton and 2 neutrons).

译　一个安全壳含有氘核（包含 1 个质子和 1 个中子）和氚核（包含 1 个质子和 2 个中子）的混合物。

39　diameter

[daɪˈæmɪtər]

义　*n.* 直径

例　Typical soil particle categories and their particle diameters are shown in Table 1.

译 典型土壤颗粒类型及其粒子的直径如表 1 所示。

40 dielectric

[ˌdaɪɪ'lektrɪk]

义 *n.* 绝缘体；电介质

例 Dielectrics are an essential constituent of capacitors.

译 电介质是电容器的重要组成部分。

41 diffraction

[dɪ'frækʃn]

义 *n.*【物】衍射

例 This phenomenon is called diffraction, and the pattern is called a diffraction pattern.

译 这种现象叫作衍射，这种图样叫作衍射图样。

42 dimension

[ˌdɪ'menʃən]

义 *n.* 尺寸；维度

例 All samples had the same dimensions.

译 所有样品的尺寸都相同。

43 dimensional

[dɪ'menʃənəl]

义 *adj.* 维度的，尺寸的

例 The particles are bound together in a 3-dimensional lattice, but are never in contact with each other.

译 这些粒子在三维晶格中聚合在一起，但彼此从不接触。

44 distilled

[dɪ'stɪld]

义 *adj.* 蒸馏得来的

例 A small amount of distilled water was added to each material.

译 每种材料中都加入少量蒸馏水。

45 effective mass

义 【物】有效质量

例 A quark's effective mass (mass when bound to other quarks) is greater than its single-quark mass (mass when unbound).

译 一个夸克的有效质量（与其他夸克结合时的质量）大于它的单夸克质量（未结合时的质量）。

46 electric field

义 【电】电场

例 Beyond the barrier are conducting plates, each of length L, that have an electric field, E, between them.

译 在屏障之外是导电板，每个长度为 L，它们之间有一个电场 E。

47 electric potential

义 电势

例 When heated, the filament emits cathode rays that are accelerated by an electric potential, V, toward a barrier having a pinhole.

译 受热时，灯丝通过电势 V 加速，向有针孔的屏障发出阴极射线。

48 electrode

[ɪˈlektrəʊd]

义 *n.* 电极

例 A standard hydrogen electrode (a hydrogen gas electrode) was placed in acid solution and connected to the voltmeter.

译 将标准氢电极（氢气电极）置于酸性溶液中，并与电压表连接。

---

49 electromagnet

[ɪˈlektrəʊmægnət]

义 *n.* 电磁铁

例 The strip was also positioned horizontally between the poles of an electromagnet.

译 这条带子也被水平放置在电磁铁的两极之间。

---

50 electron

[ɪˈlektrɑːn]

义 *n.* 电子

例 Under certain conditions, electrons can behave like waves rather than particles.

译 在某些条件下，电子能像波而不是粒子那样运动。

---

51 electronegativity

[ɪlektrəʊnegəˈtɪvɪtɪ]

义 *n.* 电负性

例 An atom's electronegativity (EN) indicates the atom's ability to attract electrons within a molecule.

译 一个原子的电负性（EN）表示该原子在分子内吸引电子的能力。

---

52 elliptical

[ɪˈlɪptɪkl]

义 *adj.* 椭圆的

例 A less elliptical orbit corresponds to a warmer climate.

译 较不椭圆的轨道对应较温暖的气候。

---

53 elution

[ɪˈljuːʃən]

义 *n.* 洗脱

例 A component's elution time is the time it takes (from the start of the flow) for 100% of the component to be eluted.

译 一个组分的洗脱时间是 100% 的组分被洗脱所花费的时间（从流动开始）。

---

54 energy shell

义 能量层级

例 A nucleus contains distinct bands of energy called energy shells.

译 原子核包含被称为能量层级的明显的能量带。

---

55 equilibrium

[ˌiːkwɪˈlɪbrɪəm]

义 *n.* 平衡

例 Two regions that are in thermal equilibrium with each other are at the same temperature.

译 两个处于热平衡的区域温度相同。

56 evaporation

[ɪˌvæpə'reɪʃn]

义 *n.* 蒸发

例 At equilibrium (when the rate of evaporation equals the rate of condensation) the pressure exerted by the vapor is called the vapor pressure, measured in millimeters of mercury.

译 在平衡状态（蒸发速率等于凝结速率）时，蒸汽施加的压力称为蒸汽压，单位为毫米汞柱。

57 exothermic

[ˌeksəʊ'θɜːrmɪk]

义 *adj.* 放热的

例 In an exothermic reaction, energy is released to the surroundings.

译 在放热反应中，能量被释放到环境中。

58 filtration

[fɪl'treɪʃn]

义 *n.* 过滤

例 The students did two experiments to study how reaction time and filtration method affected the removal of Ni^{2+} from the aqueous Ni^{2+} solution.

译 学生做了两个实验来研究反应时间和过滤方法如何影响从 Ni^{2+} 水溶液中去除 Ni^{2+}。

59 flare

[fler]

义 *n.* 闪耀的光；闪光装置信号弹，照明弹

例 A plane carrying all 4 types of flares was sent into the base of each cloud.

译 一架载有所有四种照明弹的飞机被派往每个云团的底部。

60 flask

[flæsk]

义 *n.* 细颈瓶，烧瓶

例 A 5 mL sample of water was placed in a flask, then heated until it boiled.

译 将 5 毫升的水样本放入烧瓶中，然后加热至沸腾。

61 fluorescent

[ˌflɔː'resnt]

义 *n.* 荧光 *adj.* 有荧光的；发荧光的

例 A cathode-ray tube (CRT) is a sealed, evacuated glass tube with a filament at one end and a fluorescent screen at the other end.

译 阴极射线管（CRT）是一种密封的真空玻璃管，一端有灯丝，另一端有荧光屏。

62 fraction

['frækʃn]

义 *n.* 分馏物

例 Fractions are collected at different heights in the tower.

译 在塔内不同高度收集分馏物。

63 fractionating

['frækʃəneɪtɪŋ]

义 *adj.* 分馏的

例 An auxiliary of a fractionating tower is designed to supply additional heat to the lower portion.

译 分馏塔的辅助设备用于给塔下部提供额外热量。

---

64 freezing point

义 *n.* 冰点

例 The temperature at which ice crystals first began to appear was recorded as the freezing point.

译 冰晶开始出现的温度被记录为冰点。

---

65 friction

['frɪkʃn]

义 *n.* 摩擦；摩擦力

例 Friction causes some of an object's total mechanical energy to be lost, in which case its total mechanical energy is not conserved.

译 摩擦使一个物体的总机械能损失了一部分，在这种情况下，它的总机械能就不守恒了。

---

66 frictional force

义 摩擦力

例 There was a constant frictional force between the block and the surface.

译 在物体和表面之间有一个恒定的摩擦力。

---

67 frictionless

['frɪkʃnləs]

义 *adj.* 无摩擦的；光滑的

例 Starting from rest at Point P, a 1 kg toy cart was released and allowed to move along a frictionless track in an airless vacuum chamber.

译 从静止的 P 点开始，释放一辆 1 公斤重的玩具车，让它在真空室中沿着无摩擦的轨道移动。

---

68 fume

[fju:m]

义 *n.* 烟，汽

例 When the candle is lit, the flame that lights the candle heats the candle, which causes the candle to give off fumes of wax.

译 当蜡烛点燃时，点燃蜡烛的火焰加热蜡烛，使蜡烛散发出蜡的烟雾。

---

69 furnace

['fɜ:rnɪs]

义 *n.* 熔炉

例 The crude oil is first heated to 400℃ in a furnace, then pumped into the fractionating tower.

译 首先在炉中把原油加热到 400℃，然后泵入分馏塔。

---

70 fuse

[fju:z]

义 *v.* 融合，聚变

例 The nuclei collide, fuse, and emit high amounts of energy.

译 原子核碰撞、聚变，并释放出大量的能量。

---

71 Galilean

[ˌgælɪ'li:ən]

义 *adj.* 伽利略的

例 As viewed from Earth, Jupiter's four largest moons—the Galilean moons—appear to move relative to Jupiter along an east-west line.

译 从地球上看，木星最大的四颗卫星——伽利略卫星——似乎沿着东西方向相对于木星运行。

---

72 gamma ray

义 伽马射线

例 A physicist tested various sheets for their ability to stop gamma rays (γ-rays) that had different energies.

译 一位物理学家测试了不同的薄片阻挡不同能量伽马射线(γ 射线)的能力。

---

73 generator

['dʒenəreɪtər]

义 *n.* 发电机

例 Perhaps each home will have a solar generator to provide power for lighting and heating.

译 也许每个家庭都将有一个太阳能发电机来提供照明和取暖的电力。

---

74 gravimetric

[ˌɡrævə'metrɪk]

义 *adj.* 重量的

例 In a thermo gravimetric analysis (TGA), the mass of a sample is monitored as the sample's temperature is steadily increased.

译 在热重分析(TGA)中，当样品的温度稳定上升时，样品的质量被监测。

---

75 gravitational field

义 【物】重力场

例 Earth's gravitational field extends both above and below Earth's surface.

译 地球的重力场在地表上下延伸。

---

76 gravitational potential energy

义 重力势能

例 An object's total mechanical energy is the sum of its kinetic energy and its gravitational potential energy.

译 一个物体的总机械能是它的动能和重力势能的总和。

---

77 gravity

['ɡrævəti]

义 *n.* 重力，引力

例 Einstein also predicted that light's travel time between certain planets would be increased by the Sun's gravity.

译 爱因斯坦还预言，太阳的引力会增加光在某些行星之间的行进时间。

---

78 Hall effect

义 霍尔效应

例 A physics class conducted studies of this phenomenon, called the Hall effect.

译 物理课对这种被称为霍尔效应的现象进行了研究。

---

79 harmonic

[hɑːr'mɑːnɪk]

义 *n.* 【音】泛音；【物】谐波

例 Such waves are called the string's harmonics.

译 这种波叫作弦的谐波。

80　hologram

['hɑ:ləgræm]

义 *n.* 全息图

例 A hologram is a three-dimensional image produced when light from a laser shines on a film coated with a material called a holographic emulsion.

译 全息图是激光照射在一种叫作全息乳剂的材料覆盖的薄膜上时产生的三维图像。

81　ideal gas

义 【物】理想气体

例 An ideal gas is a hypothetical gas that behaves exactly as predicted by the ideal gas law.

译 理想气体是一种完全符合理想气体定律预测的假想气体。

82　ideal gas law

义 理想气体定律

例 The ideal gas law (IGL) describes the physical behavior of gases.

译 理想气体定律描述了气体的物理行为。

83　impedance

[ɪm'pi:dns]

义 *n.* 阻抗

例 The capacitor and inductor each possess impedance, a type of electrical resistance.

译 电容器和电感器都具有阻抗，它是电阻的一种。

84　incinerator

[ɪn'sɪnəreɪtər]

义 *n.* 焚烧炉

例 The incinerator burns anything.

译 焚烧炉能把任何东西都烧掉。

85　inclination

[ˌɪnklɪ'neɪʃn]

义 *n.* 倾斜度

例 The angle of inclination of the incline was 2.3° in all three experiments.

译 三次实验中斜坡的倾斜角均为 2.3°。

86　inductance

[ɪn'dʌktəns]

义 *n.* 电感

例 An RCL circuit contains an alternating current (AC) power supply, a resistor having a resistance R, a capacitor having a capacitance C, and an inductor having an inductance L.

译 RCL 电路包括交流电源，具有电阻 R 的电阻器，具有电容 C 的电容器和具有电感 L 的电感器。

87　inductor

[ɪn'dʌktə]

义 *n.* 【电】感应器，电感器

例 The circuit has a power supply and three components: a resistor (R), an inductor (L), and a capacitor (C).

译 电路有一个电源和三个组件：电阻器（R），电感器（L）和电容器（C）。

---

88 inertia

[ɪˈnɜːrʃə]

义 *n.* 惯性

例 Inertia is the resistance of objects to efforts to change their state of motion.

译 惯性是物体对运动状态改变的阻力。

---

89 infrared

[ˌɪnfrəˈred]

义 *adj.* 红外线的

例 In general, as the atmospheric CO_2 concentration increases, more infrared radiation from Earth's surface is absorbed by CO_2, and the average global temperature rises.

译 一般来说，随着大气中二氧化碳浓度的增加，更多的地球表面的红外辐射被二氧化碳吸收，全球平均温度上升。

---

90 insulating

[ˈɪnsəleɪtɪŋ]

义 *adj.* 绝缘的

例 Both blocks were immediately placed on an insulating surface (a surface that does not conduct heat well) and connected by a given length of 1 mm diameter copper wire initially at room temperature.

译 将两个方块立即被放置在一个绝缘表面（其导热性差），并在室温下用给定长度直径为 1 毫米的铜线连接。

---

91 interval

[ˈɪntərvl]

义 *n.* 间隔；区间

例 The temperature of each block was measured at regular time intervals for 3 minutes.

译 每隔 3 分钟测量一次每个区块的温度。

---

92 irradiance

[ɪˈreɪdiəns]

义 *n.* 辐照

例 Earth's climate is affected by the total solar irradiance (TSI), the rate at which energy from solar radiation is received by Earth per unit area of the surface.

译 地球的气候受到太阳总辐照度（TSI）的影响，太阳总辐照度是地球在单位面积上接收太阳辐射能量的速率。

---

93 isoelectric point

义 等电点

例 The isoelectric point, pI, of an amino acid is the pH at which the amino acid has no net charge.

译 氨基酸的等电点 pI 是该氨基酸不带净电荷时的 pH 值。

---

94 isometric

[ˌaɪsəˈmetrɪk]

义 *adj.* 等距的；等轴的；等体积的

例 Diameter of the isometric particle is 33 nm.

译 等轴颗粒的直径为 33 纳米。

95 joule

[dʒuːl]

义 *n.*【物】焦耳（功或能的单位）

例 At various points along the track, the students determined both the cart's kinetic energy and potential energy in joules, J.

译 在轨道上的不同点，学生们确定了推车的动能和势能，单位是焦耳（J）。

---

96 kinetic energy

义 动能

例 Kinetic energy (energy that changes as an object's speed changes) and gravitational potential energy (energy that changes as an object's altitude changes) are forms of mechanical energy.

译 动能（随着物体速度的变化而变化的能量）和重力势能（随着物体高度的变化而变化的能量）都是机械能的形式。

---

97 laser

['leɪzər]

义 *n.* 激光，镭射

例 The laser provides the light at a specific wavelength.

译 激光提供特定波长的光。

List 5

1 liquid
['lɪkwɪd']

义 *adj.* 液体的，液态的

例 Freon exists both in liquids and gaseous states.

译 氟利昂既有液态也有气态。

2 lone pair

义 孤电子对

例 The influence of lone pair on bond energy cannot be an interatomic effect.

译 孤电子对对键能的影响不是原子间的效应。

3 luminous
['lu:mɪnəs]

义 *adj.* 发光的

例 Transient luminous events (TLEs) are brief flashes of light that appear above large thunderstorm clouds.

译 瞬时发光事件（TLEs）指出现在大型雷雨云上方的短暂闪光。

4 magnet
['mæɡnət]

义 *n.* 磁铁

例 The current in an electric circuit produces a magnetic field that will exert a measurable force on a nearby magnet.

译 电路中的电流产生磁场，磁场会对附近的磁铁施加可测量的力。

5 magnetic
[mæɡ'netɪk]

义 *adj.* 有磁性的

例 A magnetic force field compresses a gas of tritium and deuterium nuclei.

译 磁场压缩氚核和氘核的气体。

6 magnetic field

义 磁场

例 When an electrical current flows through a metal strip in a magnetic field, a magnetic force is exerted on some electrons in the strip.

译 当电流在磁场中流过金属片时，金属片上的一些电子就会受到磁力的作用。

7 mass
[mæs]

义 *n.* 质量

例 Photons have no mass—they are weightless.

译 光子没有质量——它们是没有重量的。

8 massless
['mæslɪs]

义 *adj.*【物】无质量的

例 When the candle is lit, the energy from the flame causes the fuel (candle wax fumes) to spontaneously decompose into a massless substance called heat.

译 当蜡烛被点燃时，来自火焰的能量使燃料（蜡烛蜡烟）自发分解成一种叫作热的无质量物质。

9　mean free path

义 【物】平均自由程

例 For gas atoms in a state of random motion, the mean free path, A, is the average distance a gas atom will travel between collisions with other gas atoms.

译 对于处于随机运动状态的气体原子，平均自由程 A 是气体原子在与其他气体原子碰撞时所经过的平均距离。

10　mechanical energy

义 机械能

例 The total mechanical energy (TME) of an object is defined as the sum of its potential energy (energy of position; abbreviated PE) and its kinetic energy (energy of motion, abbreviated KE).

译 物体的总机械能（TME）指其势能（位置能量；缩写为 PE）和其动能（运动的能量，缩写为 KE）的总和。

11　megapascal

['megə'pæskl]

义 *n.* 兆帕（压强单位）

例 1 magapascal (MPa) is equal to 145.037737797 psi (pounds per square inch).

译 1 兆帕（MPa）等于 145.037737797 磅力 / 平方英寸。

12　metallic

[mə'tælɪk]

义 *adj.* 金属的

例 All the samples were taken from a centimeter-long, extremely thin ribbon of the metallic glass.

译 所有的样品都取自一厘米长的极薄的金属玻璃带。

13　meterstick

['miːtəstɪk]

义 *n.* 米尺（指长度为 1 米的尺）

例 The light fixtures, light bulbs, blocks, foil, and the meterstick were arranged as shown in Figure 1.

译 灯具、灯泡、积木、箔和米尺的布置如图 1 所示。

14　mole

[məʊl]

义 *n.* 摩尔

例 Every mole of any substance such as molecules, atoms contains about 6.02×10^{23} particles.

译 每一摩尔的任何物质（如分子、原子）含有 6.02×10^{23} 个微粒。

15　motion

['məʊʃn]

义 *n.* 运动

例 Kepler's third law of motion relates the planet's orbital period (the time the planet takes to complete one orbit) to the ellipse's semimajor axis and the star's mass.

译 开普勒第三定律将行星的轨道周期（行星完成一次轨道运行所需的时间）与椭圆轨道半长轴和恒星的质量联系起来。

---

16 neutral

['nu:trəl]

义 *adj.* 中性的

例 Neutral solute particles do not affect the vapor pressure of a liquid.

译 中性溶质粒子不影响液体的蒸气压。

---

17 neutron

['nu:trɑ:n]

义 *n.* 中子

例 Each atomic cluster is made up of neutrons and protons.

译 每个原子团簇都是由中子和质子组成的。

---

18 newton

['nu:tən]

义 *n.* 牛顿（力学单位）

例 Therefore, any 1-cubic-meter object in air is buoyed up with a force of 12 newtons.

译 因此，空气中任何 1 立方米的物体都受到 12 牛顿的浮力。

---

19 node

[nəʊd]

义 *n.* 节

例 Each harmonic has a characteristic number of nodes.

译 每个谐波都有一个特有的节点数。

---

20 nuclei

['nju:klɪaɪ]

义 *n.* 细胞核；原子核（nucleus 的复数形式）

例 A nucleus is most stable (unreactive) when spherical; drop-shaped nuclei are more likely to undergo fission (split apart) than spherical nuclei.

译 原子核为球形时最稳定（无反应）；水滴形核比球形核更容易发生裂变（分裂）。

---

21 nucleon

['nu:klɪɑ:n]

义 *n.* 核子

例 The mass and volume of a nucleus are proportional to the number of nucleons in the nucleus.

译 原子核的质量和体积与原子核中的核子数成正比。

---

22 numerator

['nu:məreɪtər]

义 *n.* （分数的）分子；计算器

例 The numerator of the fraction is an integer.

译 这个分数的分子是个整数。

---

23 oscillate

['ɑ:sɪleɪt]

义 *v.* 摆动；振动

例 When the pendulum is displaced from its equilibrium position and then released, it oscillates (swings back and forth) about the rod, which acts as the axis of rotation.

译 当将钟摆从平衡位置移开，然后松开，它就围绕作为旋转轴的杆摆动（来回摆动）。

---

24 oscillator

['ɑːsɪleɪtər]

义 *n.* 摆动物；【物】振子

例 For a harmonic oscillator the energy levels are evenly spaced.

译 对谐振子来说，能级是等间隔的。

---

25 particle

['pɑːrtɪkl]

义 *n.* 微粒，粒子

例 A gas is composed of small particles that repel each other.

译 气体是由相互排斥的小颗粒组成的。

---

26 pendulum

['pendʒələm]

义 *n.* 钟摆

例 A physical pendulum, is an object that is suspended vertically from a rigid support.

译 物理钟摆是一个从刚性支撑点垂直悬挂下来的物体。

---

27 perpendicular

[ˌpɜːrpən'dɪkjələr]

义 *adj.* 垂直的；直立的

例 In each trial, the slide wire generator was placed perpendicular to a magnetic field of strength *B* that pointed vertically toward the ceiling.

译 在每次试验中，滑线发电机垂直放置在一个强度为 *B*、垂直指向天花板的磁场上。

---

28 pillar

['pɪlər]

义 *n.* 柱子，支柱

例 Plans for a new building show that the supporting pillars would be subject to a maximum vertical compression of 350 kg/cm^2.

译 一个新建筑的计划表明，支撑柱将能够承受最大 350 公斤每平方厘米的垂直压力。

---

29 plastic

['plæstɪk]

义 *n.* 塑料

例 Students performed the following experiments to determine the density of common plastics.

译 学生们做了以下实验来确定普通塑料的密度。

---

30 polarity

[pə'lærəti]

义 *n.* 极性

例 Molecules are attracted to other molecules based on polarity.

译 分子会因极性而相互吸引。

---

31 porosity

[pɔːˈrɑːsətɪ]

义 *n.* 孔隙度

例 The proportion of empty space in a rock is known as its porosity.

译 岩石中空隙的比例被称为孔隙度。

32 power

[ˈpaʊər]

义 *n.* 功率

例 However, because of the very high density of nuclei around the pellet, the power produced by the Laser Confinement Method can be higher than that of magnetic confinement.

译 然而，由于球团周围的核密度非常高，激光约束法产生的功率可以高于磁约束法产生的。

33 pressure

[ˈpreʃər]

义 *n.* 压强，压力

例 Pressure is highest in the inner core.

译 内核的压力最高。

34 proton

[ˈprəʊtɑːn]

义 *n.* 质子

例 Protons and neutrons are also called nucleons.

译 质子和中子也称为核子。

35 quantum

[ˈkwɑːntəm]

义 *n.* 量子

例 Classical theory and quantum theory can be used to derive two forms of distribution function (DF): a classical form and a quantum form.

译 经典理论和量子理论可用于推导两种形式的分布函数（DF）：经典形式和量子形式。

36 quark

[kwɑːrk]

义 *n.*【核】夸克

例 Quarks constitute one of the three classes of elementary particles that form all matter in the universe.

译 夸克是构成宇宙中所有物质的三种基本粒子之一。

37 radius

[ˈreɪdɪəs]

义 *n.* 半径；辐射区

例 When an ion moves through a uniform magnetic field, the ion follows a circular path having a radius R.

译 当一个离子通过一个均匀的磁场时，离子沿半径为 R 的圆形路径运动。

38 ratchet

[ˈrætʃɪt]

义 *n.* 棘轮

例 The chair has a ratchet below it to adjust the height.

译 这把椅子下面有一个棘轮来调整高度。

| 39 | **ratio** | 义 | *n.* 比率，比例 |

['reɪʃɪəʊ]

例 At each frequency, they calculated the gain, the ratio of the measured output voltage to the measured input voltage.

译 在每个频率上，他们计算增益，即测量的输出电压与测量的输入电压之比。

40　refract

[rɪ'frækt]

义 *v.* 折射

例 As we age, the lenses of the eyes thicken, and thus refract light differently.

译 随着我们年龄的增长，眼睛的晶状体变厚，因此对光线的折射也会发生变化。

41　repulsive

[rɪ'pʌlsɪv]

义 *adj.* 排斥的

例 If a gas in a closed container of fixed volume is heated, the repulsive forces between particles will increase.

译 如果在一个封闭的固定体积容器内的气体被加热，粒子之间的排斥力就会增加。

42　resistance

[rɪ'zɪstəns]

义 *n.* 阻力

例 The design of the bicycle has managed to reduce the effects of wind resistance and drag.

译 这种自行车的设计成功地减少了风的阻力和摩擦力。

43　resistivity

[ˌrɪzɪ'stɪvɪtɪ]

义 *n.* 电阻率，电阻系数

例 Resistivity is the tendency of a material to oppose the flow of an electric current, whereas conductivity is the ability of a material to carry an electric current.

译 电阻率是一种材料对抗电流流动的倾向性，而导电性是一种材料携带电流的能力。

44　resistor

[rɪ'zɪstər]

义 *n.* 电阻器

例 An RC circuit contains a resistor, a capacitor, and an input voltage source.

译 一个阻容电路包含一个电阻器、一个电容器和一个输入电压源。

45　revolution

[ˌrevə'luːʃn]

义 *n.* 旋转

例 A sample of each fuel mixture listed in Table 1 was burned in a test engine at an engine speed of 600 revolutions per minute (rpm).

译 表 1 中列出的每种燃料混合物样本在转速为 600 转 / 分（rpm）的测试发动机中燃烧。

46　rod

[rɑːd]

义 *n.* 棍棒

例 When a temperature difference exists between the ends of an insulated metal rod, heat flows from one end of the rod to the other.

| 译 | 当绝缘金属棒的两端存在温差时，热量从金属棒的一端流向另一端。 |

---

47 rotate

['rəʊteɪt]

义	***v.** 旋转*
例	When a force (such as that produced by a weight) was exerted on the surface of the platform, the hand rotated clockwise away from the zero point on the dial.
译	当一个力（比如一个重物产生的力）作用在平台表面时，指针从刻度盘上的零点顺时针方向旋转。

---

48 rotational speed

义	转速
例	They differ in their size (80 and 92 mm), their rotational speed and the airflow generated.
译	它们在规模（80 和 92 毫米）、转速和产生的气流上都是不同的。

---

49 scale

[skeɪl]

义	***n.** 秤*
例	The amount of the force, in newtons (N), required to move the brick across the table at a constant speed was measured on the spring scale.
译	用弹簧秤测量以恒定速度移动砖块从桌子的一边到另一边所需的力，单位为牛顿（N）。

---

50 sensitivity

[ˌsensə'tɪvətɪ]

义	***n.** 敏感性；灵敏度*
例	The eyes of some fish have a greater sensitivity to light than ours do.
译	有些鱼的眼睛比我们的对光更敏感。

---

51 shaft

[ʃæft]

义	***n.** 杆状物；轴*
例	These towers, or "blades", pinwheel about a triangular central shaft that holds elevators and mechanical equipment.
译	这些塔，或称"叶片"，围绕着一个三角形中心轴旋转，中心轴承载着电梯和机械设备。

---

52 sift

[sɪft]

义	***v.** 筛下，筛分*
例	The soil remaining on the screen was dried and weighed, then sifted through a series of screens, each successive screen having smaller holes than the one before, to separate the particles in different categories.
译	残留在筛面上的土壤被干燥并称重，然后通过一系列筛选，每一个筛孔都比前一个筛孔小，以将不同种类的颗粒分离出来。

---

53 spectroscopy

[spek'trɑːskəpɪ]

义	***n.**【物】光谱学*
例	X-ray spectroscopy is a way of analyzing a mineral's composition.
译	X 射线光谱学是分析矿物成分的一种方法。

54　sphere

[sfɪr]

义　*n.* 球

例　Doubly magic nuclei are the most stable nuclei and are shaped like spheres.

译　双幻核是最稳定的核，形状像球体。

55　spring

[sprɪŋ]

义　*n.* 弹簧

例　An object is dropped from a height H above the top of a spring, compressing it.

译　一个物体从高于弹簧顶部 H 的位置落下，压缩了弹簧。

56　standing wave

义　【物】驻波

例　A standing wave on a taut string is a wave that appears to vibrate without traveling along the string.

译　拉紧的绳子上的驻波是一种似乎不沿绳子传播而振动的波。

57　stiffness

[stɪfnəs]

义　*n.* 硬度，刚度

例　In three studies, students investigated the stiffness of rectangular metal beams.

译　在 3 项研究中，学生研究了矩形金属梁的刚度。

58　submerge

[səbˈmɜːrdʒ]

义　*v.* 浸泡

例　The body of a flask filled with distilled water was submerged in a cold bath at $-6℃$.

译　装有蒸馏水的烧瓶被浸泡在 $-6℃$ 的冷水中。

59　superconductor

[ˈsuːpərkəndʌktər]

义　*n.* 超导体

例　It has significance for the cryogenics, superconductor, superconducting materials and its application.

译　这对低温、超导体、超导材料及其应用技术有重要意义。

60　tared

[teəd]

义　*adj.* 去了皮重的

例　A dry 100 mL graduated cylinder was placed on an electronic balance and tared (the balance was reset to 0.000g).

译　将一个干燥的 100 毫升量筒放在电子天平上并去除皮重（天平被重置为 0.000 克）。

61　tensile stress

义　张应力

例　Tensile stress for six hours resulted in reduction of spinal cord cells and loss of neurites.

译　持续 6 小时的张应力导致脊髓细胞减少和神经突起丢失。

---

62 tensiometer

[ˌtensɪˈɑːmətər]

义 *n.* 张力计

例 Cables 1, 2, and 3, each with its own tensiometer (a device used to measure tension), were joined with a single knot.

译 拉索 1、2 和 3，每个都有自己的张力计（一种用于测量张力的设备），用一个单结连接。

---

63 tension

[ˈtenʃn]

义 *n.* 张力

例 The wall will each affect the tension, *T*, in the cable.

译 墙壁会影响拉索的张力 *T*。

---

64 terminal speed

义 自由沉降速度

例 If the net upward force on the object is equal in magnitude to the net downward force on the object, then the object will fall at terminal speed.

译 如果作用在物体上的向上的合力在大小上与作用在物体上的向下的合力相等，那么物体将以自由沉降速度下落。

---

65 thermal

[ˈθɜːrml]

义 *adj.* 热的

例 No heat is transferred between regions in thermal equilibrium with each other.

译 在热平衡状态下，区域之间没有热量的传递。

---

66 thermal conductivity

义 导热性，导热率

例 A material's thermal conductivity is a measure of its ability to transport energy from one location to another.

译 一种材料的导热率是它将能量从一个地方传送到另一个地方的能力的量度。

---

67 thermocouple

[ˈθɜːməˌkʌpəl]

义 *n.* 热电偶

例 Thermocouple is a kind of the most widely used temperature sensor.

译 热电偶是应用最广泛的一种温度传感器。

---

68 thermometer

[θərˈmɑːmɪtər]

义 *n.* 温度计

例 A 20 mL sample of H_2O was placed in a flask containing a thermometer and the flask was heated.

译 20 毫升的水样本被放置在一个装有温度计的烧瓶中，然后加热烧瓶。

---

69 torque

[tɔːrk]

义 *n.* 转力，扭矩

例 The force results in a torque on the cylinder that causes the cylinder to spin.

译 这个力产生的扭矩作用在圆柱体上，导致圆柱体旋转。

70 transformer

[træns'fɔːrmər]

义 *n.* 变压器

例 A transformer is an electrical component used to increase or decrease voltage.

译 变压器是用来增加或减少电压的电气元件。

---

71 transmitter

[træns'mɪtər]

义 *n.* 发射器，发射台

例 All data collected by the spacecraft will get beamed back to Earth using a radio transmitter and an 83-inch diameter radio antenna.

译 飞船采集的所有数据将会通过无线电发射器和直径 83 英尺的天线传回地球。

---

72 trial

['traɪəl]

义 *n.* 试验；审讯

例 Prior to each of trials 1—3, the students set the dial readings of both Scales A and B to zero.

译 在试验 1—3 中，在每次试验之前，学生都将天平 A 和天平 B 刻度盘读数归零。

---

73 vacuum

['vækjuəm]

义 *n.* 真空

例 Next, they placed one end of a shorter piece of tubing into the second hole of the 2-holed stopper and attached the other end of the shorter tubing to a vacuum pump.

译 接下来，他们将一根较短的管子的一端放入有两个孔的塞子的第二个孔中，并将较短的管子的另一端连接到真空泵上。

---

74 variation

[ˌverɪ'eɪʃn]

义 *n.* 变化

例 The dial records very slight variations in pressure.

译 该刻度盘能显示很微小的压力变化。

---

75 velocity

[və'lɑːsətɪ]

义 *n.* 速率

例 As density increases, S-wave velocity increases.

译 随着密度的增加，横波速度也增加。

---

76 venturi

[ven'tʊrɪ]

义 *n.* 文丘里管（细腰管，缩喉管）

例 As a result, the pressure in the venturi is less than atmospheric pressure, and gasoline is drawn into the venturi.

译 结果，文丘里管内的压力小于大气压力，汽油被吸入文丘里管内。

---

77 vibration

[vaɪ'breɪʃn]

义 *n.* 振动

例 The student could select the frequency, *f* (the number of cycles per second), of the oscillator's vibration.

译 学生可以选择振荡器振动的频率 f（每秒的周期数）。

---

78 viscosity

[vɪˈskɑːsətɪ]

义 *n.* 黏度

例 If a gum is added to water (such as the water in a food product), the viscosity (resistance to flow) of the resulting aqueous mixture changes.

译 如果把胶加到水里（比如食品中的水），得到的水混合物的黏度（流动阻力）就会发生变化。

---

79 void ratio

义 孔隙比

例 The porosity and the void ratio (ratio of the volume of open space to the volume of solid material) of each soil sample were calculated.

译 计算各土样的孔隙度和孔隙比（孔隙体积与材料中的颗粒体积之比）。

---

80 voltage

[ˈvəʊltɪdʒ]

义 *n.* 电压

例 The measured voltage (in volts, V) is the standard reduction potential, E°.

译 测量的电压（国际单位为伏特，符号是 V）是标准的还原电位 E°。

---

81 voltmeter

[ˈvəʊltmiːtər]

义 *n.* 电压表

例 The ends of the strip were connected to an electrical circuit containing a DC power supply, and the edges of the strip were connected to a voltmeter.

译 金属条的两端连接到包含直流电源的电路，同时金属条的边缘连接到电压表。

---

82 wavenumber

[ˈweɪvˌnʌmbər]

义 *n.* 波数

例 The students measured the absorbance, A, of a sample of pure BD and a sample of pure PD at wavenumbers from 600 cm^{-1} through 1,800 cm^{-1}.

译 学生们测量了一个纯 BD 样品和一个纯 PD 样品在波数从 600cm^{-1} 到 1 800cm^{-1} 的吸光度 A。

---

83 weight

[weɪt]

义 *n.* 重量

例 The average reduction in the weight and the volume of the original waste after burning was 58% and 70%, respectively.

译 燃烧后原废弃物的重量和体积平均降幅分别为 58% 和 70%。

List 6

1 absorbance

[əb'sɔːrbəns]

义 *n.* 吸收率

例 This is accomplished by measuring the absorbance of standard solutions.

译 这是通过测量标准溶液的吸收率来完成的。

---

2 abundance

[ə'bʌndəns]

义 *n.* 丰富度

例 Such anomalies are due to the relative abundance of the "isotopes" or varieties of each element.

译 这种反常现象是由于"同位素"的相对丰富度或每种元素的多样化造成的。

---

3 acetic

[ə'siːtɪk]

义 *adj.* 醋的

例 Paraffin wax is a nonpolar solid and acetic acid is a polar solvent.

译 石蜡是一种非极性固体，而醋酸是极性溶剂。

---

4 acid-base indicator

义 酸碱指示剂

例 A typical acid-base indicator is a compound that will be one color over a certain lower pH range but will be a different color over a certain higher pH range.

译 典型的酸碱指示剂是一种化合物，在一定的低 pH 值范围内是一种颜色，但在一定的高 pH 值范围内是另一种颜色。

---

5 adsorbent

[əd'zɔːrbənt]

义 *n.* 吸附剂

例 If the components of the mixture have different polarities, they will interact differently with the solvent and adsorbent, causing the mixture to separate into its components.

译 如果混合物的成分有不同的极性，它们将与溶剂和吸附剂发生不同的相互作用，导致混合物分离成它的成分。

---

6 aerosol

['erəsɔːl]

义 *n.* 气溶胶

例 The rest can be explained by decreases in the amount of atmospheric sulfate aerosols and increases in the stratospheric ozone content.

译 其余的可以用大气硫酸盐气溶胶数量的减少和平流层臭氧含量的增加来解释。

---

7 alkene

['ælkiːn]

义 *n.* 烯烃

例 Alkenes are carbon compounds containing at least one carbon-carbon double bond (C = C).

译 烯烃是含有至少一个碳碳双键（C = C）的碳化合物。

---

8 aluminum

义 *n.* 铝

[ə'lu:mɪnəm]

例 A small aluminum block, A, was heated to 100℃ in boiling water, and an identical aluminum block, B, was cooled to 0℃ in ice water.

译 将一个小铝块 A 在沸水中加热到 100℃，然后将一个相同的铝块 B 在冰水中冷却到 0℃。

9　ammonium

[ə'məʊnɪəm]

义 *n.* 铵

例 Next, she added 7 g of ammonium sulfate (AS), an ionic solid, to the test tube, capped the test tube, and vigorously shook it for 10 sec.

译 接着，她在试管中加入 7 克离子固体硫酸铵(AS)，盖上试管盖子后，用力摇晃 10 秒。

10　ammonium chloride

义 氯化铵

例 Students dissolved ammonium chloride (NH_4Cl) and silver cyanate (AgCNO) together in water.

译 学生将氯化铵(NH_4Cl)和氰酸银(AgCNO)溶解在水中。

11　anhydrous

[æn'haɪdrəs]

义 *adj.* 无水的

例 Dehydration (removal of all H_2O) of an MH produces its anhydrous salt (an ionic compound that has no associated H_2O molecules), which may differ in color from the MH.

译 脱水(去除所有的水)的 MH 产生其无水盐(一种离子化合物，没有相关的水分子)，其颜色可能与 MH 不同。

12　anion

['ænaɪən]

义 *n.* 阴离子

例 When salts dissolve in water, they dissociate, or break apart, into anions and cations.

译 当盐溶解在水中时，它们会分解成阴离子和阳离子。

13　antifreeze

['æntɪfri:z]

义 *n.* 防冻剂，防冻液

例 Some students were interested in the antifreeze mixed with the H_2O in a car's radiator.

译 一些学生对汽车散热器中混合了水的防冻剂感兴趣。

14　antioxidant

[,æntɪ'ɑ:ksɪdənt]

义 *n.* 抗氧化剂

例 Antioxidants are compounds that can inhibit the decomposition of oils exposed to air.

译 抗氧化剂是一种化合物，它可以抑制暴露在空气中的油的分解。

15　aqueous

['eɪkwɪəs]

义 *adj.* 水的

例 All solutions were aqueous.

译 所有的溶液都是水溶液。

16　beaker

['biːkər]

义　*n.* 烧杯

例　The beaker initially contained a solution made by dissolving a white solid in a pure, green solvent.

译　烧杯最初含有一种溶液，该溶液是将白色固体溶解在纯绿色溶剂中制成的。

17　biodiesel

['baɪəʊdiːzl]

义　*n.* 生物柴油

例　Biodiesels are renewable fuel oils typically made from soybeans.

译　生物柴油是一种可再生燃料油，通常由大豆制成。

18　bleach

[bliːtʃ]

义　*n.* 漂白剂

例　Ozone (O_3), like household bleach, can break down molecules by a process called oxidation.

译　臭氧 (O_3) 就像家用漂白剂一样，可以通过一种叫作氧化的过程分解分子。

19　bond

[bɑːnd]

义　*n.* 化学键

例　DNA is separated into two polynucleotides by breaking the bonds between the base pairs.

译　通过破坏碱基对之间的键，DNA 被分离成两个多核苷酸。

20　brittle

['brɪtl]

义　*adj.* 易碎的，脆弱的

例　AgCl is insoluble in water, and salts tend to be hard and brittle, to be nonflammable, and to have high melting points.

译　氯化银不溶于水，而盐往往又硬又脆，不易燃，且熔点高。

21　bromide

['brəʊmaɪd]

义　*n.*【化】溴化物

例　When bromide ions, Br^-, are present in the water, O_3 reacts with the Br^- to produce bromate ions, BrO_3^-.

译　当溴化物离子存在于水中时，臭氧分子与溴离子反应生成溴酸根离子 BrO_3^-。

22　buffer

['bʌfər]

义　*n.* 缓冲液

例　You can soak nails in lemon juice to nix stains, then use a nail buffer to make tips shiny.

译　你可以将指甲浸泡在柠檬汁中以去除污渍，然后用指甲缓冲液使指甲尖有光泽。

23　buffer solution

义　缓冲溶液

例　A buffer solution is a solution that maintains a stable pH.

译　缓冲溶液是一种能保持 pH 值稳定的溶液。

24 buret

[bjʊə'ret]

义 *n.* 滴定管

例 A buret is a graduated tube with a stopcock.

译 滴定管是一种带有旋塞的刻度管。

---

25 calcium

['kælsɪəm]

义 *n.* 钙

例 Calcium is found most abundantly in milk.

译 奶含钙最丰富。

---

26 carbon

['kɑ:rbən]

义 *n.* 碳

例 Organic compounds contain carbon in their molecules.

译 有机化合物的分子里含碳。

---

27 carbonate

['kɑ:rbənət]

义 *n.* 碳酸盐

例 Today, as in the past, much CO_2 is removed from the atmosphere as CO_2 becomes part of carbonates in rock and sediment on land.

译 今天和过去一样，随着二氧化碳成为陆地岩石和沉积物中的碳酸盐的一部分，大气中的大量二氧化碳被除去。

---

28 carbonation

['kɑ:rbə'neɪʃən]

义 *n.* 碳酸

例 The precipitated carbonation sludge is removed by filteration.

译 沉淀的碳酸饱和物通过过滤被清除。

---

29 catalyst

['kætəlɪst]

义 *n.* 催化剂

例 Catalysts are substances that increase the rate of reactions without being used up.

译 催化剂是一种既能加快反应速度又不会消耗殆尽的物质。

---

30 catalyze

['kætə,laɪz]

义 *v.* 催化

例 The compound imidazole catalyzes the hydrolysis.

译 化合物咪唑催化水解。

---

31 cathode

['kæθəʊd]

义 *n.* 阴极

例 A tank fitted with two electrodes—an anode (where O_2 would be produced) and a cathode (where H_2 would be produced) was assembled.

译 组装了一个装有两个电极的水箱——阳极（产生氧气）和阴极（产生氢气）。

---

32 cation

义 *n.* 阳离子

['kætaɪən]

例 Salts are composed of positively charged cations and negatively charged anions that hold together because they have opposite charges.

译 盐是由带正电荷的阳离子和带负电荷的阴离子组成的，它们因为因电荷相反而结合在一起。

---

33 cesium

['si:zɪəm]

义 *n.* 铯

例 In a particular estuary (an inlet where ocean water and river water mix), the sediment contains the radioactive isotopes lead -210 (^{210}Pb) and cesium -137 (^{137}Cs).

译 在特定的河口（海水和河水混合的入口），沉积物中会含有放射性同位素铅 -210 和铯 -137。

---

34 charge

[tʃɑ:rdʒ]

义 *n.* 电荷

例 In a covalent compound, the atoms are held together by bonds, not by their opposite charges.

译 在共价化合物中，原子是通过化学键而不是相反的电荷结合在一起的。

---

35 chelator

['kɪleɪdə]

义 *n.*【化】螯合剂

例 Iron chelators are used to remove excess iron in the blood because they can bind with and thereby remove Fe^{3+} from transferrin.

译 铁螯合剂可以去除血液中多余的铁，因为它们可以与转铁蛋白结合，从而去除转铁蛋白中的铁离子。

---

36 chemical reaction

义 化学反应

例 The rate of a chemical reaction can be measured as the change in the concentration of its products over a period of time.

译 化学反应的速率可以通过一段时间内产物浓度的变化来测量。

---

37 chemist

['kemɪst]

义 *n.* 化学家

例 Chemists used three different methods to synthesize polystyrenes.

译 化学家们用了三种不同的方法合成聚苯乙烯。

---

38 cluster

['klʌstər]

义 *n.* 群，簇

例 Additional energy is needed to break solvent molecules free from these clusters.

译 需要额外的能量使溶剂分子从这些团簇中分离出来。

---

39 composition

[ˌkɑ:mpə'zɪʃn]

义 *n.* 成分；合成物

例 Scientists study the composition of the soil.

译 科学家研究土壤的构成。

---

40 compost

义 *n.* 混合肥料，堆肥

['ka:mpəʊst]

例 Compost consists largely of organic matter that has been decomposed by bacteria that require oxygen.

译 堆肥主要由被需要氧气的细菌分解的有机物组成。

---

41 copper

['ka:pər]

义 *n.* 铜

例 Copper conducts electricity well.

译 铜的导电性能好。

---

42 corrosion

[kə'rəʊʒn]

义 *n.* 侵蚀；腐蚀

例 Zinc is used to protect other metals from corrosion.

译 锌被用来保护其他金属免受腐蚀。

---

43 covalent compound

义 共价键

例 This caused the salt to rearrange and form a more stable covalent compound.

译 这导致盐重新排列，形成一个更稳定的共价化合物。

---

44 cyanoacrylate

[ˌsaɪənəʊ'ækrəleɪt]

义 *n.* 氰基丙烯酸盐；氰基丙烯酸盐黏合剂

例 Experience had shown that accidents due to cyanocrylate are handled best by passive, non-surgical first aid.

译 经验证明，氰基丙烯酸盐引发的事故最好通过被动、非外科急救来处理。

---

45 dehydration

[ˌdi:haɪ'dreɪʃn]

义 *n.* 脱水

例 Students studied the dehydration of each of these four alcohols, which are all liquids at 25℃.

译 学生们研究了这四种醇的脱水过程，它们在 25℃时都是液体。

---

46 diffusion

[dɪ'fju:ʒn]

义 *n.* 扩散

例 CO_2 is put into Earth's atmosphere by human activities and by natural processes such as diffusion from the oceans.

译 二氧化碳是通过人类活动和海洋扩散等自然进程进入地球大气层的。

---

47 dissolved

[dɪ'za:lvd]

义 *adj.* 溶解的，可溶的

例 The concentration of dissolved oxygen (DO) in river water affects the fish in the river.

译 河水中溶解氧（DO）的浓度影响着河流中的鱼类。

---

48 distillation

义 *n.* 蒸馏

[ˌdɪstrɪ'leɪʃn]

例 Distillation means evaporation of one or more components of a liquid mixture in one vessel and condensation of the vapors in another vessel.

译 蒸馏是指一种或多种液体混合物成分在一容器内的蒸发和在另一容器内蒸气的冷凝。

---

49 electrochemical

[ɪˌlektrəʊ'kemɪkəl]

义 *adj.* 电气化学的

例 An electrochemical cell is constructed with an anode, a strip of zinc (Zn) placed in a solution of zinc ions (Zn^{2+}), and a cathode, a strip of copper (Cu) or silver (Ag) placed in a solution of copper ions (Cu^{2+}) or silver ions (Ag^+), respectively.

译 电化学电池由阳极和阴极组成，阳极是放置在锌离子（Zn^{2+}）溶液中的锌（Zn）条，阴极是放置在铜离子（Cu^{2+}）或银离子（Ag^+）溶液中的铜（Cu）或银（Ag）条。

---

50 electrolysis

[ɪˌlek'trɑ:ləsɪs]

义 *n.* 电解

例 Liquid H_2O can be broken down into hydrogen gas (H_2) and oxygen gas (O_2) by electrolysis.

译 液态水可以通过电解分解成氢气（H_2）和氧气（O_2）。

---

51 emission

[ɪ'mɪʃn]

义 *n.* 排放

例 Burning household waste in metal barrels can release harmful emissions (airborne gases and particulates), including SO_2, CO, NO_2, dioxin, lead, and mercury.

译 在金属桶中燃烧生活垃圾会释放有害排放物（空气中的气体和颗粒物），包括二氧化硫、一氧化碳、二氧化氮、二噁英、铅和汞。

---

52 emulsion

[ɪ'mʌlʃn]

义 *n.* 乳状液；感光乳剂

例 Synthetic liquids are now being substituted for oils in emulsion muds.

译 合成液体现在正在取代乳化泥浆中的油。

---

53 ester

['estər]

义 *n.* 酯

例 BD is typically prepared by reacting soybean oil with methanol in the presence of a catalyst, forming compounds called fatty acid methyl esters (FAMEs).

译 BD 的制备方法是在催化剂存在下，让大豆油与甲醇发生反应，形成脂肪酸甲酯（FAMEs）化合物。

---

54 ethanol

['eθənɔ:l]

义 *n.* 乙醇

例 The procedure was repeated using ethanol and diethyl ether.

译 使用乙醇和乙醚重复该步骤。

55 ethylene

['eθɪliːn]

义 *n.* 乙烯

例 They've developed these sensors that can detect tiny amounts of ethylene.

译 他们已经开发了这些传感器，可以检测到微量的乙烯。

56 ethylene glycol

义 乙二醇

例 They performed the following experiments to investigate the effects of the addition of ethylene glycol ($C_2H_6O_2$), the active ingredient in most types of antifreeze.

译 他们进行了以下实验来研究加入乙二醇（$C_2H_6O_2$）的效果，乙二醇是大多数防冻剂的活性成分。

57 fertilizer

['fɜːrtəlaɪzər]

义 *n.* 肥料

例 Compost is used as soil fertilizer.

译 堆肥被用作土壤肥料。

58 flammable

['flæməbl]

义 *adj.* 易燃的

例 Also, covalent compounds are much more likely to be flammable than salts.

译 而且，共价化合物比盐更易燃。

59 formic

['fɔːrmɪk]

义 *adj.* 甲酸的

例 The oil will rapidly decompose to form acidic organic compounds such as formic acid.

译 油会迅速分解，形成甲酸等酸性有机化合物。

60 fuel

['fjuːəl]

义 *n.* 燃料

例 Fuels A and B were burned separately in an engine at different speeds.

译 燃料 A 和 B 分别在发动机中以不同的速度燃烧。

61 glutaraldehyde

[ˌgluːtəˈrældəˌhaɪd]

义 *n.*【化】戊二醛

例 PG disinfectant contains 2% glutaraldehyde, alcohol and perfume.

译 PG 消毒剂含 2% 强化中性戊二醛，醇类和香料。

62 greenhouse gas

义 温室气体（如二氧化碳、甲烷等）

例 CO_2 is one of several greenhouse gases (gases that trap heat emitted from Earth's surface).

译 二氧化碳是几种温室气体（吸收地球表面散发的热量的气体）之一。

63 gypsum

义 *n.* 石膏

['dʒɪpsəm]

例 Typical evaporites are halite (NaCl), gypsum (CaSO$_4$ · 2H$_2$O), calcite (CaCO$_3$), and the mineral mixture known as bittern salts, which contains potassium (K) and magnesium (Mg) compounds.

译 典型的蒸发岩包括石盐（NaCl）、石膏（CaSO$_4$ · 2H$_2$O）、方解石（CaCO$_3$）和被称为卤水盐的矿物混合物，其中含有钾（K）和镁（Mg）化合物。

64 helium

['hiːlɪəm]

义 *n.* 氦

例 Hydrogen turns into Helium, which releases energy.

译 氢变成氦的时候会释放能量。

65 heptane

['hepteɪn]

义 *n.*【化】正庚烷

例 Heptane knocks considerably when burned and is given an octane number of 0.

译 正庚烷燃烧时震动强度很大，其辛烷值为 0。

66 herbicide

['ɜːrbɪsaɪd]

义 *n.* 除草剂

例 In wetlands, the herbicides atrazine and alachlor are removed from the water by plant uptake or by adsorption onto soil particles and subsequent bacterial decomposition.

译 在湿地中，除草剂莠去津和甲草胺通过植物吸收或吸附到土壤颗粒上和随后的细菌分解而从水中分离出去。

67 hydrate

['haɪdreɪt]

义 *n.* 水化物，水合物

例 A mineral hydrate (MH) is an ionic compound that has associated H$_2$O molecules.

译 矿物水合物（MH）是一种含有相关水分子（H$_2$O）的离子化合物。

68 hydrocarbon

[ˌhaɪdrə'kɑːrbən]

义 *n.* 碳氢化合物

例 Electric powers plants that burn fossil fuels release hydrocarbons and nitrogen oxides.

译 通过燃烧矿物发电的火力发电厂会释放碳氢化合物和氮氧化物。

69 hydrochloric acid

义 【化】盐酸

例 When a solid metal (M) such as iron (Fe), nickel (Ni), or zinc (Zn) is placed in an aqueous hydrochloric acid (HCl) solution, a reaction that produces H$_2$ gas occurs.

译 当铁（Fe）、镍（Ni）、锌（Zn）等固体金属（M）被放入盐酸（HCl）水溶液中时，会发生反应，产生氢气。

70 hydrogen

义 *n.* 氢

['haɪdrədʒən]

例 Hydrogen combines with oxygen to form water.

译 氢与氧化合成水。

---

71 hydrolyze

['haɪdrəˌlaɪz]

义 *v.* (使)水解

例 When sucrose is dissolved in an aqueous solution, it can hydrolyze (react with H_2O to break down) to form glucose and fructose.

译 当蔗糖溶解在水溶液中时，它可以水解(与水反应分解)形成葡萄糖和果糖。

---

72 hydrothermal

[ˌhaɪdrə'θɜːrməl]

义 *adj.* 热液的；水热的

例 Zinc oxide powders have been successfully prepared via hydrothermal process.

译 氧化锌粉末已经通过水热法成功制得。

---

73 hydroxide

[haɪ'drɑːksaɪd]

义 *n.* 氢氧化物

例 A particular mass of a catalyst—either sodium hydroxide (NaOH) or potassium hydroxide (KOH)—was dissolved in the flask.

译 将一种特定质量的催化剂——氢氧化钠 (NaOH) 或氢氧化钾 (KOH) 溶解在烧瓶中。

---

74 hydroxyl

[haɪ'drɑːksɪl]

义 *n.* 【化】羟基

例 If the hydroxyl bonded C atom is bonded to only one other C atom, or to no other C atoms, the alcohol is a primary alcohol.

译 如果羟基碳原子只与另一个碳原子相连，或者不与其他碳原子相连，这种醇就是伯醇。

---

75 increment

['ɪŋkrəmənt]

义 *n.* 增量

例 The NaOH solution was slowly added to the HCl solution in small increments.

译 缓慢地将氢氧化钠溶液少量地加入盐酸溶液中。

List 7

1 inorganic

[ˌɪnɔːrˈɡænɪk]

义 *adj.* 无机的

例 All of Earth's petroleum has formed from simple, inorganic carbon compounds at depths from 100 km to 200 km below Earth's surface.

译 地球上所有的石油都是由简单的无机碳化合物在地球表面以下 100 至 200 千米处形成的。

2 iodine

[ˈaɪədaɪn]

义 *n.* 碘；碘酒

例 For example, tellurium comes before iodine in the periodic table, even though its atomic mass is slightly greater.

译 例如在元素周期表中，碲排在碘之前，尽管它的原子质量略大一些。

3 isooctane

[ˌaɪsəʊˈɑːkˌteɪn]

义 *n.*【化】异辛烷

例 Isooctane knocks very little and is given an octane number of 100.

译 异辛烷燃烧时震动强度低，其辛烷值为 100。

4 isopropyl

[ˌaɪsəˈprəʊpɪl]

义 *n.* 异丙基

例 During a demonstration, a teacher placed 20 mL of water, 10 mL of isopropyl alcohol (IPA), and one drop of blue food coloring into a test tube, capped the test tube, and inverted it six times.

译 在示范过程中，教师将 20 毫升水、10 毫升异丙醇（IPA）和 1 滴蓝色食用色素放入试管中，盖上试管盖，倒置 6 次。

5 isotope

[ˈaɪsətəʊp]

义 *n.* 同位素

例 However, isotope evidence from certain sedimentary rocks (rocks made of sediments deposited in liquid water) formed around that time indicates that Earth's surface temperature was well above freezing.

译 然而，大约在那个时期形成的某些沉积岩（由液态水沉积而成的沉积物构成的岩石）的同位素证据表明，地球表面的温度远高于冰点。

6 krypton

[ˈkrɪptɑːn]

义 *n.*【化】氪

例 Three experiments were done using CO_2, krypton (Kr), or O_2.

译 用二氧化碳、氪（Kr）或氧气做了三个实验。

7 lattice

[ˈlætɪs]

义 *n.* 晶格，点阵

例 If a gas is released into an evacuated container, the particles in the lattice will move apart from each other until the gas completely fills the container, then stop moving.

译 如果一种气体被释放到真空容器中，晶格中的粒子将彼此分离，直到气体完全充满容器，然后停止移动。

8　lead

[led]

义　*n.* 铅

例　In a particular estuary (an inlet where ocean water and river water mix), the sediment contains the radioactive isotopes lead-210 (210Pb) and cesium-137 (137Cs).

译　在特定的入海口（海水和河水混合的入口），沉积物中会含有放射性同位素铅 -210 和铯 -137。

9　leucine

['luːˌsiːn]

义　*n.*【生化】亮氨酸

例　In each of five trials (Trials 1—5), paper electrophoresis was performed on leucine (an amino acid) using a solution of known pH.

译　在五个实验中（实验 1—5），使用已知 pH 的溶液对亮氨酸（一种氨基酸）进行纸电泳。

10　lithium

['lɪθɪəm]

义　*n.* 锂

例　It was dissolved from lithium cobaltate.

译　它是从钴酸锂中溶解出来的。

11　material

[mə'tɪrɪəl]

义　*n.* 材料，物质

例　Four different materials were selected for composting—coffee grounds, pine needles, crushed eggshells, and alfalfa (a plant).

译　选择了四种不同的材料进行堆肥——咖啡渣、松针、碎蛋壳和苜蓿（一种植物）。

12　melting point

义　熔点

例　Covalent compounds are generally not as brittle as salts and tend to have lower melting points.

译　共价化合物一般不像盐那样脆，而且往往熔点较低。

13　metal

['metl]

义　*n.* 金属，合金

例　The procedure was repeated for each of the other metals and their respective nitrate salt solutions.

译　对其他每种金属和它们各自的硝酸盐溶液重复这一步骤。

14　methane

['meθeɪn]

义　*n.*【化】甲烷

例　Methane and propane are alkanes.

译　甲烷和丙烷都属于烷烃。

15　mixture

['mɪkstʃər]

义　*n.* 混合物

例　The mixture was stirred as it was cooled in a low-temperature bath.

译　混合物在低温浴中冷却时被搅拌。

16 molar

['məulər]

义 *adj.*【化】【物】摩尔的

例 A strip of Ag was placed in 1 molar $AgNO_3$ solution at 25℃ and connected a voltmeter.

译 将银条置于 25℃的 1 摩尔 $AgNO_3$ 溶液中，并连接电压表。

---

17 molecule

['mɑ:lɪkju:l]

义 *n.*【化】分子

例 Polarity is a measure of the separation of charge in a molecule.

译 极性是分子中电荷分离的量度。

---

18 monohydrate

[ˌmɒnəʊ'haɪˌdreɪt]

义 *n.* 一水合物

例 Because the monohydrate is a solid, it can be filtered from the solution.

译 因为一水合物是固体，它可以从溶液中过滤出来。

---

19 nickel

['nɪkl]

义 *n.* 镍

例 When a solid metal (M) such as iron (Fe), nickel (Ni), or zinc (Zn) is placed in an aqueous hydrochloric acid (HCl) solution, a reaction that produces H_2 gas occurs.

译 当铁（Fe）、镍（Ni）、锌（Zn）等固体金属（M）被放入盐酸（HCl）水溶液中时，会发生反应，产生氢气。

---

20 nitrate

['naɪtreɪt]

义 *n.* 硝酸盐

例 When a nitrate salt is dissolved in water, it separates into metal ions and nitrate ions.

译 当硝酸盐溶于水时，它会分离成金属离子和硝酸盐离子。

---

21 nitrazine

['naɪtrɑ:zɪn]

义 *n.* 硝嗪

例 An acid-base indicator solution of nitrazine yellow was also used.

译 还使用了硝嗪黄的酸碱指示剂溶液。

---

22 nitrogen

['naɪtrədʒən]

义 *n.*【化】氮

例 For each type of compost, the pH, and the nitrogen, phosphorus, and potassium contents were then determined.

译 对每种堆肥进行了 pH 值和氮、磷、钾含量测定。

---

23 nonpolar

[nɒn'pəʊlə]

义 *adj.* 非极性的

例 Nonpolar molecules, like those that make up mineral oil, do not have differently charged regions.

译 非极性分子，比如那些组成矿物油的分子，没有不同的带电区域。

24 nonvolatile

['nɒn'vɒlətaɪl]

义 *adj.* 不挥发的

例 Differences in the nonvolatile content of the paints are taken into account in the calculation of results.

译 计算结果时需要考虑涂料中不同的不挥发物。

25 octane

['ɑːkteɪn]

义 *n.* 【化】辛烷

例 The octane number of a fuel is a measure of how smoothly the fuel burns in a gasoline engine.

译 燃料的辛烷值是汽油发动机中燃料燃烧平稳程度的量度。

26 oxalate

['ɑːksə,leɪt]

义 *n.* 草酸盐

例 As calcium oxalate hydrate ($CaC_2O_4 \cdot H_2O$) is heated, it first dehydrates to yield calcium oxalate (CaC_2O_4).

译 水合草酸钙（$CaC_2O_4 \cdot H_2O$）受热时，首先脱水生成草酸钙（CaC_2O_4）。

27 oxidation

[,ɑːksɪ'deɪʃn]

义 *n.* 氧化（反应）

例 Scientists use an accelerated oxidation apparatus, AOA, to model this process on a short time scale.

译 科学家在短时间内使用加速氧化装置（AOA）模拟这一过程。

28 oxide

['ɑːksaɪd]

义 *n.* 氧化物

例 Heating this chemical compound drives off carbon dioxide gas, leaving calcium oxide.

译 加热这种化合物会析出二氧化碳气体，留下氧化钙。

29 ozonation

[əʊzəʊ'neɪʃn]

义 *n.* 臭氧化；【化】臭氧化作用

例 This process is called ozonation.

译 这个过程叫作臭氧化。

30 peroxide

[pə'rɑːksaɪd]

义 *n.* 过氧化物

例 When an oil is exposed to air, small amounts of reactive peroxides can form in the oil.

译 当油暴露在空气中时，油中会形成少量的活性过氧化物。

31 petroleum

[pə'trəʊlɪəm]

义 *n.* 石油

例 Petroleum (crude oil) is brought to Earth's surface from large underground deposits that are mostly 0.5—0.7 km below Earth's surface.

译 石油（原油）是从地下 0.5—0.7 千米深处的大型地下矿床中被带到地球表面的。

32 photodecomposition

义 *n.* 【化】光解（作用）

[ˌfəʊtəʊdiːˌkɑːmpəˈzɪʃən] 例 To undergo photodecomposition, a pesticide must first absorb light energy.

译 农药要进行光解，必须得先吸收光能。

---

33 pigmentation

[ˌpɪɡmenˈteɪʃn]

义 *n.* 着色；色素沉淀

例 In corn snakes, pigmentation is determined by Genes O and B.

译 玉米蛇的色素沉淀是由 O 和 B 基因决定的。

---

34 polar

[ˈpəʊlər]

义 *adj.* 极性的

例 An H_2O molecule is polar because it has a region of positive charge and a region of negative charge.

译 水分子是极性的，因为它有一个带正电荷的区域和一个带负电荷的区域。

---

35 polymer

[ˈpɑːlɪmər]

义 *n.* 聚合物

例 In SEC a sample solution of polymer molecules is injected into a flow of solvent.

译 在色谱分离中，聚合物分子的样品溶液被注入流动的溶剂中。

---

36 polystyrene

[ˌpɑːlɪˈstaɪriːn]

义 *n.* 聚苯乙烯

例 Polystyrene is a polymer made up of identical subunits.

译 聚苯乙烯是由相同的亚基组成的聚合物。

---

37 potassium

[pəˈtæsɪəm]

义 *n.* 钾

例 A known mass of potassium iodide (KI) was dissolved in a known mass of H_2O.

译 已知质量的碘化钾（KI）溶于已知质量的水中。

---

38 primary alcohol

义 【化】伯醇

例 There were more carboxyl groups, condensed guaiacyl units and guaiacyl primary alcohol in the waste ASP liquor than those in KP waste liquor.

译 与 KP 相比，ASP 废液中木素含有较多的羧基、缩合型愈创木基结构以及愈创木酚型的伯醇醚。

---

39 reactive oxygen species

义 活性氧

例 Biological aging is caused solely by the reactive oxygen species (ROS) produced by cellular respiration.

译 生物衰老仅仅是由细胞呼吸产生的活性氧（ROS）引起的。

---

40 reduction

义 *n.* 还原反应

[rɪ'dʌkʃn]

例 The higher the value of E°, the more easily the metal ions undergo reduction (the gain of electrons) to form a metal.

译 E°值越高，金属离子越容易发生还原反应（电子的增益）并形成金属。

---

41 saline

['seɪliːn]

义 *adj.* 含盐的；咸的

例 Ten milliliters of a mixture of nutrient medium (NM) and saline solution (SS) that was 5% SS by volume was put in a test tube.

译 将 10 毫升的营养培养基（NM）和生理盐水（SS）的混合物置于试管中，其中生理盐水含量为 5%。

---

42 salt bridge

义 盐桥

例 The solutions are connected by a salt bridge (a tube filled with a solution containing nitrate ions).

译 这些溶液由盐桥（一根充满硝酸盐离子溶液的管子）连接起来。

---

43 saturate

['sætʃəreɪt]

义 *v.* 使饱和

例 Each tray was placed in shallow water for 24 hours to saturate the sample.

译 每个托盘要在浅水中放置 24 小时使样品饱和。

---

44 saturated

['sætʃəreɪtɪd]

义 *adj.* 饱和的

例 If the jar is placed over the lit candle, the candle will soon stop burning because the O_2 in the air under the jar will quickly become saturated with heat.

译 如果把罐子放在点燃的蜡烛上面，蜡烛很快就会停止燃烧，因为罐子下面空气中的氧气很快就会被热量饱和。

---

45 saturation

[ˌsætʃə'reɪʃn]

义 *n.* 饱和；饱和度

例 The method can be used for measuring the vertical saturation permeability coefficient of the soil out doors quickly and accurately.

译 该方法可用于迅速准确测定野外土壤的垂向饱和渗透系数。

---

46 sediment

['sedɪmənt]

义 *n.* 沉淀物

例 A six meter long hollow tube was dropped to the ocean floor at five different sites around the volcanic islands to collect cores of undisturbed ocean floor sediments.

译 在火山岛周围的 5 个不同地点，将一个 6 米长的空心管投到海底，收集未受干扰的海底沉积物的岩心。

---

47 selenium

[sə'liːnɪəm]

义 *n.* 【化】硒

例 In some locations, drainage water from agricultural areas contains selenium (Se), a substance that can be harmful to wildlife.

译 在一些地方，农业地区的排水中含有硒(Se)，这是一种对野生动物有害的物质。

---

48 separation

[ˌsepəˈreɪʃn]

义 *n.* 分离；离析

例 The experiments were done to study how using solvents and adsorbents of differing polarities affects the separation of a mixture.

译 实验是为了研究不同极性溶剂和吸附剂的使用如何影响混合物的分离。

---

49 silica

[ˈsɪlɪkə]

义 *n.* 二氧化硅，硅土

例 The samples were analyzed for their percent silica and potassium oxide contents.

译 对样品进行了二氧化硅和氧化钾含量的分析。

---

50 sodium

[ˈsəʊdɪəm]

义 *n.* 钠

例 Four liters (4.0 L) of a 25% by mass aqueous solution of sodium hydroxide (NaOH) was added to the tank.

译 将 4 升(4.0 L)质量分数为 25% 的氢氧化钠(NaOH)水溶液加入罐中。

---

51 sodium hydroxide

义 【化】氢氧化钠

例 Two titration experiments were done at 25℃ using a 0.10 M sodium hydroxide (NaOH) solution and either a 0.0010 M hydrochloric acid (HCl) solution or a 0.0010 M acetic acid solution.

译 使用 0.10 摩尔的氢氧化钠(NaOH)溶液和 0.0010 摩尔的盐酸(HCl)溶液或 0.0010 摩尔的醋酸溶液在 25℃下进行了两次滴定实验。

---

52 solubility

[ˌsɑːljʊˈbɪlətɪ]

义 *n.* 可溶性；溶解度

例 They differ in solubility and chemical reactivity.

译 它们在溶解度和化学反应活性上有差别。

---

53 solution

[səˈluːʃn]

义 *n.* 溶液

例 The solution was added to the graduated cylinder until the volume was 50.0 mL.

译 将溶液添加到量筒中，直到体积为 50 毫升。

---

54 solvent

[ˈsɑːlvənt]

义 *n.* 溶剂

例 Solubility is the maximum amount of a compound that will dissolve in a given volume of solvent.

译 溶解度是一种化合物在一定体积的溶剂中溶解的最大质量。

---

55 stability

[stə'bɪlətɪ]

义 *n.* 稳定性

例 The stability of a nucleus is related to its shape.

译 原子核的稳定性与它的形状有关。

56 sterilize

['sterəlaɪz]

义 *v.* 灭菌

例 Beech tree leaves were collected, air-dried, and sterilized.

译 采集山毛榉树叶，风干并杀菌。

57 stopcock

['stɑːpkɑːk]

义 *n.* 止水栓

例 Liquid flows out of the buret when the stopcock is opened.

译 当止水栓打开时，液体从滴定管流出。

58 sulfate

['sʌlˌfeɪt]

义 *n.* 硫酸盐

例 This reaction begins when hot fluid containing methane (CH_4) rises from a source deep beneath the ocean-floor surface and mixes with seawater containing sulfate.

译 当含有甲烷（CH_4）的热流体从海底表面深处的源头上升并与含有硫酸盐的海水混合时，这个反应就开始了。

59 sulfur

['sʌlfə]

义 *n.* 硫

例 Volcanoes put sulfur into the troposphere and the stratosphere, where the sulfur reacts to form sulfate aerosols (liquid droplets suspended in air).

译 火山将硫喷射至对流层和平流层，硫在那里发生反应形成硫酸盐气溶胶（悬浮在空气中的液滴）。

60 synthesis

['sɪnθəsɪs]

义 *n.* 合成

例 Each fragment serves as a template for the synthesis of a new complementary fragment.

译 每个片段都作为合成新互补片段的模板。

61 titration

[tɪ'treɪʃn]

义 *n.* 滴定

例 Acid-base titration is a technique in which precise volumes of a titrant (an acid or base solution) are added incrementally to a known volume of a sample solution (a base or acid solution, respectively).

译 酸碱滴定法是一种将精确量的滴定液（酸或碱溶液）递增地加入已知体积的样品溶液（分别为碱或酸溶液）中的技术。

62 toxic

['tɑːksɪk]

义 *adj.* 有毒的

例 The remaining ash also may contain toxic substances.

译 剩余的火山灰也可能含有有毒物质。

63 transition range

义 转变范围

例 In the small range between these pH ranges—the transition range—the indicator's color will be an intermediate of its other colors.

译 在这些 pH 值范围之间的小范围内，即过渡范围内，指示剂的颜色将是其他颜色的中间色。

---

64 volatile

['vɑːlətl]

义 *adj.* 不稳定的；易挥发的

例 When a volatile liquid is in a closed container, the liquid at the surface is constantly evaporating (forming a vapor) and condensing (reforming a liquid).

译 当挥发性液体在一个封闭的容器中，其表面的液体不断蒸发（形成蒸汽），然后冷凝（重新形成液体）。

---

65 volume

['vɑːljuːm]

义 *n.* 体积，容量

例 Ethanol was added to the graduated cylinder until the volume of liquid was 50.0 mL.

译 在量筒中加入乙醇，直至液体体积为 50.0 毫升。

---

66 well plate

义 孔板

例 Assays can be executed in 96-well plate or cuvet.

译 可采用 96 孔板或比色皿检测。

---

67 zinc

[zɪŋk]

义 *n.* 锌

例 Zinc is used to protect other metals from corrosion.

译 锌被用来保护其他金属免受腐蚀。

List 8

1	**Antarctic**	义 *adj.* 南极的
	[æn'tɑːrktɪk]	例 The atmospheric CO_2 concentration that existed at any given time over the past 160,000 years can be determined from air trapped in bubbles in Antarctic ice formed at that time.
		译 在过去的 16 万年中，任何给定时间存在的大气二氧化碳浓度都可以通过当时形成的南极冰层气泡中捕获的空气来确定。

2	**Atlantic**	义 *adj.* 大西洋的
	[æt'læntɪk]	例 Snow crab is a subarctic species of crab that is commercially fished in the Atlantic Ocean.
		译 雪蟹是一种亚北极蟹类，人们在大西洋对其进行商业捕捞。

3	**average**	义 *n.* 平均数
	['ævərɪdʒ]	例 There has been below average rainfall this month.
		译 这个月的降雨低于平均降雨量。

4	**basin**	义 *n.* 盆地；流域
	['beɪsn]	例 Discharge is affected by several factors, including the area of the river's drainage basin and the spatial relationship of the river to other rivers.
		译 流量受几个因素的影响，包括河流的排水流域的面积和河流与其他河流的空间关系。

5	**bedrock**	义 *n.* 基岩
	['bedrɑːk]	例 Friction between the glacier and bedrock is reduced.
		译 冰川和基岩之间的摩擦减少了。

6	**channel**	义 *n.* 通道；渠道
	['tʃænl]	例 Water velocity through the channel and water flow depth could be controlled.
		译 流经渠道的水流速度和水流深度可以控制。

7	**deposition**	义 *n.* 沉积
	[,depə'zɪʃn]	例 This process is known as wet deposition.
		译 这个过程称为湿沉积。

8	**discharge**	义 *n.* 流量
	[dɪs'tʃɑːrdʒ]	例 A river's discharge is the volume of river water flowing past a location in the river in a given amount of time.

译 河流流量是指在给定的时间内流经河流中某一地点的水量。

---

9 downstream

[ˌdaʊn'striːm]

义 *adv.* 朝下游方向

例 Over the 12 days following the rainfall event, as the flood caused by the rainfall moved downstream, the discharge was continuously measured.

译 在降雨后的 12 天内，随着降雨引起的洪水向下游移动，持续测量了流量。

---

10 drainage

['dreɪnɪdʒ]

义 *n.* 排水；排水面积，流域面积，流域

例 The area of each river's drainage basin is given in square kilometers.

译 每条河流的流域面积以平方公里为单位。

---

11 ecliptic

[ɪ'klɪptɪk]

义 *n.* 黄道

例 The small inclinations of short-period comets' orbital planes with respect to the ecliptic plane are consistent with an origin in the KB (Kuiper Belt).

译 短周期彗星轨道面相对于黄道面的小倾角与柯伊伯带的起源是一致的。

---

12 elevated

['elɪveɪtɪd]

义 *adj.* 抬高的

例 An elevated inclined plane makes an angle, with a floor.

译 一个升高的斜面与地面形成一个角度。

---

13 eruption

[ɪ'rʌpʃn]

义 *n.* 爆发；喷发

例 Wind spread ash from a volcanic eruption eastward over a large area.

译 风把火山喷发的火山灰向东吹散，覆盖了大片地区。

---

14 faint

[feɪnt]

义 *adj.* 微弱的

例 Their instruments detected very faint radio waves at a frequency of 3 kilohertz.

译 他们的仪器探测到了频率为 3 千赫兹的非常微弱的无线电波。

---

15 fossil

['fɑːsl]

义 *n.* 化石

例 Human activities, primarily the burning of fossil fuels, have added significant additional CO_2 to the air (6 billion tons per year at present).

译 以燃烧化石燃料为主的人类活动使空气中的二氧化碳大量增加（目前每年增加 60 亿吨）。

---

16 glacier

['gleɪʃər]

义 *n.* 冰河，冰川

例 The lake was formed when a large glacier dammed several rivers.

译 该湖是在一个大冰川阻断了几条河流后形成的。

---

17 groundwater

['graʊndwɔːtər]

义 *n.* 地下水

例 Groundwater trapped in lake and glacial sediments provides information about the climate at the time the sediments were deposited.

译 湖泊和冰川沉积物中的地下水提供了沉积物沉积时的气候信息。

---

18 hectare

['hekteər]

义 *n.* 公顷

例 A hectare (10,000 m^2) area of forest was equally divided into Plots X and Y.

译 1公顷等于10 000平方米的森林面积被平均划分为X和Y两个地块。

---

19 ice cap

义 冰盖

例 This global warming has caused ocean surface temperature increases and the melting of parts of the polar ice caps.

译 全球变暖导致海洋表面温度上升和极地冰盖部分融化。

---

20 moisture

['mɔɪstʃər]

义 *n.* 水分；湿度

例 A 0.5 mL sample of soil gas was collected from each diffusion well and the water content of the soil was read from each moisture sensor.

译 从每个扩散井采集0.5毫升土壤气体样本并从每个湿度传感器读取土壤含水量。

---

21 population density

义 种群密度

例 Its aggregation degree increased with the increase of population density.

译 其聚集程度随种群密度的升高而增大。

---

22 pore

[pɔːr]

义 *n.* 毛孔；小孔；空隙

例 Pore water is water in the pores of subsurface material.

译 孔隙水是地下物质孔隙中的水。

---

23 runoff

['rʌnˌɔːf]

义 *n.* 径流量

例 Green roofs help control runoff during rain events.

译 屋顶绿化有助于控制降雨期间的径流量。

24　silt

[sɪlt]

义 *n.* 淤泥，泥沙；粉尘层，泥沙层；粉砂

例 Loam is a soil with roughly equal proportions of clay, sand and silt.

译 壤土是由大约等比例的黏土、沙和粉砂合成的。

25　stream

[striːm]

义 *n.* （小）河，水流

例 Two streams, Stream A and Stream B, are identical in all respects, except that water flows rapidly in Stream A.

译 水流 A 和水流 B 两条水流，除了水流 A 的水流很快之外，在所有方面都是相同的。

26　threshold

[ˈθreʃhəʊld]

义 *n.* 界限，阈值

例 When surface temperatures rise to a comfortable threshold, they emerge.

译 当地表温度上升到一个舒适的阈值时，它们就会出现。

27　volcano

[vɑːlˈkeɪnəʊ]

义 *n.* 火山

例 Lava is extruded from the volcano.

译 熔岩从火山中喷出。

List 9

1 asthenosphere

[æs'θiːnɜːˌsfɪə]

义 *n.* 软流圈

例 The lithosphere, asthenosphere, and transition zone boundaries were determined using speed changes in S waves, a type of earthquake wave.

译 利用 S 波（一种地震波）的速度变化来确定岩石圈、软流圈和过渡带的边界。

2 basalt

[bə'sɔːlt]

义 *n.* 玄武岩

例 Most crystalline rocks are much more solid, but a common exception is basalt, a form of solidified volcanic lava, which is sometimes full of tiny bubbles that make it very porous.

译 大部分结晶岩石都非常坚硬，但也有例外，最常见的就是玄武岩，它是一种火山岩浆凝固后的形态，内部充满了微小的气泡，因此也具有多孔渗水的特点。

3 cement

[sɪ'ment]

义 *n.* 水泥

例 The cement and water react chemically to form a hard paste, which binds the aggregate together.

译 水泥和水发生化学反应并形成坚硬的膏体，将骨料黏结在一起。

4 chalcanthite

[kæl'kænθaɪt]

义 *n.* 胆矾

例 It shows the mass of a sample that was converted from chalcanthite to $CuSO_4$ as its temperature was increased from 0℃ to 350℃.

译 它显示了当温度从 0℃升高到 350℃时，由胆矾转化为硫酸铜的样品质量变化。

5 coarse

[kɔːrs]

义 *adj.* 粗糙的

例 By contrast, dry soils are sandy and porous, their coarse textures permitting water to drain rapidly.

译 相比之下，干燥的土壤是砂质的、多孔的，粗糙的质地使得水分迅速流失。

6 concrete

['kɑːŋkriːt]

义 *n.* 混凝土

例 Concrete is a mixture of cement, water, and aggregate (usually sand or gravel).

译 混凝土是水泥、水和骨料（通常是砂或砾石）的混合物。

7 continent

['kɑːntɪnənt]

义 *n.* 大陆，洲

例 The famine threatened to depopulate the continent.

译 饥荒导致该大陆人口剧减。

8　crater

['kreɪtər]

义　*n.* 火山口

例　The lava will just ooze gently out of the crater.

译　熔岩会从火山口缓缓涌流出来。

9　crust

[krʌst]

义　*n.* 地壳

例　The crust is thinner under the continents.

译　大陆下面的地壳比较薄。

10　earthquake

['ɜ:rθkweɪk]

义　*n.* 地震

例　Earthquakes produce seismic waves that can travel long distances through Earth.

译　地震产生的地震波可以在地球上传播很长一段距离。

11　element

['elɪmənt]

义　*n.* 元素，成分

例　Rock types can often be differentiated by the rare earth elements (REEs) they contain.

译　岩石类型通常可由其所含的稀土元素（REEs）成分来区分。

12　evaporite

[ɪ'væpə,raɪt]

义　*n.*【地】蒸发岩，蒸发盐

例　Evaporites are minerals that precipitate (crystallize) during the partial or total evaporation of seawater.

译　蒸发岩是在海水的部分或全部蒸发过程中沉淀（结晶）的矿物质。

13　geologic time

义　地质时期，地质年代

例　The geologic time scale is divided into long time frames called eras and shorter time frames called periods.

译　地质年代尺度分为长时间框架（代）和短时间框架（期）。

14　geologist

[dʒɪ'ɑ:lədʒɪst]

义　*n.* 地质学家

例　A geologist conducted three studies using an artificial river channel 15 meters long, 1 meter wide, and 0.6 meters deep.

译　一位地质学家利用一条长 15 米、宽 1 米、深 0.6 米的人工河道进行了 3 次研究。

15　hot spot volcano

义　热点火山

例　Unlike most volcanoes, hot spot volcanoes (HSVs) develop far from tectonic plate boundaries.

译　与大多数火山不同，热点火山（HSVs）的形成远离构造板块边界。

16　igneous

义　*adj.*（指岩石）火成的；火的

['ɪgnɪəs]

例 Igneous and metamorphic rocks are more compact, commonly crystalline, and rarely contain spaces between grains.

译 火成岩和变质岩比较紧密，通常是结晶性的，颗粒之间很少有空隙。

---

17 lahar

['lɑːhɑː]

义 *n.*【地】火山泥流

例 A lahar is a flow of water-saturated volcanic ash and rock.

译 火山泥流是由充满水分的火山灰和岩石形成的。

---

18 lahar deposit

义 火山泥流沉积

例 A lahar deposit, formed once the flow stops, consists of clasts (rocks having diameters ≥ 16 mm) embedded in a matrix (a mixture of particles having diameters ≤ 8 mm).

译 一旦水流停止，就会形成火山泥流沉积，由嵌入基质（直径 ≤ 8 毫米的颗粒混合物）中的碎屑（直径 ≥ 16 毫米的岩石）组成。

---

19 lava

['lɑːvə]

义 *n.* 熔岩

例 HSVs erupt iron-rich lavas that are chemically similar to mantle rocks.

译 热点火山喷发出富含铁的熔岩，其化学性质与地幔岩石相似。

---

20 lithosphere

['lɪθəsfɪr]

义 *n.* 岩石圈

例 The lithosphere includes the crust and part of the mantle.

译 岩石圈包括地壳和部分地幔。

---

21 magma

['mægmə]

义 *n.* 岩浆

例 The ascending magma causes earthquakes and creates networks of large fractures in crustal rocks.

译 上升的岩浆引起地震，并在地壳岩石中形成巨大的裂缝网络。

---

22 magnitude

['mægnɪtuːd]

义 *n.*（地震）级数；星等

例 A star's brightness is described by its magnitude.

译 一颗恒星的亮度用星等来描述。

---

23 mantle

['mæntl]

义 *n.*【地】地幔

例 Earth's interior is divided into four primary layers of different chemical composition: the crust, mantle, outer core, and inner core.

译 地球内部的结构可以分为四个主要的化学成分层：地壳、地幔、外核和内核。

---

24 mantle plume

义 地幔柱

例 In the mantle beneath an HSV, at depths between 200 km and 400 km, hot magma rises toward Earth's surface in one large column called a mantle plume.

译 在热点火山下的地幔中，深度 200 到 400 公里之间的地方，炽热的岩浆以一个巨大的柱状上升到地球表面，称为地幔柱。

---

25 mineral

['mɪnərəl]

义 *n.* 矿物

例 Therefore, the iodine dissolved in the mineral oil, but not in the H_2O.

译 因此，碘溶于矿物油，而不溶于水。

---

26 neodymium

[ˌniːəʊ'dɪmɪəm]

义 *n.* 钕

例 In each rock type, the average neodymium concentration is lower than the average samarium concentration.

译 在各岩石类型中，钕的平均浓度均低于钐的平均浓度。

---

27 olivine

[ˈɑːlɪ'viːn]

义 *n.* 橄榄石

例 Olivine and pyroxenes are the most abundant minerals in mantle rocks and in the lavas erupted at HSVs.

译 橄榄石和辉石是地幔岩石和热点火山喷发的熔岩中含量最丰富的矿物。

---

28 ore

[ɔːr]

义 *n.* 矿石

例 The processing of sulfur-rich ore (rock containing valuable metals) from mines produces liquid waste, which is often stored in a pond.

译 从矿山开采的富硫矿石（含有有价金属的岩石）会产生废液，废液通常储存在池子里。

---

29 pyroxene

['paɪrɑːkˌsiːn]

义 *n.* 辉石

例 Olivine and pyroxenes are the most abundant minerals in mantle rocks and in the lavas erupted at HSVs.

译 橄榄石和辉石是地幔岩石和热点火山喷发的熔岩中含量最丰富的矿物。

---

30 seismic

['saɪzmɪk]

义 *adj.* 地震的

例 Two types of seismic waves are P waves and S waves.

译 地震波有两种，纵波和横波。

---

31 seismograph

['saɪzməgræf]

义 *n.* 地震仪

例 A seismograph records earthquakes.

译 地震仪记录地震。

---

32 serpentine

['sɜːrpəntiːn]

义 *adj.* 弯曲的　*n.* 蛇纹石

例 Hot fluids circulate through basalt (an igneous rock) and alter it to produce a mineral known as serpentine.

> 译 热流体在玄武岩（一种火成岩）中循环，并将其改变，产生一种叫作蛇纹石的矿物。

---

33 tectonic

[tek'tɑːnɪk]

义 *adj.* 【地】地壳构造（上）的

例 Most petroleum deposits exist along tectonic plate boundaries.

译 大多数石油矿床沿着地壳构造板块边界存在。

List 10

1 albedo

[æl'bɪdəʊ]

义 *n.* 星体反照率

例 One way we keep track of the radiation budget is by looking at the albedo of the different surfaces on the planet.

译 我们观察辐射收支的方法之一就是观测地球不同表面的星体反照率。

---

2 asteroid

['æstərɔɪd]

义 *n.* 小行星

例 When an asteroid hits the surface of a planet or moon, an impact crater is formed.

译 当小行星撞击行星或月球表面时，就会形成陨石坑。

---

3 astronomy

[ə'strɑ:nəmɪ]

义 *n.* 天文学

例 An astronomy class is given the facts about stellar evolution.

译 天文学课上给出了关于恒星演化的事实。

---

4 atmosphere

['ætməsfɪr]

义 *n.* 大气

例 The Martian atmosphere contains only tiny amounts of water.

译 火星的大气层只含有微量的水。

---

5 collapse

[kə'læps]

义 *v.* 崩塌

例 Gravity causes part of a cloud of gas and dust to collapse and heat up, creating a pre-MS star.

译 重力导致部分气体云和尘埃云崩塌并升温，形成前主序星。

---

6 comet

['kɑ:mət]

义 *n.* 彗星

例 Comets are complex mixtures of ices and dust that orbit the Sun.

译 彗星是冰和尘埃的复杂混合物，它围绕太阳旋转。

---

7 cosmic

['kɑ:zmɪk]

义 *adj.* 宇宙的

例 NASA plans to launch a satellite to study cosmic rays.

译 美国国家航空航天局计划发射一颗卫星来研究宇宙射线。

---

8 deflected

[dɪ'flektɪd]

义 *adj.* 偏离的

例 Albert Einstein predicted that light passing by a massive object would be deflected from its original direction of motion.

译 阿尔伯特·爱因斯坦曾预言，光经过一个大质量物体时，会偏离其最初的运动方向。

9 elevation

[ˌelɪ'veɪʃn]

义 *n.*（某地方的）高程；（尤指）海拔；立视图

例 As elevation increases, narrow, deep channels of water form throughout the marsh.

译 随着海拔的升高，沼泽中形成了又窄又深的水渠。

---

10 galaxy

['gæləksɪ]

义 *n.* 银河，银河系；星系

例 Because it takes so long to form gas-giant planets like Jupiter, they are very rare in our galaxy.

译 因为像木星这样的气态巨行星需要很长时间才能形成，所以它们在我们的银河系中非常罕见。

---

11 Jupiter

['dʒuːpɪtər]

义 *n.* 木星

例 Two scientists discuss how gas-giant planets like Jupiter form from planet cores in stellar nebulae.

译 两位科学家讨论像木星这样的气态巨行星是如何从恒星星云的行星核心形成的。

---

12 Mercury

['mɜːrkjərɪ]

义 *n.* 水星

例 Mercury, the planet, is the fastest moving heavenly body that naked eyes can see.

译 水星是肉眼能看到的运动得最快的天体。

---

13 meteorite

['miːtɪəraɪt]

义 *n.* 陨石，流星

例 Meteorites, taken as a group, are used to calculate the relative concentration because their composition is distinctly different from any Earth rock.

译 陨石，作为一个群体，被用来计算相对浓度，因为它们的组成明显不同于任何地球岩石。

---

14 methyl

['meθɪl]

义 *n.* 甲基

例 Large deposits of the material known as methyl hydrate are present at specific locations beneath Mars's surface.

译 这种被称为甲基水合物的物质的大量沉积于火星表面下的特定位置。

---

15 nebula

['nebjələ]

义 *n.*【天】星云

例 Planet formation begins when some of the solid material within a stellar nebula clumps together to form a spherical body called a planet core.

译 当恒星星云中的一些固体物质聚集在一起，形成一个叫作行星核的球形物体时，行星就开始形成了。

16 orbit

['ɔːrbɪt]

义 *n.* 轨道 *v.* 绕轨道运行

例 The orbit of this comet intersects the orbit of the Earth.

译 这颗彗星的轨道和地球的轨道相交。

---

17 orbital

['ɔːrbɪtl]

义 *adj.* 轨道的

例 The newly discovered world followed an orbital path unlike that of any other planet.

译 这个新发现的天体的运行轨道不同于其他任何行星。

---

18 parsec

['pɑːrˌsek]

义 *n.* 秒差距（表示天体间距离的单位）

例 A star's absolute magnitude is the magnitude that would be measured 10 parsecs from the star.

译 一颗恒星的绝对星等是距离该恒星 10 秒差距的星等。

---

19 planet

['plænɪt]

义 *n.* 行星

例 Kepler's third law also describes a moon's orbit around a planet.

译 开普勒第三定律也解释了卫星围绕行星的轨道运行。

---

20 planetary

['plænəterɪ]

义 *adj.* 行星的，有轨道的

例 As planetary mass increases, planetary orbital speed increases.

译 随着行星质量的增加，行星轨道的速度也会增加。

---

21 protoplanet

[prəʊtə'plænɪt]

义 *n.*【天】原行星

例 Gas clusters that push the protoplanet outward can sometimes exert stronger forces than those that push inward.

译 气体星团推动原行星向外的推力可能在某些时候强于那些使它向内的推力。

---

22 protostar

['prəʊtəstɑːr]

义 *n.*【天】原恒星

例 A protostar (forming star) affects gas in the surrounding portions of the cloud in two ways.

译 原恒星（正在形成的恒星）通过两种方式影响星云周围的气体。

---

23 Saturn

['sætɜːrn]

义 *n.* 土星

例 Radar observations of Saturn's moon Titan have revealed landforms that resemble longitudinal sand dunes found in some deserts on Earth.

译 对土星卫星土卫六的雷达观测显示，土卫六的地形与地球上一些沙漠中发现的纵向沙丘相似。

24 solar eclipse

义 【天】日食

例 Scientists observed the stars appearing at the Sun's edge during a total solar eclipse, and they plotted the stars' positions in the sky.

译 在日全食期间，科学家们观察到了出现在太阳边缘的恒星，并绘制出了这些恒星在天空中的位置。

---

25 solar system

义 太阳系

例 The KB has a small inclination with respect to the ecliptic plane and is located in the solar system between 30 AU and 50 AU from the Sun.

译 柯伊伯带相对于黄道面有一个小倾角，位于太阳系中距离太阳 30 到 50 个天文单位之间。

---

26 stellar

['stelər]

义 *adj.* 星球的

例 Gas-giant planets form within stellar nebulae—large, flattened clouds of gas and dust that surround newly formed stars.

译 气态巨行星形成于恒星星云——在新形成的恒星周围的那些巨大的、扁平的气体云和尘埃内。

---

27 Venus

['viːnəs]

义 *n.* 金星

例 They found that in some cases, Mars and Venus collided with the Earth.

译 他们发现在有些情况下，火星和金星会与地球相撞。

List 11

1　air current

义 气流

例 Wind tunnel experiments show that the shape of the female Zamia cones creates air currents that facilitate the horizontal movement of pollen into these cones.

译 风洞实验表明，雌性泽米属植物球果的形状产生了气流，促进花粉水平移动进入这些球果。

2　anemometer

[ˌænɪˈmɑːmɪtər]

义 *n.* 风速计

例 At each site, four anemometers (devices for measuring wind speed) were attached to a vertical pole at different heights above the ground, and a sand trap was placed at the base of the pole.

译 在每个地点，将 4 个风速计（测量风速的装置）安装在离地面不同高度的垂直杆上，并且在杆的底部放置了一个沙坑。

3　atmospheric

[ˌætməsˈferɪk]

义 *adj.* 大气层的

例 A beaker containing 100 mL of water was heated at atmospheric pressure (760 mm Hg).

译 在大气压（760 毫米汞柱）下加热装有 100 毫升水的烧杯。

4　condense

[kənˈdens]

义 *v.* 浓缩，凝结

例 When air cools to its dew point, the water vapor in the air can begin to condense and form clouds.

译 当空气冷却到露点时，空气中的水蒸气就会开始凝结并形成云。

5　consecutive

[kənˈsekjətɪv]

义 *adj.* 连续的

例 In July, on the last of 14 consecutive days of fair weather, 100 mL water samples were collected.

译 在 7 月连续 14 天的好天气的最后一天，采集了 100 毫升水样。

6　cumulus

[ˈkjuːmjələs]

义 *n.* 积云

例 Over a year, two studies of cloud-seeding were done at a subtropical location, using every cumulus cloud that was isolated from other clouds, that had a top at an altitude between 3,350 m and 4,900 m, and that had a liquid water content of at least 0.5 g/m^3.

译 在一年多的时间里，在一个亚热带地区进行了两项人工降雨研究，研究了从其他云层中分离出来的积云，这些积云的顶部海拔在 3 350 米到 4 900 米之间，液态水含量至少为 0.5 g/m^3。

7　dew

[duː]

义 *n.* 露水

例 Air at its dew point temperature (or dew point) is saturated with water vapor.

译 在露点温度（或露点）的空气处于水蒸气饱和状态。

8 droplet

['drɑːplət]

义 *n.* 小滴

例 A cloud droplet grows by attracting more water droplets until it becomes a raindrop, which then falls from the cloud.

译 云里微小的水滴通过吸引更多的水滴而积聚，直到它变成雨滴，然后雨滴从云中落下。

---

9 flux

[flʌks]

义 *n.* 流量

例 Cloud cover may increase because of an increase in the cosmic ray flux.

译 由于宇宙射线通量的增加，云量可能也会增加。

---

10 global warming

义 全球变暖

例 Global warming is caused by human activities that have significantly increased the atmospheric concentration of CO_2 above the concentration prior to 1880.

译 全球变暖是由人类活动造成的，人类活动使大气中的二氧化碳浓度大大增加，超过了 1880 年之前的浓度。

---

11 humidity

[hjuːˈmɪdətɪ]

义 *n.* 湿度

例 The humidity is relatively low.

译 湿度相对较低。

---

12 microgram

['maɪkrəʊɡræm]

义 *n.* 微克

例 During one dust storm, airborne aluminum concentrations exceeded 1,400 micrograms per cubic meter.

译 一场沙尘暴中，空气中的铝浓度会超过 1 400 微克每立方米。

---

13 ozone

['əʊzəʊn]

义 *n.* 臭氧

例 Ozone (O_3) is concentrated in a part of Earth's atmosphere called the ozone layer.

译 臭氧（O_3）集中在地球大气层的一部分，称为臭氧层。

---

14 precipitation

[prɪˌsɪpɪˈteɪʃn]

义 *n.* 沉淀；降雨量

例 Precipitation is influenced by topography among other things.

译 除其他因素外，降水还受到地形的影响。

---

15 prediction

[prɪˈdɪkʃn]

义 *n.* 预言；预测

例 Weather prediction has never been a perfect science.

译 天气预报从来都不是一门准确无误的科学。

---

16 radiation

[ˌreɪdɪ'eɪʃn]

义 *n.* 辐射

例 O_3 absorbs harmful high-energy solar radiation.

译 臭氧(O_3)吸收有害的高能太阳辐射。

---

17 stratosphere

['strætəsfɪr]

义 *n.* 平流层

例 The tropopause is the transition between two layers of Earth's atmosphere: the troposphere (the layer that begins at Earth's surface) and the stratosphere (the layer just above the troposphere).

译 对流层顶是地球大气层两层之间的过渡：对流层(从地球表面开始的一层)和平流层(对流层的上方)。

---

18 thunderstorm

['θʌndərstɔːrm]

义 *n.* 雷暴雨

例 Franklin conducted his dangerous kite experiment in a thunderstorm, founding the science of atmospheric electricity.

译 富兰克林在雷雨中进行了危险的风筝实验，从而奠定了大气电学的基础。

---

19 tornado

[tɔːr'neɪdəʊ]

义 *n.* 龙卷风

例 The tornado disrupted broadcasting along the entire coast.

译 龙卷风使整个沿海的广播都中断了。

---

20 tropopause

['trəʊpəˌpɔːz]

义 *n.* 对流层顶

例 The tropopause is the transition between two layers of Earth's atmosphere: the troposphere (the layer that begins at Earth's surface) and the stratosphere (the layer just above the troposphere).

译 对流层顶是地球大气层两层之间的过渡：对流层(从地球表面开始的一层)和平流层(对流层的上方)。

---

21 troposphere

['trəʊpəsfɪr]

义 *n.* 对流层

例 The height of the top of the troposphere varies with latitude (it is lowest over the poles and highest at the equator) and by season (it is lower in winter and higher in summer).

译 对流层顶部的高度随纬度的变化而变化(它在两极处最低，在赤道处最高)和随季节的变化而变化(它在冬季较低，在夏季较高)。

图书在版编目（CIP）数据

ACT答案词 / 盛会杰，王鑫编著. --北京：中国人
民大学出版社，2022.10
ISBN 978-7-300-30769-5

Ⅰ.①A… Ⅱ.①盛… ②王… Ⅲ.①英语-词汇-高
等学校-入学考试-美国-自学参考资料 Ⅳ.①H313

中国版本图书馆CIP数据核字（2022）第107651号

- 本书中所有理论、概念均系作者原创，如果引用需注明出处。
- 本书著作权归作者所有，出版权归中国人民大学出版社，任何复印、引用均需征求著作权人及
  出版权持有人同时同意。

ACT答案词

盛会杰 王鑫 编著

ACT Da'anci

出版发行	中国人民大学出版社			
社　　址	北京中关村大街31号	**邮政编码**	100080	
电　　话	010-62511242（总编室）	010-62511770（质管部）		
	010-82501766（邮购部）	010-62514148（门市部）		
	010-62515195（发行公司）	010-62515275（盗版举报）		
网　　址	http://www.crup.com.cn			
经　　销	新华书店			
印　　刷	唐山玺诚印务有限公司			
规　　格	185mm×260mm　16开本	**版　次**	2022年10月第1版	
印　　张	26.5	**印　次**	2022年10月第1次印刷	
字　　数	608 000	**定　价**	66.00元